HISTORY OF
PHOTOGRAPHY

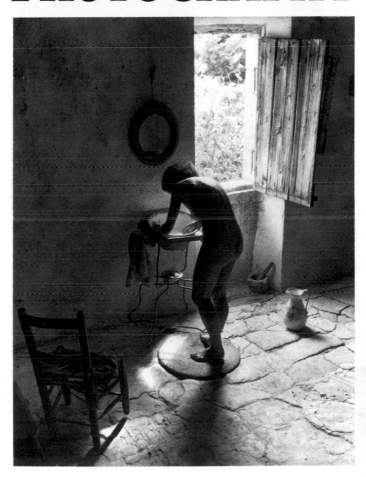

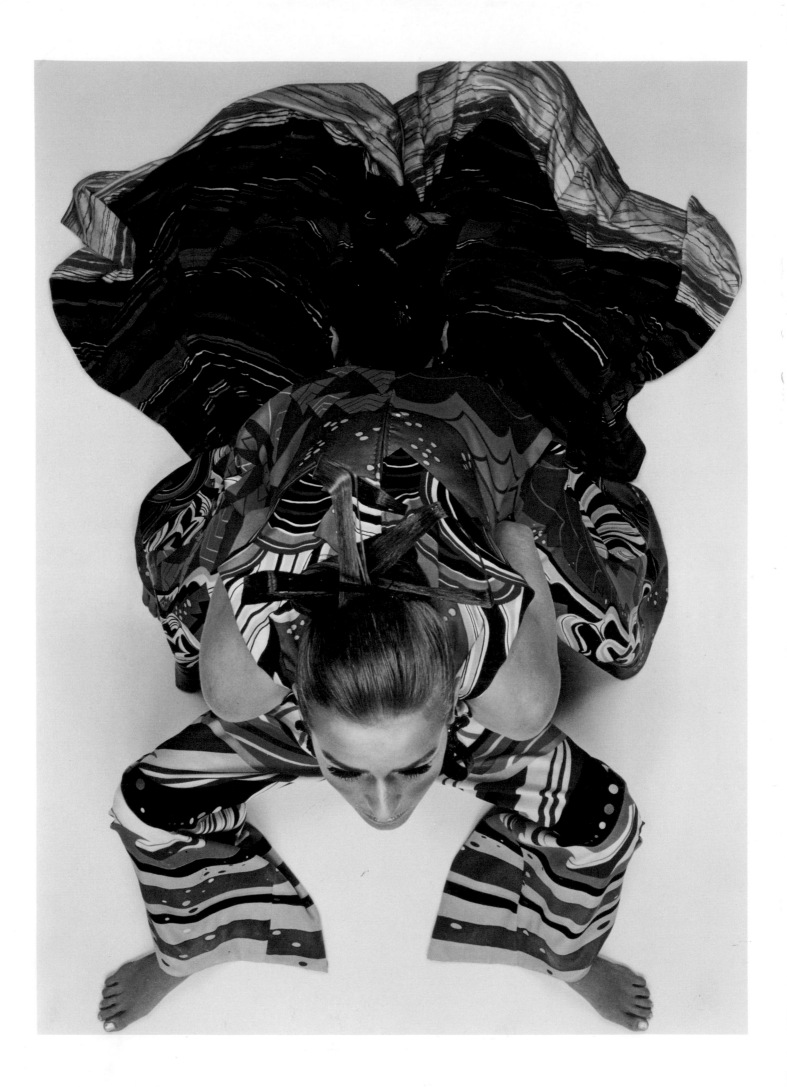

Peter Turner

HISTORY OF PHOTOGRAPHY

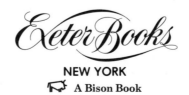

NEW YORK

A Bison Book

Copyright © 1987 by Bison Books Corp

First published in USA 1987
by Exeter Books
Distributed by Bookthrift
Exeter is a trademark of Bookthrift Marketing, Inc.
Bookthrift is a registered trademark of Bookthrift Marketing
New York, New York

ISBN 0-671-08923-4

Printed in Hong Kong

Designer: Martin Bristow
Editor: Jane Laslett
Picture researcher: Wendy Sacks
Assistant picture researcher: Mandy Little

Page 1 *La Nue Provinciale, Marie-Anne at Gordes, c 1949*, by Willy Ronis, one of France's most regarded reportage photographers. (Willy Ronis/Rapho.)

Page 2 *Three figures in silk by Julian Tomchin*, 1967, by Hiro – a fashion photographer adding visual skills to the idea of selling style. (© Hiro, 1967; courtesy of the photographer.)

Page 5 *Rumania*, 1975, a classic image by Henri Cartier-Bresson, who set his style in the 1930s and influenced three generations of photographers. (© Henri Cartier-Bresson/Magnum; courtesy John Hillelson Agency.)

Author's Acknowledgments

Unlike many projects I have undertaken, requiring specific research, this book represents 20 years of general enquiry. The people who have helped me en route – photographers, curators, historians and friends – are too numerous to mention individually. However, they know who they are and to all of them goes my warmest gratitude. This said, Mark Haworth-Booth and Chris Titterington of the Victoria & Albert Museum, London, deserve especial thanks for giving so much time to my frequent visits and making available to me their magnificent collection. From Australia, Gael Newton helped in selecting nineteenth-century material, as did William Main in New Zealand. Working with me were Wendy Sacks as picture researcher, who performed minor miracles in locating sources for the works published, and Jane Laslett as editor who never complained about my spelling and induced me to give more than I thought possible. Both have been assets. Let me acknowledge also Heather Forbes, my partner, who accepted my preoccupation with the project with more affection and good grace than I deserve, and Eileen Pilkington of *Creative Camera* magazine, whose capacity to hold the fort enabled this work to be completed.

Graham King has written widely on aspects of popular culture, from the fiction of the French author Emile Zola to the sociological impact of British comic strips. He is also a student and collector of snapshots, and his book *Say 'Cheese'!*, published in America and Britain, is a pioneer study of the snapshot as art and social history. A professional scriptwriter, he has published poetry and several novels, one of which won a 1974 Royal Society of Literature Award. (Chapter 4: You Press the Button . . .)

Martin Harrison was director of the Olympus Gallery, London, from 1982-5. He organized the 'Shots of Style' exhibition at the Victoria and Albert Museum in 1986 and is the author of Part I of a retrospective on David Bailey, *Black and White Memories*. (Chapter 9: The Selling Image)

Except where otherwise noted, all prints are silver-gelatin.

Contents

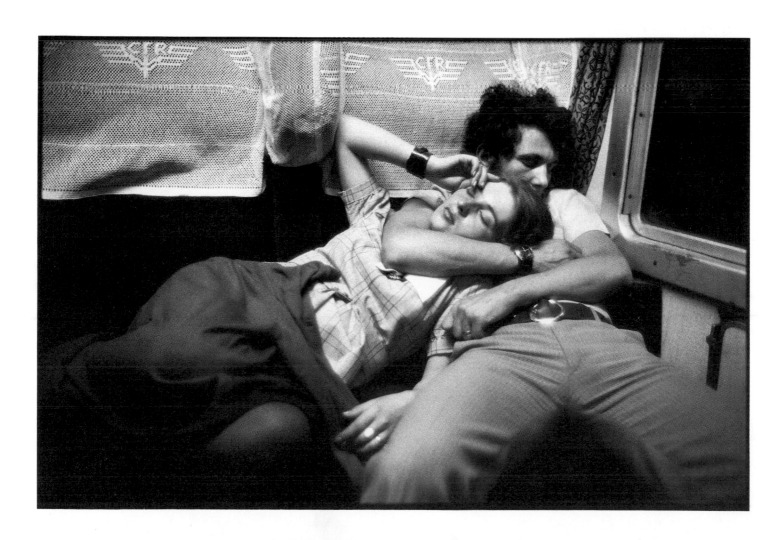

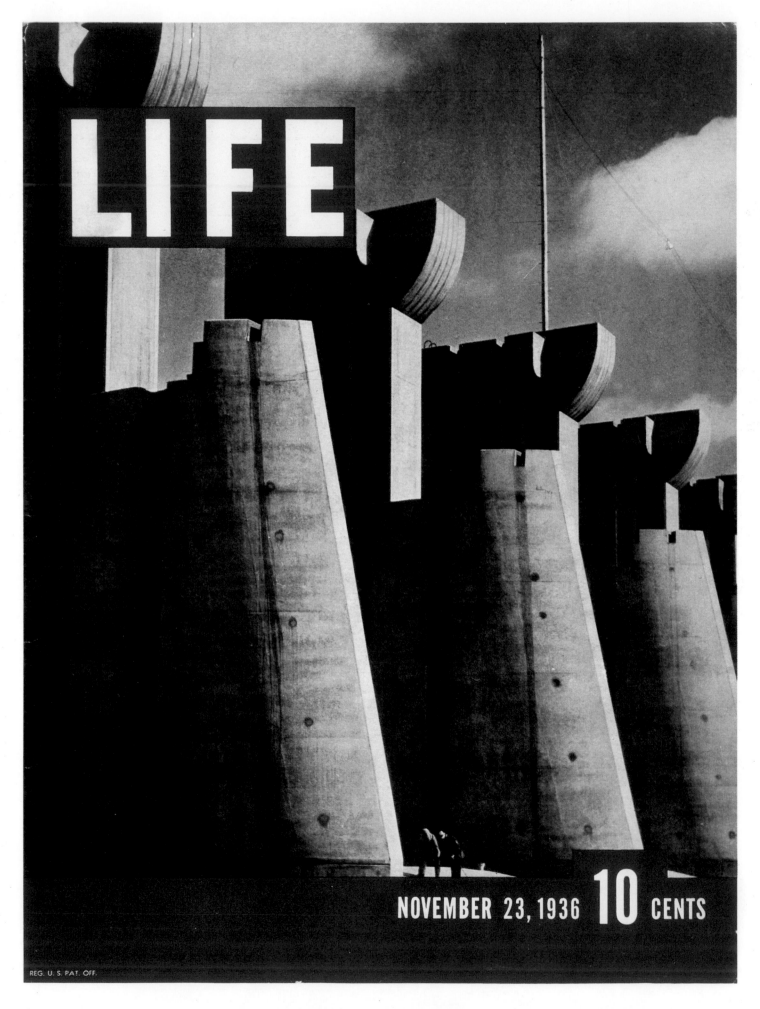

Introduction

I was told once that more photographs exist than bricks. A careless, off-hand little statistic perhaps – but extraordinary none the less. The very suggestion of such a vast image bank fills me with wonder. Photographs, like bricks, are everywhere. Can there be anyone left who has not seen a photograph? And what number of the world's population has not been in a photograph? In the West, at least, photography records the essential rites of passage. From snapshots to billboards, from the cradle to the grave, we give and receive through images on a daily basis. Photography is a remarkable medium and all the more so for its part in our lives.

A history of photography, then, could almost be a story of the world since 1839. That was the year a means of making these fascinating, small-scale replicas of reality was first announced. But such a project, were it attempted, would fill many volumes. Outside direct representation of the dramas, crises, wars, revolutions and political upheavals we might associate with such a work, photography has another axis. As a small medium it is uniquely sited at an intersection between art and science, commerce, philosophy and technology. That point, that meeting place, seems a more appropriate beginning to an examination of its own history. The ideas of the intersection have been my point of departure.

Technology has played a secondary role in photography's visual history – for all their micro-chip sophistication today's cameras are close relatives of the humble wooden apparatus made for William Henry Fox-Talbot (England's inventor of the negative/positive process) by his village carpenter. I have provided an introduction to the topic, but photo-technology from invention to today's electronic imaging systems is a subject in itself and needs its own, specialist history. Photography and science too requires separate examination. The two combined have massively expanded what we know of our environment, terrestrial and celestial. A brief overview is contained in Chapter 10. Similarly photography and its relationship with commerce, another specialist subject, is overviewed in Chapter 9. Art and philosophy comprise the main thrust of this history.

More photographs than bricks ... and more photographers than a single book could possibly hope to cover. Photography is such a new medium that contributors to its history are uncovered almost daily. Many will never surface – their work remains only in fragments, the rest neglected, lost, destroyed. Many are known only to a few intimates. This acknowledged, there is so much material to choose from that it is possible to construct separate and self-contained pictures of photography's past – a history of Russian photography; women's photography; portrait photography; photography as propaganda. Such a list is as long as one's imagination or short as one's goal. However, the history here is largely Western and is concerned, mainly, with an accepted

Left The first front cover of *Life*. Photograph by Margaret Bourke-White, *Fort Peck Dam, 1936*. (Margaret Bourke-White, *Life* Magazine © 1936 Time Inc.)

Below Photographic history recognized in the US Civil War. Albumen stereo card of a dead soldier, 1865, by Timothy H O'Sullivan. (Gordon D Hoffman.)

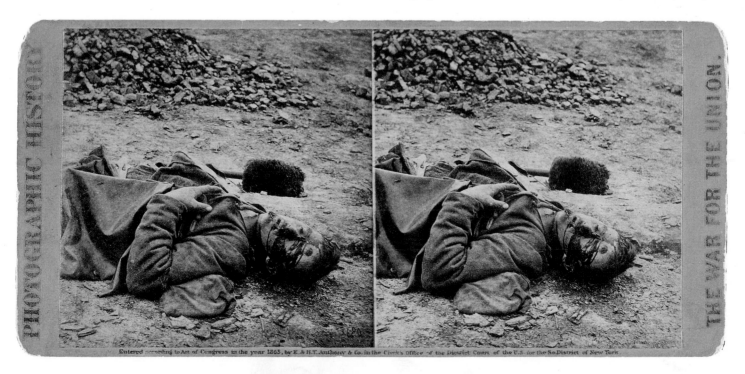

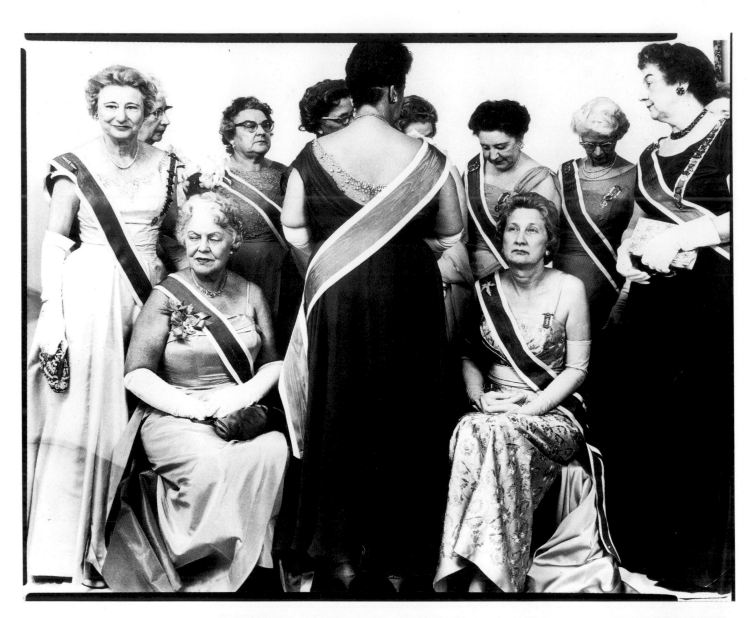

Above *The Generals of the Daughters of the American Revolution, Washington DC*, 1963, by Richard Avedon, doyen of US portraitists. (Copyright © by Richard Avedon Inc. All rights reserved.)

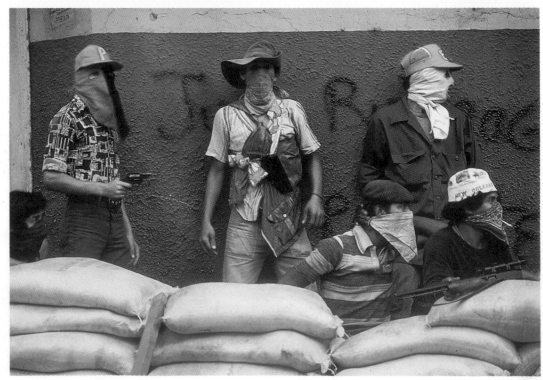

Right From her book *Nicaragua*, 1981, by Susan Meiselas, a contemporary photojournalist who lends political awareness to her skills as a visual reporter. (© Susan Meiselas/Magnum; courtesy John Hillelson Agency.)

canon: images transcending utility, dull record or simplistic statement; the people who made them, their circumstances and some reasons why and how the pictures look the way they do.

Much of the book's structure is based on my experience teaching photography. In history sessions I discovered how tracing ideas and relationships rather than a broad then-to-now scenario made the subject more interesting to students curious to know where our concepts of what makes a 'good' picture came from. To know where you are going it is useful to know where you have come from. Teaching too taught me. I have stressed here the notion of photography as an art, in part because this is what I know best, in part because the 'other' general history – one in which ideological concepts subsume images into a determinist's tale – leaves little room for photographers (and I was teaching photographers), only for photography. Little room as well for photography as an expressive medium. The 'other' history is of photography as a mass medium and a means of control rather than personal liberation. In time this 'other' history will be written.

Most chapters in this history have been conceived of as relatively self-contained examinations of some enduring strand of photography written around the image makers who contributed most to its development. Not all the photographers mentioned can be represented by their works and some whose pictures are shown do not feature in my text. This is no accident. My words are not illustrated by the pictures, nor has what I write been conceived of as a narrative to support selected pictures. My aim is for images and text to form a partnership – each complementing the other in unfolding a changing idea of photography's contribution to visual culture.

I hope you find the pictures here stimulating and sometimes surprising. Some of the photographers mentioned or

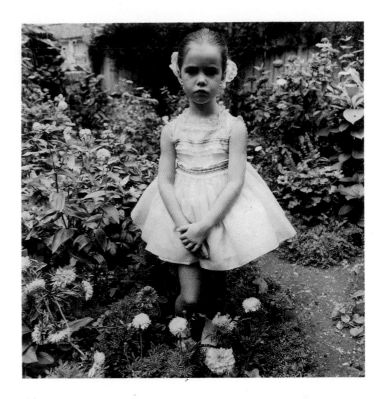

shown have been subjects of monographs – the bibliography on page 221 should aid tracking down more information and more pictures. The latter is particularly important – photography is a serial art and the final picture often lies in many images. Lastly a note on reproductions. We have come to believe that when reproduced photographs are true facsimiles. This is not the case. Color (even in monochrome images), scale and texture all contribute to a photograph's meaning. There are substantial national or regional collections in most Western countries. Visit them and see fine photographs first hand.

PETER TURNER

Above right *Petal Pink for Little Parties,* fashion photograph by Diane Arbus, 1962. Arbus was later to become acclaimed for her deeply personal portrayal of American society. (Copyright © Estate of Diane Arbus 1962. Courtesy of *Harper's Bazaar,* The Hearst Corporation.)

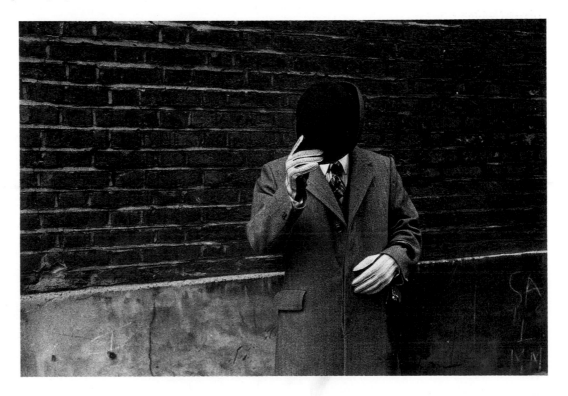

Right A portrait of the author as a young photographer, by Peter Turner, 1976. (© Peter Turner.)

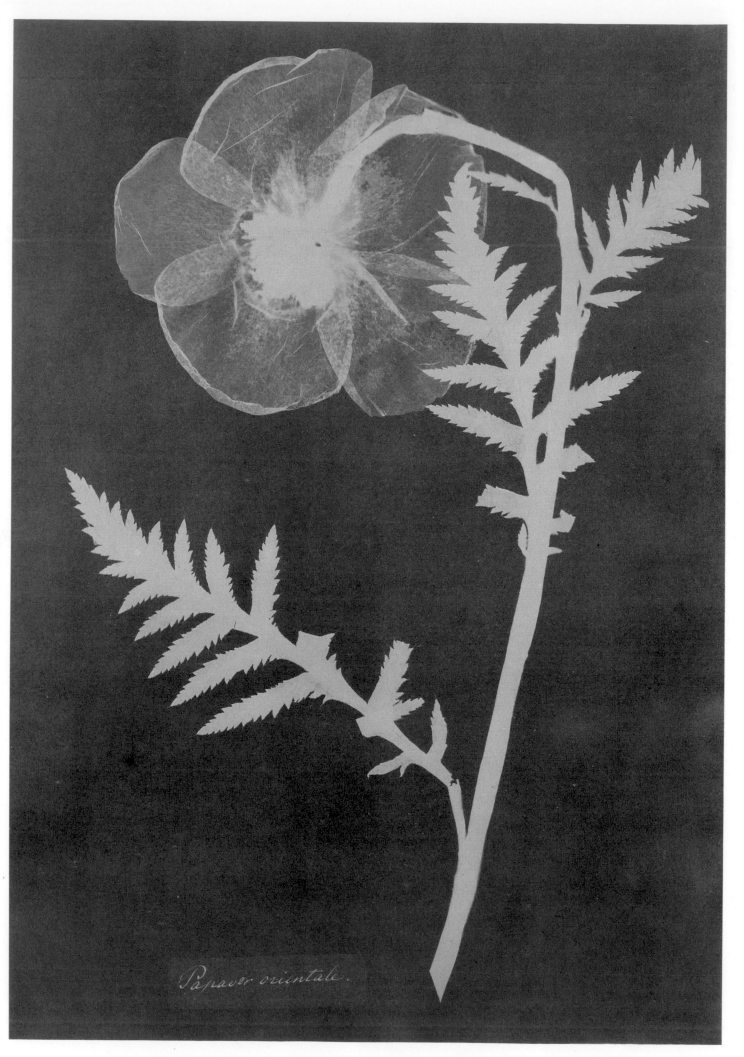

Papaver orientale.

CHAPTER ONE

Through a Glass Darkly

The Beginnings of Photography

'And this led me to reflect,' wrote a nineteenth-century English gentleman, 'on the inimitable beauty of the pictures of nature's painting which the glass lens of the Camera throws upon the paper in its focus – fairy pictures, creatures of a moment, and destined as rapidly to fade away.' The gentleman was William Henry Fox Talbot, a sometime scientist and politician, the year 1833. On a Grand Tour of Europe he was supplementing his poorly developed skills as an artist with the aid of a mechanical and optical device called a camera obscura. Known for centuries as a means of producing an image from reality which could be traced on paper, the camera obscura was a likely addition to the luggage of a well-to-do tourist. Like many of his generation Talbot used it to sketch views, to record his travels and to provide an accurate if shaky rendering of what lay before its lens. But unlike many who must have thought similarly, Talbot's muse continued, to suggest 'how charming it would be if it were possible to cause these natural images to imprint themselves durably and remain fixed upon paper!'

When Talbot returned to England and his home, Lacock Abbey in Wiltshire, he set about the problem. His aim, quite simply, was to capture and preserve the camera-made image and he began to experiment. In a world filled with the excitements of discovery and invention – from Darwin's voyage on the *Beagle* to Morse devising the telegraph – the invention of photography can be seen as a natural extension of nineteenth-century appetites for advancement and innovation. It comes as small surprise then, to learn that as Talbot worked at Lacock using silver salts that darkened under light, so too were pioneers in France and Brazil. Unknown to Talbot he

was by no means the first to attempt 'Photogenic Drawings' as he began to call his pictures. The quest for a means of mechanical reproduction had begun during the Renaissance and was reaching its climax at the very time he wrote, in 1835, that he had 'obtained very perfect, but extremely small pictures, such as without great stretch of the imagination might be supposed to be the work of some Lilliputian artist.'

Cameras obscura were described by Leonardo da Vinci and in some detail by Giovanni Battista della Porta in his book *Magiae Naturalis* (Natural Magic) published in 1558. The phenomenon they spoke of was one which had been observed as far back as the fifth century BC – when the rays of light reflected from an object pass through a tiny hole and into a darkened chamber, the object can be seen as an inverted replica projected in smaller size on a white wall. In 1569 Daniello Barbaro, a professor in Padua, Italy, noted in his treatise 'La practica della perspecttiva' that an optical lens might improve the result. 'Close all shutters and doors,' he instructed, 'until no light enters the *camera* except through the lens, and opposite hold a sheet of paper which you move forward and backward until the scene appears in sharpest detail. There on the paper you will see the whole view as it really is. By holding the paper steady you can trace the whole perspective with a pen.'

Cameras obscura were an aid to drafting, a means of gaining a sense of perspective in drawings and paintings. Medieval artists thought of their medium as a means of narrative, a way of illustrating some perception of their world. Their sense of linear representation was far removed from our own – people of importance were given status by being shown

Right Engraving of a portable camera obscura made by Athanasius Kirchner in 1646. An artist would have the camera carried to a suitable vantage point then trace the inverted image thrown up as light reflected from the subject passed through a tiny hole. (Gernsheim Collection, Harry Ransom Humanities Research Center, the University of Texas at Austin.)

Left *Papaver (Oriental)*, a cyanotype or blueprint by Anna Atkins *c* 1853. Cyanotype was one of the earliest photographic processes and Atkins possibly the first woman photographer. (Victoria and Albert Museum.)

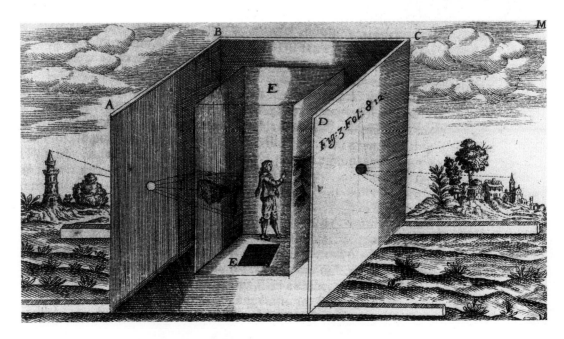

Right A table camera obscura engraved by Georg Brander, 1769. As cameras obscura progressed in design they became more versatile. This one used a 45° angle mirror which projected the image upwards, making tracing easier. It could be focused via a series of tightly fitting boxes which telescoped back and forth until the image was sharp. (Gernsheim Collection, Harry Ransom Humanities Research Center, the University of Texas at Austin.)

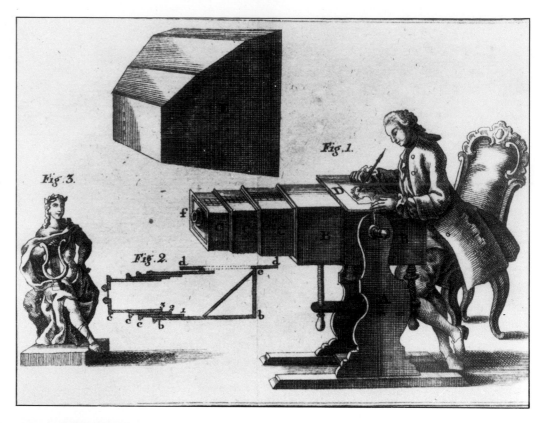

Below *Joseph Nicéphore Niépce,* maker of the world's first surviving photograph, from a painting by Leonard-François Berger, 1854. (Science Museum, London.)

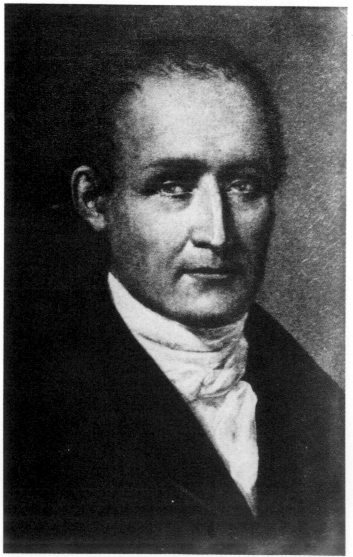

larger and the same person might appear several times in one painting as the story unfolded. As this visually effective but otherwise unsatisfactory means of showing the world came into question, so artists developed 'one point perspective,' the view that one person had of a scene from a single standpoint at a particular moment. It looked 'realistic' but required a high level of skill to take it beyond the confines of geometry and absolute precision and place it back in a world of constant flux. Realism wanted 'naturalism' to make it work. And the camera obscura was on hand to inform the artist's hand.

At first the cameras were adapted rooms, which limited their use. The artist would enter and work from within, but once a transcription had been made of the view from that point, the system had nothing but novelty to commend it. By the seventeenth century they had become portable and by the eighteenth century cameras obscura were in common use by artists throughout Europe. Thus the stage was set for photography, literally 'drawing with light.' All that remained was to find a way to preserve the images from life contained within the camera. It was a problem which suited what is called 'The Age of Reason' yet its solution lay in the past. Fabricus, an alchemist, had discovered that the sun's rays would darken certain silver compounds in 1552. However it was not until almost 200 years later that the first serious step was made towards the invention of photography. In 1727 Johann Heinrich Schulze published a paper at the Nuremburg Academy of Natural Philosophers. 'Scotophorous Discovered Instead of Phosphorous or, A Noteworthy Experiment of the Action of the Sun's Rays' describes how he had accidentally come up a mixture of silver nitrates that darkened when exposed to light. As phosphorous means 'bringer of light,' so Schulze named his discovery 'bringer of

Right *Intérieur d'un Cabinet Curiosité,* daguerreotype still-life by Louis Jacques Mandé Daguerre. Made in 1837, two years before photography was made public, stillness was a prerequisite for the first photographers – this image needed an exposure of over an hour. (Collection Société Française de Photographie.)

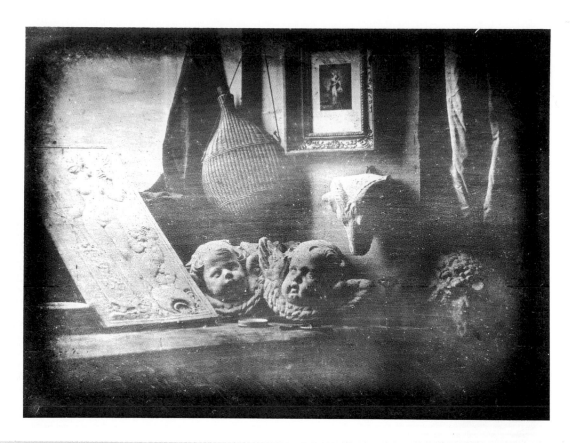

Below *View from a Window at Gras,* 1827, a heliograph by Joseph Nicéphore Niépce, the oldest photographic image extant and the result of an eight-hour exposure. Heliography differed in broad detail from Daguerre's process but Niépce may fairly be called the first to make 'an image from nature.' (Gernsheim Collection, Harry Ransom Humanities Research Center, the University of Texas at Austin.)

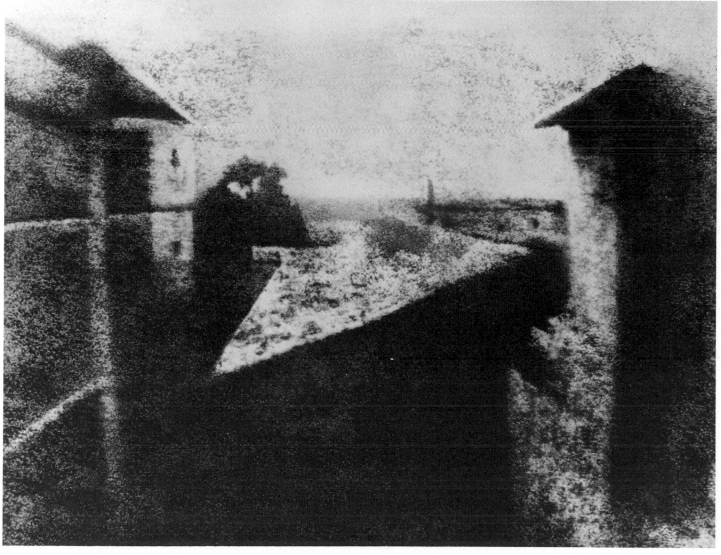

darkness.' It marked a turning point. For the first time there was proof positive that the sun could be used to imprint its energy.

Professor Schulze was not alone in his endeavors; other chemists throughout Europe were also experimenting. At the close of the eighteenth century all that was needed to preserve the fleeting pleasures of the camera obscura was known, but in rudimentary form. Not until 1802 did the first primitive images emerge. Thomas Wedgwood and Sir Humphry Davy working in England described a process by which they attempted to copy paintings made on glass on to paper or white leather. 'When the shadow of any figure is thrown upon the prepared surface, the part concealed by it remains white, and the other parts speedily become dark.' Sadly their 'sun prints' contained two fatal flaws – they were impermanent and could be viewed only by candlelight. It was Davy who wrote, 'Nothing but a method of preventing the unshaded parts of the delineation from being coloured by exposure to the day is wanting, to render the process as useful as it is elegant.' From the time of the Industrial Revolution and a rising middle-class hungry for newness, his words have an almost plaintive ring. Had Wedgwood and Davy discovered a fixative, they would most certainly have enjoyed the wealth of invention. As it was, this went to France and Louis Jacques Mandé Daguerre.

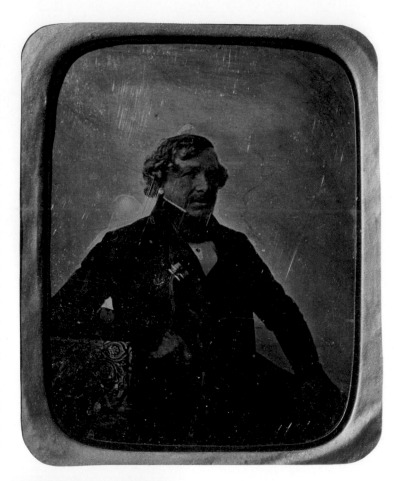

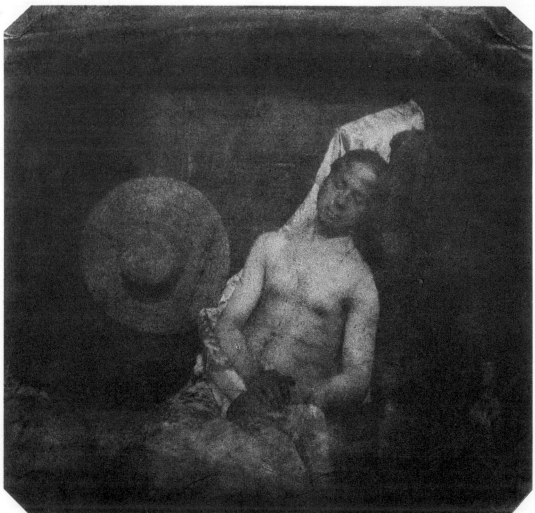

Above *Portrait of Louis Jacques Mandé Daguerre, c* 1844, first to be credited with photography's invention, by Jean Baptiste Sabatier-Blot. (Collection Société Française de Photographie.)

Left Hippolyte Bayard, *Portrait of the Photographer as a Drowned Man*, 1840. Bayard, another significant French inventor of photography, had his direct-positive process suppressed by his government in favor of the daguerreotype. In mock despair (for he went on to make exceptional images) he made this, the first photographic self-portrait. (Collection Société Française de Photographie.)

Right *Fishing at Flaipool*, daguerreotype by Horatio Ross, 1847. An extraordinary example of early photography outside the studio. Photographing his son with John Munro, Ross created something similar to a snapshot. Massive over-exposure of the sky caused it to partially reverse and so turn blue. (Victoria and Albert Museum.)

It was Daguerre who in 1839 made public the discovery of photography, but it is to his fellow countryman and business partner Joseph Nicéphore Niépce that true credit must go for making the first successful photograph. Niépce was an inventor. From a family of standing in the provincial town of Chalon-sur-Saône, he tried his skills in such diverse projects as the internal combustion engine and a means of improving the then-infant lithography before coming upon the concept we call photography. In a letter dated 1 April 1816 to his brother Claude who lived in Hammersmith, now a London suburb, he wrote, 'The experiments I have done up till now make me believe that, as far as the principal effect, my process will work well; but I need to arrive at some way of fixing the color: this is what is concerning me at the moment, and it's the thing which is most difficult.' In another letter dated 5 May the same year, he mentions again the 'great difficulties . . . in fixing the colors' and goes on to describe what can only be a black-and-white negative. Two weeks later Claude received a letter with 'two prints made by the process you know about.' In short, while 1839 is the official year for the invention of photography it is clear that photographs were made at least as early as 1816, and that attempts were being made to produce them in color!

How then did Daguerre enter the arena? And what of Talbot and his experiments?

Louis Jacques Mandé Daguerre, born just outside Paris in 1787, began his working life as an apprentice painter of panoramas; enormous landscapes, battle scenes or cityscapes, some over 100 meters long, they were exhibited as public entertainments in the capitals of Europe. Shown in semidarkness and painted with consummate skill, they gave an astonishing illusion of reality. From panoramas Daguerre turned to the theater proper and in 1816 became a stage designer and creator of theatrical illusions. He was highly successful and in 1821 combined his talents in new kind of show – the Diorama. Here massive paintings on semitransparent paper were subjected to a cleverly changing lighting which formed a display so apparently real that contemporary reporters almost refused to believe the cathedrals and sweeping vistas they witnessed were mere representations. This venture, too, was a great success and Daguerre won a great reputation and public acclaim. However, he remained unsatisfied. 'My dioramas are perishable,' he is reputed to have said, 'to win immortality I need a second, more permanent, renown.'

As part of his apprenticeship Daguerre would almost certainly have used the camera obscura for perspective drawing. By 1824 his appreciation of this aid to accuracy had developed into a search for some means of retaining its images. His quest seemed obsessional and touched with madness. In 1827, it is reported, Madame Daguerre approached the famous French

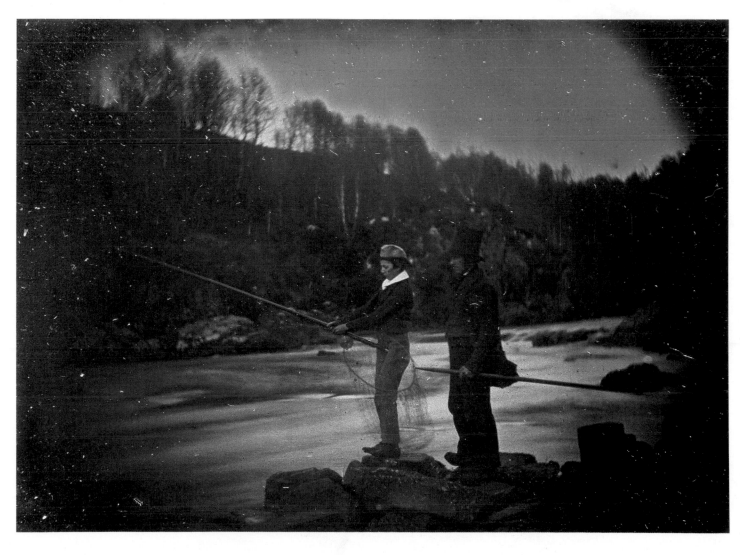

chemist Dumas, 'I have to ask you a question of vital importance to myself. I am the wife of Daguerre, the painter. He has for some time been possessed by the idea that he can fix the images of the camera. He is always at the thought, he cannot sleep at night for it. I am afraid he is out of his mind. Do you, as a man of science, think it can ever be done, or is he mad?' 'It cannot be done,' Dumas replied, 'but I cannot say it will always remain impossible, nor set the man down as mad who seeks to do it.'

It was about this time that Daguerre learned of Niépce and his experiments. The two began a correspondence which culminated in a partnership, Daguerre hoping to pair his entrepreneurial skills and flair for showmanship with Niépce's advanced techniques. In 1833, however, Niépce died and Daguerre, still chasing the elusive fixative, continued alone. Isidore, Niépce's son, inherited rights to the partnership but was unable to contribute to further experiments. Two years later, under pressure from Daguerre, Isidore signed an agreement which recognized technical advances made by Daguerre alone. In 1837 a final agreement was put before the now-impoverished Isidore. Using a salt solution, Daguerre had finally succeeded in making his images permanent! The process, Daguerre insisted, was new and should bear his name. *Heliography*, Niépce's discovery, faced obscurity. So different were the two means of making pictures, claimed Daguerre, that they should be offered for sale separately. Torn between the certain knowledge that without Niépce Daguerre would not have succeeded, and the financial gains he felt sure would follow what seemed to him a modification of his father's invention, Isidore signed.

It was, then, to an excited gathering at the Paris Académie des Sciences on 7 January 1839 that the announcement was made of Daguerre's invention. As it shocked Paris (Paul Delaroche the painter is said to have exclaimed 'from today painting is dead') the news was to shake others too. William Henry Fox Talbot in England was one, Hippolyte Bayard, a French civil servant, another. Bayard had dabbled in the idea of photography for some time. Unlike Niépce and Daguerre, who worked with polished metal plates as the support for a light-sensitive emulsion, Bayard chose paper. Sensitized with silver chloride and potassium iodide, it was bleached by light in a camera obscura. The result was a positive paper print. Like daguerreotypes each image was unique and like the process that Talbot was investigating, they were on paper. Bayard worked alone and was distressed to find his independent invention eclipsed by Daguerre's. Daguerre, backed by François Arago, a highly influential scientist, had sold his process to the French government in return for a pension for life of 6000 francs per annum for himself and 4000 francs annually for Isidore Niépce. Bayard, more diffident by nature, was given 600 francs and asked in the most diplomatic terms not to interfere with the promotion of the daguerreotype. Saddened in retrospect by his treatment, for he had displayed his work in public before any but a select group had seen Daguerre's pictures, Bayard nevertheless continued to photograph. His feelings might be judged by a self-portrait he produced in 1840 – the photographer as a drowned man. On the back of this print he wrote 'The body you see is that of Monsieur Bayard ... The Academy, the King, and all who have seen his pictures admired them, just as you do. Admiration brought him prestige, but not a sou. The Government which gave M. Daguerre so much said it could do nothing for M. Bayard and the poor wretch drowned himself. Oh! the vagaries of human life!'

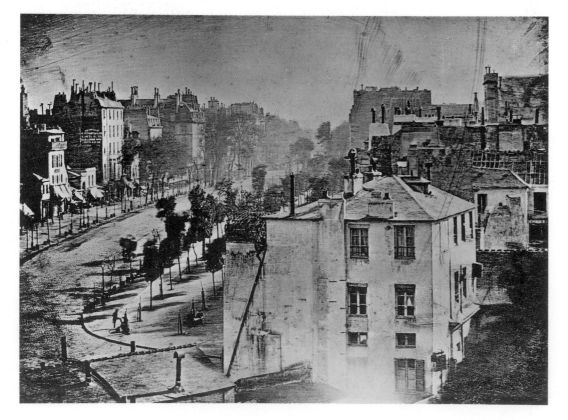

Left *Boulevard du Temple, Paris, c*1838, a daguerreotype by Louis Jacques Mandé Daguerre, one of the earliest known photographs to look outside the studio. Significant, because of long exposure, is the lack of people in this normally busy street – except for the boot black and his shadowy customer. (Bayerisches Nationalmuseum.)

Right Photography's invention and popularity attracted satirical comment. From an 1840 engraving we see the technical problems of image making, with a camera sending the new kind of artist to sleep while waiting for the sun to do his work for him. (Gernsheim Collection, Harry Ransom Humanities Research Center, the University of Texas at Austin.)

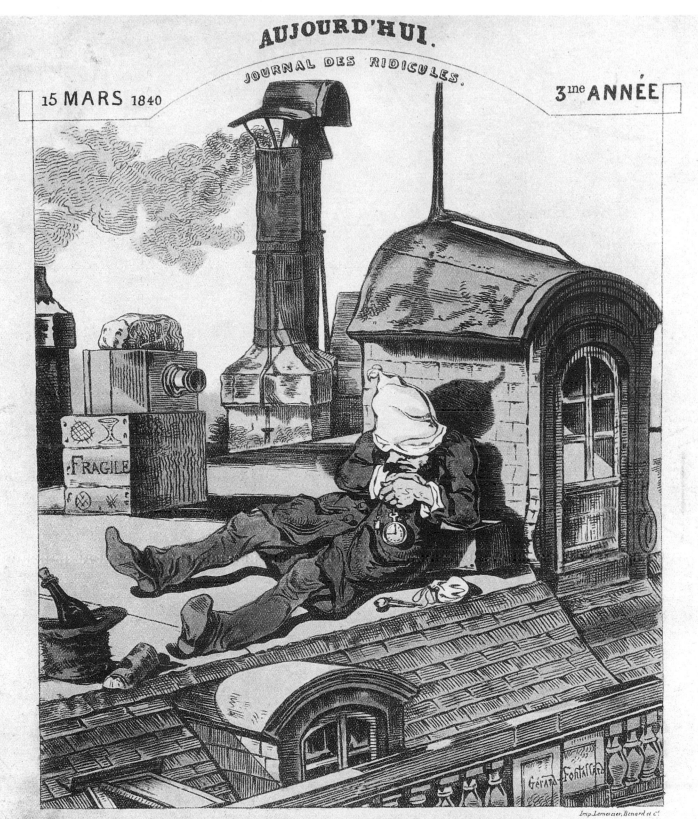

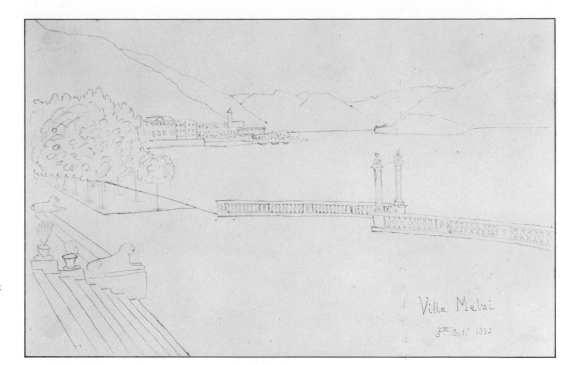

Villa Melzi

5th Oct.r 1833

Right A camera lucida sketch, 1833, by William Henry Fox Talbot, made while travelling in Italy. (Science Museum, London.)

Below *Game Keeper, c* 1844, by Fox Talbot, one of many similar pictures made by the inventor of the negative/positive process at Lacock Abbey in Wiltshire. (Science Museum, London.)

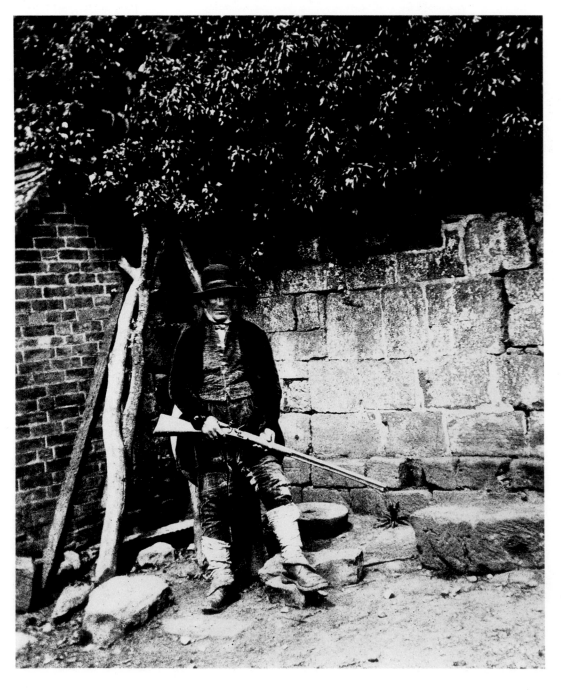

Right *The Reading Photographic Establishment,* Fox Talbot's workshop for volume production of calotypes. Taken in 1844 it shows Talbot (right) and his assistant Nicholaas Henneman. (Science Museum, London.)

If the luckless Bayard compared his fortune with that of Daguerre and found his position wanting, Talbot was stunned to find himself pipped at the post. He had been experimenting little between 1835 and 1838, devoting his time instead to writing. Now, fearing that his labors might prove valueless, he swept into action. To the French scientists who had supported Daguerre he wrote notes claiming the invention of photography as his own. Then, some 18 days after publication of Daguerre's news, he made a presentation to the Royal Institution in London. The works consisted of 'flowers and leaves; a pattern of lace; figures taken from painted glass; a view of Venice copied from an engraving; some images formed by the Solar Microscope, viz a slice of wood highly magnified ... Another Microscopic sketch, exhibiting the reticulations on the wing of an insect. Finally: various pictures representing the architecture of my house in the country; all these made in the summer of 1835. And this I believe to be the first instance on record of a house having painted its own portrait.' A week later he made available a paper entitled 'Some Account of the Art of Photogenic Drawing, or, the Process by which Natural Objects May be Made to Delineate Themselves without the Aid of the Artist's Pencil.'

Talbot had presumed, incorrectly, that his process and Daguerre's were identical. Daguerre's works, described by a contemporary observer as 'Nature itself,' were positives made on copper plates. Talbot's were negatives, made on paper and subject to the coarseness of the paper's fibers. Both, however, had an electrifying effect on those who saw them. Samuel Morse, in Paris to patent his telegraph when the daguerreotype was announced and interested because he too had made photographic experiments with a camera obscura, wrote back to his brothers in America, 'they are produced on a metallic surface, the principal pieces about 7 inches by 5, and they resemble aquatint engravings, for they are in simple chiaro scuro, and not in colors. But the exquisite minuteness of the delineation cannot be conceived. No painting or engraving ever approached it.' Sir John Robinson as a member of a party invited to Paris to inspect the new camera-made images reported back to the Society of Arts in Edinburgh that 'the perfection and fidelity of the pictures are such

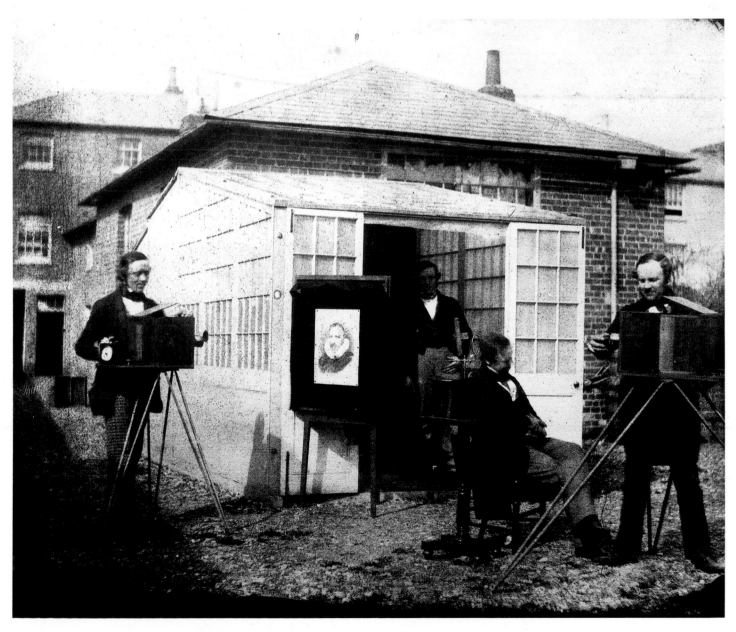

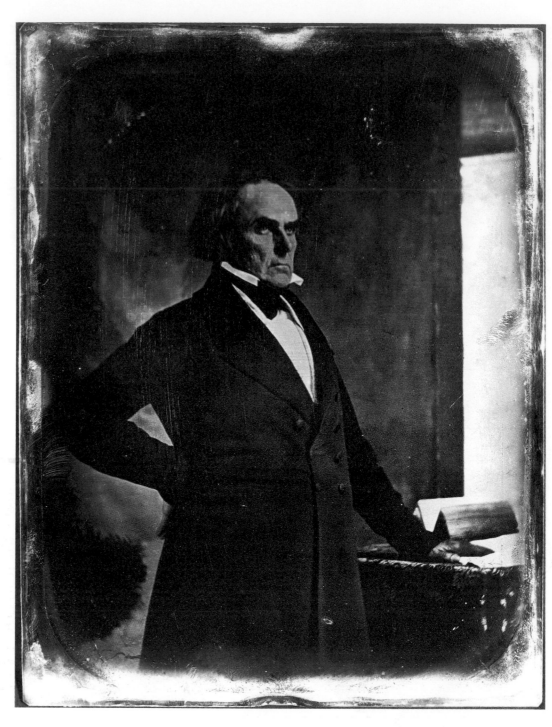

Right *Daniel Webster,* nd, daguerreotype by Albert Southworth and Josiah Hawes. (Courtesy, Museum of Fine Arts, Boston. Gift of Edward Southworth Hawes in memory of his father Josiah Johnson Hawes.)

that on examining them by microscopic power, details are discovered which are not perceivable to the naked eye in the original objects: a crack in plaster, a withered leaf lying on a projecting cornice, or an accumulation of dust in a hollow moulding of a distant building.'

On seeing Talbot's first exposition at the Royal Institution, Michael Faraday remarked that 'no human hand has hitherto traced such lines as these drawings display; and what man may hereafter do, now that Dame Nature has become his drawing mistress, it is impossible to predict.' It was Talbot's friend Sir John Herschel, however, who picked up the true difference between the methods. Invited to Paris with Sir John Robinson, he too was deeply impressed by daguerreotypes but noted that despite their clinical accuracy (in comparison Talbot's were 'vague, foggy things') there was

no means of duplicating the image once made. It was Herschel, a brilliant man, who named Talbot's originals 'negatives' and the generation made from them 'positives.' He also coined the term 'photography,' discovered an improved means of fixing photographic images permanently by using sodium thiosulphate – known then and now as 'hypo' – and independently 'invented' photography in three days. Following the news from Paris and London but with no details of how either process worked, he set to in January 1839 and made 'something of the same kind.' His recognition of 'hypo' (known by Herschel in 1819) was almost as important to photography's future as the inventions of Talbot and Daguerre. Without it our inheritance of the photographic wonders of the nineteenth-century world would be little more than faded relics of a bygone age.

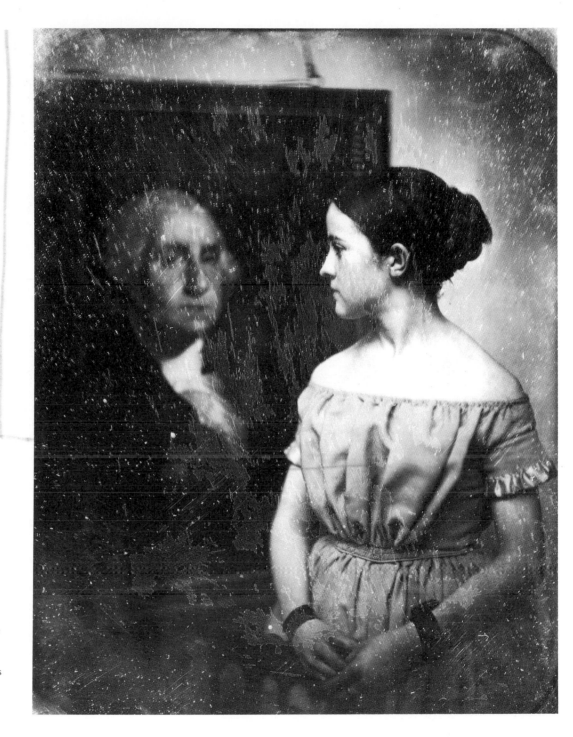

Right *Girl with portrait of Washington,* nd, daguerreotype by Albert Southworth and Josiah Hawes. (The Metropolitan Museum of Art, Gift of I N Phelps Stokes, Edward S Hawes, Alice Mary Hawes, Marion Augusta Hawes, 1937. 37.14.53.)

The world was amazed by photography, seeing it as a triumph of human inventiveness and a means of placing art in the hands of all who could master its techniques and chemistry. Exposures were long, as much as 30 minutes in bright sun, and the processes hazardous to health, but the infant medium attracted devotees in large numbers. In return for his pension, Daguerre had been required by the French government to make his process public; indeed it was given free to the world. Except Britain. Five days before that shattering announcement to the Academy in Paris, the wily Daguerre had patented his process in Britain. So great was the sense of competition between the two nations that licenses were to be sold to would-be daguerreotypists across the Channel. And so great was Talbot's sense of accomplishment that he proceeded to patent his process, but not until 1841. By then he had improved his original methods via the discovery of a latent image that could be chemically developed to equal the density of his original negatives. Previously the negative had been exposed until it became visible within the camera. Now much shorter exposures, perhaps half a minute, were possible. He named the changed process calotype, from the Greek for 'beautiful,' and used a mixture of gallic acid and silver nitrate as his developer. With an exposure of just thirty seconds, portraiture would be possible.

Having little hope of receiving financial recognition from the British government in the manner France had honored Daguerre, Talbot was eager to see some return for his efforts and, like his rival, began selling licenses. The first was purchased by Henry Collen, a painter of miniatures who hoped to capitalize on the process's receptivity to retouching.

Right *The Butterfly Collector,* *c* 1850, a daguerreotype by an unknown photographer. (International Museum of Photography at George Eastman House.)

Below *Portrait of Egerton Cleeve,* a hand-tinted daguerreotype in papier-mâché case, late 1840s. (Victoria and Albert Museum.)

Opposite left *Portrait of Martha Emma Roper,* *c* 1851 by William Edward Kilburn, a hand-tinted daguerreotype in a plush-lined papier mâché case. (Victoria and Albert Museum.)

Opposite right *Members of the Roper Family* photographed by William Edward Kilburn *c* 1851. Hand-tinted daguerreotype. (Victoria and Albert Museum.)

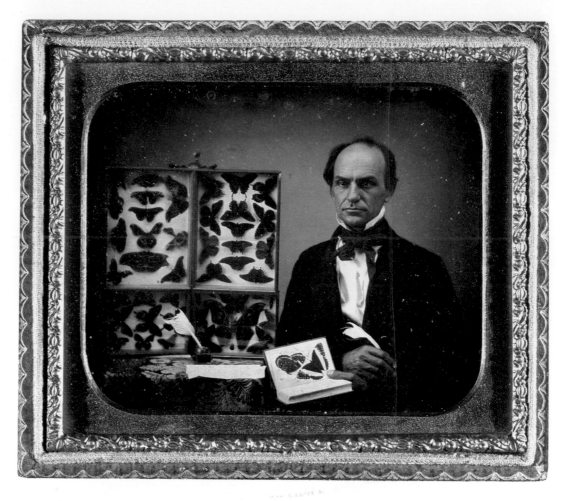

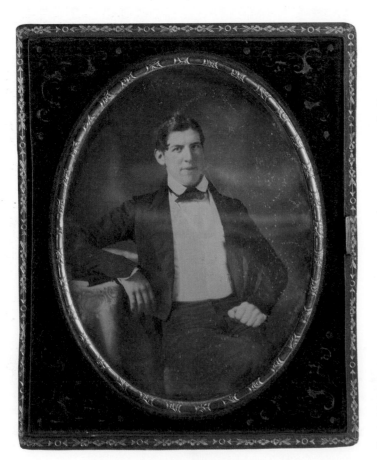

Daguerreotype portraits (Daguerre had also come upon the possibility of a latent image and reduced exposure times) were becoming established in Europe, America and England. With an acute eye for the marketplace, Collen saw their drawbacks. For all their exactness and fidelity they were, to quote from a contemporary account, 'so absolutely fearful, that we have but little hope of ever seeing anything tolerable from any machine ... its best likeness can be only that of a rigid bust or corpse.' Conversely, calotypes had 'a rough air of truth about them ... full of broad effects and vigour.' Made on paper they could be 'improved' by the judicious use of pen and pencil and so combine the newness of photography with established artistic values. Collen was not successful. His daguerrean rivals were taking £60 a day but Collen's first annual royalty to Talbot, an agreed 30 per cent of turnover, amounted to a miserable £70 2s 9d. By his own admission he was not sufficiently skilled in the theory or practice of photography. In 1844 his license lapsed and Talbot, who had been seeking a more able partner since 1842, sold calotype rights to Antoine Claudet, a banker turned daguerreotypist from France.

Despite patent restrictions, the daguerreotype had gripped public attention in England. Claudet, then resident in London, had travelled to Paris and bought rights to the process directly from Daguerre (others had to deal with his English agent, Miles Berry). He paid the then-huge sum of £200 for his license and in June 1841 opened a studio known as the 'Glass House' at the Adelaide Gallery off the Strand, London. (The site of this studio is still known today as Glasshouse Street.) Although Claudet was the second, not the first, to open a photographic portrait studio – that honor going to Richard Beard – unlike his commercial rival he was a scholarly person whose attempts to go beyond commercial utilization of photography must have appealed to Talbot. Their negotiations were long and complex, taking 18 months before both parties reached agreement even though Claudet felt Talbot's method had a 'beauty which the other has not' and that it was possible to 'send them through the post, stick them in albums ... and obtain an unlimited number of copies.'

Claudet struggled and failed to make a commercial success with the calotype. In order to cover the costs of his studio he needed to make five portraits a day and the public preferred daguerreotypes. The process of being portrayed was less arduous because exposure times were shorter, more detail was visible and the finished picture was presented, jewel-like, in a very handsome closing case. Daguerreotype studios flourished – in London, Paris, Berlin and many other European cities.

The United States too was seduced by the silvery verisimilitude of photography. As early as 1839 Samuel Morse began to take daguerreotypes in New York and in 1840 'the first daguerreotype gallery for portraits' opened in that city. It was run by two associates of Morse, Alexander Wolcott and John Johnson. This enterprise opened so soon after France's gift to the world that it must have run on novelty value alone, for the improvements that also restrained commercial calotype exploitation were yet to be made and the process was agonizingly slow. One of Wolcott's early sitters recounts in a letter dated 2 February 1840 that he sat 'for eight minutes with strong sunlight shining on my face and tears trickling down my cheeks.' Technology improved at a rapid rate, however, and exposure times soon came down to a manageable 30 seconds. A new lens was designed by the Austrian Josef Petzval with an aperture of f3.6 – 22 times faster than the one

used by Daguerre. Then, despite the inventor's indifference to bettering his process, others discovered how to increase the light sensitivity of plates. Finally ingenious methods were devised using mirrors to increase the amount of sunlight that fell on the subject. Thus the stage was set for daguerreotypes to find a place in daily life and the United States grasped the new medium with all the force it could muster.

Just as photography's invention can be seen as one part of a nineteenth-century technological revolution embracing manufacture, transportation and communications, its welcome in the United States can be similarly understood. Daguerreotypes were clear and unadorned records that mirrored reality at a time when the United States was coming to terms with its new-found nationhood. These little pictures could capture the face of a country excitedly experiencing its sense of place in the world. As a new medium in a new country it was offered easy acceptance and the frankness a daguerreotype displayed was in accordance with an established tradition of realism in American painting. And photography was a product of mechanization. Its arrival was timed perfectly on the crest of the wave that was to take the agriculturally-based society of the United States into the technological age. Finally, and perhaps most importantly, there was a sense of relationship between those miniature replicas of the world as it was known, with their seeming truthfulness, and a growing feeling that god and nature were intertwined. Picture the latter and you represent the former. Photography seemed the point where American practicality, democracy and spirituality joined forces. By 1853 86 daguerreotype

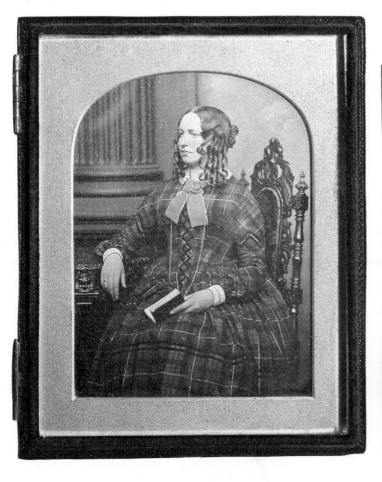

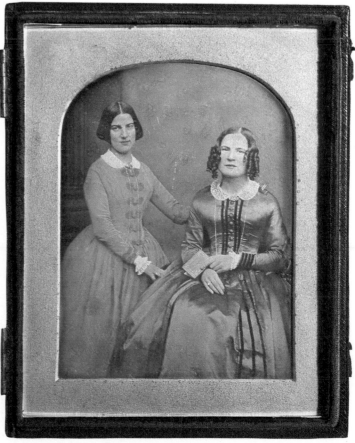

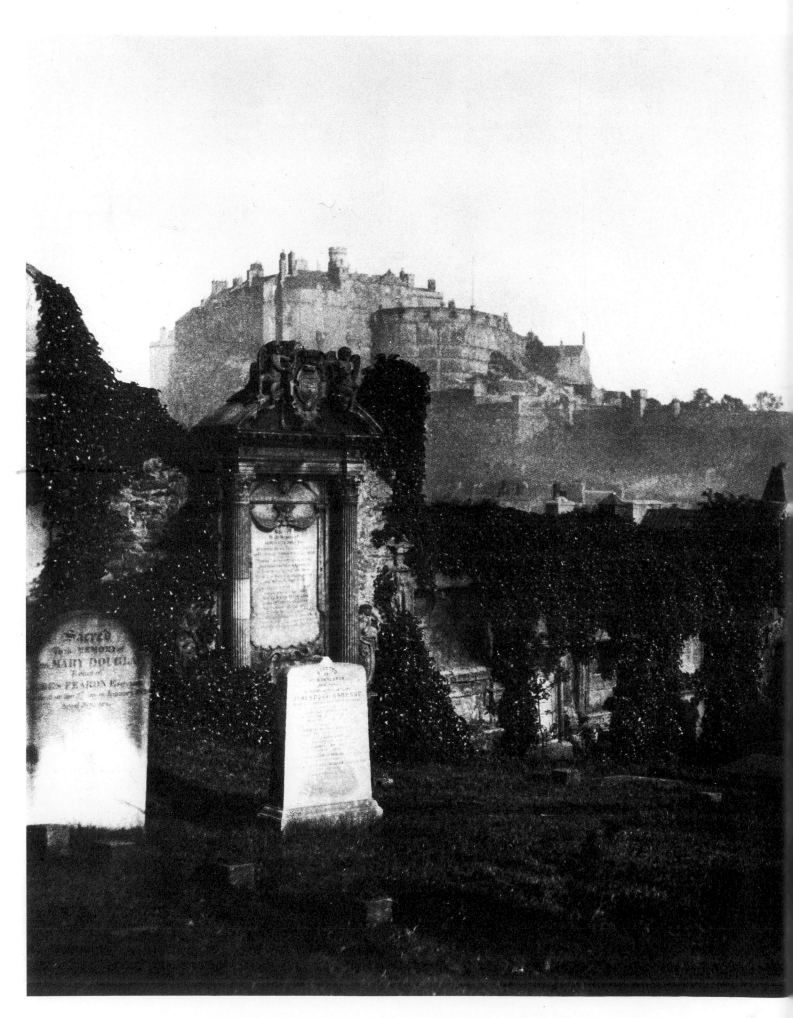

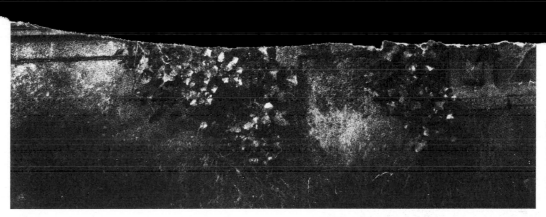

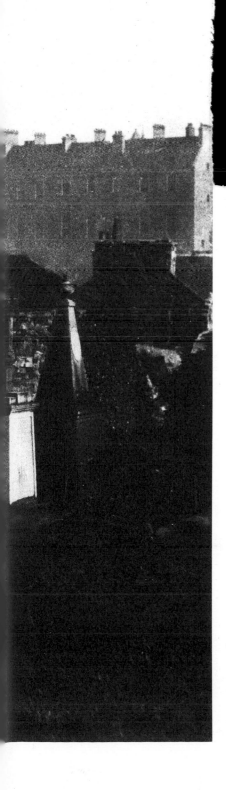

Above *Grayfriars Churchyard, Edinburgh.* Calotype by Dr Thomas Keith, 1853–5. Keith. A Scots surgeon and amateur photographer, he practiced photography for only two years, during which he produced some of the most visually impressive early photographs. (Private collection.)

Left *Grayfriars Churchyard, Edinburgh,* 1853–5. Calotype by Dr Thomas Keith; the churchyard was one of his major subjects. (Private collection.)

studios existed in New York alone, one claiming a daily output of between 300 and 1000 portraits. In the year prior to 1 June 1855 it was recorded that 403,626 daguerreotypes had been made in the state of Massachusetts.

Most daguerreotypists were little more than technical operators and their pictures dull. Even with a decrease in exposure times, portrait subjects were required to maintain a rigid position which did not lend itself to spontaneity. Head clamps were used to ensure that no movement took place. Hands, which might tremble with anxiety, were often placed gripping the arm of the studio chair. Backgrounds were generally conventional, sometimes painted with classical columns to suggest august surroundings. The pictures surviving, with their stiff formality, have contributed greatly to our image of the Victorian era as a time of solemn propriety. As Edward Bradley wrote, under the pseudonym Cuthbert Bede, in his delightful book *Photographic Pleasures*, published in 1855, 'it is of no use your going to have your portrait taken by our friend Camera unless you can sit still . . . If you are addicted (as I hope you are not) to the worship of Bacchus and

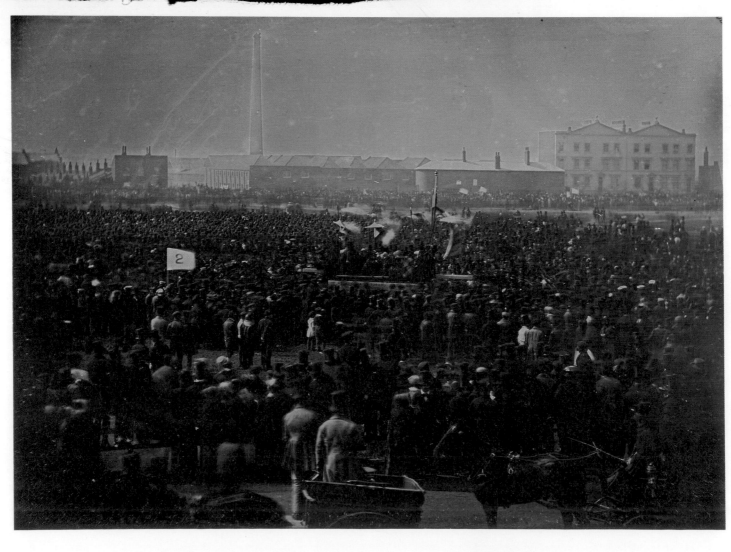

should, on a certain evening, make an undue number of libations to your deity, I should advise you not to call on our friend Camera the next morning, but to tarry until the tremulous motion of your head and hands shall have subsided into sober steadiness.'

Some daguerreotypists worked to overcome the limitations of such a prescribed method of picture making. In England Antoine Claudet, Talbot's erstwhile partner who became 'photographer-in-ordinary' to Queen Victoria, produced portraits of surprising intensity and graceful family groups. Claudet's sometime assistant, T R Williams, took equipment out of the studio and photographed the wonders of the Crystal Palace, the site of The Great Exhibition of the

Works of Industry of All Nations in London 1851. After it was destroyed by fire, Philip Delamotte was commissioned to record its reconstruction and reopening. Further north Horatio Ross, later to help found the Photographic Society of Scotland, photographed his family fishing – the closest daguerreotypes have ever come to contemporary snapshots.

Medals were awarded for daguerreotypes at The Great Exhibition. Three of the five presented went to Americans. With technical ingenuity New World photographers had so improved their methods that European practitioners advertised that they were using 'The American Process.' The promise of fortunes to be made from satisfying public demand for portraits attracted many American entrepreneurs

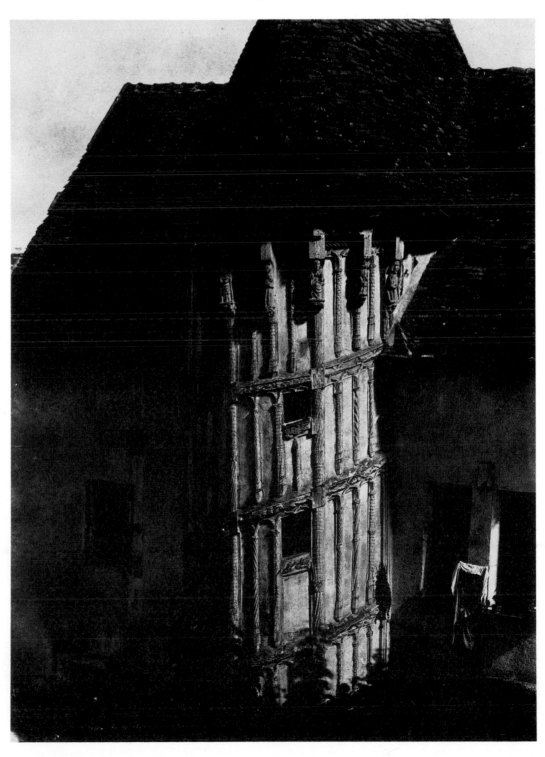

Right *Stairtower, Rue de la Petite Boucherie, Chartres*, 1852. Contemporary print by Edward Steichen (1937) from a calotype negative by Henri Le Secq. (Collection, the Museum of Modern Art, New York. Courtesy Victor Barthélemy.)

27

to the new profession, but few had the ability to transcend utilitarianism. An exception was the Boston-based partnership of Albert Southworth and Josiah Hawes, which began in 1843. Viewed down the corridor of time, their portraits display an advanced sensibility, but it seems the partners knew precisely what they were doing, as one of their advertisements shows: 'We will reserve and claim by right the name of our establishment, "The Artists' Daguerreotype Rooms." One of the partners is a practical Artist and as we never employ *Operators*, customers receive our personal attention.' The gibe at '*Operators*' may well have been directed at a competitor, Mathew Brady, who ran three studios, in New York and Washington and used his own name on all the pictures his employees made. Southworth and Hawes produced portraits of considerable sophistication. Their compositional strategies were a far cry from the painterly imitations of their rivals. In place of classicism they utilized the realism of their medium to create powerful portraits of such diverse sitters as Lola Montez, the courtesan and mistress of Mad King Ludwig of Bavaria, shown posing in demimonde style with a risqué cigarette; Ralph Waldo Emerson; and Daniel Webster pictured as the indomitable elder statesman.

If commercial success seemed certain for daguerreotypists in Europe and the United States, it still eluded the luckless Talbot. Having failed to interest the public in calotype por-

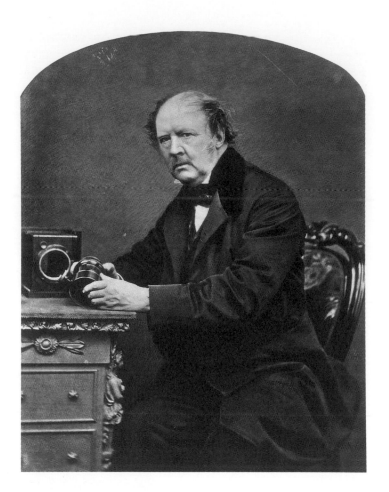

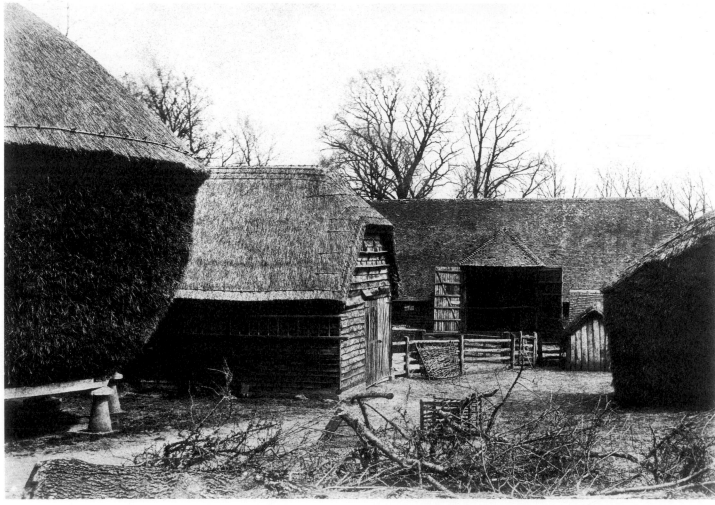

traits and benefiting little from the sale of licenses for his process, he turned to an exploration of its qualities of reproducibility. In 1843 he set up The Talbotype Establishment in Reading and began volume production of calotypes from his own negatives. In June 1844 the first part of a six-instalment work, *The Pencil of Nature*, was published, the world's first photographically illustrated book. Each of its 24 plates was an original calotype and the text offered a history of Talbot's discovery and an explanation of each picture's significance. For all his seeming lack of business acumen, Talbot was quick to grasp the aesthetic potential of photography. Many of his pictures were of everyday subjects transformed by the camera. Reduced from three dimensions down to two and then written in the brownish tonalities of his process, Talbot's photographs seem both explicit records and works of feeling and perception. He wrote in *The Pencil of Nature* that 'a

casual gleam of sunshine, or a shadow thrown across his path, a time-withered oak, or a moss-covered stone may awaken a train of thoughts and feelings, and picturesque imaginings.' With uncanny prescience the English pioneer had explained what was to become and remain a fascination for photographers – how an interaction between things of the material world might gain a new meaning when passed through their medium's mediator, the camera. That meaning comes in part from the selection by the photographer of what to include and part from the viewer and his or her association with the subject of a picture.

All Talbot's attempts to gain financially from his discovery were to come to nothing. He recorded eventually that he spent a total of £5000 on the medium, of which he recovered less than half. But if public response to calotypes was poor, the process won a positive reception among Talbot's family,

Left *Portrait of William Henry Fox Talbot*, by Nicholaas Henneman. (Science Museum, London.)

Below left *At Compton, Surrey*, 1852–4. Albumen print from a waxed paper negative by Benjamin Brecknell Turner. Turner, an amateur, was described by *The Times* in 1852 as one of England's best photographers. (Victoria and Albert Museum.)

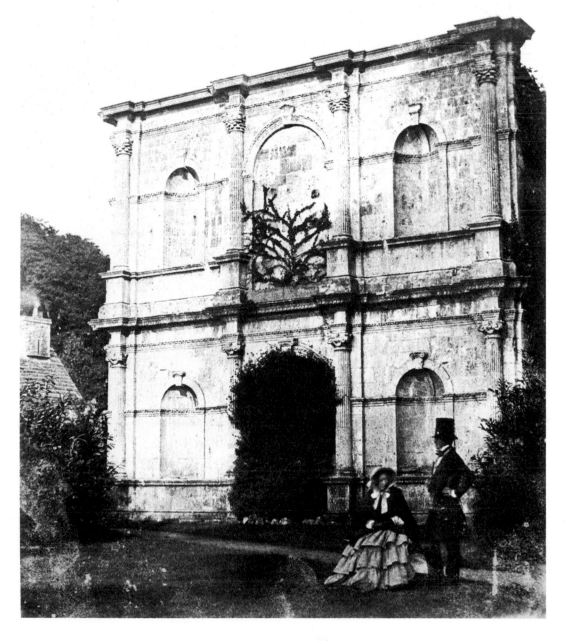

Right *Couple Posed Before a Classical Arch*, 1846–7. Calotype by the Rev Calvert Jones. Jones, a neighbor of Fox Talbot's cousin in Wales, practiced photography as early as 1839. (Victoria and Albert Museum.)

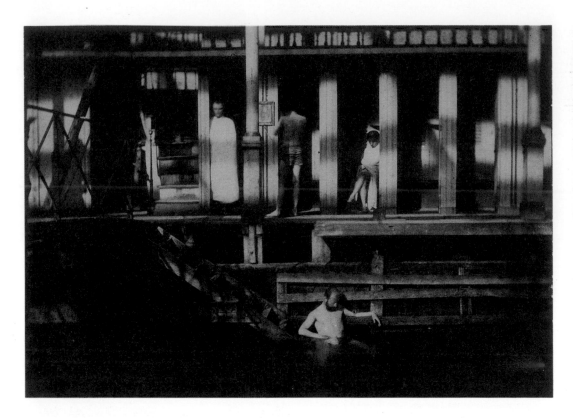

Above *Public Bathhouse,* Paris, 1852. Salt print from a calotype negative by Henri Le Secq. (Collection Bibliothèque des Arts Décoratifs, Paris.)

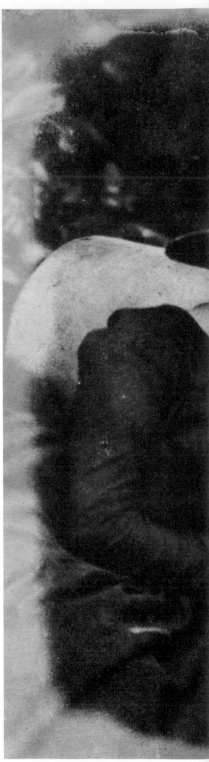

friends and colleagues. His patents restricted use to licensees, though on advice from Sir David Brewster (a close friend and Principal of the University of St Andrews) no patent was taken out to cover Scotland. Sensing that severe prohibition was not the best route to acknowledgment of calotypes, Talbot altered his patent in 1846 to include an 'amusement only' license costing one guinea – one fifth of the cost of a nonprofessional Daguerreotype license. He had also sent details of the invention to cousins in Wales, who began to

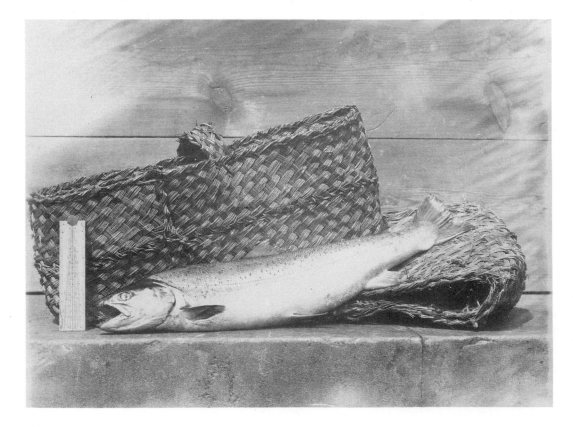

Above *The Sleeping Flowergatherers – Study – The Misses McCandlish,* c 1843–6. Calotype by D O Hill and Robert Adamson. (Victoria and Albert Museum.)

Left *Sewin,* c 1855. Salted paper print from a collodion negative by John Dillwyn Llewelyn, one of Fox Talbot's circle of friends. (Victoria and Albert Museum.)

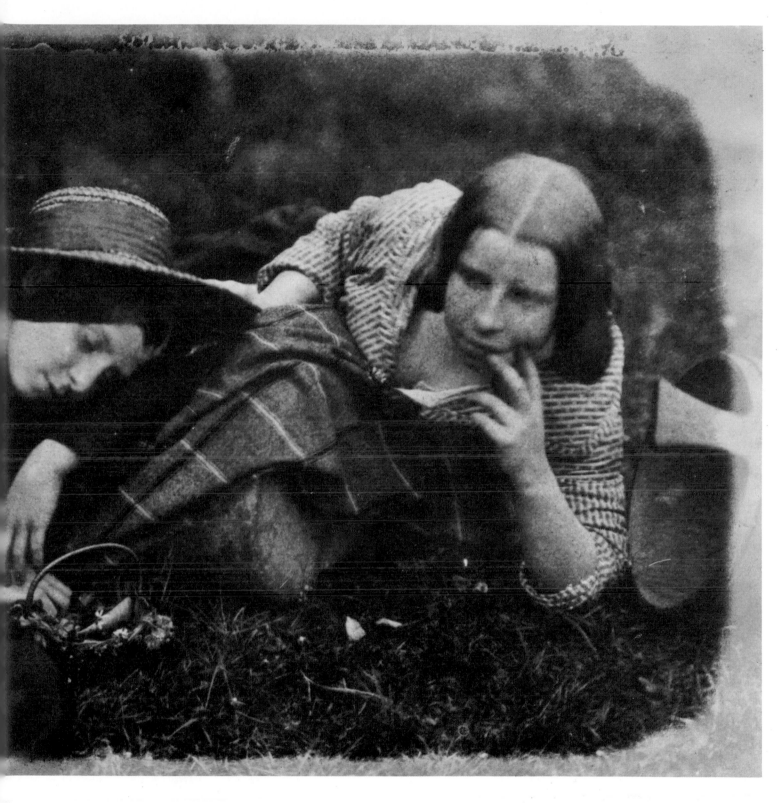

photograph with considerable enthusiasm. They in turn passed on their knowledge to owners of adjoining estates and a
coterie of Welsh amateur calotypists quickly emerged. Tal-
bots in Wales were joined by the Llewelyn and Jones families.
As early as February 1839 Talbot's cousin Charlotte Traherne
was excitedly reporting that 'John Llewelyn has been making
some paper according to your process and they have all been
trying little scraps of paper and succeeding very well before
breakfast . . . Mr Calvert Jones is quite wild about it.' The
pictures they made and their endeavors to advance the quality
of their work is testimony to the importance of Talbot's

discovery. A fascinating correspondence was exchanged as
all concerned began to uncover the possibilities of photography. Botanical and marine photography were discussed, particularly by Jones. He visited Hippolyte Bayard in 1845 and
reported to Talbot that 'his system is of course a secret, but he
told me it was much more simple and easy of manipulation
than yours . . . his paper . . . comes out very even . . . he was
kind enough to give me a few sheets for you.' Not content to
investigate photography for his own amusement, Jones was
interested in assisting Talbot in commerce – he suggested that
Queen Victoria's German tour of 1845 should be photographed

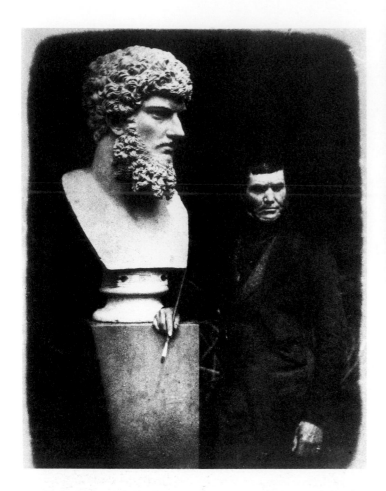

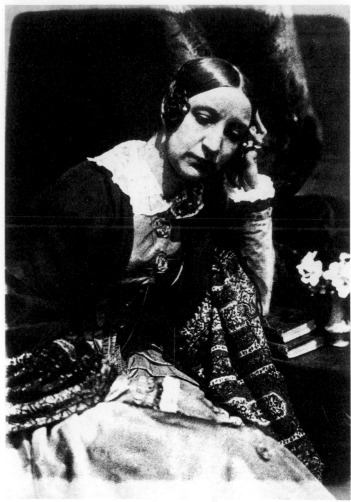

and he collaborated with Mr Newton of Winsor and Newton, a company manufacturing artists' materials, in trying to improve calotypes by varnishing the surface.

As amateurs, those who practiced calotypy went far beyond the studio inclinations of the majority of commercial daguerreotypists. Jones made pictures in Italy and Malta, Talbot photographed in France, others went to Greece, Egypt and the Holy Land. They made 'views,' the contemporary equivalent of postcards, to be printed and distributed by Talbot's works in Reading. One calotypist, the Reverend George Bridges, almost succeeded in introducing the process to the United States (patents again prevented it from taking off), but it was in restriction-free Scotland that negative/positive photography began to come of age.

Sir David Brewster had exhibited Talbot's 'photogenic drawings' at the Literary and Philosophical Society of St Andrews in 1839. Thereafter he maintained a keen interest in the system's development, corresponding frequently with Talbot and promoting knowledge of the discovery among his scientific colleagues. It is clear from Brewster's letters that he found the process troublesome – in fact he failed to produce any pictures despite Talbot sending him essential chemicals. These chemicals and information on making 'sun pictures' were passed on to two of Brewster's university associates and one of them, Dr John Adamson, Professor of Chemistry, succeeded. In 1841 Adamson, who was already familiar with daguerreotypy, made the first calotype portrait in Scotland. And in August 1842 Brewster wrote to Talbot telling him that 'a brother of Dr Adamson . . . is willing to

practise the calotype in Edinburgh as a profession. Mr Adamson . . . has been well drilled in the new art by his brother.'

Almost simultaneously negative-positive photography arrived in Scotland and began to be practiced as a profession. The younger Adamson, Robert, opened a studio in Rock House, Calton Hill, and by July 1843 Brewster was again in contact with Talbot, reporting that there were 'crowds every day at his Studio.' Amateurs delighted in the new medium too, and Brewster gathered about him a group of enthusiasts who formed the Calotype Club, to share an interest in depicting architecture and landscapes. Scotland, then, became a center for photography on paper, but it was to be a professional partnership that marked it as a place of vital importance to the medium's future, a place where art and commerce came together, and the pictures produced were considered as photography's first masterpieces.

In 1843 a dramatic event occurred within the General Assembly of the Church of Scotland. Some 155 members of the clergy, almost a fifth of those present, resigned. Their grievance was growing interference in church matters from secular bodies like the Crown. In a cleverly managed display, the dissenters marched through Edinburgh to Tanfield Hall where they established the Free Church of Scotland. Crowds gathered to see the spectacle, among them painter and book illustrator David Octavius Hill. Hill determined to paint a group portrait of the historic gathering and was advised by Sir David Brewster (an ordained minister and participant in the affair) that calotype portraits might serve as a more useful aide-memoire than sketches. Robert Adamson was called in and he and Hill began a collaboration. The partnership was to last almost five years, until the death of Adamson in 1848, and was to give rise to pictures of a quality and kind that have retained their power into the present. Where an amazed public had gasped at daguerreotypes and 'the perfect clearness of every object,' calotypes by Hill and Adamson resonate beyond the simple appearance of things. In the main they made portraits, with Hill acting as 'art director' and his partner handling technical matters. They made much of light and shade, with their subjects, often notables of the day, emerging as rugged individuals seen strongly sunlit against a dark, fibrous-textured background that is so characteristic of calotypes. But beyond their flair for drama, Hill and Adam-

son worked with another possibility few of that generation aside from Talbot had recognized. Light and shade were seen as symbols. Not surprisingly, perhaps, as the partnership arose from disagreements within an established church, they utilized a sense of spirit within the photographs. Light triumphed over dark and lack of detail enhanced the effect. What was suggested became as much part of a picture as what was stated. Through an incomplete outer description we are invited to consider some kind of interior life. Or, as Hill was so eloquently to express it later in his career when comparing calotypes with daguerreotypes, 'they look like the imperfect work of man . . . and not the much diminished perfect work of God.'

Left *Miss Elizabeth Rigby* (later Lady Eastlake), *c* 1843-6. Calotype by D O Hill and Robert Adamson. (Victoria and Albert Museum.)

Far left *John Stevens RSA*, *c* 1843-6. Calotype by D O Hill and Robert Adamson. (Victoria and Albert Museum.)

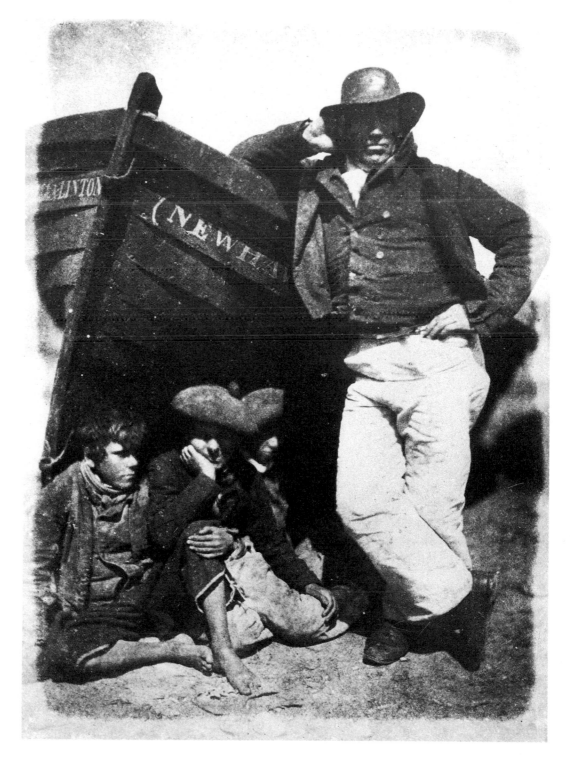

Right *Sandy (James) Linton, his boat and his bairns, c* 1845. Calotype by D O Hill and Robert Adamson. (Victoria and Albert Museum.)

Early Photographic Processes

What characterizes many nineteenth- and early twentieth-century pictures is the actual process that was used. Development, changes and improvement were rapid – literally dozens of modifications followed photography's invention and subtly altered the look of photographs.

Like many of the Polaroid processes today, Daguerreotypes were unique, and could not be copied. Daguerreotypes were made on silvered polished copper plates, sensitized with iodide vapor in a wooden box then placed in the camera. After exposure the plate would be developed in a mercury vapour. This process attached mercury to the silver iodide in proportion to the amounts of light each part of the plate had received and a positive image appeared containing tremendous detail. Following development, the image, now a silvery monochrome, would be fixed (first in common salt, but soon after in sodium thiosulphate) and sealed behind glass to prevent the silver from tarnishing. Finally it was placed in a case, which was sometimes elaborately decorated.

Daguerre's process, for all its faithful detail, had serious drawbacks. Mercury vapour was highly dangerous and deaths were recorded from less than careful photographers, and, of course, the image was unique. If more copies were needed then more exposures had to be made. William Henry Fox Talbot, who made talbotypes or calotypes, overcame the problem of reproduceability when he invented the negative/positive process. A sheet of paper (generally writing paper) would be carefuly brushed with silver nitrate solution and dried. Then followed a bath of potassium iodide which combined with

the first chemical to form silver iodide. Finally, before the paper was exposed it would be floated on a bath of gallo-nitrate of silver and placed in the camera's back ready for exposure. After the negative was made it was developed in gallo-nitrate silver and fixed in sodium thiosulphate (known as 'hypo'). The image produced was tonally reversed (the paper blackened in proportion to the light falling on it). The image would then be dried and printed in contact with another sheet of prepared paper so that the tones once again reversed and areas which had received most exposure would become the brightest in the finished positive. As many copies as wanted could be made from a single negative. A variation was the salt or salted paper print. This involved brushing the paper with a solution of common salt (sodium chloride) and then silver nitrate to create silver chloride.

Various improvements were made to Talbot's original methods to increase the sensibility of the paper and thus reduce exposure times. The clarity of the resulting picture was increased by waxing the paper to reduce the effect of its fibers which gave the image a rather granular appearance.

For all their infinite repeatability, paper negatives gave pictures lacking in detail when compared to Daguerreotypes. In 1848 Frederick Scott Archer began making negatives using glass as a support and detail was massively improved. This wet collodion process involved pyroxyline dissolved in a mixture of alcohol and ether to which was added bromide and iodide salts. This was coated on glass plates and when dry the plate was placed in a bath of silver nitrate. While still wet, the plate was exposed in the camera and developed in proto-sulphate of iron or pyrogallic acid. Despite being cumbersome to use, wet collodion was the major negative/positive

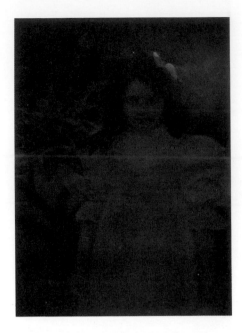

Above *Peggy Warburg, c* 1909, by J C Warburg, an autochrome. (Royal Photographic Society.)

process used from the early 1850s until 1878 when dry plates with silver halides suspended in gelatine came on the market.

Throughout this period silver had reigned supreme as the light-sensitive agent, but experiments were also being made with non-silver processes – notably in platinum and gum bichromate. Platinum prints were absolutely permanent and offered an exquisite tonal range beyond the reach of silver. Both factors helped in their popularity among serious photographers, especially after a company was established to make the paper commercially in 1878. Platinotypes were sized, coated with

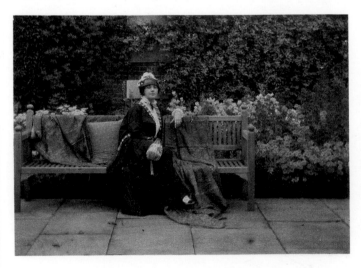

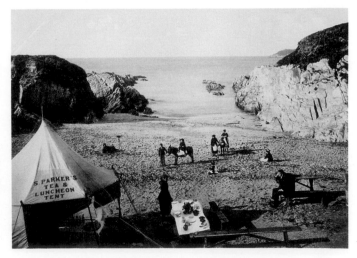

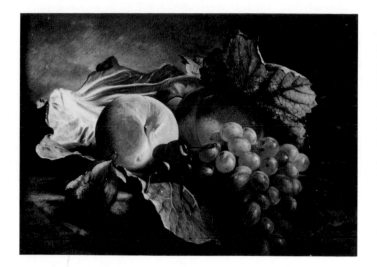

Above *Fruit Study*, c1885, by John Moffat. This is a tri-color carbro image, a pigment process made up of three separate colored layers. (Edinburgh Photographic Society.)

potassium chloroplatinate and ferrec oxy-late and dried. In use they were partly printed out (light turned the ferrec oxylate to ferrous oxylate) then developed in potassium oxylate which reduced the chloroplatinate to its metallic state. Fixing involved solutions of hydrochloric or cit-ric acid followed by washing. The subtle-ties of platinotypes attracted many leading late nineteenth-century photographers.

Gum bichromate, involving no metallic salts, had come to prominence briefly in the 1850s as an answer to lack of perma-nence in photographs and again in the 1890s for its potential for manipulation (gum prints could be made to look like

Below *Mayfield roofs from the Middle House garden*, c1933, a tri-color carbro image by Agnes Warburg. (Royal Photographic Society.)

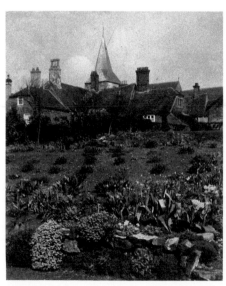

paintings). It utilized a solution of gum arabic mixed with potassium bichromate (which was sensitive to light and would harden with exposure) and watercolor paint. This was brushed onto sized paper, dried and exposed with a negative. Next came 'development' in a tray of water which dissolved the non-hardened areas, leaving an image drawn in the chosen pig-ment. Finally the image would be treated with potash-alum, or, if the printer wished, the process could be repeated to gain a deeper tone or even to make a print in more than one color. This means of print making survived into the 1930s and enjoyed a revival in the 1970s.

Gum prints could give the appearance of color, but actual color photographs were the desire of many who found mono-chrome too limiting a medium. Niépce, one of the earliest experimenters with the idea of photography who had (before his death) shared resources with Daguerre, was trying to invent color photography as early as 1816, but it was not until the be-ginning of the twentieth century that dreams became realities. In 1904 the brothers Augusta and Louis Lumière patented a process called 'autochrome' which offered glass transparencies in full color that could be used by all photo-graphers. Their invention involved dying tiny grains of starch in the primary colors of red, green and blue, attracting an even mixture of the grains onto a glass plate and backing it with a monochrome emulsion. The plate was exposed with the color grains toward the camera lens. As light passed through them they acted as filters, exposing the monochrome emulsion selectively according to the color (through a red grain, for example, only red would pass onto the emulsion). After exposure the plate was developed conventionally, passed through a reversal process (potas-

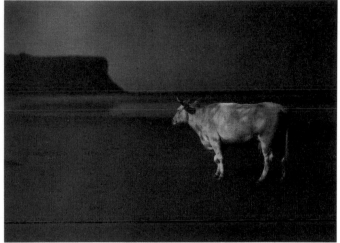

Above *Cow on Saltburn Sands*, c1909, an autochrome by J C Warburg. (Royal Photographic Society.)

sium permanganate and sulphuric acid) then re-exposed to white light and rede-veloped. The first part of the process got rid of unexposed metallic silver, the second brought up the image as a positive transparency. When held up to the light or projected, light would pass through the grains of color and the black-and-white image to produce a color picture. The re-sult was granular (because of the starch grains) but visually highly attractive. Autochromes were followed by Dufy col-our from another French Company, and Agfa color from Germany, but they re-mained market leaders until the 1930s when Kodachrome was introduced.

Below *Woman at Pump*, c1920, a more modern approach, an early Agfa color picture. (Agfa-Gevaert, Leverkusen.)

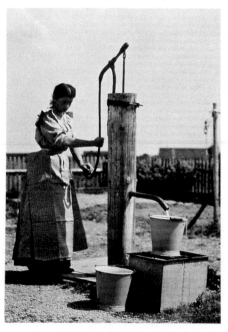

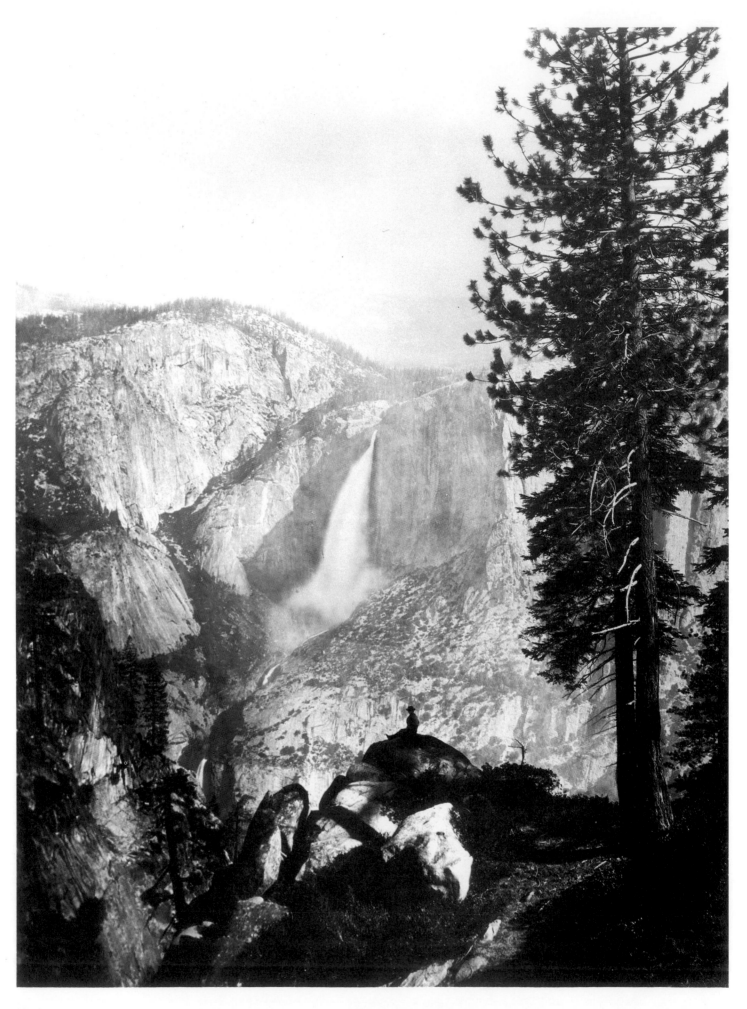

CHAPTER TWO

Travellers with a Camera

The Photographer Abroad

Photography's invention, as we have seen, was no accidental discovery. It came at a period when the Western world was going through fast and fundamental changes. It was simultaneously expanding and shrinking. Technology was contributing to an enlarged view of man's domain while improved communications were bringing the remote and far-flung to Europe's doorstep. Increasing industrialization too had shown effect, not simply as a radical alteration to national economies but in the ways people thought. One sign of its force was a change from an existing understanding of the landscape simply as the area which surrounded one and so of minor concern into concepts of 'city' and 'country.' Another was the growth of an affluent middle class and a corresponding rise in working-class poverty. As sail gave way to steam, travel became more widespread. For some it was an expression of wealth and leisure, for others a means to an end. Ironically both groups sought escape, the former from sights of grim 'satanic mills,' the very cornerstones of their wealth, the latter to avoid almost almost certain penury. They chose different destinations; one group travelling for travel's sake in search of the exotic, the other enduring a long miserable voyage to the United States, Africa or the Antipodes for a chance of fortune. Whether motivated by

thoughts of poetic adventure or hopes for a better future, the Europeans who were witness to photography's birth were adventurous and cameras were soon to be in every corner of the world. Industrialization created new levels of leisure. It was from the beneficiaries of change, the bourgeoisie, that photography's first practitioners arose, and from their consciousness came the first photographs. One part of that thinking revolved around what Talbot described as 'picturesque imaginings.' Not only did this notion involve the viewer of a photograph as an essential contributor to its meaning, it was concerned with a concept of what might be photographed. Prior to the Industrial Revolution ideas of 'land' were all-embracing. From the land came life. Land was life. Afterwards, when many had migrated to new work centers growing up around industry, the countryside came to represent something else. Land could be dissociated from the everyday. It was poetic, romantic, sometimes gothic . . . Land in its association with freedom represented an admired past. In the nineteenth-century, it was to take on another meaning.

In Europe it was acquiring a symbolic quality referring back to a time before industry when man and land were thought to be in harmony. In the newly colonized countries of Africa, Asia and the Pacific, with no past as far as Europe

Left *Falls of the Yosemite from Glacier Rock,* 1872. Albumen print by Eadweard J Muybridge, an English photographer working in California. (Department of Special Collections, UCLA.)

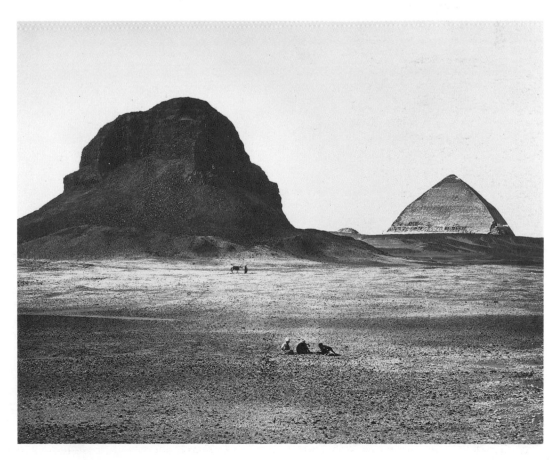

Right *The Pyramids of Dahshoor,* 1858. Albumen print by Francis Frith, made on the second of his three trips to Egypt. (Victoria and Albert Museum.)

was concerned, the land offered a new and vast physical openness; a perfect parallel to opportunity and an ideal antidote to city soot, confining crowds and the yet-to-be-adjusted-to pressures of urban life.

As early as 1839, indeed one day before that conclusive official pronouncement of the medium's arrival to the Académie des Sciences, a French journalist had published an article on photography. He wrote that 'travellers may perhaps soon be able to procure M. Daguerre's apparatus and bring back views of the finest monuments and of the most beautiful scenery of the whole world.' Before the year was out he was proved correct. An enterprising French optician and publisher, Noël Lerebours, equipped a group of artists with daguerreotype cameras and sent them as far as the Holy Land to provide material for a partwork *Excursions Daguerriennes: vues et monuments les plus remarquable du globe*. With no means

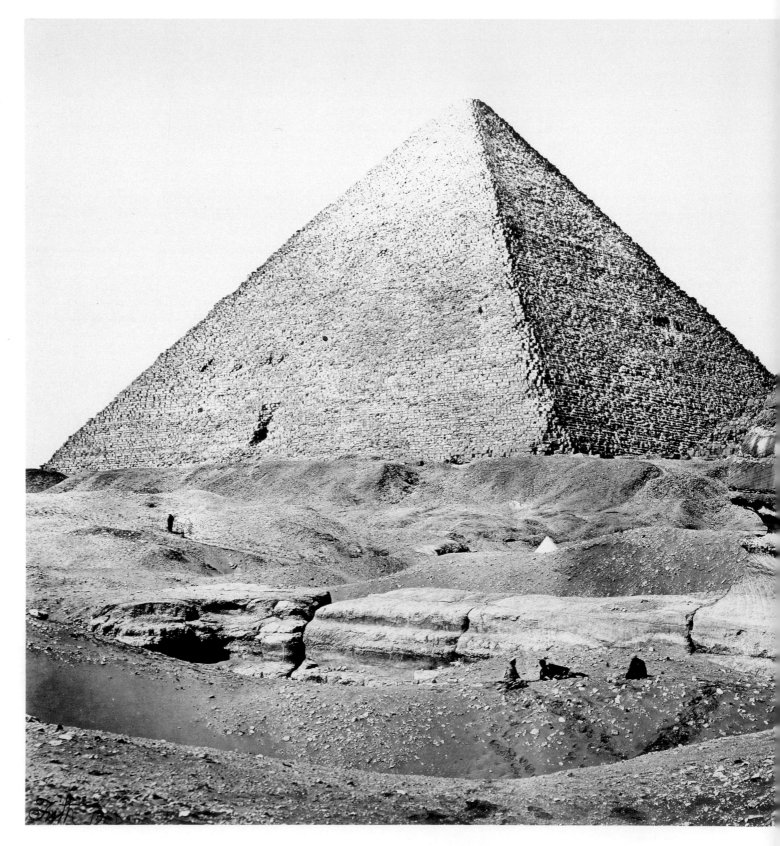

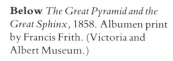

Below *The Great Pyramid and the Great Sphinx*, 1858. Albumen print by Francis Frith. (Victoria and Albert Museum.)

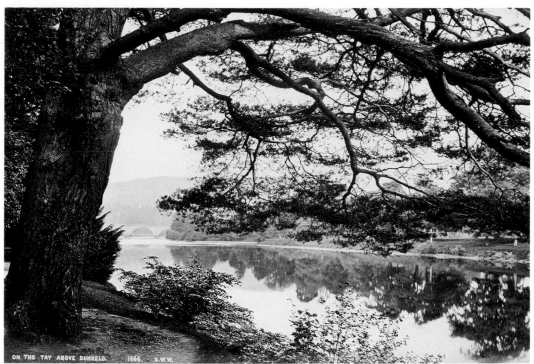

ON THE TAY ABOVE DUNKELD. 1666. G.W.W.

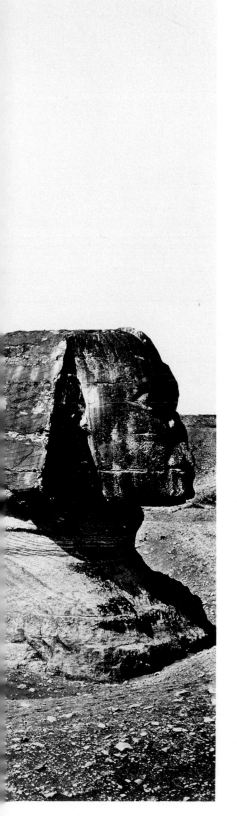

of reproducing these early pictures, they were used as a source for engravings. Lerebours added to his team's work, collecting daguerreotypes from travellers to Russia, the United States and the Orient. By 1841 he is reputed to have acquired more than a thousand pictures to satisfy an incredible public curiosity for knowledge of the world.

It is almost certain that Lerebours prompted the first travel pictures, but his idea of using photographs to circulate dreams of adventure in exploration was swiftly followed. In 1840 Dr Alexander Ellis, an English philologist, borrowed the concept and published *Italy Daguerreotyped*. Daguerreotypists roamed as far as Japan and the Pacific, calotypists to Greece, Turkey and even Burma. Photography and exploration seemed good partners, as did photography and the process of colonization. Empires could be brought into clear focus and the massiveness of, say, the American West, given some comprehensible form.

Commerce was as much a motivation for the mid-century travelling photographer as any thoughts of Empire. The invention of wet collodion by Frederick Scott Archer in 1848 made finely detailed paper prints a possibility and the public bought them in large numbers. As Britain reached towards the zenith of its imperial era a sense of correspondence between British might and the classical civilizations – Greece and Rome – began to grow. The British at home, with a sense of assured possession, revelled in images documenting the origins of a style now to be seen reflected in the columns and façades of new buildings going up around them. Egypt too was a source of considerable interest as a major power remembered by its monuments, pyramids and gigantic statues. As early as 1812 the Egyptian Hall had been opened in Piccadilly, London, a tribute to the Napoleonic Egyptian campaign of 1798. An enduring Egyptian style was to follow (Cleopatra's Needle, for example, was erected beside the

Above *On the Tay above Dunkeld*, 1880s. Albumen print by George Washington Wilson; his company in Aberdeen was the largest publisher of topographic views in Britain. (Roger Taylor.)

39

Thames in 1878) and extend to furniture as well as architecture and the visual arts. No surprise, then, that Egypt became a focus of photographic attention.

France also has long nurtured an interest in Egypt. It went back to the campaigns of Napoleon in 1798 and was manifest in the building of the Suez canal – designed and largely financed by the French. In 1843 the writer Gerard de Nerval photographed in Egypt (without success, the heat upset his chemicals and caused him to return to written descriptions of the wonders he saw). Others followed – significantly Auguste Saltzmann and Maxime Du Camp. Saltzmann arrived in 1854, hoping to use photography as an adjunct to archaeological theories, and made pictures of considerable visual perception. Du Camp had come earlier, in 1849, in the company of friend and novelist Gustave Flaubert. Du Camp was also a writer, but entranced by photography. His scheme, like many of the first photographers of this fabulous and concentrated memorial to man's ability to triumph over impossible odds, was to compile a catalogue. A single photograph could replace time-consuming pen and pencil transcription of statues, reliefs and hieroglyphs. Du Camp, however, sensed a possibility beyond scientific record. While

Flaubert dreamed of the intricacies of *Madame Bovary* his companion translated the wonders of an ancient world into fine images of ruin, the kinds of ruin that would mesh with gothic European tastes.

French photographers had national reasons for an interest in Egypt. Flaubert and Du Camp, for example, had travelled on official Government missions. For the British it was more romantic – Egypt was both mysterious and biblical, a lure for bold empire builders turned tourist. One such was Francis Frith, the epitome of a Victorian self-made man. After an undistinguished academic career which ended when he was 16, Frith went into commerce. Variously apprentice to a manufacturer, a wholesale grocer and a printer, he emerged at 34 as a man of means and leisure. Leisure for such a person could not be equated with idleness. As the Romantic poet Wordsworth wrote in 1807:

The world is too much with us; late and soon,
Getting and spending, we lay waste our powers:

And, as Frith himself recorded, 'the spirit in which money earning work is done is very often and largely a cursing spirit. It may easily become a means of crushing out the little germ

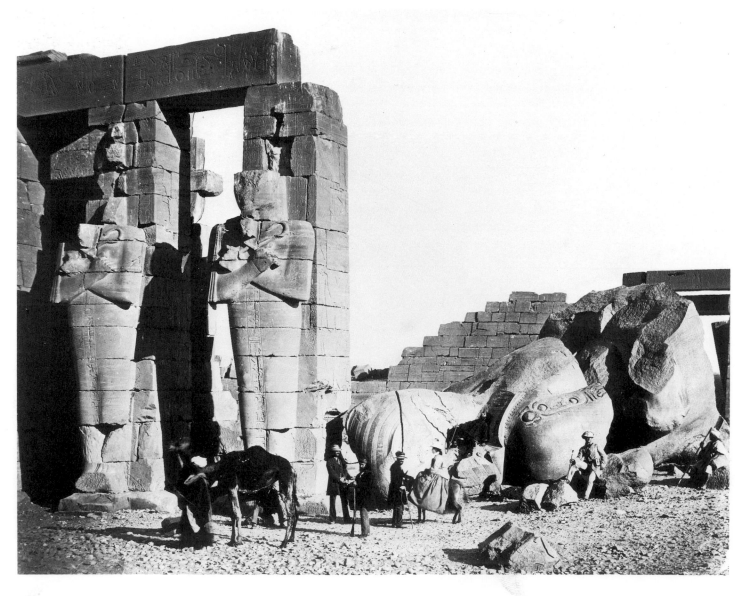

Right *Crocodile on a bank of the Nile,* 1857. Albumen print by Francis Frith. (Royal Photographic Society.)

Below *Along the Salween River,* *c* 1875. Albumen print by Samuel Bourne. (Royal Photographic Society.)

Below left *The Rameseum of El-Kurneh, Thebes,* 1858. Albumen print by Francis Frith. (Victoria and Albert Museum.)

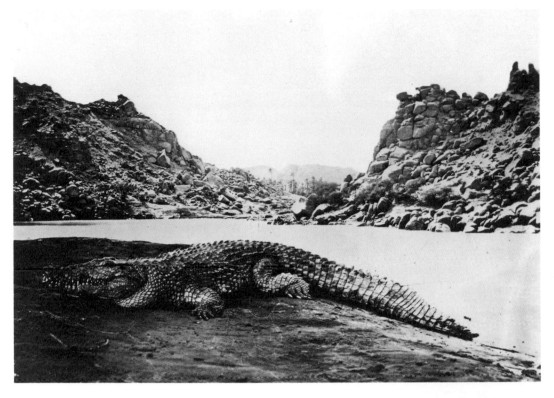

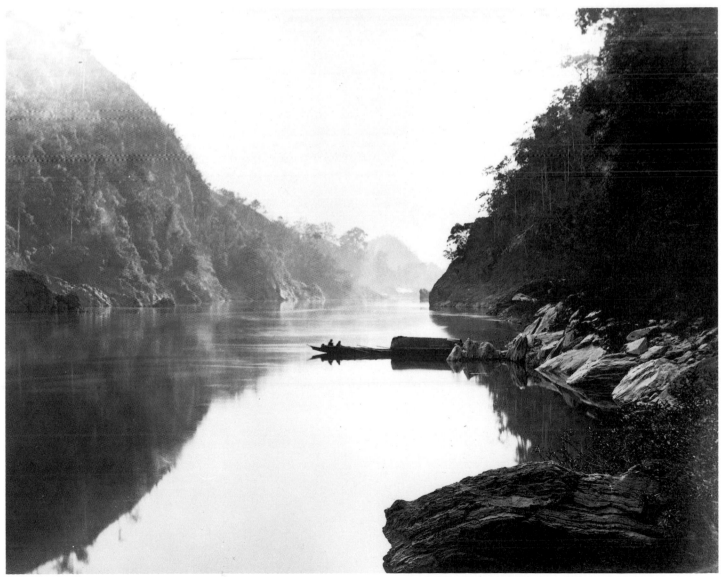

of generous, true, spiritual life and noble aspiration which God and nature have planted in a man.' Thus armed with considerable capital, a desire to grow closer to 'noble aspirations' and a hatred for the 'cursing spirit' of money for its own sake, he resolved to amalgamate his talents as an entrepreneur with a burgeoning interest in travel and photography. As a devout Christian, the bible played a part in his decision to

visit Egypt and the Holy Land. In 1856 he fulfilled his dreams and landed in Alexandria.

Between 1856 and 1860 he made three journeys, going further into Africa than any photographer before him – to the borders of Egypt, Nubia and Ethiopia and across the desert to the Sixth Cataract of the Nile. He ventured too across the Sinai, tracing Moses' journey and photographing under

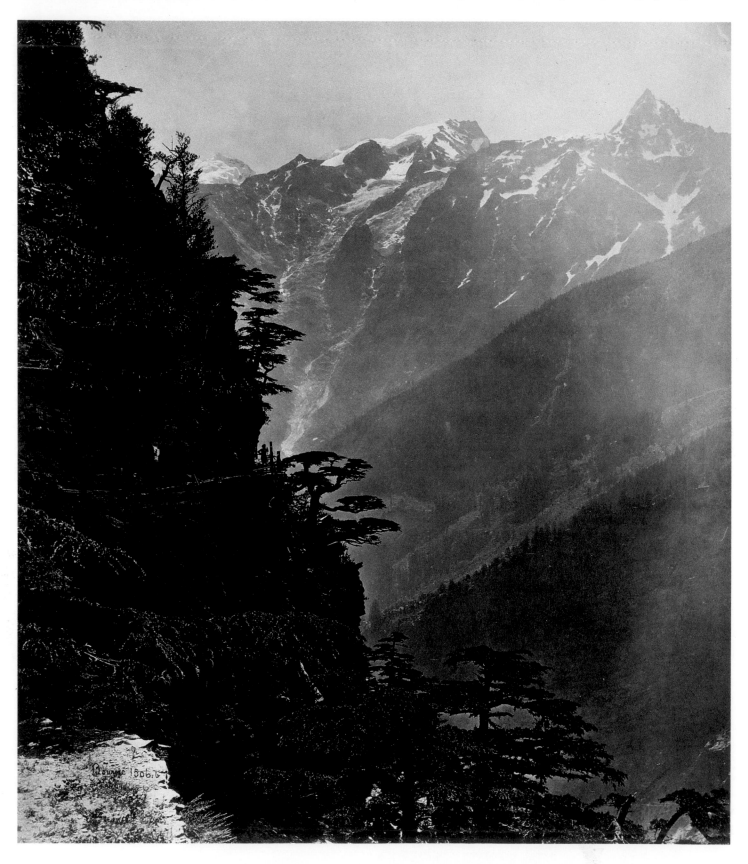

appalling conditions; in 1860 he wrote that he was 'devoured by thousands of sandflies . . . the water very bad and the heat great . . . the temperature in my little tent could not be less than 130 degrees Fahrenheit.' Frith used Archer's wet-collodion process which, for all its gains over the calotype, was difficult and time-consuming to manipulate. A sheet of glass was cleaned and made immaculate, then collodion (pyroxyline dissolved in alcohol and ether) was poured across the surface. Once set, the plate was placed in a solution of silver nitrate and, while still wet, into a light-tight container. This operation complete, the photographer would rush to his camera, make an exposure and return to the darkroom to develop the negative while its emulsion was still damp. In the heat and dust of the desert technical problems became enormous. Frith recorded the stifling heat of his dark tent, so hot that at times his collodion boiled, and his attempts to find less punishing methods. On one occasion he began his chemistry in a pharaoh's tomb, only to be driven out by dust, bats and mounting claustrophobia. And photographic problems aside, he had to contend with bandits, sometimes-hostile natives, and even packs of wild dogs that roamed the desert. Frith's achievement, on grounds of endurance alone, was considerable. When one takes account of the quality and kind of his pictures, it rises. Francis Frith was the premier photographer of his kind.

While Frith was applauded in London, given medals and cited by *The Times* as producer of the best photographs ever taken, his fellow countryman Samuel Bourne, a sometime bank clerk from Nottingham, was also beginning to gain attention in photographic circles. In 1862, after a period spent picturing the landscape of Scotland and Wales as well as his native England, he set sail for India; a professional photographer about to experience the jewel in the imperial crown. Britain was amazed by the very idea of this vast subcontinent, a remote and wondrous treasure house of exotic animals, precious cloth, spices, jewels and ivory. Here snakes could be charmed, holy men could levitate and fortunes could be made. Little wonder, then, that Queen Victoria rejoiced in the title Empress of India and pioneer photographers were drawn to record for themselves (and an interested public) the mysteries of so rich a possession. Bourne was not the first to take his equipment into Britain's prize. In the 1850s Dr John Murray, keen on photography and treating cholera, made fine pictures of Mogul architecture. Captain Linnaeus Tripe also preceded Bourne. Leaving his military career for photography, Tripe was employed by the British East India Company to record Indian antiquities. Murray and Tripe both attempted works of pictorial merit, sometimes more successfully than others. Bourne, however, seemed bent on nothing less. His market was to be the wealthy British in India and at home and his search, which involved major expeditions, was for a landscape which might somehow match that of England for 'picturesqueness or beauty.'

Where Frith photographed to emphasize monumentality, Bourne was drawn to romance. Both, unconsciously, recorded lands that matched a Victorian ideal: Egypt and the

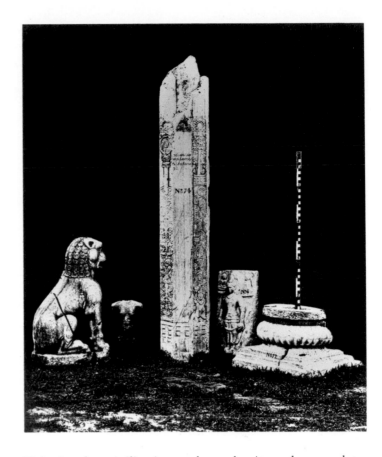

Holy Land – civilizations whose demise only served to emphasize the present greatness of Britain; India – a subcontinent whose extractable richness enhanced notions of British supremacy. By 1897, when Queen Victoria celebrated 60 years of rule, the British Empire controlled one quarter of the world, larger than any empire in history. In the 1860s, when Samuel Bourne was at work photographing the Himalayas,

Above *The Elliot Marbles, Central Museum, Madras,* 1858. Albumen print by Captain Linnaeus Tripe. (Victoria and Albert Museum.)

Right Apparatus carried by a travelling wet-collodion photographer, from an 1874 engraving. The process involved chemically coating a glass plate immediately before exposure. (Science Museum, London.)

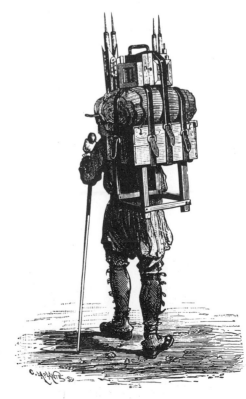

Far left *A 'bit' on the new road near Rogi,* 1866. Albumen print by Samuel Bourne, made on the last of three major expeditions. (Victoria and Albert Museum.)

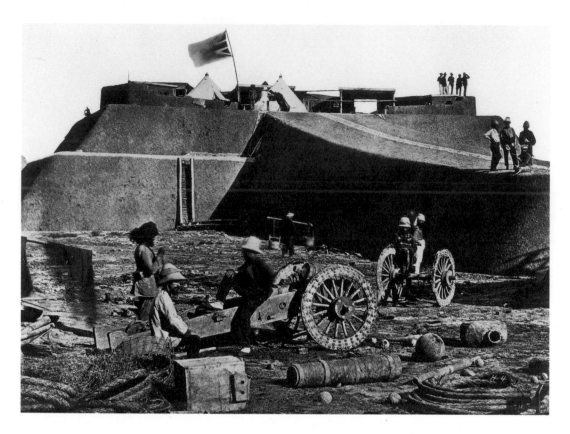

Right *Fountain of Ahmael III, Constantinople,* 1853. Albumen print from the partnership of James Robertson and Felice Beato. (Victoria and Albert Museum.)

Left *Pehtang Fort,* headquarters of the British Army, China War, 1860. Albumen print by Felice Beato. (Victoria and Albert Museum.)

Below *The Taj Mahal from the River Bank, Agra,* 1850s. Albumen print by John Murray. (Victoria and Albert Museum.)

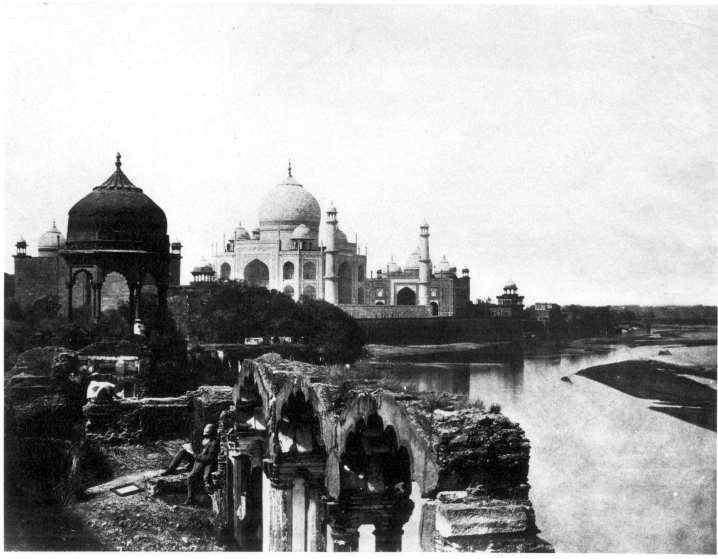

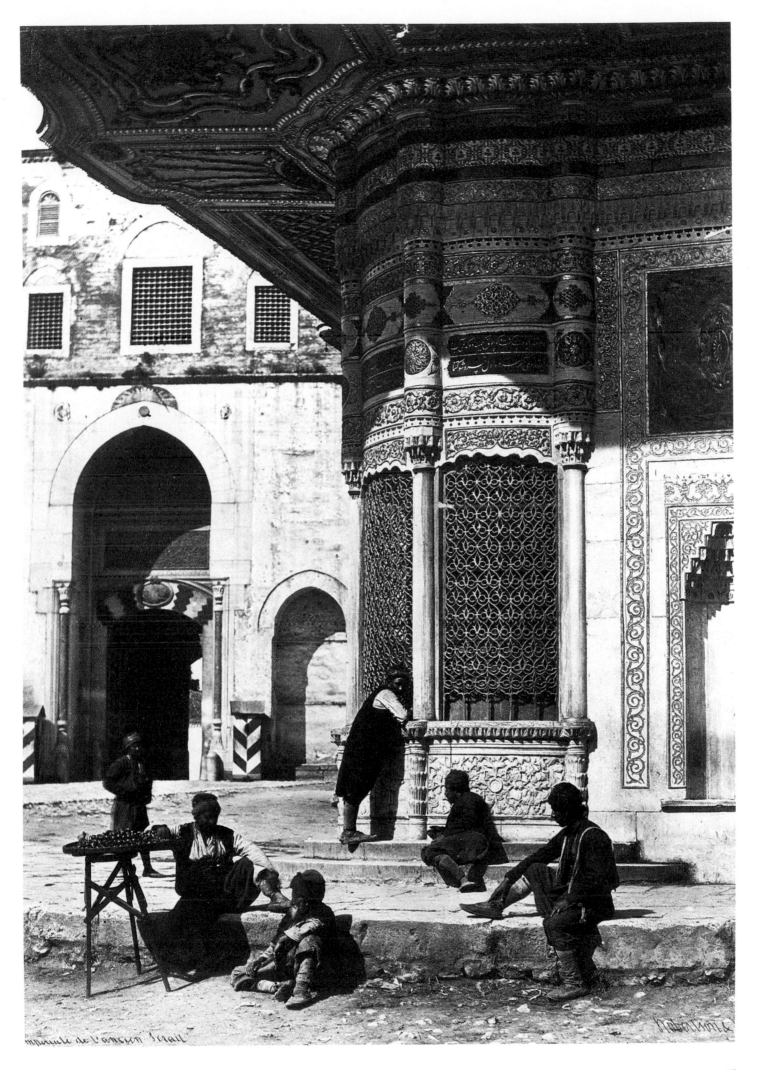

péristyle de l'ancien Sérail

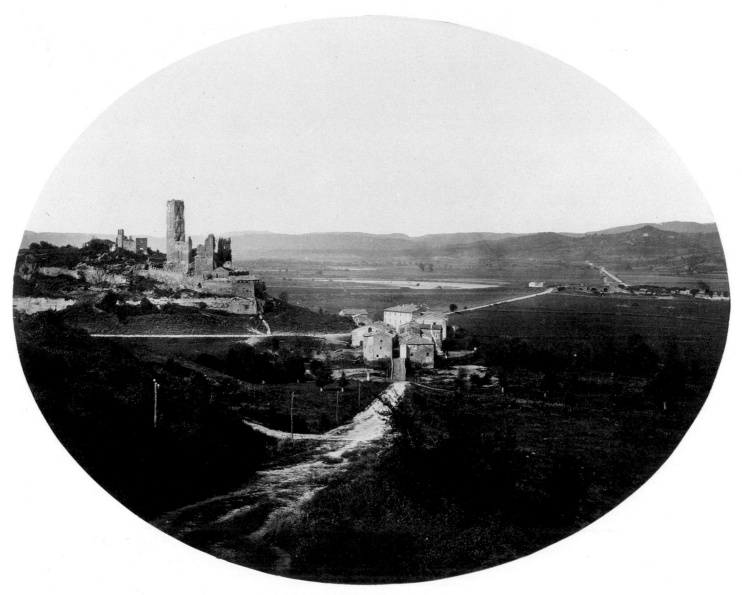

that sense of ascendency was increasing. To make the landscape comprehensible to his audience, Bourne looked for views to correspond with his audience's preconceptions, views which he would 'not be ashamed to send to England.'

Bourne's first Indian exploration was from Calcutta, where he disembarked in 1863, to Simla, summer home of British administration. It was 1200 miles and not once did he find a visual match for his expectations. But like Frith he had a will to succeed, and trip was to follow trip. In 1864 Bourne went into partnership with Charles Shepherd, who owned the first photographic business in India, and this enhanced his desire to make pictures of the finest kind.

Conditions were not conducive to making photographs. Collodion was hard to find (one ingredient was gun-cotton, a prohibited import) and the climate difficult. Bourne needed physical agility to reach the viewpoints he wanted and incredible stamina to withstand the extremes of heat and cold which became his lot. In regular dispatches to *The British Journal of Photography* he described ideas, ideals and realities: 'As I sat down to rest on a grassy mound contemplating this scene a feeling of melancholy seemed to steal over me. Here was I, a lonely wanderer, going Heaven knows where, sur-

rounded by the gloomy solitude of interminable mountains . . . to grasp or comprehend their extent was impossible . . . How often have I lamented that the camera was powerless to cope with these almost ideal scenes, and that with all its truthfulness it can give no true idea of the solemnity and grandeur.' The 'ideal' he remarks on was that of a landscape formed only by nature; a form of universality where nature and truth became intertwined, 'Beauty is truth, truth beauty' as the poet Keats expressed it in 1819.

Bourne's realities were some way from imagined concepts of romance. In pursuit of the picturesque he suffered. It could be hot, but more often it was cold – freezing cold. As Frith endured flies and dogs so Bourne took on the rigors of Indian alpine conditions. In February 1864 *The British Journal of Photography* published one part of his account of an expedition to Chini, close to the border with Tibet. He recounts 'immense difficulty, sundry bruises and great personal fatigue under a scorching sun.' Later the same month, after Bourne had climbed to 15,282 feet – the greatest altitude at which a photograph had been taken – he wrote 'I was compelled to wait in that freezing and ice-bound spot for three dreary days and nights without a particle of fire . . . I could only keep myself from freezing by lying in bed.' His problem had been created by a snowfall which caused his coolies to desert. Bourne travelled with a team of at least 30 and sometimes as many as 60 natives who carried his equipment, chemicals, glass for plate-making, tents, food and a Winchester quart of 'spirits of wine' (brandy). On this occasion, luckily, replacements arrived and Bourne was able to continue.

Bourne spent three years in India, made 1500 or so pictures and undertook three major expeditions. The first, to Chini, took 10 weeks. The second was to Kashmir and lasted 10 months. His final journey through the Manirung Pass to the source of the Ganges involved six months of unremitting effort. His Kashmir trip, where 'sylvan beauty' reminded him of 'the hills and valleys, green fields, parks and pastures of England' involved an almost daily 'reinvention' of the collodion process to cope with new extremes. He would wait hours, sometimes days, in temperatures as low as -22 degrees Fahrenheit to make a negative; if his chemical predictions of how the process might react were wrong, that time was wasted. With hands numbed by cold but still pained from chemicals such as cyanide of potassium he would coat his 12 x 10-inch plates, sometimes in winds almost of hurricane force, risking as he did so human error and calamities of other kinds. On one occasion a pack pony 'lost his footing and came right down upon the tent and me! Down went the table and smash went the bottles, collodion, developers, fixer and measures!' Another time two coolies slipped while maneuvering a box of glass plates and 'the box rolled down a declivity about a thousand feet. The men were carried with it.' Describing this event, Bourne notes with a true pioneer's pride that some glass fragments were large enough for him to cut down to 8 x 4½-inch plates for his 'small camera' and with seeming callousness that it caused one coolie 'a broken arm, and the other a fracture of one or two ribs.' One account even included a technical failure probably never equalled in photographic history. In the village of Dunkar Bourne found that his plates had been spoiled by chemical fogging. The reason, as he described it, was 'from the ammonia and other noxious fumes with which the air was reeking.' The fumes came from the villagers who believed that washing (for those over the age of four) would rob them of their possessions. But all was not so bleak. Before the climb to Manirung Pass Bourne paused at a village where the natives advised him against his attempt. It would involve great danger, they told him, probable death and, even if he did succeed, the village across the pass was infected with smallpox. Unconvinced, he made clear his intention to go on. To Bourne's amazement the villagers responded by giving him sheep and goats for fresh meat, a group of additional bearers for his 'dandy' (a mobile hammock) and a yak.

Samuel Bourne made some of the finest, most memorable topographical photographs of the nineteenth century, under conditions that today seem little short of lunatic. Of his success there is no doubt. (One record of that was the purchase by the South Kensington Museum, now the Victoria and Albert, of every one of 1666 views listed in Bourne and Shepherd's 1867 catalogue.) Yet the very facts of his achievement, both technical and aesthetic, beg a question. Why? Why endure months of discomfort and physical danger for the sake of making photographs? One answer lies in Victorian concepts, both of work and the meaning of empire and colonial power. Another, more revealing, answer rests with Bourne himself. A twentieth-century landscape photographer, Robert Adams, asking the same question of himself as we have of Bourne, decided that he did it 'for the view.' Time and again in reports to the *British Journal of Photography*, Bourne writes of a similar motivation. 'For the view' may sound naive. It is not. 'The view' represents a complex, metaphysical response to landscape. Bourne describes it sometimes as 'mysterious,' sometimes as 'awesome' sometimes as 'splendid.' In one article he mentions photographing the source of the river Ganges and says he 'ought to consider (himself) a privileged mortal in being permitted to gaze on this' and that he wished to 'pay my respects to some objects around me.' Each description uses emotive expressions, each somehow likens landscape to a notion of supreme power, to a vision of God made material, God perceived in nature. 'The view' was one that harmonized a nineteenth-century struggle to reconcile the wilderness and its natural aesthetic to a new

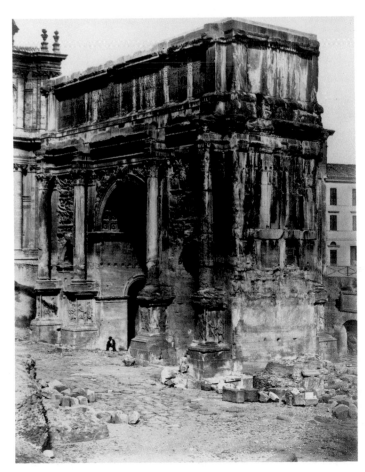

Above left *Valley of the Tiber at Point Felice*, late 1850s. Albumen print by Robert MacPherson. (Victoria and Albert Museum.)

Right *The Arch of Alexander Severus, Rome*, after 1856. Albumen print by Robert MacPherson. (Royal Photographic Society.)

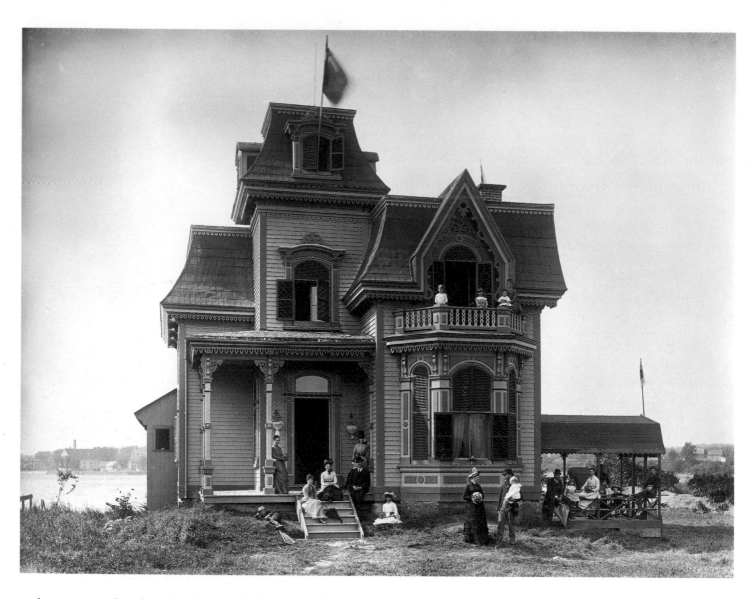

and man-created order. For Bourne, India was a place to rediscover his understanding of England and of life.

Fascination with wilderness and photographing it were not confined to Bourne and his vision of an imperial picturesque. As he and his coolies climbed through the Himalayas in search of grandeur, photographers were searching for a similar viewpoint many thousands of miles distant in the American West. And like Bourne, while they often travelled in the name of survey their real goal was one of search. Underpinning the documentary precision of their works was a sense of wonder – as if the gigantic scale of the landscape before them, an immensity approaching infinity, was indeed evidence of God. Before them were mountains, lakes, waterfalls, bubbling geysers, grotesque rock formations; a trackless wonderland that seemed close to creation itself. Many photographers worked in the American West, recording man's hand on the land as well as nature's majesty, but four stand out – William H Jackson, Eadweard Muybridge, Carlton E Watkins and Timothy H O'Sullivan. With piercing clarity they documented one of the last remaining frontiers.

Photographing the West began in earnest at the close of the Civil War in 1865. An uneasily united nation needed to be surveyed and opportunities were growing for picture makers

who could stand the harsh life of the interior. Some, like Jackson and O'Sullivan, had been toughened by the war. Others, including Muybridge and Watkins, learned endurance for the sake of commerce. Muybridge, according to one contemporary report, would wait days for perfect lighting (he favored drama) and would fell trees if that improved his view. He called himself 'Helios, the Flying Camera,' and swaggered. Watkins, who began his photographic life as a daguerreotype portraitist in San Jose, near San Francisco, used a mammoth plate camera making negatives 18 x 22 inches, boasted a mule train to carry his equipment and advertised a life spent hauling himself and his massive camera to the most inaccessible peaks in pursuit of fine views. Watkins and Muybridge (an Englishman from Kingston upon Thames) were commercial rivals. Both courted a varied clientele (from government departments to painters) and both tried to live from their landscape work. Sadly, but perhaps inevitably, one was to win over the other. In 1868, a year after he opened his Yosemite Art Gallery to sell photographs in San Francisco, Watkins gained a medal for his pictures shown at the Paris International Exposition – a rare European honor for a photographer from California. Five years later the Vienna International Exposition showed both

Watkins and Muybridge, awarding the latter a medal of progress for landscape. The year after Watkins was bankrupt. His failure came through lack of foresight: as the railroad made Pan-American transport possible it also defined what people might see. An artist by nature, the much-lauded Watkins could not grasp that his market had changed. Where once his viewers had been excited by sights of exotic natural grandeur beyond their reach, they now demanded nothing more than souvenirs, mementos of what they had seen. Tourists could be satisfied with uninspired pictures produced by journeymen photographers while Watkins searched virgin territory beyond the railroad's reach.

His rival was more successful. In 1873 a columnist wrote that the 'Watkins photographs are too well known to require comment; but I should like to mention that Mr Muybridge, a photographer not so long before the public, will exhibit this spring a series of large YO-Semite views, finer and more perfect than any which have ever before been taken.' These pictures owe a debt to Watkins' vision, even though they are romantic in inclination. Sadly the debt was unseen by contemporary critics and while Watkins declined, Muybridge ascended, though not in the field of landscape. His photographic concerns were wider and in 1872 Leland Stanford, the millionaire governor of California, gave him an unusual commission. Muybridge was asked to settle a wager photographically. His patron was keen on horses and owned 200 thoroughbreds. Instinct told Stanford that a horse at gallop lifted all four feet off the ground during some part of its stride. A friend wagered $25,000 that it was impossible and Muybridge was employed to settle the matter. He began work only to be halted when brought to trial for shooting his wife's lover. Muybridge pleaded insanity, borne out by witnesses who spoke of the irrationality involved in balancing off a rock face 3400 feet above sea level to make photographs more pleasing, and was acquitted. After the trial, which gained considerable publicity, Muybridge made a tactical withdrawal from San Francisco and reappeared in 1875. He resumed his investigations on behalf of Governor Stanford. By 1878 he had devised a 12-camera method of recording equestrian locomotion; to Stanford's satisfaction all four feet *did* leave the ground. Photography proved it, even more it showed that the horse's legs were tucked underneath and not thrust out front and back as popularly believed. It was a triumph. From his 12-camera beginnings, Muybridge improved the system, eventually arriving at something he called a Zoöpraxiscope. Functioning like a primitive cinema projector, it utilized a human quality, the persistence of vision, to give a series of still images taken in short succession the appearance of movement. Muybridge received praise and attention worldwide for his studies of motion. Artists and scientists were equally fascinated and he abandoned landscape for ever.

Outside commerce and satisfying an ever-growing picture-buying public lay the need for survey. The West was opening up and government teams were sent to explore, study and map the region. Although on no official payroll, Watkins was the first photographer to be used, by the California State Geological Survey who were working in Yosemite Valley in 1866. In 1867 a Geological Exploration of the Fortieth Parallel began. Led by Clarence King, a scientist, it was to chart the land between the Sierra Nevada Mountains and the Rocky Mountains, a massive undertaking costing $100,000. Timothy O'Sullivan, a Civil War veteran who had worked with Mathew Brady and Alexander Gardner (see

Left *Mr Gurd's Country House, Canada*, 1886, by William Notman. Contemporary print from a collodion negative. (Notman Photographic Archives, McCord Museum, McGill University.)

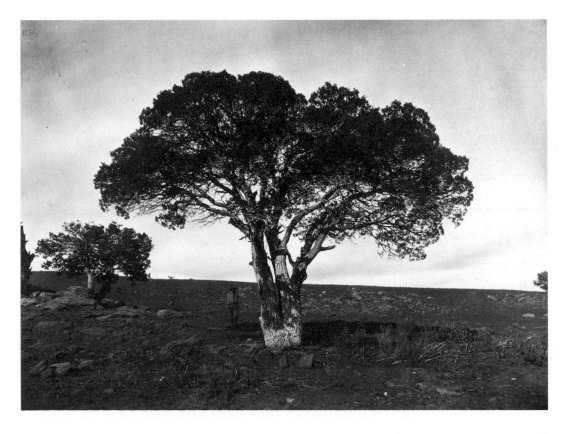

Right *Oak Grove, Sierra Blanca Range, Arizona*, 1873. Albumen print by Timothy H O'Sullivan. (United States National Archives.)

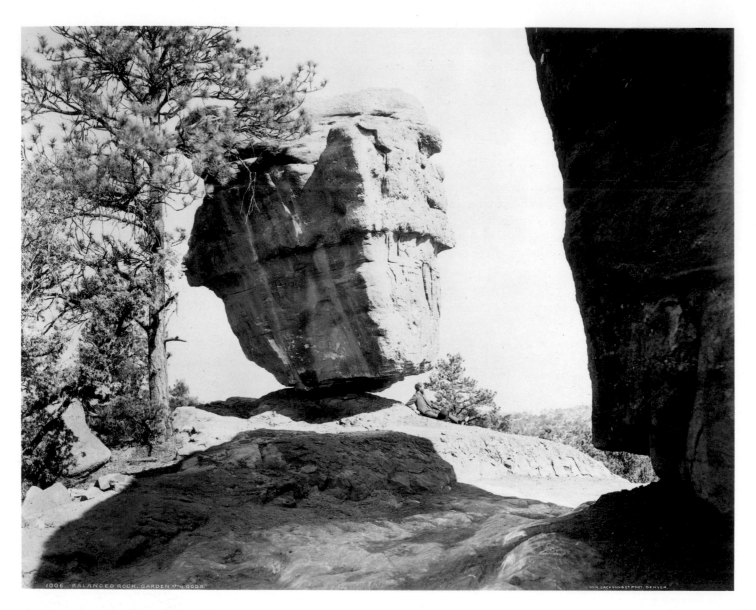

Chapter 6), was employed to record visually the expedition's findings. No records exist to explain the choice of O'Sullivan; however it seems possible that King was looking for more than a mere recorder. He was a founder member of the Society for Truth in Art and as a geologist he held to a theory known as 'catastrophism' which mingled science and theology. Slow geological evolution, he maintained, was interrupted by periods of rapid change. These were shattering, awful, life-threatening and catastrophic. They were God's work, designed to 're-create' the earth and force change or extinction. What better a photographer to picture divine power written in the corrugations and crumples of mountain ranges than one who had experienced the catastrophies of war? For King the Civil War had been a human equivalent to geological change – mighty powers of destruction had been unleashed when a nation turned against itself. If his theories sound eccentric, his choice of O'Sullivan was sound. Experienced in the hardships of photography in the field from his Civil War years, O'Sullivan had a photographic vision that matched King's expectations. Unlike his contemporaries Watkins and Muybridge, O'Sullivan was no romantic in search of an ideal but an honest gatherer of evidence. Much of

what lay before him seemed awesome, inhospitable, sometimes terrifying. It was nature in her raw state, unmarked, wild, larger and more mysterious than man, no place for the picturesque. Thus O'Sullivan documented it in terms of blinding light and harsh shadow: a battlefield of contrasts that threatened to overcome the hapless explorers with its hostile magnificence.

The Fortieth Parallel Survey went on for two hard years. O'Sullivan endured many of the same agonies as Bourne in India; his wet-collodion equipment, cameras and darkroom were carried in a converted mule-drawn ambulance and he would go to any lengths to make the pictures necessary to record their findings. At one point he recalled 'the most voracious and particularly poisonous mosquitoes' and 'the entire impossibility to save one's precious body from frequent attacks of that most enervating of all fevers, known as the mountain ail.' Such effort was rewarded, part financially – a salary of $100 a month – and part with more work. In 1869 he became photographer to the Darien Survey exploring routes for a possible canal through the Isthmus of Panama and in 1871 he joined a military survey mapping 'West of the One Hundredth Meridian.' His task for the latter was less a scientific document than a public relations exercise designed to divert funding from civil to military use. Again personal hardship was the order of the day. Under the leadership of Lieutenant George Wheeler of the Corps of Engineers, the team surveyed the Southwest – parts of California, Nevada and Arizona. Their route included Death Valley, where O'Sullivan's chemicals boiled in the heat, and the Colorado River which they attempted to ascend via the Grand Canyon. In two boats (one named 'The Picture' by O'Sullivan) a small party rowed and towed themselves up 260 miles of treacherous water. The trip involved near-drownings and eventual starvation. No lives were lost, however, and Wheeler commented in his report 'in the face of all obstacles [Mr O'Sullivan] made negatives at all available points.' It was a triumph, not just of human survival but of art. Carefully composed, the pictures step beyond record and become instead evocation, filled with an austere and beautiful wonder at discovery.

His pictures have a curious sense of being modern, as if this nineteenth-century photographer had rejected all contemporary notions of landscape as a sublime subject and worked instead with a knowing sense of abstraction and of how content and form might re-present themselves in silent timelessness, shaped by the camera into a view that is exact and mysterious.

By contrast, William H Jackson, sometime cowboy and now official photographer to the Hayden Survey (1870-78) had a more romantic sensibility. Like O'Sullivan he had been involved in the Civil War, but as a sketcher rather than as a photographer. On return to civilian life he found himself bored and broke. He went West in search of excitement and a job, joined a cattle drive and became a $20-a-month cowboy known as 'Mustang Jack.' In 1867 'Mustang Jack' resumed life as William Jackson when he joined his brother Edward in Omaha to set up Jackson Brothers, a photographic studio. Omaha was a bustling, thriving place, headquarters of the Union Pacific Railroad, and work was plentiful. The brothers made portraits, photographed groups, pictured shop and hotel fronts and did an occasional interior. But the ex-cowboy grew restless with studio work and in 1869 he joined another photographer, A C Hull, to work along the

Left *Balanced Rock, Garden of the Gods,* after 1880. Albumen print by William H Jackson. (The J Paul Getty Museum.)

Below *Yosemite Valley from the 'Best General View,'* c1866. Albumen print by Carlton E Watkins. (American Geographical Society, University of Wisconsin – Milwaukee Library.)

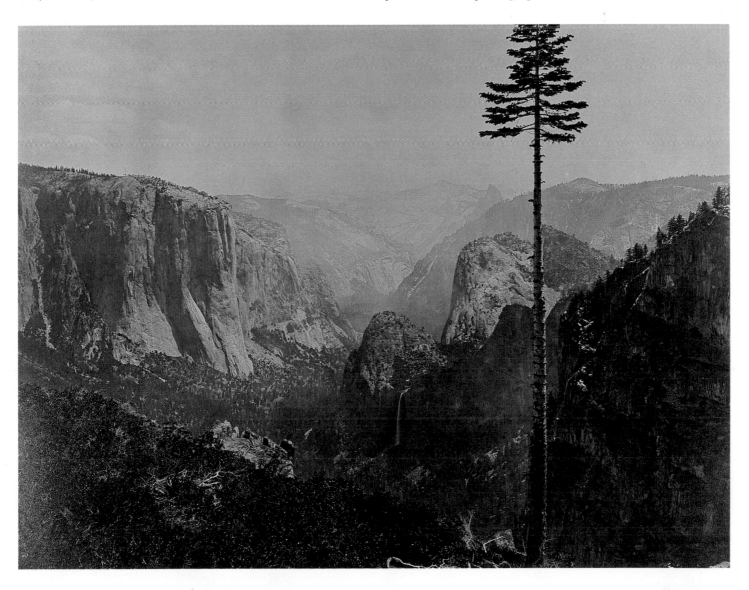

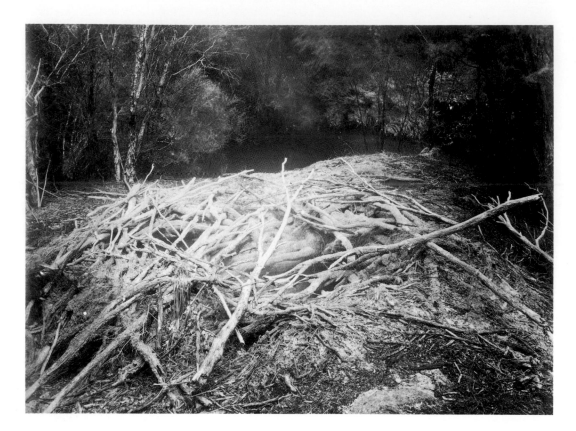

railroad's route. They sold their pictures as they went and their subject matter was much the same as Jackson was used to in Omaha. He did, however, add landscapes to his repertoire – enough to impress Ferdinand Hayden, leader of the US Geological and Geographical Survey of the Territories. Hayden had begun his work without a photographer, but seeing O'Sullivan's pictures used to aid King's case for a renewal of government funding, he changed his mind. Jackson seemed to have the qualities needed and was hired. For the itinerant photographer it was good fortune indeed, for, as he wrote later, 'it gave me a career.' For his employer luck and judgment came together. When Hayden examined Jackson's landscapes he assumed them to be a selection of his best work. In fact they were all Jackson had made, the majority taken to satisfy an order for 1000 views made by a railroad porter in Cheyenne. In 1869 Jackson had taken 45 landscapes. In 1870 he set off into the wilderness, an official Government survey photographer charged with documenting mountains and valleys and canyons which no white American had ever seen.

Jackson was a prolific diarist. From his notes we learn of the day-to-day routine of surveys. He rose at three in the morning, breakfasted on black coffee and made the day's plans. For every mile that was surveyed three were travelled and Jackson used a mule named Hypo to carry his 11 x 14-inch camera, plates and chemicals. Like King, Hayden had high regard for art and Jackson gained a new pictorial education from the painters Gifford and Moran who were part of the team. He learned too how to match geological needs with his own developing visual sensibilities and produce photographs that gave a poetic edge to their scientific value. His days were spent finding vantage points from which to properly convey the wonders Hayden's survey uncovered and

nights were given over to writing up his dairy, cleaning guns and drinking coffee (this time laced with whiskey) by lamplight. Supper was at six (food was provided by hunters who were important members of the party) and bed at eight. Sometimes Jackson would sleep miles from the camp in order to take advantage of early-morning light; like his contemporaries he was a perfectionist.

Each winter the expeditioners would leave the wilderness for Washington, where reports were written, maps drawn, negatives numbered and prints made. When spring arrived it was back into the field, back to *terra incognita*. Hayden's team pushed further into the interior, fuelled by stories from trappers and prospectors. One story, which proved spectacular in its outcome, was of 'Colter's Hell.' John Colter, escaping from hostile Indians, had come upon an other-worldly landscape of heat, evil smelling gas and steaming springs. Hayden determined to discover the truth behind these fabulous tales. All was revealed in 1871 when they penetrated the Yellowstone region. Its geysers, steam, sulphurous mud and boiling water enticed them back in 1872, as if they could not believe their eyes or even Jackson's pictures. Re-photographed and presented in handsome leather-bound albums to members of Congress, the facts of this amazing landscape were enough to create a phenomenon in themselves. The same year saw President Grant signing the bill making Yellowstone America's first National Park – a place where the forests, mountains and wildlife should be preserved from man's destructive influence.

Jackson's career went on. In 1873 the Hayden expedition trekked Colorado where Jackson sought to locate and photograph the Mountain of the Holy Cross, first seen by William Brewer in 1869. On this peak, so Brewer said, could be seen a crucifix – sure indication of the relationship between God, man and nature. Unknown to Jackson the cross was formed by snow caught in rock crevices, but after 'Colter's Hell' it seemed a worthy subject. The best place, he surmised, to make his photograph would be from Notch Mountain to the northeast. Some 1500 feet from its 14,000-foot summit, the mules could go no further and Jackson and two assistants completed the climb. His picture became legend. As the poet Longfellow wrote, photograph in front of him:

> There is a mountain in the distant West
> That, sun-defying in its deep ravines
> Displays a cross upon its side.
> Such is the cross I wear upon my breast
> These eighteen years, through all the changing scenes
> And seasons, changeless since the day she died.

Longfellow had *Mountain of the Holy Cross* hung next to a portrait of his dead wife. Government offices displayed it and the picture sold in thousands as confirmation of might and man in alliance. It was America, the United States.

Jackson's tale is a long one; he lived to be 99 and even though his work for Hayden's survey ended in 1878 he continued to photograph for railroad companies across the United States, Canada and Mexico. In 1894 the World Transport Commission asked him to supply landscapes and people pictures from around the globe. Jackson visited England, Egypt, India, Australia, New Zealand, China, Russia and Japan. Later still he resumed his sketching and worked as a muralist. Finally, as the time he had experienced and pictured became legend as the 'Old West,' he was rediscovered. In 1942 The Museum of Modern Art, New York, mounted an exhibition selected by Ansel Adams, 'Photographers of the Civil War and the American Frontier.' Jackson and O'Sullivan were included and Jackson, just short of his hundredth birthday, was a guest at the opening. 'That's a pretty good picture,' he said to Ansel Adams, gazing at one of his own creations, 'who took it?'. 'You did, Mr Jackson!' came the reply. 'Well, so I did,' said Jackson, 'but I can do better now and in color.' Having said that, he pulled out a 35mm camera, laughed and added that there was 'no need for a string of mules.'

While American pioneers faced a magnificent and unknown landscape, so did their counterparts around the world. Photography was a kind of fever which gripped all

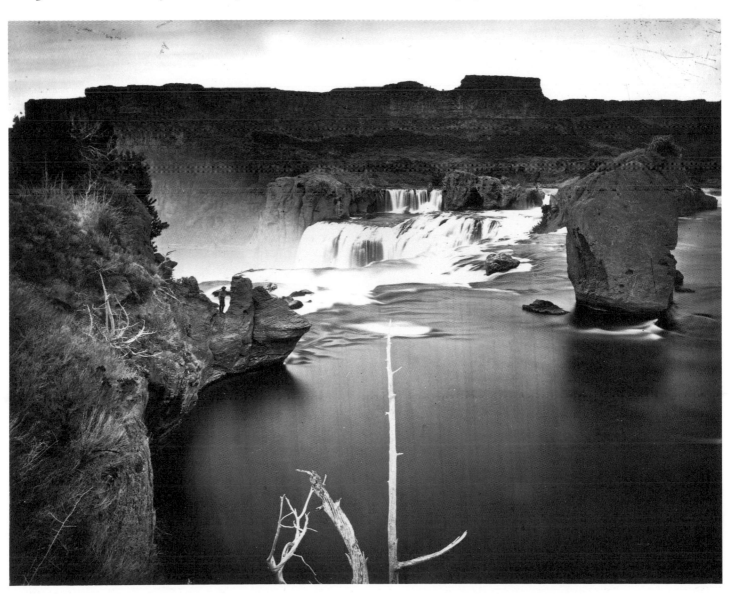

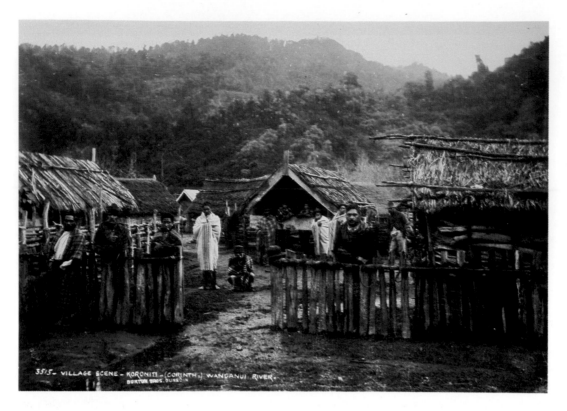

who practiced it and drove them to the most inaccessible corners of the globe in search of pictures. From the Australian outback to the Arctic and Asia photographers sought images to amaze and delight an image-hungry audience. The majority made views, generally picturesque and romantic studies that borrowed heavily from painting for their visual effect. Some saw further and realized their medium could do more than transcribe nature and be sold to tourists. One such was John Thomson, a Scot born in 1837. Thomson grew up with photography and perhaps because of this he saw making pictures as a natural extension of human curiosity. While O'Sullivan confronted the American West and wrestled with King's concepts of an intersection between geology and theology, Thomson was eagerly exploring China, docu-

menting a culture rather than recording a landscape. *Illustrations of China and Its People*, a four-volume work, was published in 1873-74. It was the first major pictorial survey of people, and as a stranger in a strange land Thomson became the first photoreporter, bringing social comment to a vision of an exotic nation so far removed from Victorian Britain that it might well have been the moon.

Thomson had originally studied chemistry and began to travel when he was 24. By 1865 he had opened a studio in Singapore and in 1868, or thereabouts for little is known of Thomson's early life, he moved to Hong Kong. This rocky island was one of Britain's prizes from the Opium Wars when colonial opportunism prevailed over a mighty civilization. Opium, which brought China to a dreamy, drug-induced

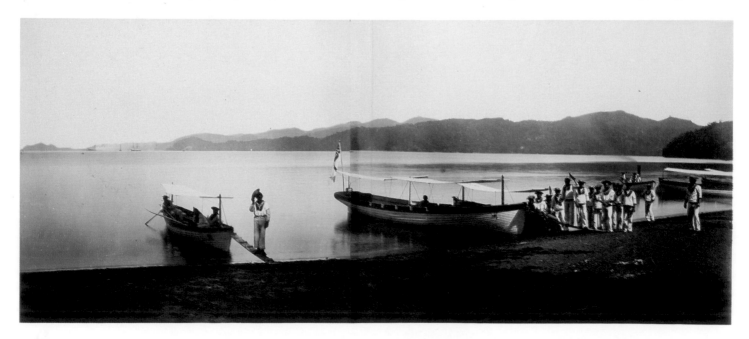

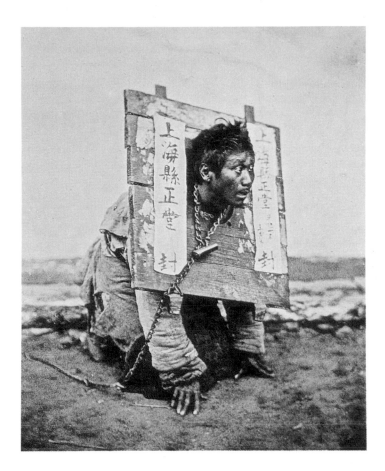

Treaty of Nanking made Hong Kong a Crown Colony and provided 21 million dollars in silver by way of restitution for opium destroyed in China's clean-up campaign. Hong Kong boomed as the West poured into the land of tea and silk, porcelain and lacquer work. Thomson, however, was not content to trade as a simple portrait photographer – surely his reason for moving to Hong Kong – and in 1868 he began what was to become a five-year, 5000-mile journey across the Chinese mainland into regions where white men were unknown.

Because we lack information on John Thomson's early life, only speculation can provide clues as to why he made a break with the practice of photographing people only in studios. It seems possible that culture might provide an answer. The Chinese were intensely wary of his camera, seeing it as some agent of evil that could see through things; at times Thomson was stoned when trying to take pictures. To overcome these fears he would talk to the people he wanted to picture, gain details of their lives and try to understand their social position. When they and he were satisfied, a picture was taken with 10- to 20-second exposure. As he gained information that comes aside from just looking, Thomson must have decided that reassembling these scenes in a studio could not show the whole truth. He was talking to and photographing the poorest people he had ever seen. More interesting than any landscape, they lived on life's margins, a people who had customs and traditions that were alien to the West. For the sake of authenticity they must be pictured where they stood. And so began a tradition that exists to this day – the photographer as cultural interpreter and witness to the world.

collapse, made millions for European drug dealers who brought it from India's poppy fields. The emperor ordered opium smugglers to be executed and banned trade with Britain. Britain reacted by sending gunboats and attacking the Chinese mainland and was eventually victorious. In 1842 the

Above *Punishment in China*, *c* 1870. Albumen print by John Thomson. (Hans Christian Adam.)

Right *Bound feet of Chinese Ladies*, *c* 1870. Albumen print by John Thomson, who bribed his subjects to reveal their deformities, considered by the Chinese to be a mark of beauty. (Hans Christian Adam.)

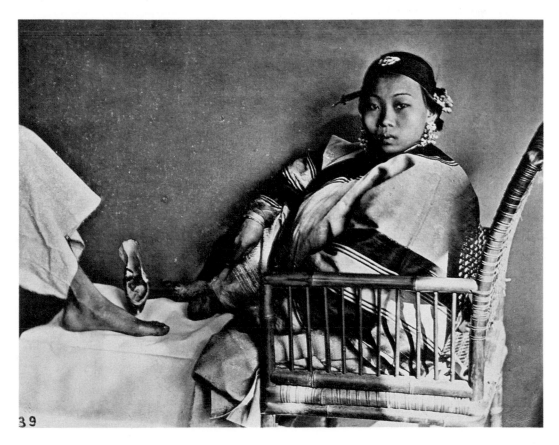

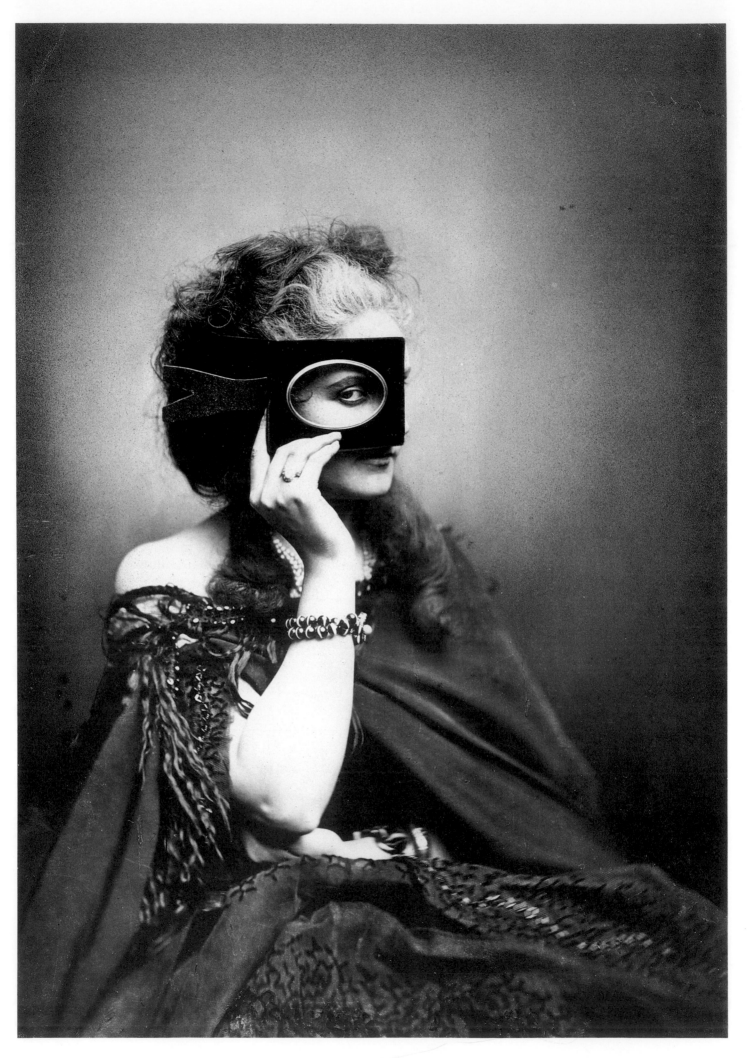

CHAPTER THREE

Beauty and Truth

Pictorialism, Realism and the Fight for Photography as a Fine Art

Looking back almost 150 years to photography's birth, distinctions between concepts of art, commerce and status become blurred. Whatever the motives for a picture being made, given the respect we accord early images, our impulse is to view art and commerce almost as one – the past is made present and holds its own fascination. At the time these photographs were made, however, lines were being sharply drawn and divisions set up. As wonder at the very production of a photograph faded, the question arose is photography art? When painter Paul Delaroche exclaimed 'from today painting is dead' he seemed certain that photography would overtake pencil and pen, brush and canvas. Others were not. Within the infant photographic community, at least in Britain and France, the question seemed more directed towards establishing what *kind* of photography was art. Could the truthfulness of this medium be equated with the ideals of painting?

The very idea of a machine (the camera) intervening between art, sublime and beyond reach of the industrial age, and pictures seemed foolish. The notion caused controversy, even argument. Contemporary reports give the best flavor of these debates, and provide an important insight to the nineteenth-century mind and how contemporary thinking contributed to visual imagery.

In 1853 Sir William Newton read a paper to the newly formed Photographic Society of London. He was a painter and talked of 'Photography in an Artistic View.' Having explained that one cannot find a 'true representation of light and shade in Photography, which is to be found in fine work of art' Sir William asked what course a photographer ought to pursue. The answer, he thought, was that pictures should 'not to be so *chemically*, as *artistically* beautiful . . . I do not conceive it to be necessary that the whole of the subject should be what is called *in focus*; on the contrary, I have found . . . that the object is better obtained by the whole subject being a little *out of focus*, thereby giving a greater breadth of effect, and consequently more *suggestive* of the true character of nature.' Sir William's idea that a somewhat misty appearance might transform the ordinary and make it art was controversial, but his mention of 'nature' is indicative of the then-prevailing view of art. As we shall see, this concept was to haunt photography for years to come.

Lady Eastlake, a contemporary of Newton and wife of the Photographic Society's first president, was to present a counter. In an article published in *Quarterly Review* in 1857, she denounced Sir William's views. Her essay, stunning in its grasp of photography's potential, proclaimed that picture making by camera was 'a new medium of communication.'

Left *The Countess Castiglione,* *c*1860. Albumen print by Louis Pierson. (The Metropolitan Museum of Art. Gift of George Davis, 1948. 48.188.)

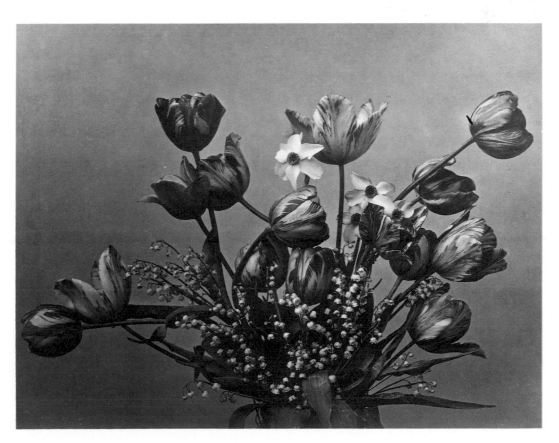

Right *Still Life, c*1855. Albumen print by Adolphe Braun, a prolific French photographer and print publisher. (Victoria and Albert Museum.)

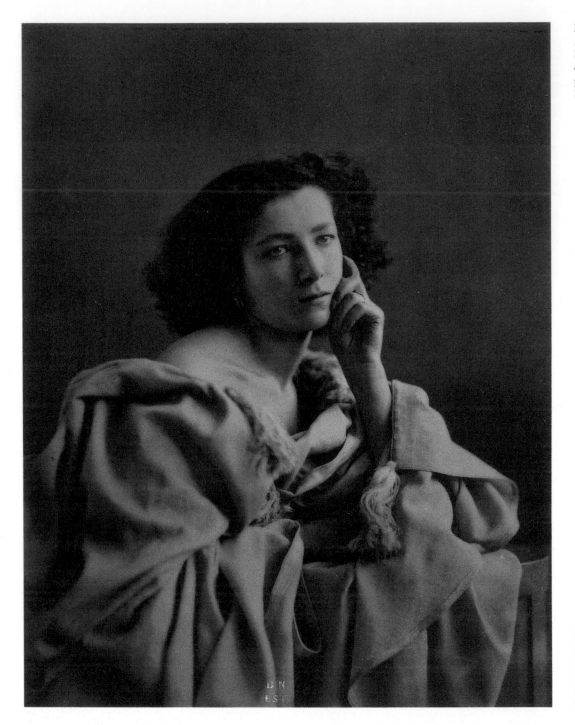

Lady Eastlake argued that Newton was guilty of 'propounding the heresy that pictures taken slightly out of focus . . . would be found more *artistically* beautiful . . . As soon could an accountant admit the morality of a false balance . . . (could) your merely scientific photographer be made to comprehend the possible beauty of "a slight *burr*."' For Lady Eastlake photography was 'made for the present age, in which the desire for art resides in a small minority, but the craving, or rather necessity for cheap, prompt, and correct facts is in the public at large. Photography is the purveyor of such knowledge to the world. She is the sworn witness of everything presented to her view . . . Every form which is traced by light is the impress of one moment, or one hour, or one age in the great passage of time. Though the faces of our children may not be modelled and rounded with that truth

and beauty which art attains, yet *minor* things – the very shoes of one, the inseparable toy of the other – are given with a strength of identity which art does not even seek . . . Here, therefore, the much lauded and much abused agent called Photography takes her legitimate stand. Her business is to give evidence of facts, as minutely and as impartially as, to our shame, only an unreasoning machine can give . . . If, therefore, the time should ever come when art is sought, as it ought to be, mainly for its own sake, our artists and our patrons will be of a far more elevated order than now: and if anything can bring about so desirable a climax, it will be the introduction of Photography.'

As Sir William Newton asked for photographs to take on the look of painting, so Lady Eastlake insisted that it should be itself and explore the qualities that set it apart as a medium.

Painters, she maintained, had nothing to lose and everything to gain from its presence. Others disagreed, they viewed photography as a science which threatened to corrupt art. In 1859 Charles Baudelaire, the French poet wrote: 'As the photographic industry was the refuge of every would-be painter, every painter too ill-endowed or too lazy to complete his studies, this universal infatuation bore not only the mark of a blindness, an imbecility, but also the air of a vengeance.' Summing up arguments to date he continued his attack. 'During this lamentable period, a new industry arose which contributed not a little to confirm stupidity in its faith and to ruin whatever might remain of the divine in the French mind.

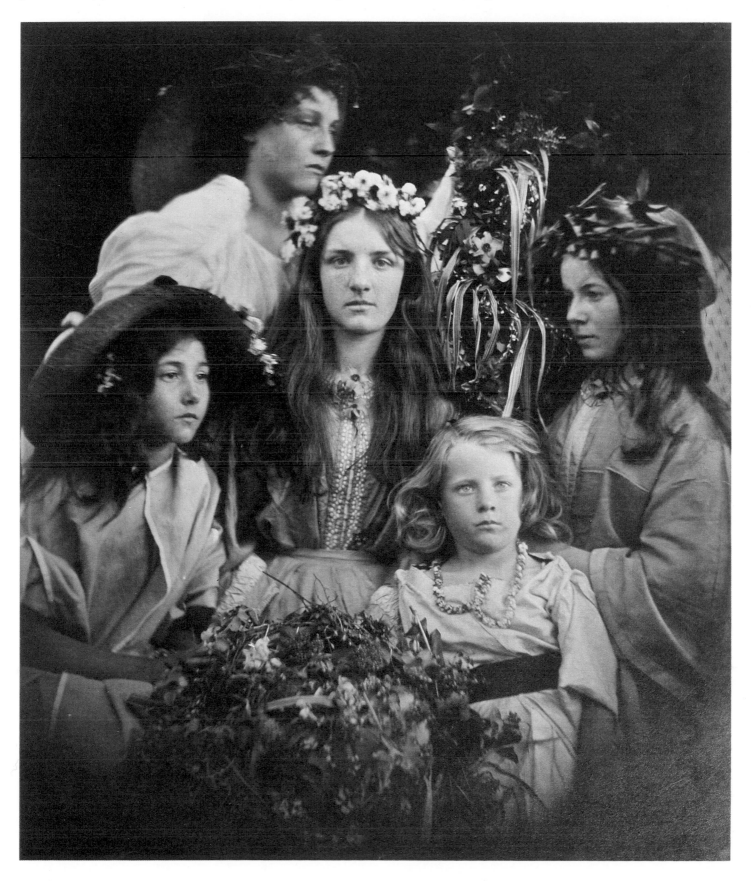

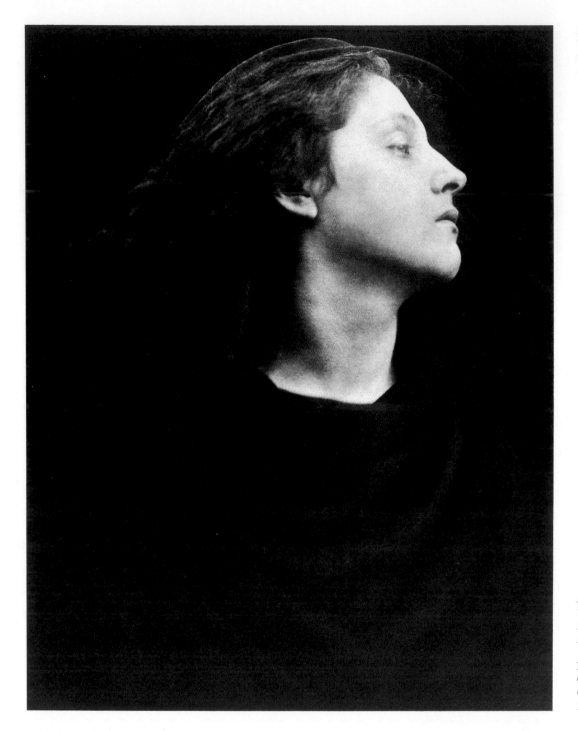

Left *Portrait of Mary Hiller*, 1865–75. Carbon print by Julia Margaret Cameron. (Victoria and Albert Museum.)

Above right *Sir John Herschel*, 1869. Carbon print by Julia Margaret Cameron. (Victoria and Albert Museum.)

Right *Sir Henry Taylor*, c1866. Carbon print by Julia Margaret Cameron. (Victoria and Albert Museum.)

The idolatrous mob demanded an ideal worthy of itself and appropriate to its nature – that is perfectly understood. In matters of painting and sculpture, the present-day *Credo* of the sophisticated, above all in France . . . is this: "I believe in Nature, and I believe only in Nature . . . I believe that Art is, and cannot be other than, the exact reproduction of Nature (a timid and dissident sect would wish to exclude the more repellent objects of nature, such as skeletons or chamber-pots). Thus an industry that could give us a result identical to Nature would be the absolute of Art". A revengeful God has given ear to the prayers of this multitude. Daguerre was his Messiah. And now the faithful says to himself: "Since photography gives every guarantee of exactitude that we could desire (they really believe that, the mad fools!), then photography and Art are the same thing". From that moment our squalid society rushed, Narcissus to a man, to gaze at its trivial image on a scrap of metal.' Art, Baudelaire went on to declare, is the stuff of dreams and photography its 'most mortal enemy.'

Baudelaire's main concern was not photography itself; one of his great friends was Nadar, a photographic portraitist. What troubled him was the notion of its popularity and the unthinking commercialism that followed. Should such a vulgar medium overtake art in the public's mind, then a bitter blow would be struck against civilization. His arguments, like those of Sir William Newton and Lady Eastlake, are reiterated to this day. Is photography an art? If so what *kind* of art? Can what Fox Talbot called 'the imitation of nature' suffice to lift a mechanical form of picture making into the realms of human expression? Another Victorian, Jabez

Hughes, believed he had found a solution to such problems when he spoke to the South London Photographic Society in 1860. He proposed that photography 'should be divided into three classes: Mechanical photography, Art-photography, and, for want of a better term, High-Art photography. Mechanical photography will include all kinds of pictures which aim at simple representation of objects to which the camera is pointed . . . This branch, for obvious reasons, will always be the most practised: and where literal, unchallengeable truth is required, is the only one allowable. [A restatement of Lady Eastlake's position, if lacking her foresight in the visual power of such images.] Art-photography will embrace all pictures where the artist, not content with taking things as they may naturally occur, determines to infuse his mind into them by arranging, modifying, or otherwise disposing them, so that they may appear in a more appropriate or beautiful manner. [A minor version of Sir William Newton's argument.] High-Art photography [the Victorian ideal] . . . pictures which aim at higher purposes . . . [their] aim is not merely to amuse, but to instruct, purify, and ennoble.' By 1860, then, basic fields had been established in an intellectual debate. On the one hand photography was a popular means of reproducing the material world, on the other it had aspirations towards 'the exercise of individual genius.' As mass-market concerns consumed the former, so a disjointed group of artist-photographers began exploring the latter, hoping to develop photography as a serious contender to painting.

If we look back, briefly, to the medium's beginnings, to Fox Talbot, Bayard and Daguerre, the concepts which informed their picture making can be seen entangled in similar

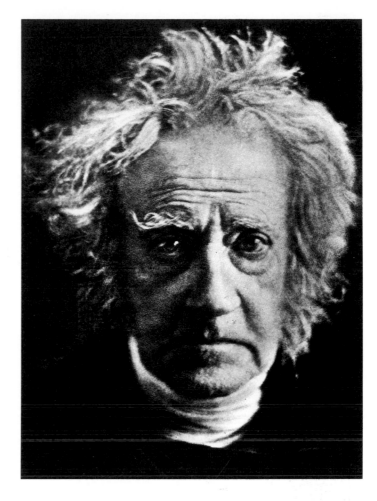

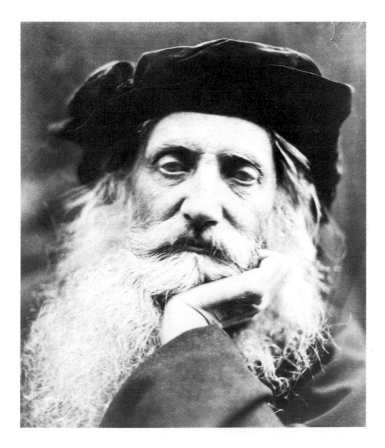

concerns. Was their invention for artists or artisans? And how does one go about making or taking a photograph when no guide-lines to its content or appearance exist? Daguerre, a man of commerce, favored the artisan route. If the public wanted fact first, he could provide it. Bayard, the world's first 'amateur photographer,' saw art as his goal. He grieved for lack of recognition but continued to photograph for the sake of his pictures. Fox Talbot, typically British, vacillated. He wanted financial reward but in his own photography veered towards a pictorial aesthetic that satisfied 'artistic' notions.

Following in the wake of these originators came photographers in their hundreds, eventually thousands. Many were dabblers, content with mastering chemical and technical aspects of this new way of picturing the world. Some, however, were more purely visual in their approach, taking their cue from an area they already knew – sketches, watercolors and prints. For mid-century Victorians, photography was an opportunity to blend the successes of their age, bringing seemingly uncomplicated ideas of art to the science now making its presence felt in Europe and the United States. Both groups had the financial means necessary to indulge their interest, and time in which to exercise their fascination for this latest marvel. Photography was a mingling of art and science and suited their liberal viewpoints. As Europe attuned itself to new industry, new mobility and new wealth, photography, with its power to appear truthful, was ideally suited to presenting a view of stability within a period of change.

Favored subject matter, then, emphasized rural beauty, ruined abbeys, castles, churches and venerable trees. The old order seemed intact.

But even as photography came into being its relationship with new ways of viewing the world became clear. Anna Atkins, now recognized as the earliest woman photographer, made sketches, fine drawings, lithographs, and paintings before the invention of photography. Inspired by Fox Talbot, she turned to the cyanotype process to make publicly available her concern for the minutiae of plant life. Atkins' pictures, now called photograms, were made by laying botanical specimens on light-sensitive paper. The plant appeared as a white silhouette against a blue background. The image avoided any vagaries of the human hand and was scientific in its exactness. More than this, it had beauty. In Atkins' work, art and science came together – as it did in photograms made by Thereza Llewelyn (daughter of Fox

Talbot's cousin). These works were botanically accurate and aesthetically pleasing; they displayed photography's gift to perfection. At its inception photography was an interweaving of visual matters with the high planes of science, at least science as was understood by part-time scientists. It also offered the capacity to bring a more rounded vision to those who felt beauty, truth and nature to be essential components of art.

As these ideas fed into the mainstream of photographic thinking, so the arguments and debates outlined above took hold. And, as Jabez Hughes noted in his contribution, 'mechanical photography' seemed by far the most popular to public taste. As leaders in the photographic community were quick to see, the public were persuaded by novelty and lacked discrimination. An antidote to such vulgarity was sought by those who saw themselves in the essentially Victorian role of gentlemen-scholars; men of learning and science, art

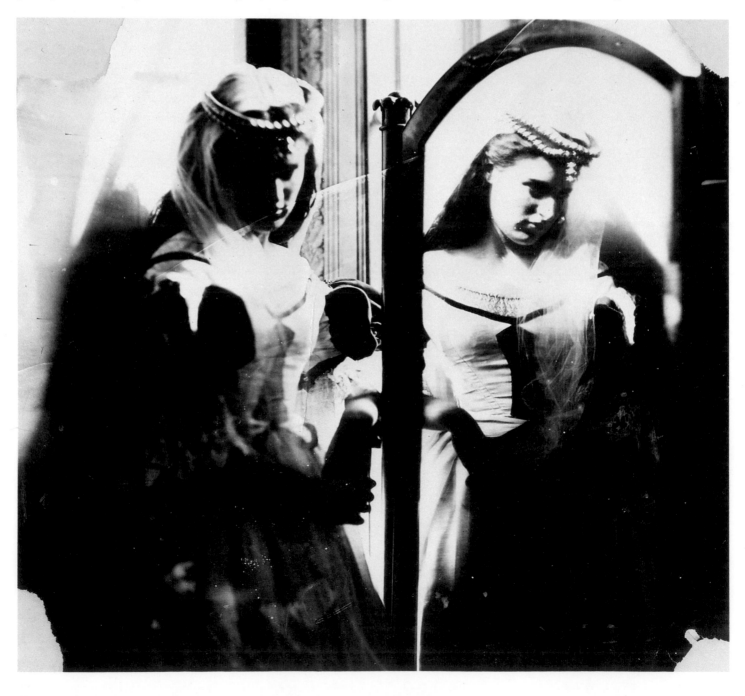

Right *The Briar Rose,* 1909. Autochrome by John Cimon Warburg. (Royal Photographic Society.)

Left *Photographic Study,* early 1860s. Albumen print by Clementina, Viscountess Hawarden, awarded a Photographic Society medal in 1863 as 'best amateur exhibitor.' (Victoria and Albert Museum.)

Below *Two Ways of Life,* 1857. Combination carbon print by Oscar G Rejlander whose work was greatly appreciated by Queen Victoria. (Royal Photographic Society.)

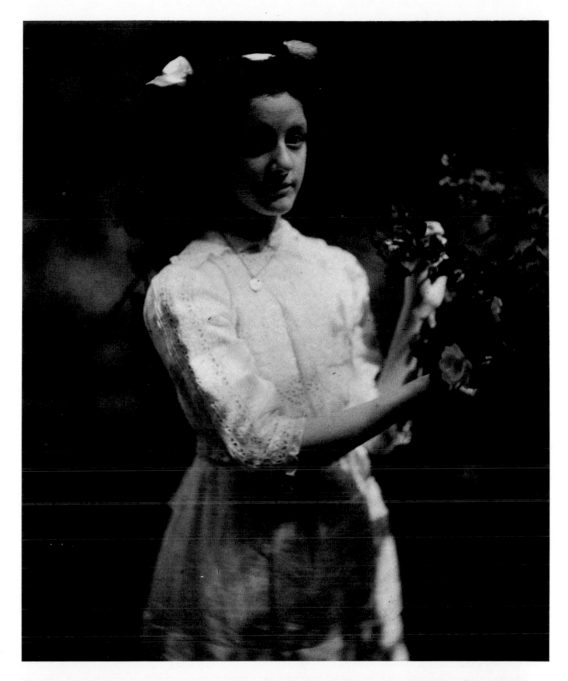

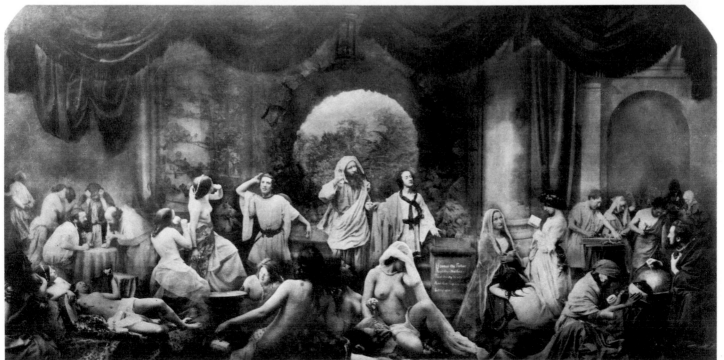

appreciators. In 1852 Roger Fenton, painter, photographer and lawyer, had proposed a Photographic Society for 'all those gentlemen whose taste has led them to the cultivation of this branch of natural science.' Fenton, once a student of the painter Delaroche in Paris, returned to France to check on the formation of the Societé Héliographique. Britain should have the same, he determined, and in 1853 Sir William Eastlake was elected first president of the now-established group (Fox Talbot had declined the invitation). Fenton (whose considerable contribution to photography is examined in Chapter 6) became secretary. With an august society to make plain differences between the work of artist and artisan, a divide took place within photography. The public, or so it seemed, were allowed the plebeian products of 'mechanical photographers' while those of more refinement would concern themselves with art photography. As in a cricket match there were 'gentlemen' and 'players.'

With photography now firmly established in its new location as an art/science comes a return to the question if an art, what kind? Art was understood to embrace certain areas – landscape, portrait, still-life, figure studies, genre studies and so on. Many photographers thought the same should apply to their medium. But how to deal with truth when it appeared less than beautiful was a problem when art was equated with notions of 'the ideal.' Far-sighted critics realized that 'what makes an artist is not the process but the feeling.' On the whole photographers were not convinced. If photography was to be art, it should look like painting. Two solutions were found. One lay in the idea of *effect* – Newton's idea of a retreat from realism into the realms of soft focus

which banished the indelicacies of truthfulness to a misty blur. The other was in composite photographs. It was becoming fashionable to construct genre photographs, visual narratives, often telling a moral tale. Such pictures involved the amateur theatricals of dressing models or friends in appropriate costume, finding or constructing a background and then arranging the players in a re-enactment of some scene from the classics or a re-creation of imagined bucolic bliss. Such storytelling, with all its overtones of the 'higher purposes' Hughes had proposed as photography's zenith, could be constructed in the darkroom by using several negatives – a sky from one, figures from another, background from a third and so on. Thus composite photographs came into currency. They joined ideas of craft and a display of the artist's hand to an escape from inevitable realism.

Once again, distinctions between attitude, idea and realization are not clear cut, but work from two photographers – Julia Margaret Cameron and Henry Peach Robinson – highlight the situation. Cameron, who described photography as 'mortal but yet divine,' crossed her knowledge of painting with a firm sense of Christian right and explored an image making optically smoothed of 'the little frets of life.' Robinson, feeling himself part of the Pre-Raphaelite movement in painting, took to ideas of absolute imagination and made photographs consisting of several negatives. Originally a painter, he would make sketches of an ideal picture, find backgrounds, models and costumes to fit the ideal, then blend each with the other until photographic accuracy met his vision. For his first public success, a young girl dying from consumption called *Fading Away* (1858), Robinson combined

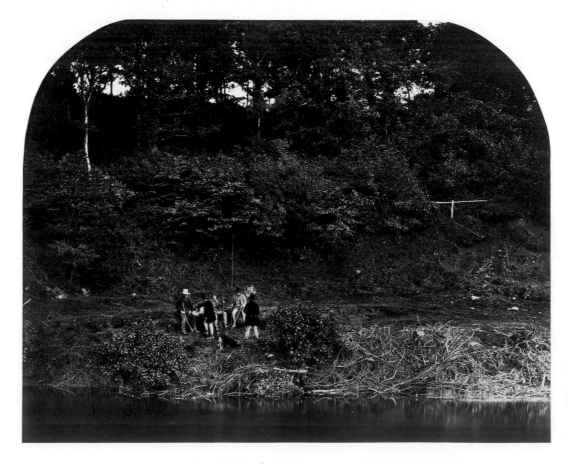

Left *The Keeper's Rest, Ribbleside*, 1858. Albumen print by Roger Fenton, whose visual accomplishments ranged from still-life to photography of war. (Victoria and Albert Museum.)

Right *The Lady of Shalott,* 1861. Albumen print by Henry Peach Robinson, who encouraged the imitation of Pre-Raphaelite painting. (Royal Photographic Society.)

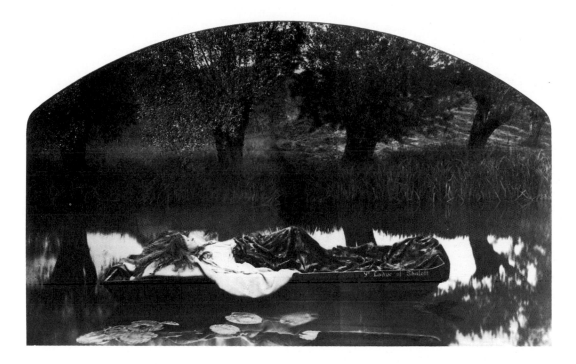

Below *Haymaker and Rake,* 1888. Photogravure by Peter Henry Emerson, chief protagonist in the fight for photography's visual independence. (Victoria and Albert Museum.)

five negatives. This combination technique had been learned from another photographer, Oscar Rejlander, who sought subjects in a less social and more classical mode. Rejlander's tour de force was *Two Ways of Life* (1857), an upholding of morality which showed in allegorical form good and evil, work and idleness in opposition. Rejlander used some 30 negatives to make his composite. It seemed very close to a painting, even though contemporary art critics dismissed it as being made by a machine. Robinson wanted none of this. He set about constructing a theoretical basis from which to work, wrote articles and books on aesthetics and stated directly that 'a method that will not admit of modifications of the artist cannot be art.'

Such constructions were not confined to Britain, nor were the strivings made by photographers for *effect*. Painters borrowed wholesale from photography's verisimilitude and photographers in several countries wanted similar license in respect of the art they knew. However, it was in empire-confidant Britain that the idea flourished. Newton had asked for photographs that were 'suggestion' rather than statements of fact and Cameron was on hand to provide just such a form of image making.

Cameron came late to photography; she was 49 years old when, in 1863, her daughter gave her a camera as a gift. Despite a lifestyle involving house parties and entertaining, Cameron was lonely. Her husband was abroad, her children grown up or away at school. Photography was fashionable, and her daughter thought it might amuse her 'to try to photograph' during her solitude at Freshwater. The Camerons lived on the Isle of Wight in a house next door to their friend Alfred Lord Tennyson, Poet Laureate. Among their circle were members of an intellectual elite: the painter G F Watts and his wife, Ellen Terry; the astronomer Sir John Herschel; Charles Darwin; and the poets Browning and Longfellow. It was to such famous faces that Cameron was to turn with her camera, but first she needed to master the

chemical aspects of photography. With considerable energy, for she was now 50, she converted a coal hole into a darkroom and there learned how to coat her plates with wet-collodion. They were 10 x 15 inches and she would contact print them the same size. Her darkroom had no running water; when the process was over, the finished prints would be washed in a well. Technical matters seemed of small concern, indeed

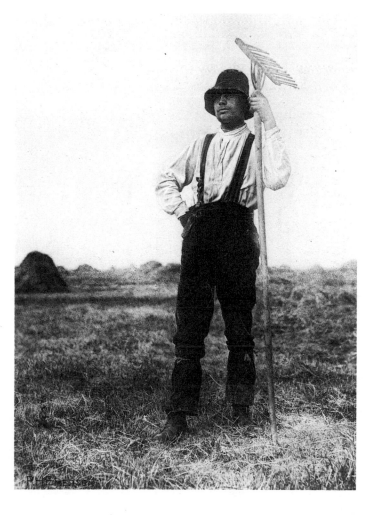

surviving prints show a degree of carelessness, but it took her a year of trial and error to make what she described as her 'first success' and three years to become proficient to the point where she was willing to begin the series of portraits that some consider photography's finest.

Cameron was unconventional in the ways in which she used the medium. At first she favored allegorical subjects, using models to make, for example, a madonna and child (*Divine Love, c* 1865) or *Return after Three Days*, where Christ at 33 is played by the same 12-year old boy who was the infant Jesus in *Divine Love*. Then she turned to portraits of extraordinary compositional boldness, filling her frame with a head in a way Herschel described as 'thrusting from the paper into the air.' Next came illustrations to poetry, children dressed as angels, and more theater. Finally, when she and her husband left England for Ceylon (now Sri Lanka), Cameron turned to a more naturalistic portrayal of natives. Whatever her subject matter, lack of photographic convention marks Cameron's works apart. She preferred soft focus, writing 'when focussing and coming to something which to my eye, was very beautiful, I stopped there instead of screwing on the lens to the more definite focus which all other photographers insist upon.' And she pressed the chemistry of photography into support of her desires for pictures to express rather than explain. The result outraged other photographers for whom perfection in technique was all-important. As Professor Wilhelm Vogel said of her display at the 1867 Universal Exhibition in Paris: 'Those large unsharp heads, spotty backgrounds and deep opaque shadows looked more like bungling pupils' work than masterpieces. And for this reason many photographers could hardly restrain their laughter, and

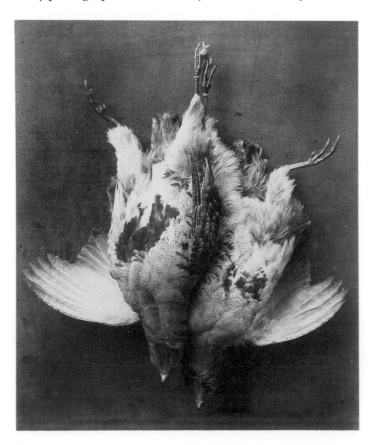

mocked.' Unlike Robinson, who simply dismissed Cameron's work as 'badly defined,' Vogel saw some virtues. He noticed photographers laughing but saw too how interested were artists who came to the exhibition; they 'praised their artistic value, which was so outstanding that technical shortcomings hardly count.' Art was important to Cameron, and though she dearly wished for praise from her British photographic peers, which was not forthcoming, she found joy in the response from her writer, poet and painting friends. Where Robinson thought himself somehow a Pre-Raphaelite he missed their spirit and took his lead directly from contemporary genre painters, Cameron looked for greater breadth for influence. She was inspired by Pre-Raphaelite painters, many of whom were part of her circle, but, under the influence of G F Watts – a maverick among Pre-Raphaelites – she also looked to Rembrandt, Titian and Giotto. And while her works bear all the hallmarks of photography in painting's footsteps, they have qualities far beyond imitation. Perhaps this is because she saw beyond an inevitable intertwining of beauty and truth, even when, like Robinson's, it was created in the darkroom, and settled instead for beauty alone.

Cameron was not the only photographer to be dismissed by Robinson. His was the most powerful voice of the period. Not only did the technical virtuosity of such constructed photographs as *Fading Away* impress, but his writing left a deep mark on nineteenth- and twentieth-century photography. As late as the 1950s magazines in Britain and the United States were rewriting the advice he offered in 1869 in *Pictorial Effect in Photography*, a manual of composition that borrowed freely from books for painters. In 1886 a young photographer called Emerson began to lecture and condemn Robinson's mimicry of painting as outmoded, and began a debate that was to last several years. And like the previous division of photographers into 'gentlemen' and 'players,' this factioning was to have far-reaching consequences.

Peter Henry Emerson, who was later to applaud Cameron and publish her works, was a man of many parts – Doctor of Medicine, naturalist, billiard player, writer and photographer. His writings, which include novels and detective stories, are sadly neglected – except for one, *Naturalistic Photography for Students of the Art*. Published in 1889 it served as a counter to Robinson's supremacy in the field of theory, at least as far as late-Victorian progressives were concerned. Where Robinson stressed that a photographer's duty was 'to avoid the mean, the base, and the ugly; and to aim to elevate his subject, to avoid awkward forms, and to correct the unpicturesque,' Emerson opined that 'nature is so full of surprises that, all things considered, she is best . . . as she is.' Just as Robinson was to influence generations of photographers with remarks like 'it is the purpose of the artist to represent agreeable truth,' so Emerson bellowed back 'the realist makes no analysis . . . the naturalist's work we should call true to nature.' He was opinionated, frequently contradictory and convinced that naturalism rather than artifice was the means of bringing his medium to full flower. He saw naturalism as reality perceived rather than recorded.

Right *Gathering Water Lilies*, 1886. Photogravure by Peter Henry Emerson. (Victoria and Albert Museum.)

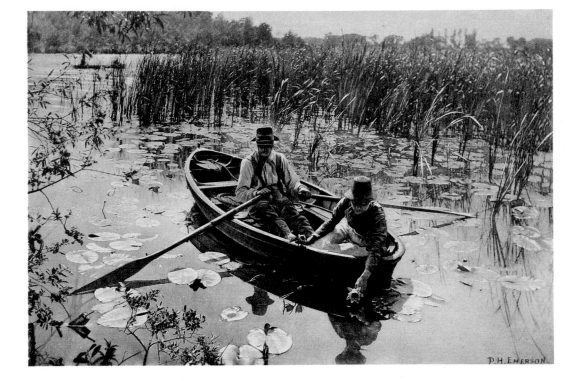

Below left *The First of September*, *c*1885. Albumen print by William Lake Price, who in 1858 wrote the first treatise on photography as an aesthetic pursuit. (Victoria and Albert Museum.)

Below *River Seine, France*, 1858. An albumen print by Camille Silvy, which was praised in Britain for its 'exquisite and varied detail.' (Victoria and Albert Museum.)

Like his liberal-minded predecessors, Emerson saw art and science joining together in an enlightened age. Using *Physiological Optics* by Hermann von Helmholtz as a guide, his theoretical and practical aim was to show how art had a scientific basis. Not optical sharpness as a synonym for truth, 'an impersonal mathematical plotting,' but the more complex case of human perception where 'everything is seen against something else ... its outlines fade into that something else, often so subtly that you cannot quite distinguish where one ends and the other begins.' It was Emerson's

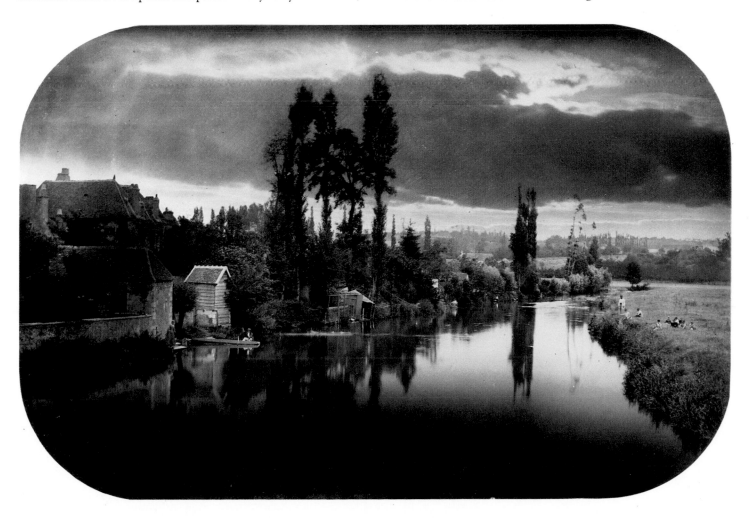

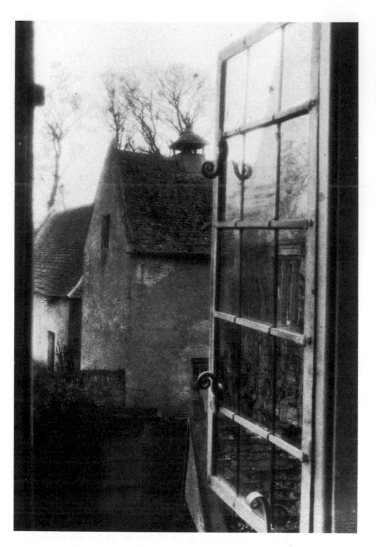

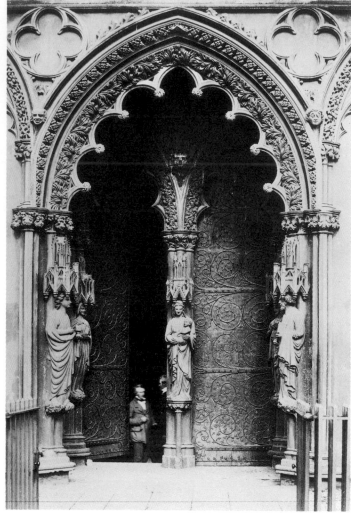

contention that human vision was so unlike camera vision that the only way to make photographs truthful was by a slight softness to all except the main subject because 'in this mingled decision and indecision, this lost and found, lies all the charm and mystery of nature.' Like Cameron, who upset the establishment by making pictures with soft edges, the antithesis of photography's understood strength, Emerson ventured on to dangerous ground when he advocated a move away from fashion. But like the French naturalist painters from whom he took his cue, Emerson thought that nature and truth were interwoven. Photography, used correctly, could display that truth and record how an individual viewed the world and responded to its charms. It was in the wilds of Norfolk that he made his pictures. They show an England many thought had vanished, a desolate landscape where peasants pulled a hard living from the soil, set snares and traps for meat and seemed unknowing of city squalor. To Emerson it was idyllic, it contained all the elements an artist in search of truth might want; this life was real and he photographed with passion.

Photographs aside, it was in the political arena that Emerson made his name, through his *Naturalistic Photography*, his bickering with Robinson and the shock waves his theories sent through the photographic world. Concepts of naturalism which many seemed to think simply involved a less than

sharp result caused a division: it means 'no focus at all, a blur, a smudge, a fog, a daub, a thing for the gods to weep over and photographers to shun' cried one authority; 'it is not in man, even in f64 man, [the aperture giving greatest sharpness] to overlook the unnaturalness of joinings in photographic pictures, and the too visible drawing-room drapery air about attractive ladies playing at haymaking' was the retort, making direct reference to Robinson's habit of dressing friends as peasants for his pictures. Two camps emerged, with Robinson and Emerson as their respective champions. Followers of Robinson persisted with what Emerson called 'literary fallacies and art anachronisms' while the naturalistic school took up making what their opponents called 'fuzzygraphs.' Sadly, few who thought Emerson was bringing freshness and vigor to a staid medium, truly listened to his advice. He asked for truth, for 'pictures from nature' and warned against 'that so-called "fuzziness" . . . destroying the structure of any object, otherwise it becomes noticeable.' They saw soft focus as the road to photographic impressionism and another proof of their medium's claim to be an art. However, the fight was to continue even without Emerson. To the surprise of his followers he made an announcement in 1891. A 'great painter' (probably his friend Whistler) had convinced him that art and nature were not one. Further, recent experiments by two pioneers of photographic sensitometry, Ferdinand Hurter and Vero Driffield, showed that the absolute tonal control he believed possible in a picture was not. Five years after he began to shake photography with a new kind of picture and a storm of invective, Emerson privately published a sad epitaph, *The Death of Naturalistic Photography*. In this black-bordered pamphlet he wrote: 'The individuality of the artist is cramped – control of the picture is possible to a *slight* degree . . . But the all-vital powers of selection and rejection are totally limited, bound in by fixed and narrow barriers. No differential analysis can be made, no subduing of parts, save by dodging – no emphasis – save by dodging, and that is not pure photography, impure photography is merely a confession of limitations. I thought once (Hurter and Driffield have taught me differently) that true values could be *altered at will* by development. They cannot; therefore to talk of getting

values . . . true to nature is to talk nonsense . . . I have, I regret it deeply, compared photographs to great works of art and photographers to great artists. It was rash and thoughtless and my punishment is having to acknowledge it now.'

Emerson's insistence on a 'pure' photography is notable for while he took his lead from painting and admired artists like Jean-François Millet and Jules Bastien-Lepage to the point of imitation, he had a clear view of photography as its own medium. Not a counter to painting but a parallel, using actuality as its basis and avoiding the excesses of sentiment that so pleased his colleagues. His recanting was a public gesture and typical of the brave if high-handed way in which he tried to overturn contemporary attitudes; in private he continued to photograph. But even without his influence new developments, based on similar principles, continued.

Far left *From a Window at Kelmscott Manor,* 1896. Platinum print by Frederick H Evans, a leader in the move from pictorialism. (Royal Photographic Society.)

Left *Litchfield Cathedral: The West Porch, c*1858. Albumen print by Roger Fenton. (Victoria and Albert Museum.)

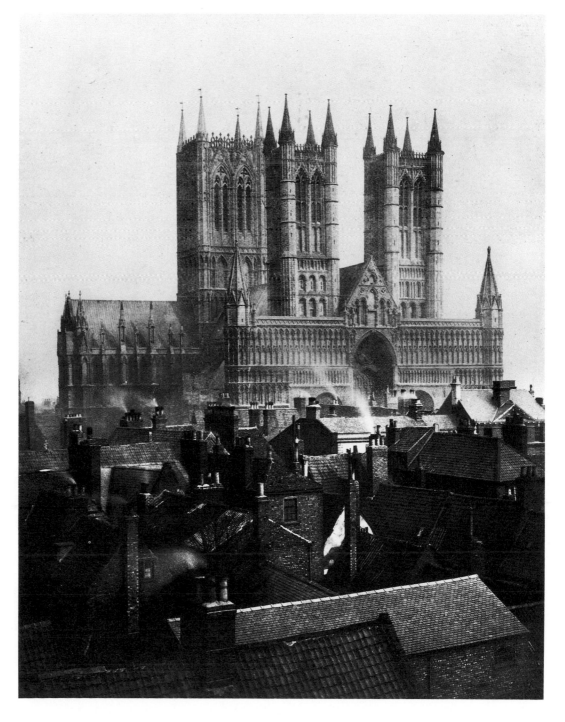

Right *Lincoln Cathedral, c*1895. Platinum print by Frederick H Evans. (Victoria and Albert Museum.)

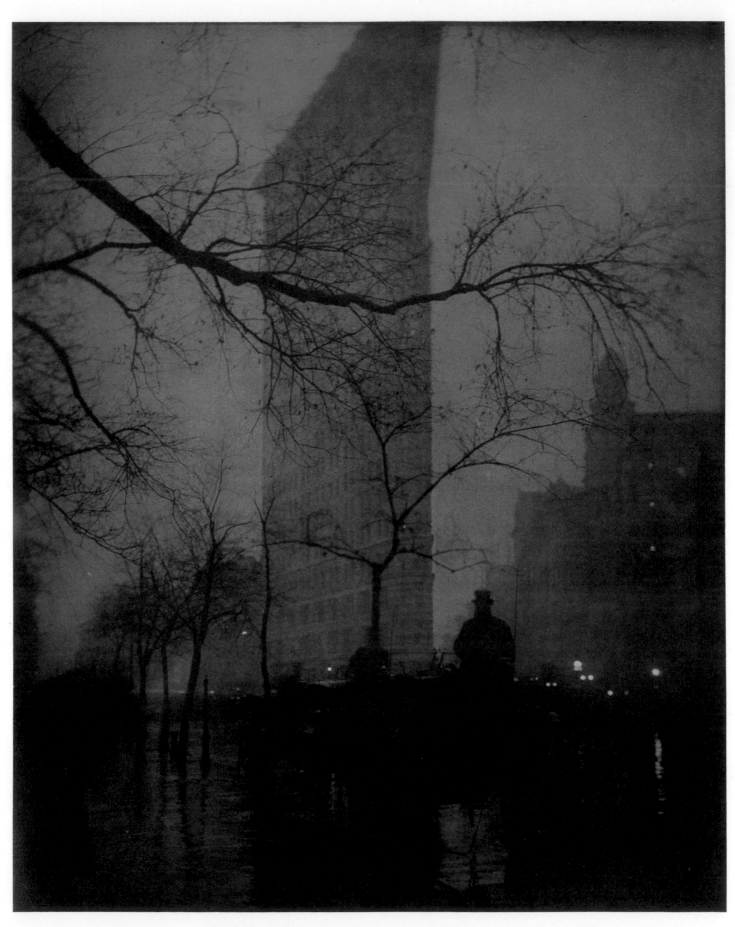

Above *The Flatiron*, 1909. Gum bichromate over platinum print by Edward Steichen. This building symbolized all that was new in the twentieth century. (The Metropolitan Museum of Art, The Alfred Stieglitz Collection, 1933. 33.43.39.)

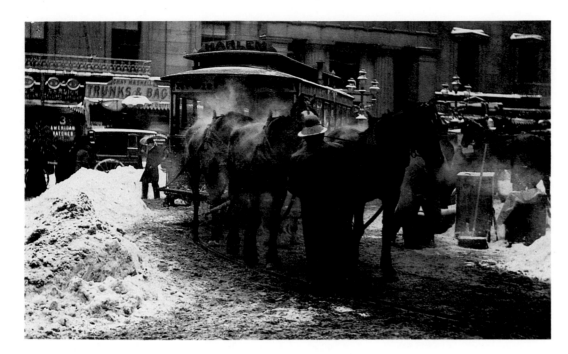

Left *The Terminal, New York, 1892,* by Alfred Stieglitz who demanded that photography be linked with realism. (Courtesy, Museum of Fine Arts, Boston. Gift of Alfred Stieglitz.)

Below *The Steerage,* 1907. Photogravure by Alfred Stieglitz. (© Estate of Alfred Stieglitz; Victoria and Albert Museum.)

Emerson had inspired a new confidence in the medium, a sense that it had the potential to be seen as a unique, fine art.

In 1887 Baron von Liebig showed 10 of Emerson's pictures to the newly formed Kamera Klub in Vienna. It was, he said, 'the first time that art lovers had been offered a series of original photographs of interest not in the objects they represent, but in the interpretation and handling.' In 1891 the club held an exhibition based on the aesthetic merits of photographs, a bold step as previous shows throughout Europe had used technical excellence as the criteria for selection (hence the laughter at Cameron in London and Paris). Because aesthetics were the issue it was thought proper to ask painters and sculptors to act as the jury. The photography world at large reacted with shock, the very idea of mingling art and photography so closely seemed alien when most photographers wanted little but technical perfection. Some 600 prints were hung, and a trend was set in motion.

In 1893 London witnessed the first showing of works by a break-away group from the Photographic Society. Named The Linked Ring, this group called for 'the complete emancipation of pictorial photography, properly so called, from the retarding and nanizing bondage of that which was purely scientific or technical.' Their exhibition of 300 prints brought forward mixed reactions but *The Studio,* a leading magazine declared, 'photography as a medium for artistic expression is now established for ever.' That same year the Photo-Club de Paris announced the 'First Exhibition of Photographic Art,' where only work presenting 'real artistic character' would be shown. And again in 1893, this time in Germany, the public were amazed to find 600 photographs on the walls of the Kunsthalle in Hamburg. Hanging photographs in an art museum was an unknown and dangerous precedent!

Across Europe photographers were becoming excited, not only at the controversy they caused but also by new visual potentials that were springing up. As Hughes' 'mechanical photographers' plodded dutifully on, artist-photographers

felt ready to take on the art world as a whole. In the United States and Australasia things moved a little slower, the former content with the existing order, the latter waiting to see and digest the flood of catalogues, books and magazine articles written in promotion of 'pictorialism' – a descriptive term growing in usage. The United States, however, was soon to get the message of a new photography. In 1890 an American student, Alfred Stieglitz, was in Vienna. He had gone to Europe nine years previously to study engineering in

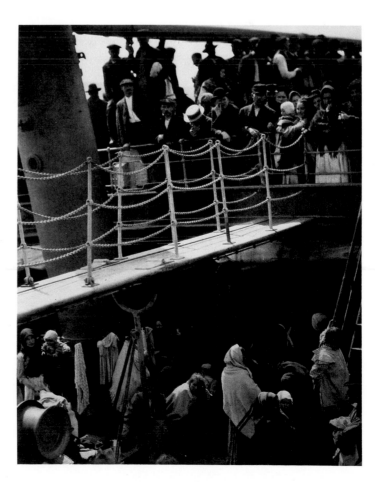

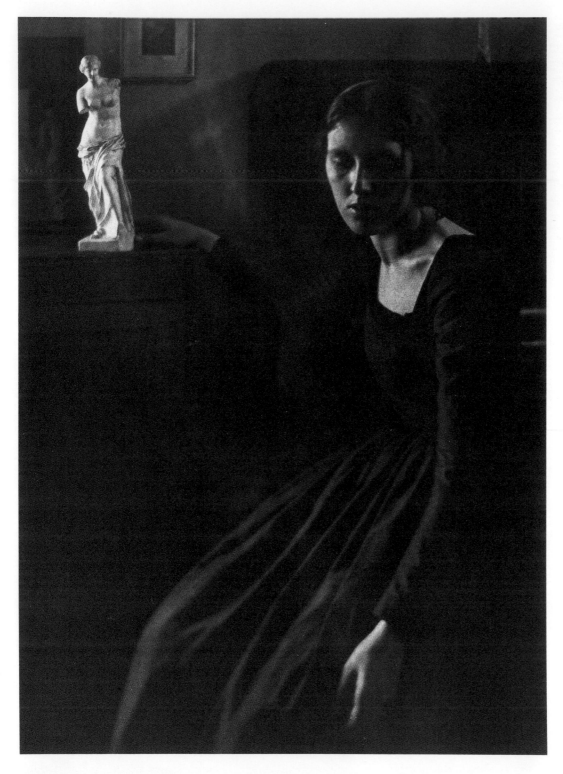

Right *The Cleft of the Rock*, 1912, by Anne Brigman. (International Museum of Photography at George Eastman House.)

Far right *Portrait (Miss N.)*, c 1898 by Gertrude Kasebier. (International Museum of Photography at George Eastman House.)

Left *Lady in White with Statuette*, 1898, by Clarence H White. Brigman, Kasebier and White were all part of Stieglitz's circle of Secessionists. (International Museum of Photography at George Eastman House.)

Germany but became interested in photography and turned to it with vigor. Vigor brought some success, a silver medal, for example, awarded by the English magazine *The Amateur Photographer* for a competition judged by Emerson in 1887. By 1890, hoping to continue as a student at a newly founded school in Austria, he was helping organize Vienna Kamera Klub's important exhibition when news reached him of his sister's death. He hurriedly returned to New York, there to begin a revolution in photography that would reverberate around the world.

A man of passionate beliefs, Stieglitz was bewildered to find his homeland indifferent to the new art photography.

With missionary zeal he launched himself into the task of raising awareness of a picture making based on aesthetic principles. 'The work shown by Englishmen,' he wrote in 1893, 'is proof positive that we Americans are "not in it" with them when art photography is in question . . . Our best men would be about at the top of the second class in England.' In response to his energy and rising international reputation, Stieglitz was elected president of the Society of Amateur Photographers of New York which he swiftly merged with the New York Camera Club to form a new and stronger body, The Camera Club of New York. His ambitions for the medium were enormous; he lectured, organized exhibitions

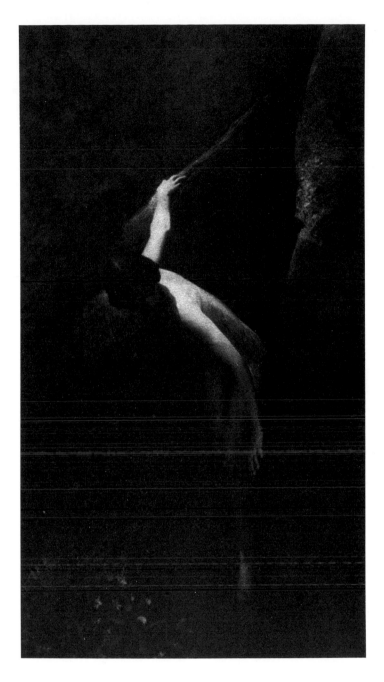

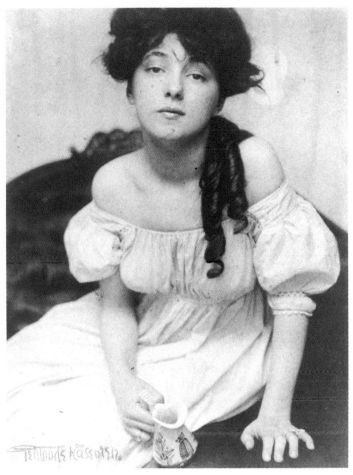

and transformed the club's magazine *Camera Notes* into an international quarterly. Stieglitz, for all his commitment, was not universally admired. Many felt his championing this new style of photography, which had moved from naturalism to symbolism, to be too forward, too far removed from popular taste. After all, roll film had been invented in 1880 and non-professional photography was moving into a wider orbit. They were hurt, too, by his ignoring all but work conforming to a pictorialist aesthetic. Undeterred, Stieglitz pressed on. In 1902 he formed his own group, the Photo-Secession, named after European artists' groups who seceded from their overbearing academies in favor of independence. Twelve photographers joined him and stated that their aims were: To advance photography as applied to pictorial expression; To draw together those Americans practicing or otherwise interested in art; To hold from time to time, at varying places, exhibitions not necessarily limited to productions of the Photo-Secession or to American work.

Stieglitz had found his fellow secessionists via exhibitions he mounted in earlier years, among them photographers who would become highly influential. The society stood as a direct threat to The Camera Club, for Stieglitz as photographer and as promoter of photography as art was gaining attention beyond the confines of his medium. Under pressure from the Club coupled with malicious comments concerning the reliability of his accounting for their funds he resigned as editor of *Camera Notes* in 1902. By 1903 the first issue of a new publication appeared – *Camera Work*. The years marking its existence, 1903 to 1917, were to see radical changes in the visual arts and photography alike – in painting the rejection of naturalism in favor of symbolism gave way to cubism and dada; in photography pictorialism bowed under pressure from the first stirrings of modernism.

Stieglitz was a partner in a firm of engravers, a position he loathed, but it gave him access to the finest possible production and reproduction facilities. *Camera Work* was luxurious. Tipped-in gravures were mounted on tinted paper and surrounded by pages of elegant typography. Design and typography were by Eduard Steichen, a 21-year-old photographer and painter who was a founder member of the Photo-Secession. Issue 1 was a monograph on work by Gertrude Kasebier, a 50-year-old who ran a studio on Fifth Avenue, had been elected to The Linked Ring in England and was admired for the boldness of her compositions. Successive issues featured Steichen, Stieglitz himself, other secessionists such as Fred Holland Day and Alvin Langdon Coburn and

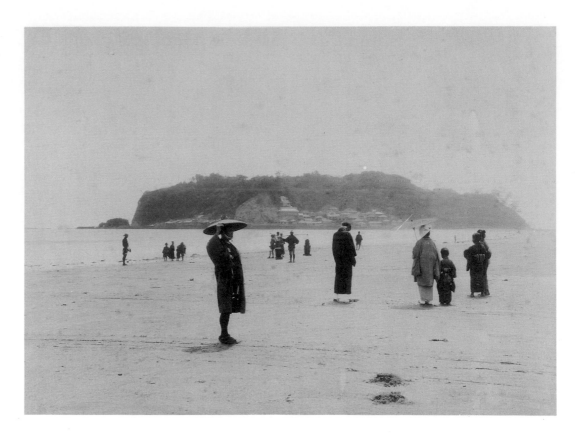

Right View of Enoshima, Japan, c1888. Hand-colored albumen print, photographer unknown. From an album sold to tourists. (Private collection.)

pictorialists from Europe – Frederick Evans from England, Robert Demachy from France, Heinrich Kühn from Germany. The magazine was a *tour de force*, matching leading photographers with critics and leading writers. Before long *Camera Work* was publishing contributions from people like George Bernard Shaw and H G Wells while mixing drawings from Matisse, Picasso and Rodin with photographs which looked back to Hill and Adamson and Julia Margaret Camer-

on (all but forgotten) and then forward to what Stieglitz called 'The New Color Photography.' *Camera Work* has never been equalled, nor did Europe ever find so articulate a champion of the avant-garde as Alfred Stieglitz. As early as 1906 one critic wrote that 'the chief purpose for which the Photo-Secession was established has been accomplished – the serious recognition of photography as an additional medium of pictorial expression.' Stieglitz was not to remain content

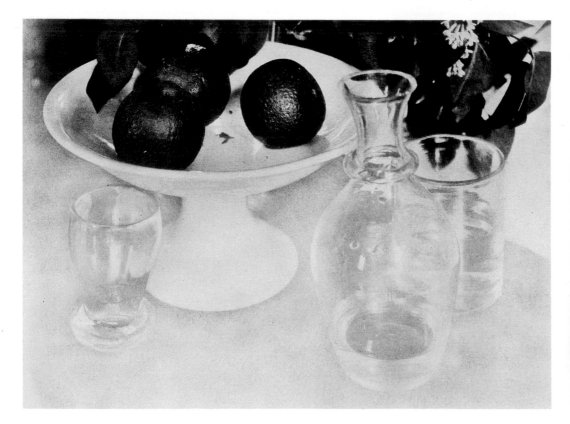

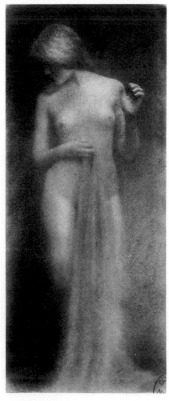

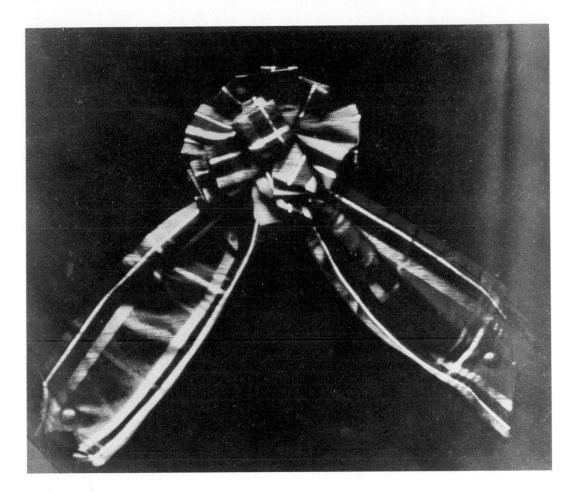

Right James Clerk Maxwell's *Tartan Ribbon*, 1861. The earliest reproduction of color. Reproduction print from a photographic projection. (Science Museum, London.)

with such applause, as we shall see later his work went on and his influence can be clearly discerned in photographs produced in 1986. Nevertheless in those crucial years, marked and marred by World War I, he thrust photography into the twentieth century. Gentlemen and players, art and artifice were all changed in the bloody conflict that began with tradition and ended in technology. In this period, when Victorian values finally gave way to the twentieth century,

Stieglitz, 'the seer,' led the medium through. The question of whether photography is an art had been answered. The question of what kind of art had also been met head on. In Stieglitz' own words the 'dry bones of a dead art are rattling as they never rattled before.' Photography was a new medium in a new century and a new way of picturing the world. It would forge its own aesthetic and never depend on imitation for success.

Far left *Still Life with Oranges*, 1903. Bromoil print by Heinrich Kühn, a European secessionist who fought for photography as an art. (Museum Folkwang, Essen.)

Left *Untitled*, c 1900. Bromoil print by Robert Demachy, a leading French pictorialist who manipulated his prints to show artistic intervention. (Collection Société Française de Photographie.)

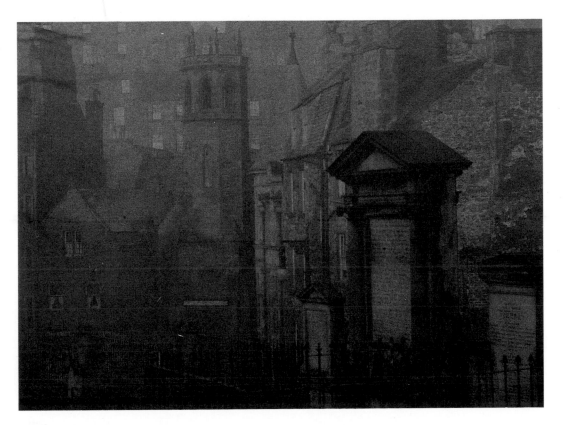

Right *Grayfriars Churchyard, Edinburgh*, c 1912. Autochrome by James Russell. (Edinburgh Photographic Society.)

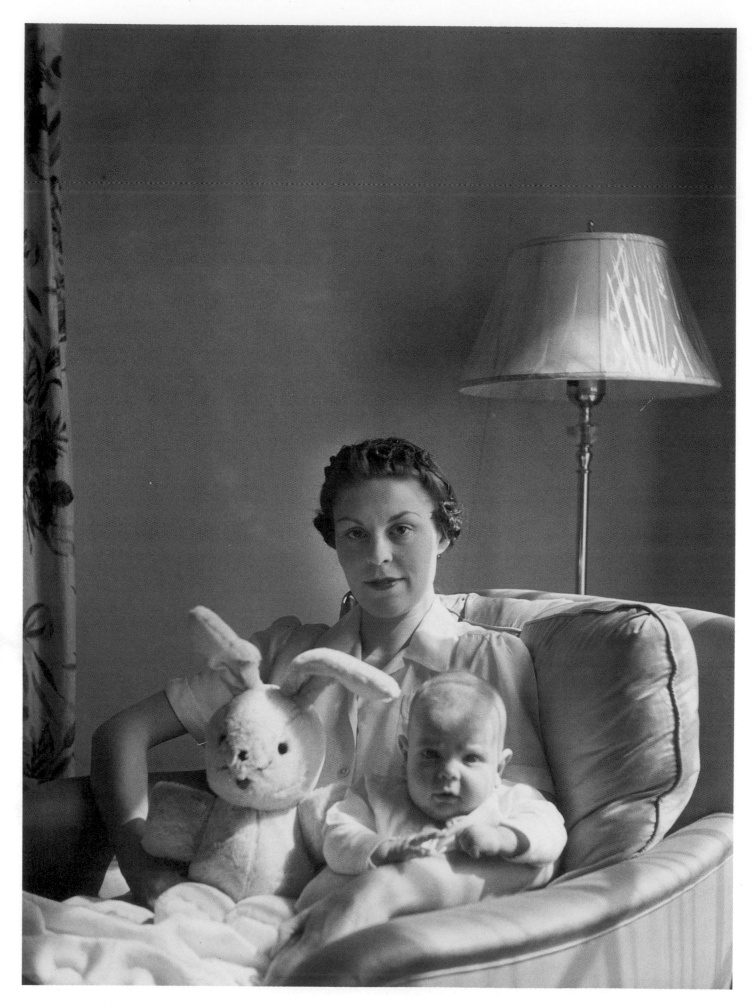

CHAPTER FOUR

You Press the Button ...

Snapshots and Photography for All

For 50 years from its invention, photography was a serious business. The extensive paraphernalia needed for even a simple outdoor photograph was enough to cripple both the backs and the enthusiasm of all but the most determined amateurs. And even had it been possible, the very idea of a snapshot simply did not exist in those early days. A snapshot, after all, implies that something is shot or captured instantaneously, an action impossible with the long exposures required by early cameras and glass plates.

Then something happened that almost overnight brought a light-hearted and even playful aspect to the new medium – the possibility of universal popular photography. And this, in turn, was due to the invention of dry plates and film which accepted an image in a second or less. The term 'snapshot' entered the language, and so did a name that is permanently associated with the snapshot: Kodak. The name, in dozens of manifestations – Brownie, Instamatic, Verichrome, Kodachrome, Ektachrome – has been synonymous with snapshot photography for a century.

The Kodak story began in 1878 in Rochester, New York, with George Eastman's invention and manufacture of gelatin dry plates. These handy plates and the later even more convenient film did not change things a lot, but Eastman's first

camera certainly did. Introduced in 1888, it sold for $25, and was called the Kodak camera. It was factory loaded with a roll of film to take 100 exposures, which was returned to the factory for developing, and it was the progenitor of millions of simple, cheap family cameras that dominated the market for decades. It was in the advertising for these early cameras that the famous phrase, 'You press the button – we do the rest!' first appeared. 'We furnish anybody,' Eastman proclaimed, 'man or woman or child, who has sufficient intelligence to point a box straight and press a button ... with an instrument which altogether removes from the practise of photography the necessity for exceptional facilities or, in fact, any special knowledge of the art.'

Subsequently, Kodak kept to the forefront in providing for the amateur photographer's needs and aspirations; it produced the first transparent roll film, the first folding camera, and, in 1900, the first of the famous and long-lived range of Brownie cameras, which sold for a dollar and used film costing only 15 cents a roll. The Box Brownie gave the world a new eye; cheap roll film gave it folk art in gelatin.

And the world was ready and eager. The pastime of photography was a craze that caught on like a forest fire. The boom in amateur photography at the turn-of-the-century coincided

Left This snapshot could be entitled 'Mother and Child with Bunny,' an amusing variation on a stock theme. Babies and children bring out an irresistible photographic urge in most people. (Ken Graves.)

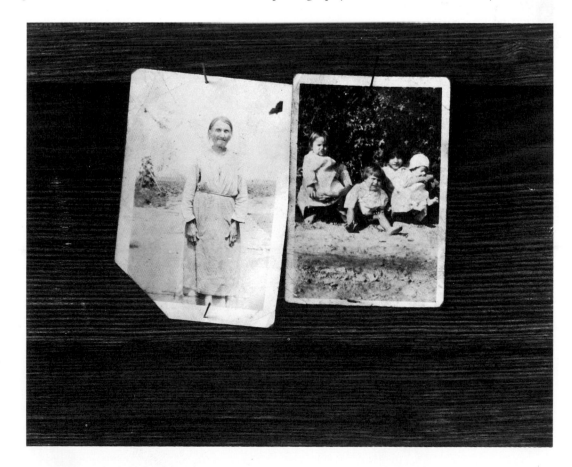

Right To symbolize the poignancy of an Alabama sharecropper's life during the Depression, Walker Evans photographed this pair of well-handled snapshots tacked to the wall of the family shack, 1936. (Library of Congress.)

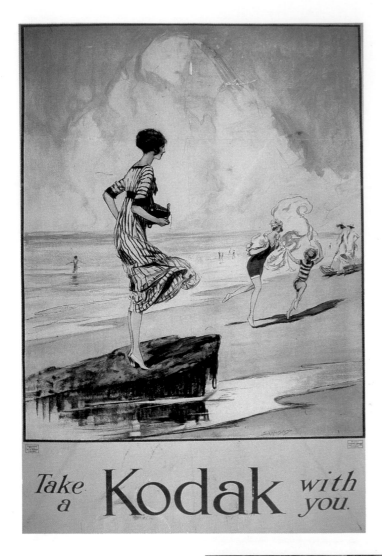

Take a **Kodak** with you.

with the emergence of the family as the emotional and also the material center of life. Tremendous social and economic pressures were exerted on every adult to marry, acquire a home, furnish and embellish it, and to begin a family. The snapshot played a vital role in idealizing this phenomenon. The comforts enshrined in a family album rationalized human purpose; and one's daily grind, mortgages, debts and family crises all became bearable when balanced against the anodyne album with its contented, glowing faces, its happy occasions and material and social achievements.

Thus dawned the 'Golden Age' of the snapshot, arbitrarily between 1910 and 1950, and corresponding to the period when cheap cameras were in universal use, with ordinary people busily recording their private lives and converting them – using trillions of exposures in the process – into a rejuvenating source of imagery from which they experienced a range of satisfying responses.

These responses fall into several quite distinct groups, the most fundamental of which concerned a family's need for some expression of its assets. Of the average family's possessions, the home, above all else, most impressively symbolized achievement. Its size, style and state of repair all offered evidence of a family's relative prosperity and well-being. This need, incidentally, was not a new phenomenon; for centuries the English gentry had had themselves painted against the backdrop of their grand country houses. The snapshot equivalent was somewhat more humble but its purpose was the same: to reassure and impress. Millions of identical compositions were cherished in albums, showing one or more family members posed against the house, by the

Above A mid-1920s poster for Kodak; by this time most people could afford a camera. (Kodak Ltd.)

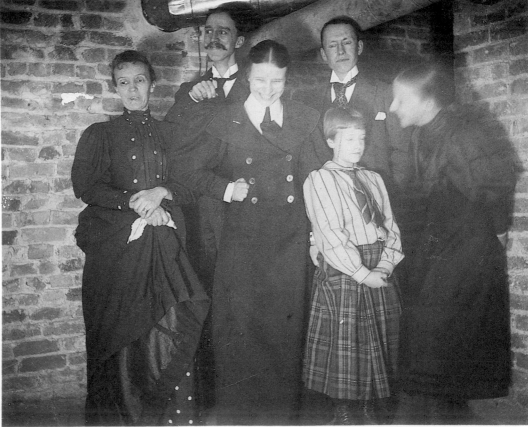

Right An early example of a flashlight snapshot, 1894. Magnesium flash equipment opened up new possibilities for the amateur, allowing snapshots to be taken indoors. (Graham King Collection.)

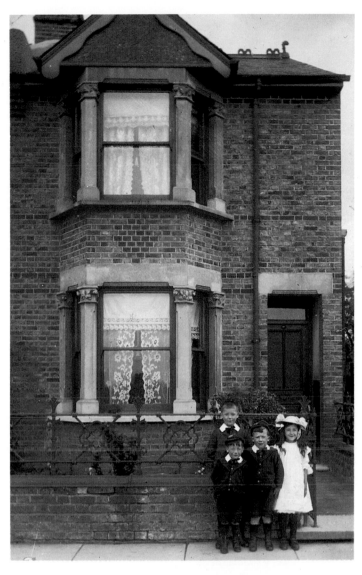

front gate, or in a doorway. These simple shots are far more revealing than studio portraits.

As we move away from the 'Golden Age,' the house photo has become less important as flattering evidence of a family's affluence, perhaps reflecting a fact of modern life, the slippage of traditional family values. In its place, however, are new vogue subjects: swimming pools and two-car garages and, enhanced by the arrival of color film, the garden.

Next in line on the family balance sheet of resources was, from the 1920s anyway, the automobile. Possession of a car not only implied the family could afford one (or at least the monthly payments!) but also that at least one of its members had the skill to drive it and the time to take it on jaunts across the country. The automobile joined other possessions like pets and garden gnomes that were duly recorded and sent to relatives and friends as status reminders. When material possessions ran out, a family typically resorted to promoting the achievements of its members. Prize-giving and graduation snapshots obviously fall into this category, representing intellectual achievement, but even more common are all those hunting and fishing snapshots, expressing something more primitive. Snapshots of people holding fish exemplify human achievement in its most folksy and basic form; while shots that include not only the game but also the house *and* car, are surely the epitome of the 'Golden Age' family snapshot.

Apart from its ability to record and confirm a household's material milestones, the snapshot was also utilized during a family's journey through life to celebrate and immortalize. These two functions were most commonly expressed by the wedding photo and portraits of mother and child – less often the father, because he was customarily the one who took the snapshot.

Above A charming family façade, England, *c*1905. The intention of snapshots like this was to reassure and impress. The exemplary dress of the children and the meticulously arranged curtains convey pride and respectability. (Graham King Collection.)

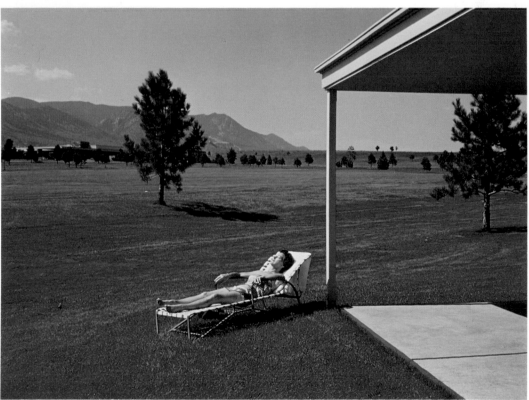

Right *Garden of the Gods Club, Colorado Springs, Colorado,* 1974. Occasionally artlessness is transformed into art, as in this example. Although an amateur casual snapshot, it entrances the eye with its compelling composition and striking color. (Ken Graves.)

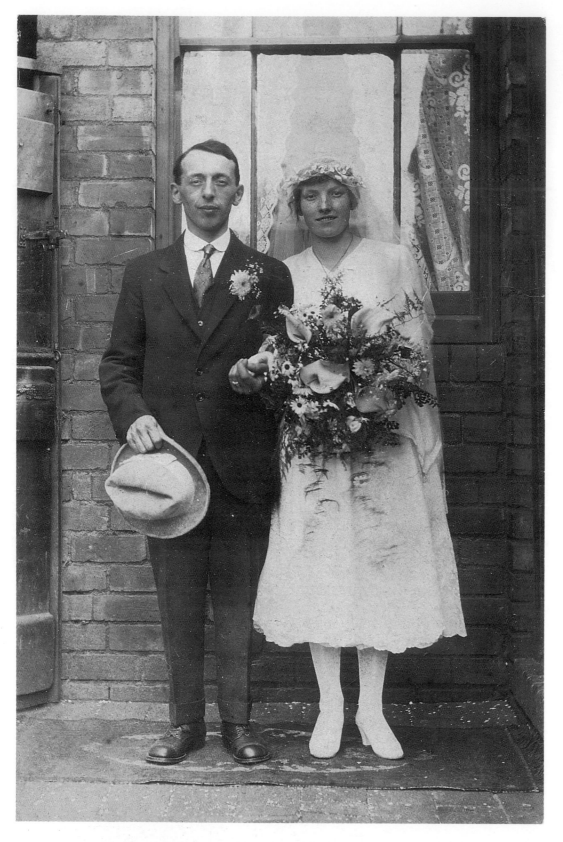

Right A typical 'motherless child' snapshot, English, c1940. The framing of the baby and the cropping of the mother emphasize the photographer's preoccupation with the baby. Such compositions could be intuitive. (Graham King Collection.)

Far right A sepia-toned print snapshot, English, c1910. A superb study of a mother and child in the drabbest of surroundings. One can see the swept brick pathway and polished chair are an attempt to hide the signs of poverty. (Graham King Collection.)

Left Although this 1920s snapshot strives for formality – note the stiff poses, the ambivalent expressions, the neat floor mat – this backyard bride and her husband are betrayed by the grim ordinariness of their surroundings. (Graham King Collection.)

A marriage and its public celebration was and probably still is the most personally important ceremony in most people's lives and, with its welter of traditional trappings, demanded to be eternalized with photographs. Wedding photos are rarely found before the 1870s and for several decades after that they were almost always studio posed and about as animated as the wedding cake. But because considerable cost was involved, the informal wedding snap came into being, especially among the poorer members of society. The most instructive of these wedding snapshots are the 'backyard' photos taken by family and friends at no cost at all. The yard was tidied and swept clean and the bridal couple, in all their finery, were stood on a mat or seated on chairs brought from the house. The fantasy was the wedding group; the backyard environment was the drab reality.

Today, snapshot weddings are the norm, except that the

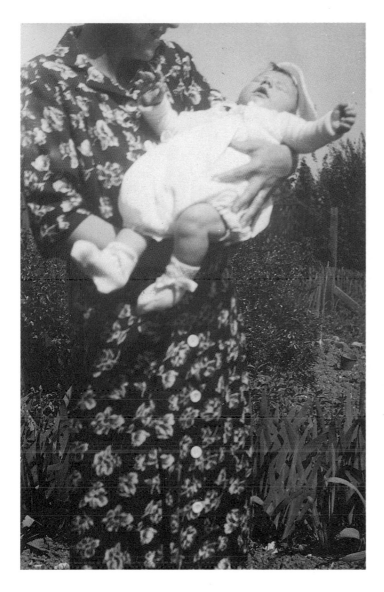

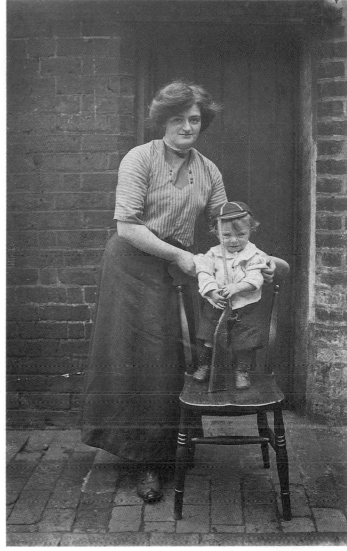

snapshots – called 'casuals' – are professionally taken, often from the first fitting of the bridal gown to the stock shot of the couple's shoes outside the bedroom door of the honeymoon hotel. But these have not by any means daunted the amateur photographer, who defiantly brings the fairytale occasion down to earth by capturing the bride with a fly on her nose.

If a wedding can unleash a hundred shutters, the addition of a baby to a household stirs the photographic impulse in parents to an insatiable fervor. Perhaps there is a correlation between birthrate and the profits of the photographic industry, for the birth of a child is a compelling reason for many people to buy a camera, and snapshots of babies roll out of photo-finishing laboratories by the millions every day. Snapshots of young children, in particular, are possibly more interesting and revealing than any other kind. They possess, however indefinable, an intrinsic appeal. Such snapshots record a period of a child's existence that is beyond that individual's memory, thus filling a vital gap, the first years of a human life.

The 'Golden Age' family album, then, contained no grandeur or great events, no horror or hatred, no sex or sadness, a tradition that continues strongly today. You will never, for example, see an amateur camera at a funeral. Instead, what was created for the viewer was a family continuum: visual snippets of private lives that ran their course in a milieu of apparent felicity and fulfilment. These snapshots, of picnics and parties and vacations, vernacular records of people at play, form easily the largest group of family photographs. This group is probably best represented by seaside photographs: snapshots taken by the sea.

For a century or more, during the summer months, it has been the habit of a good proportion of the world's population to rush, lemming-like, towards the sea: in the United States, to the boardwalks, surf beaches and fashionable beachfront enclaves; in Britain to the dozens of pebbly watering places popular since Edwardian times. The snapshot, in fact, played an important role in the creation of seaside mythology. When the sun shone – as of course it always does in our memories of childhood – it literally unleashed the recording power of millions of Kodaks. Vacations by the sea were always redolent of hot sand and warm seas, sunburn lotion and ice cream, bare flesh and joyous faces. When the clouds loomed, when the wind turned cold and the sea turned grey and choppy, those same shutters were mostly silent; few people take snapshots in the rain. Seaside snapshots are invariably sunny ones.

It will be obvious by now that the world of the snapshot is that part of it which the taker wants the world to see – at least, that is the intention. But what the majority of snapshots actually *reveal* is quite another matter. This is particularly true with snapshots of people – 'portrait' snaps of family and friends.

A portrait, in the painterly sense, is a visual impression of the sitter's appearance and personality, sometimes with overtones of flattery, satire, or psychological observation. It is custom-made according to the skill and intentions of the artist and the wishes of the subject.

A photographic portrait, however, differs in an important way: it is *taken*. A professional portraitist will, as part of his task, impose his own skill and artistry on the finished result, and erase any signs of discomfort or embarrassment on the part of the sitter. With a snapshot, however, a sitter is as often a framed victim as a willing subject.

The ancestor of the snapshot portrait is the studio portrait, which came into vogue in the mid-nineteenth century. The apparatus for such a likeness was formidable: formal appointments, mysterious actions under a black cloth, and all the heroic props of grand portraiture – massive antique furniture, classical backdrops, flowing draperies, fake tree trunks, moss and grass, artificial floral displays. From a hundred thousand studios from Austria to Australia, from Prague to Peoria, poses and expressions as predictable and repetitive as the tide flowed out in an endless cardboard stream.

Such portraits, obscured under layers of make-believe, offer few clues to the sitters' personalities, or to what they did and how they lived. Compared with the numbing uniformity of the studio portrait, however, its snapshot equivalent is replete with insights. The amateur, with only the slenderest control of his instrument, abandoning his negatives to the mercy of impersonal developing, allows the transcendent power of the camera itself to record whatever it is pointed at.

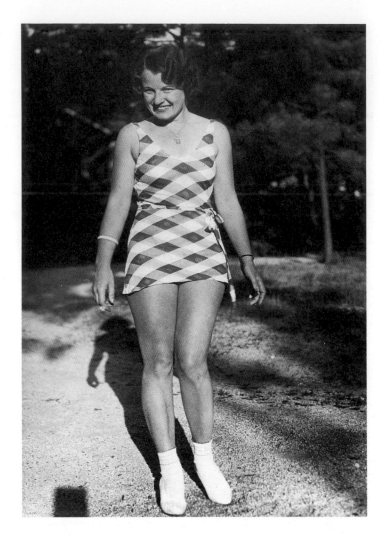

Perhaps aware of this, the human subject is frequently not a little unnerved.

It is possible that, even today, despite over a century of familiarity with the camera, we still retain vestiges of some instinctive fear of having our image taken from us. Our

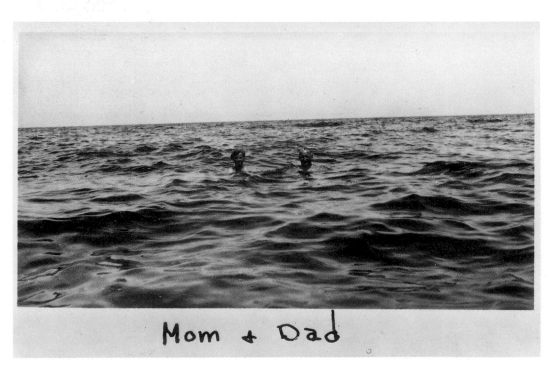

Mom + Dad

Above A prewar American snapshot captures the mood of an age. (Graham King Collection.)

Right Snapshots of vacations by the sea are invariably sunny and replete with joyous faces; few cameras click when the cold winds blow or when it rains. Billions of snapshots like this contribute to the myth that the sun always shone at the seaside. (National Museum of Photography, Film and Television, Bradford.)

Left *Cape Cod, Massachusetts, c1943.* Surely the epitome of the humble snapshot, transformed into an anonymous icon. (Ken Graves.)

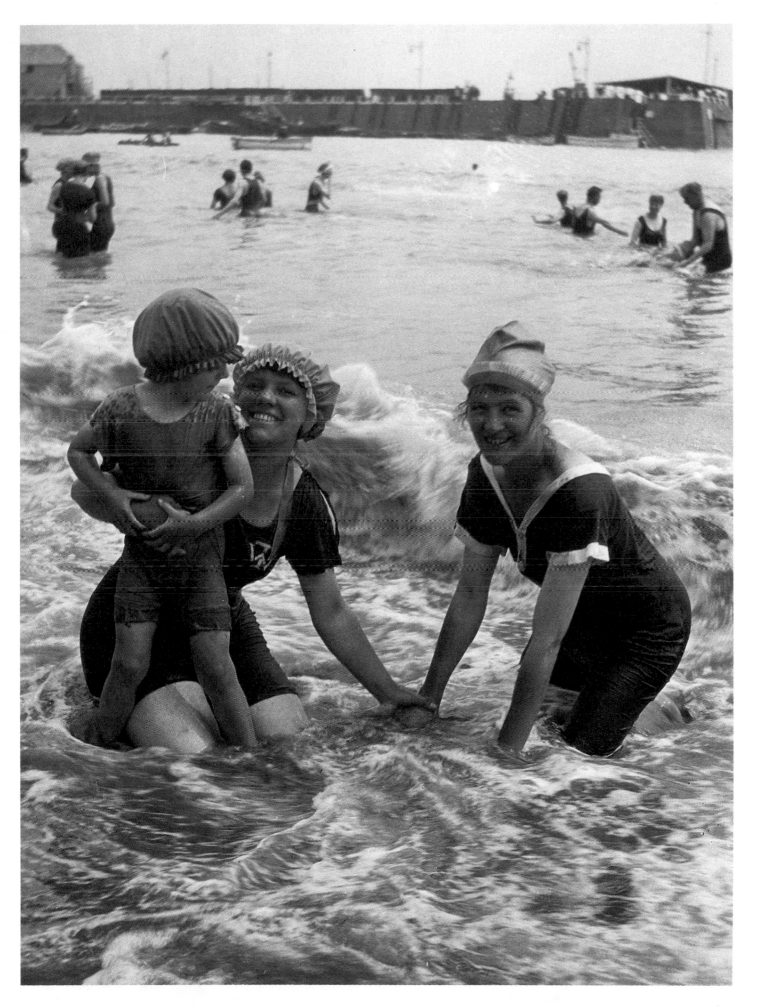

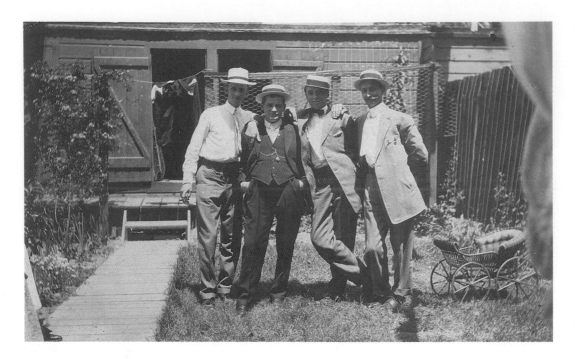

Left A 1920s American snapshot shows a group of men avoiding embarrassment by joky posing. (Graham King Collection.)

Below A carefully staged American snapshot, *c* 1920. The visual joke was a common stratagem to avoid a full frontal confrontation with the camera. (Ken Graves.)

snapshot photographer, lacking the skills of a professional, leaves us with a dilemma. We worry about the quality of the result; we are concerned about what might happen to it. Will people make fun of our image?

Most of us, though, have come to terms with cameras, and we have evolved various ploys to avoid being caught in the act of being afraid or embarrassed or 'showing our bad side.' Nevertheless there are plentiful signs, when we study snapshots, that the amateur and the camera frequently win. Evidence of this is revealed in blinking; behavioral scientists tell us that we blink at a faster rate when we are nervous, which explains why many snapshots show people with their eyes closed.

A common stratagem to avoid displaying nervousness is to fool around, and many people, confronted by a camera, spontaneously pull faces, strike an absurd pose, stand on one leg or embrace a statue or a post – anything to deflect the camera's scrutiny. Even more intriguing as a stratagem is the

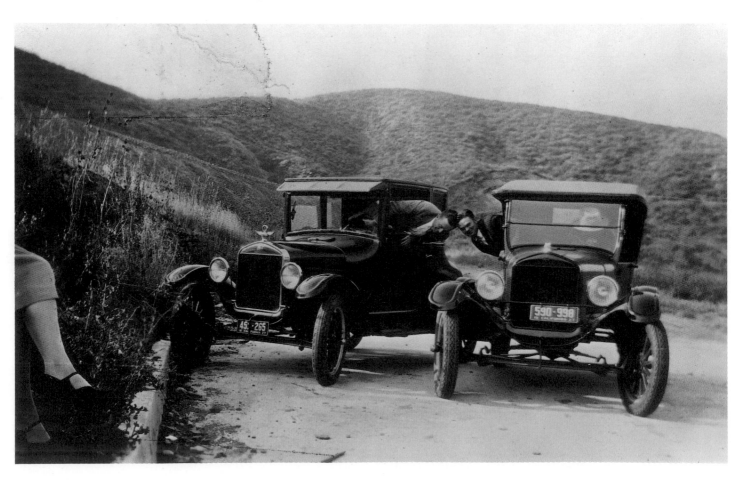

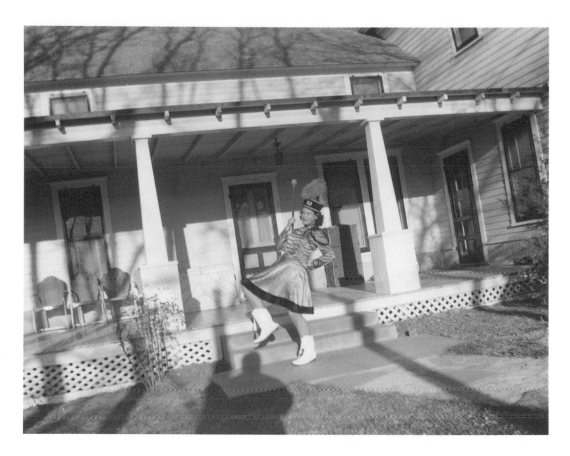

Right This shows many common snapshot mistakes – tilted horizon, intruding shadow, banal subject. Yet this snapshot is no less charming for all its ineptness. (Ken Graves.)

conscious or even unconscious selection of a background. With snapshots, plain backgrounds are relatively rare. Acting, it would appear, in concert, the amateur and his subject invariably create a composition loaded with visual clutter. From the subject's point of view, the more bizarre and distracting the backdrop, the less intense is the viewer's gaze. Thus we find snapshot portraits that melt into the background, or are effectively camouflaged by some intervening effect like dappled shade.

The snapshot victim is also immeasurably helped in the flight from the camera's pursuing eye by the ineptitude of the amateur. This results in a range of aberrations that, in a superficial way, almost define what a snapshot is. We have all seen these amusing mistakes in snapshots and have committed many ourselves – the tilted horizon, the blurred or out-of-focus shot, the subject anonymously lost in the distance, or having a tree growing out of his or her head – all these are time-honored snapshot foibles. Eccentric framing and inadvertent cropping are also common and they occasionally produce compositions so arresting that the characteristics have been widely copied by both painters and contemporary photographers. And we all know that we must take snapshots with the sun behind us, which is why we see so many frowning faces with black pits instead of eyes. It is also the reason why the shadow cast by the photographer insists on creeping along the ground and up into the picture.

But despite all these stratagems, blunders and technical barriers, snapshots have the knack of capturing and conveying the unadorned truth – 'humanity with its pants down.' Or, in the rather more elegant words of the distinguished New York photographer, Lisette Model, 'I am a passionate lover of the snapshot, because of all photographic images it comes closer to the truth. The snapshot is a specific spiritual moment.'

Yet, in all its honesty, a snapshot can also be a veritable mountain of *hidden* truths and ambiguities. It could be said that every snapshot has ambivalent layers which must be penetrated for the truth of the image. A branch of psychoanalysis is already at work breaking through these ambiguous veils, in which patients' personal snapshots are used as an aid to psychotherapy. A technique has been created called photoanalysis, with which one may, from clues in snapshots – body positioning in group shots, the way people touch or avoid one another, the way arms hang – divine the nature of family relationships, sibling rivalry, aggressive tendencies and so forth.

The snapshot also preserves a mine of information, not only of how we and our ancestors looked, but how things and places looked. It is widely accepted that the snapshot has helped revolutionize our way of seeing the world. Our family albums serve as instruction manuals for a greater awareness of photographic imagery, of our own lives and of our past. As American historian John Kouwenhoven observed, 'The cumulative effect of one hundred and thirty years of man's participation in the process of running amuck with cameras was the discovery that there was an amazing amount of significance, historical and otherwise, in a great many things that no one had ever seen until snapshots began forcing people to see them.'

We may, however, be witnessing a change in the *purpose* of taking snapshots. As we have seen, for past generations this purpose has been fairly clearly defined: to prove something

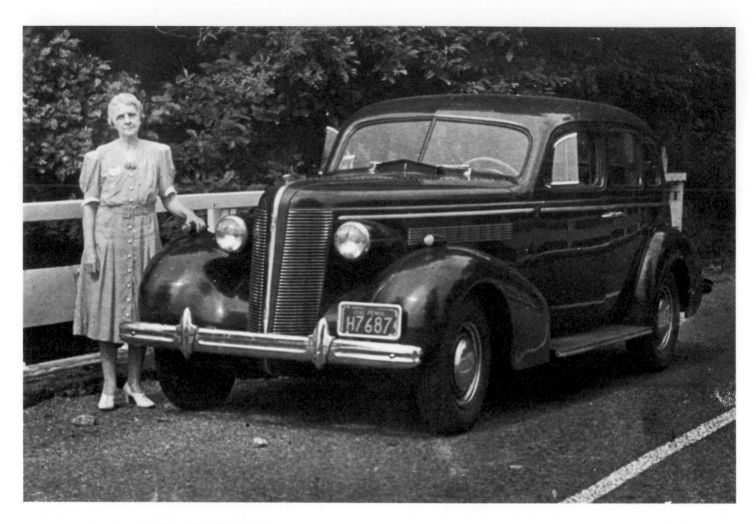

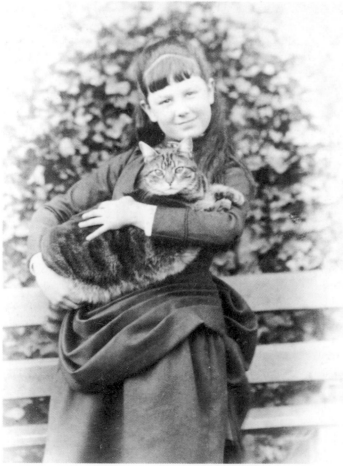

('That's me with Bill on the beach at St Tropez'); to record something ('That's Jeremy. See his curly hair as a baby?'); and to immortalize something ('That's Helen at her graduation'). And if we examine family snapshots spanning several generations in a chronological sense we will detect a certain stratification. When cameras were skill intensive and film relatively expensive, picture taking was much more of an orchestrated event than it is today. The picture had to be 'worth taking,' and taking it was treated with a sense of occasion. Then came semi-automatic cameras, faster film, Polaroid and cheap flash units. The snapshots of this period undoubtedly capture more candid moments but, not requiring subjects to stand still, are generally less thoughtful and less composed – although no less attractive or truthful for that. One does not see so many 'Dad with his new car' pictures; 'pride pictures' (people in uniform, fancy dress, newly bought clothes); trick shots (distant figure 'standing' on close-up hand); or dynasty pictures (assemblies of several generations of a family).

Today, the snapshot has irreversibly entered the electronic age. Microchips control automatic exposure and focusing, even in the cheaper cameras. Flash units are computer controlled. One camera even shouts verbal commands to help the user avoid common mistakes (Load film! Check distance! Too dark use flash!). The 'point and shoot' amateur now holds in unsteady hands wonder toys that would have seemed inconceivable a decade ago. They have the ability to shoot

Left After the home, the automobile was the most conspicuous status symbol. (Graham King Collection.)

Below left With the introduction of faster film and smaller, more portable cameras, nineteenth-century amateurs could capture their subjects in a more relaxed manner. This picture dates from *c*1895. (Graham King Collection.)

Right Any owner of a camera equipped with motor drive will recognize this snapshot ... and the next one, in which the subject has disappeared into the water! (Graham King Collection.)

Below For some obscure reason, people seem prepared to risk life and limb when having their photographs taken. Snapshots of people in trees are peculiarly common. This dates from *c*1910. (Graham King Collection.)

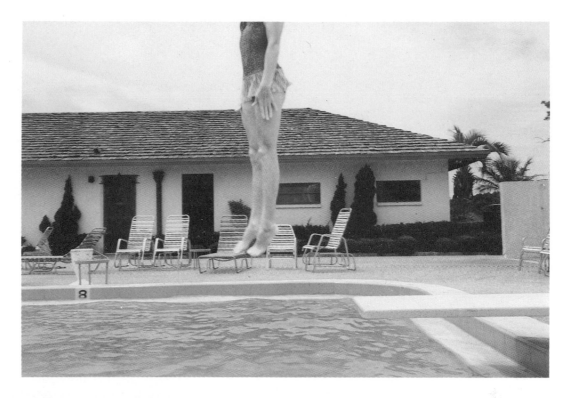

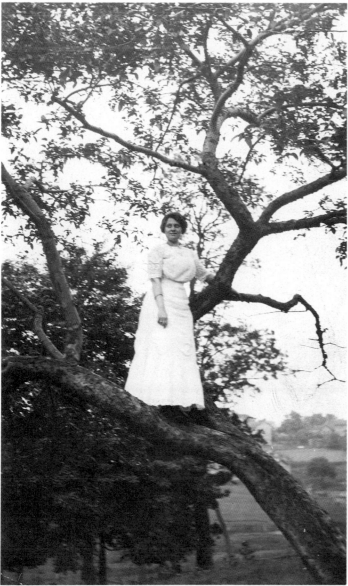

almost anything, stationary or moving, in an instant, even in appalling light conditions, with 'laser sharp pictures from thirty-three inches to infinity,' according to one manufacturer's claim. One would think that we had seen the last of those silly snapshot mistakes, but while today's snapshots are sharper, brighter, closer, bigger, more detailed, more candid and more colorful, the high-tech toys have introduced a fresh range of quirks. With its hungry, wide-angle lens, the modern camera positively lusts after detail, and contemporary snapshots are havens for irrelevant detail – minutiae which, incidentally, may fascinate historians of the future. And fast, cheap processing has encouraged waste. In the 'Golden Age,' rarely was a snapshot discarded; today, the snapshooter has moved a step closer to the professional, selecting perhaps three or four prints from a roll of 36 and rejecting the rest. The motor drive, too, contributes to the waste. With this attachment the amateur has come close to losing all control of his camera – with its *Zzap! Zzap! Zzap!* promising more, it invariably achieves less.

Essentially, however, the purpose of taking snapshots has not really changed. Children, homes, pets, parties, weddings, bar mitzvahs and sunsets continue to be the stuff of snapshots and continue to provide confirmation of our existence. Except in some remote corners of the world, photography is universal; there cannot be many people alive today who have not been photographed. And to anyone doubting the universality of the snapshot, even the Duchess of York took snapshots of her own royal wedding to Prince Andrew. She sent them to a druggist for development and received her wedding snaps back the same evening. This prompted a testy letter to *The Times*. Noting the unusually fast service given the Duchess, the writer complained he was still waiting ten days for his own to arrive. 'Ah well,' he concluded, 'perhaps one day *my* prints will come.'

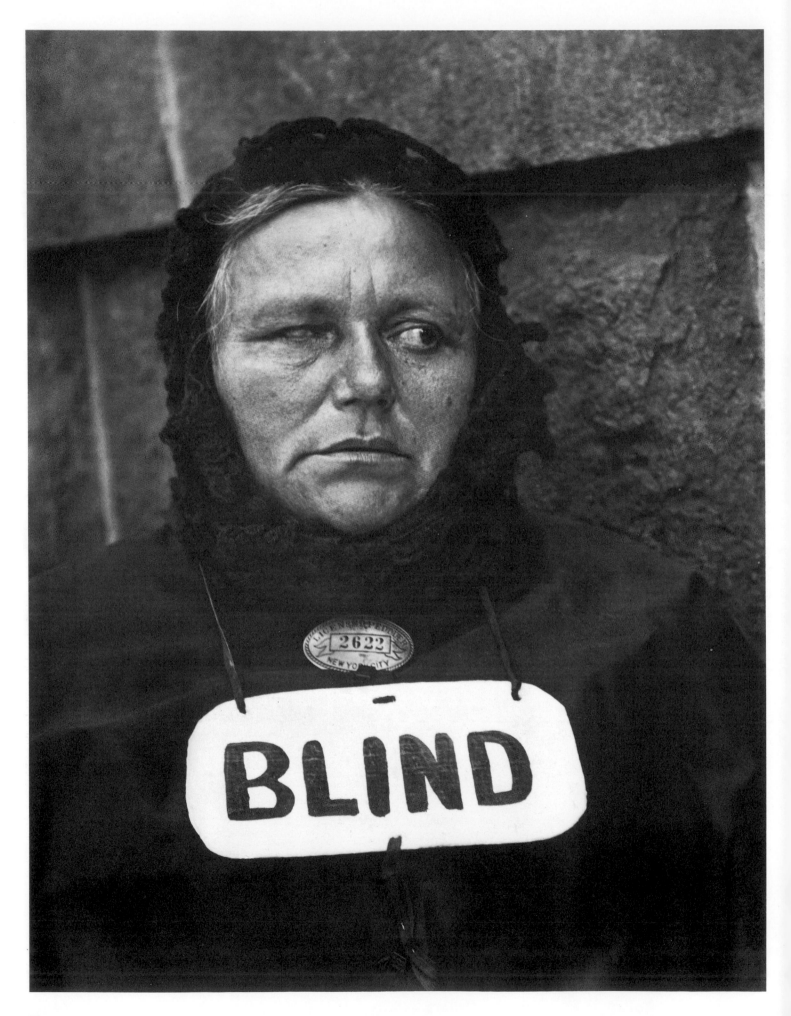

CHAPTER FIVE

Brave New World

The Rise of Modernism

When Britain declared war against Germany in 1914, it was in expectation of a brief conflict. Like wars before it was to be conducted by professionals according to time-honored tactics and methods, but as it turned out, the war rapidly became disturbing for all concerned. Those imagined months turned to unthought of years and old rules no longer seemed to apply. World War I began with tradition and ended in modernity; in four ghastly years tanks replaced horses, aerial and chemical warfare came to challenge the foot soldier's long-held might and on the home front women were to find new roles and freedoms as a workforce. The war can be viewed as a watershed in social and intellectual terms as well as changing military concepts: before it the world struggled to come to terms with the twentieth century and after it all that was new was embraced with a fervor and intensity that shook cultural foundations. Futurism, constructivism and surrealism, for example, turned ideas of what constitutes art on its head. Poets like Ezra Pound and T S Eliot found new languages hidden within an English once thought familiar and composers such as Stravinski did the same for music.

The genesis of such experimentation had begun within the avant-garde prior to World War I, but the war's influence was profound; rattling sabers against the might of tanks had exposed the twentieth century, and the arts wanted new technology and a new world. Those lessons learned in destruction could now be turned around: machines would build the structures of a new society. Nowhere was this more keenly felt than in Germany, where defeat created a mistrust of things past and a desire for all that was new. In Russia, too, the Revolution of 1917 turned the past aside. The United States also experienced radical changes which, for photography, can be observed through the pages of Alfred Stieglitz's *Camera Work*. His quarterly acted as a chronical of shifting consciousness, it charted the end of nineteenth-century visual ideas and the struggle to drag the United States, unwillingly, into line with a European notion of the avant-garde. Issues in 1913 and 1914 show secessionist work, full of nature, mood and soft atmosphere, then comes a break; photography does not seem up to the task of embracing a new vision and cubist drawings are published. In 1916 photographs reappear and they are different – six pictures by Paul Strand exchange pictorialist charm for a more sharply focused view bringing elements of cubist abstraction to visions of the city. Then, in 1917, in what was to be *Camera Work*'s final issue, the journal is filled with photographs by Strand. Stark formality, geometry and a sense of boldness prevail. Stieglitz wrote in

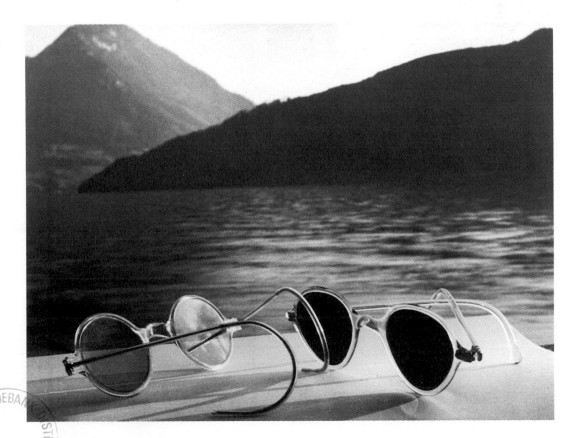

Left *Blind Woman, New York, 1916,* by Paul Strand, a powerful example of the medium's change from pictorial romanticism. (Copyright © 1971, Aperture Foundation, Paul Strand Archive.)

Right *Lake Lucerne,* 1936, by Herbert List, who introduced elements of metaphysical concern into otherwise ordinary scenes. (Max Scheler.)

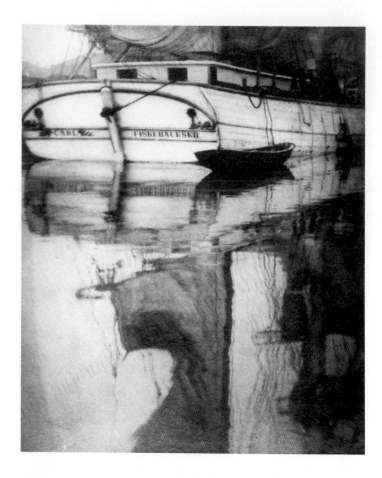

the same issue: 'The work is brutally direct. Devoid of flim-flam; devoid of trickery and any "ism;" devoid of any attempt to mystify an ignorant public, including the photographers themselves. These photographers are the direct ex-precession of today.' In fewer than 30 years the medium as practiced by those who valued its aesthetic potential had dramatically thrown off its mimicry of painting's traditions and thrown in its lot with an international avant-garde.

The year 1917 also saw Alvin Langdon Coburn, whom Stieglitz had published as a pictorialist, experimenting with abstraction in London. He was involved with the vorticist movement of English cubists and his 'vortographs,' made through something similar to a kaleidoscope, were the short-lived outcome of an earlier plea. 'Why,' Coburn had asked, 'should not the camera artist break away from the worn-out conventions, that even in its comparatively short existence have begun to cramp and restrict his medium, and claim the freedom of expression which any art must have to be alive?' Coburn, like Strand, had been exposed to the most contemporary art from Europe in exhibitions Stieglitz and Steichen had organized at '291' (The Little Galleries of the Photo-Secession). Unlike many of their fellows they had not howled in dismay when expected photographs were replaced by unexpected paintings. Rodin, Cézanne, Matisse, Brancusi, Picasso and Braque were all shown to initial bewilderment but ultimate effect. For Strand, who absorbed the conceptual complexities of these artists' works, art, photography and life itself were joined together. Photography was 'born of actual living'; it was not some misty incantation

evoking the ethereal spirit of nature but a direct expression of reality that followed 'a real respect' for the thing in front of the photographer. A visual revolution was in the air.

As Paul Strand experimented with new ways of seeing in New York, exploring high viewpoints, using his camera to compress space and looking to everyday, functional subject matter from which to extract some sense of modern times, his counterparts in Europe were doing likewise. In Britain the power of a pictorialist convention remained supreme (Alvin Langdon Coburn and a few others excepted), but on the Continent it seemed vital to re-present the world in new terms, to attract attention to a proposed new society where the artist, architect, engineer and designer would interact on equal levels. What was characteristic should be turned inside out – high viewpoints, made possible by new-style architecture and industrial structures, allowed a plan view of the world; switching to the opposite extreme introduced a mix of reality and distortion; mirrors and reflections could interrupt accepted spatial understandings and confuse standard visual references; close-ups made the familiar un-real. Through photography the world could be shown in a whirl of change where everything was possible, because it could be photographed.

However, some artists felt that simple representation, however dynamically it showed new thinking and the new order, was insufficient to bring forth a powerful response. They turned to a technique reminiscent of Henry Peach

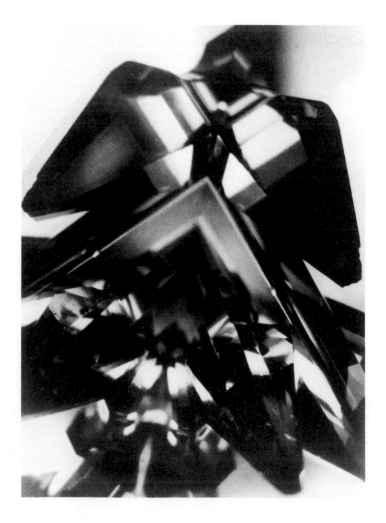

Far left *Reflections*, 1909, by Malcolm Arbuthnot, who was to join the English vorticist movement. (Royal Photographic Society.)

Below left *Vortograph No. 3*, 1917, by Alvin Langdon Coburn. Mounting interest in abstraction and cubism can be seen by comparing this and Arbuthnot's work. (Royal Photographic Society.)

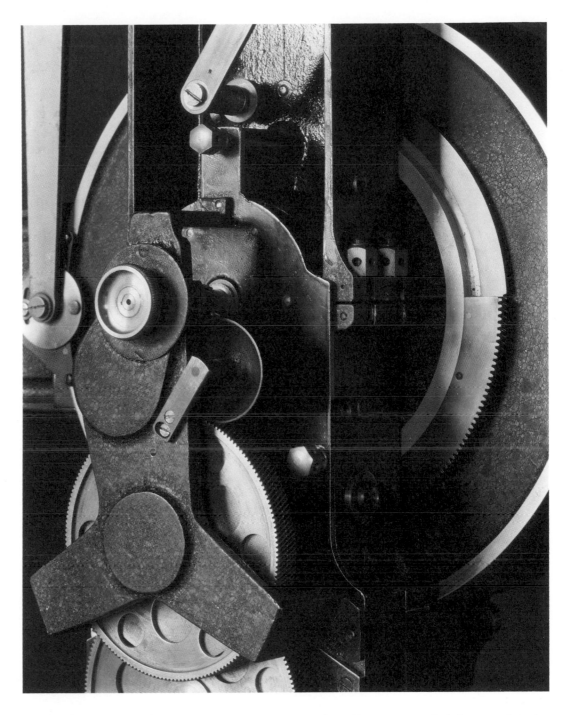

Right *Double Akeley, New York, 1922*, by Paul Strand shows modernism and the machine age intertwined. (Copyright © 1971, Aperture Foundation, Paul Strand Archive.)

Robinson's combination printing, photomontage. Montage involved bringing together a variety of elements – photographs, drawings, illustrations and words and combining them in a seamless, photographic whole. Obviously 'created' as opposed to 'seen' or 'found,' montages looked to unlikely juxtaposition for their effect. They were designed to startle, then inform. Photomontage attracted image makers of some diversity – from dadaist artists in Paris and Germany, and futurists in Italy to the revolutionary constructivists of the newly formed Soviet Union. Often their work reflected political issues of the day (Russia's revolution had inspired artists worldwide), though sometimes the motivation was purely aesthetic. Behind it all, however, was a desire to show new realities, the realities of an exciting, fast-moving new world of change and promise.

Germany was the center of what was becoming known as the New Photography. Change was vital for a nation depressed by defeat in war and the future assumed fresh importance. As one contemporary critic put it, 'Germany has suddenly become endowed with an intense "modern consciousness" and looks forward more eagerly than other nations because it does not care to look back.' National pride might be re-established in a changed society where technology, brought forward by the war, could contribute to human progress. The old was banished and the new welcomed in acts of reconstruction designed to create a machine-based industrial society. Foremost among the institutions which fostered change was the now-legendary Bauhaus, a school of design and architecture set up in 1919. Founded by architect Walter Gropius and employing many of the most original talents of the day, the Bauhaus taught multidiscipline thinking and practice. Using modern materials and methods

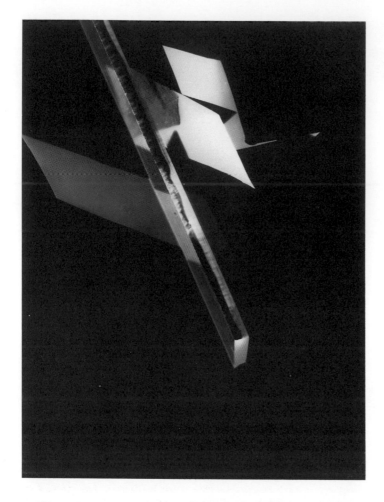

graphy played a dynamic role as a visual art born of machines. The very precision, mechanical and optical, of cameras could reconcile art with technology; it seemed a truly modern medium. Laszlo Moholy-Nagy, painter, sculptor, film-maker, graphic and stage designer, taught at the Bauhaus and encouraged wide-ranging experiments with photography. Some involved a simple use of light and photographic paper to explore fluid forms, others emphasized scrutinizing what was known in the world to find ways of presenting it afresh.

Bauhaus ideas, particularly those of Moholy-Nagy, left a deep impression on the 'New Photography.' Similarly the work of Albert Renger-Patzsch became highly influential. A commercial photographer, he concentrated on taking pictures for books and his third, *Die Welt Ist Schön* (The World is Beautiful), was viewed as the epitome of photography's contribution to a new Germany. Precise, ordered and dispassionate, Renger-Patzsch's works were objective records that used design, composition and formal unity to emphasize relationships between things, whether they be brick textures in a factory building, the qualities and feel of steel in a machine, or patterns thrown up in close-ups of plant life. In order lay a form of beauty that seemed to extend human perception and bring it closer to notions of a new society that worked in harmony, each part interlocking to form a smoothly running whole. Analysis was what counted, not a photographer's personality. *Die Welt Ist Schön* was published in 1928 and was a perfect reflection of the Weimar Republic, where terms like 'the romance of engineering' conjured up a fitting marriage between man and machine. Renger-Patzsch made much of patterns, using repeated motifs to lend a visual rhythm to his pictures just as the industrial culture of which he was a part rejoiced in the wonders of repetition in mass production.

students were encouraged to think across fields of specialization – the architect would confront sculpture, the sculptor examined furniture design, the designer would look to painting. It was a new and exhilarating concept in which photo-

Above Untitled photogram *c* 1925 by Laszlo Moholy-Nagy, who experimented with the plasticity possible in cameraless images. (Museum of Fine Arts, Houston. Museum purchase with funds provided by the S I Morris Photography Endowment Fund.)

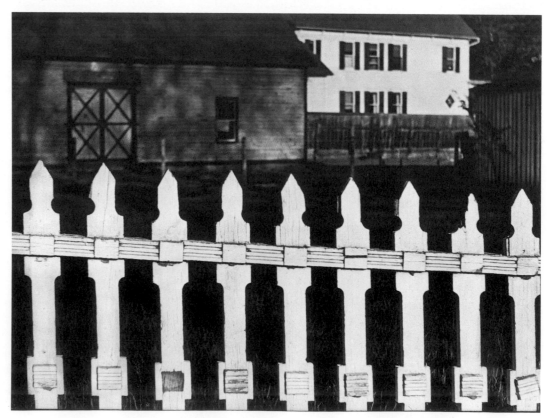

Right *The White Fence, Port Kent,* 1916, by Paul Strand, often cited as the first modernist photograph. (Copyright © 1971, Aperture Foundation, Paul Strand Archive.)

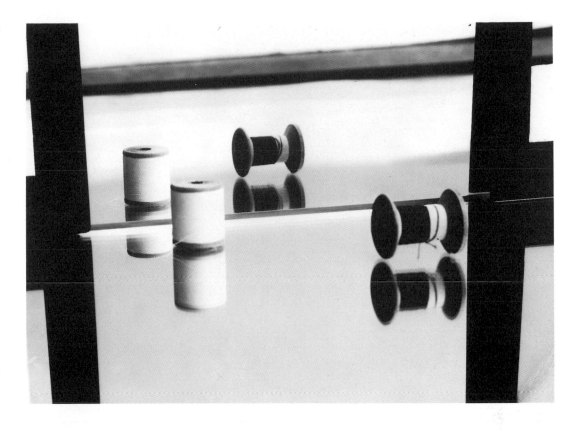

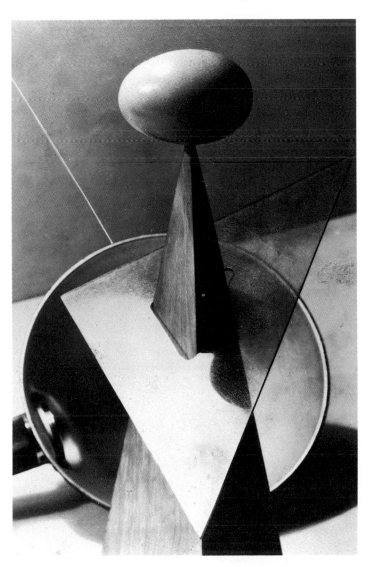

Germany's vanguard position in the arts was signalled in the curiosity of writers, painters and poets who saw Paris in decline and Berlin as a center of radical thought and liberal mores. Photography's status within this hothouse of experimentation was shown in a major exhibition, 'Film und Foto,' held in Stuttgart in 1929. In a magazine article published the same year, the show's director, Gustaf Stotz, succinctly expressed photography's new approach: 'We see things differently now, without painterly intent in the impressionistic sense. Today things are important that earlier were hardly noticed: for example shoe laces, gutters, spools of thread, fabrics, machines, etc. They interest us for their material substance, for the simple quality of the thing-in-itself; they interest us as a means of creating space-form on surfaces, as the bearers of the darkness and the light.' 'Film und Foto' brought together photographic modernists from around the world and crossed avant-garde filmmaking with still images as interacting forms of visual culture and technology. Edward Weston (whose work will be discussed later) was asked to select and submit photographs from the United States. Weston's choice included pieces from Steichen, who aided him in selection and whose work was now far removed from his pictorialist beginnings; Weston's son, Brett; Charles Sheeler, a painter and photographer fascinated by industry's visual structures; Imogen Cunningham, who showed plant forms; and pictures by Paul Outerbridge, who, like a number of his colleagues, translated the exactness of photographic seeing into a form of abstract imagery for advertising. Work came from all over Europe and included pictures from artists not normally associated with photography – Max Ernst, El Lissitzky, George Grosz and several others. Forceful but anonymous press pictures were also exhibited alongside

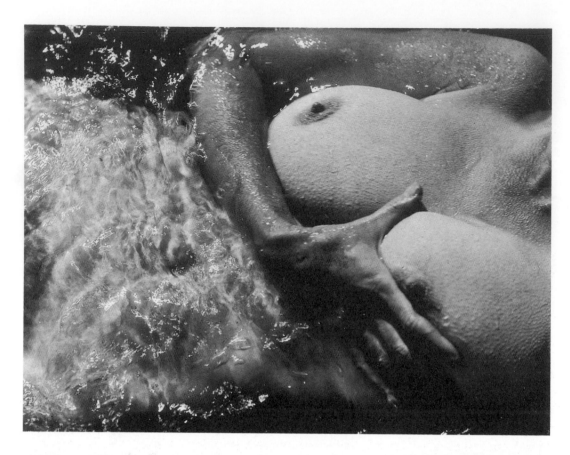

visually remarkable medical photographs, photomicrographs, primitive space pictures and sophisticated photomontages. It was a *tour de force* for photography as the medium which crossed all frontiers. New realism found company with surrealism, constructivists with montagists, photographers with cinematographers. 'New Photography' and the twentieth century formed a natural alliance.

Among the tightly cropped portraits and geometrically composed cityscapes of 1920s modernism, one group of pictures in 'Film und Foto' stood out as singular, different. Aside from their subject matter, which seemed to belong to an earlier era, their maker had the dubious distinction of being the only dead photographer represented. That this work stood apart was somehow heightened by its being presented as a separate historical exhibit; surely such old style, brown-toned depictions of times past, for these were how they appeared, belonged with the pre-modernists. No record exists to explain why Eugene Atget, depictor of an almost vanished Paris, found himself in the company of photography's new avant-garde. His pictures had been chosen by Man Ray, an American photographer and surrealist working in Paris who lived a few doors from Atget. Those selected picked up on photography's capacity for chance juxtaposition and obviously appealed to Man Ray for their surrealist qualities. But two years after the exhibition Walter Benjamin, a German critic, wrote that Atget was: 'the first to disinfect the stifling atmosphere . . . He cleanses this atmosphere, indeed he dispels it altogether: he initiates the emancipation of object from aura which is the most single achievement of the latest school of photography. When avant-garde periodicals like *Bifur* or *Variété* publish pictures

captioned *Westminster, Lille, Antwerp* or *Breslau* but showing only details, here a piece of balustrade, there a tree whose bare branches criss-cross a gas lamp, or a gable wall, or a lamppost with a lifebuoy bearing the name of the town – this is nothing but a literary refinement of themes Atget discovered. He

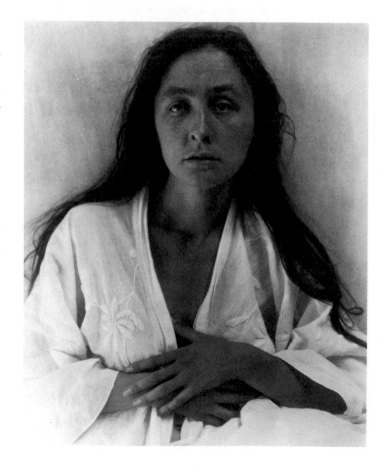

looked for what was unremarked, forgotten, cast adrift, and thus such pictures too work against the exotic, romantically sonorous names of the cities; they pump the aura out of reality like water from a sinking ship.'

Eugéne Atget, who lived and died in virtual obscurity, could be described as the father of modernist photography. His materials, working methods and indeed subject matter all seem firmly rooted in the nineteenth century. But as Walter Benjamin points out, his vision, his way of seeing and using photography mark him apart, a man who sensed the future while photographing the past. At the time of his death in 1927 he was known to a few intimates and had seen his work appreciated by the Paris surrealists. By the mid-1980s he had been hailed as possibly the most significant photographer of the twentieth century. Within his career and events later, paradox abounds. How, for example, could a photographer who concentrated on the plain forms of documentary be taken up by a visual avant-garde? Why was his work, a record of an old Parisian land- and cityscape, so admired by critics like Benjamin who was to argue for photography as a revelation and condemnation of contemporary society? And what is contained in Atget's photographs that now makes him seemingly easily divisible (depending on one's viewpoint) between great artist and humble artisan? In Atget's work,

Right *At Coffee,* nd by Laszlo Moholy-Nagy opens up a way of seeing beyond normal vision. (The Museum of Fine Arts, Houston. Museum purchase with funds provided by Max and Isabell Herzstein.)

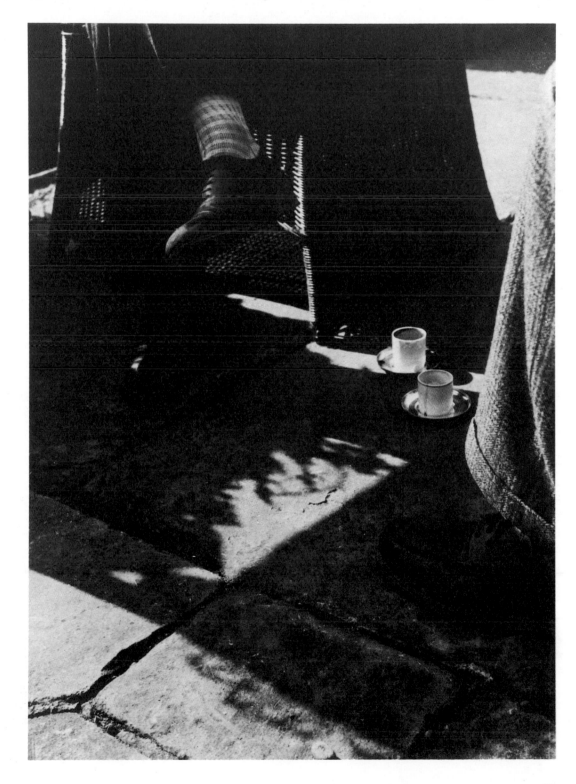

Left *A Portrait (1),* 1918, by Alfred Stieglitz. His subject was Georgia O'Keeffe the painter of whom he made a 'collective portrait' over a period of more than 16 years. (Courtesy, Museum of Fine Arts, Boston. Gift of Alfred Stieglitz.)

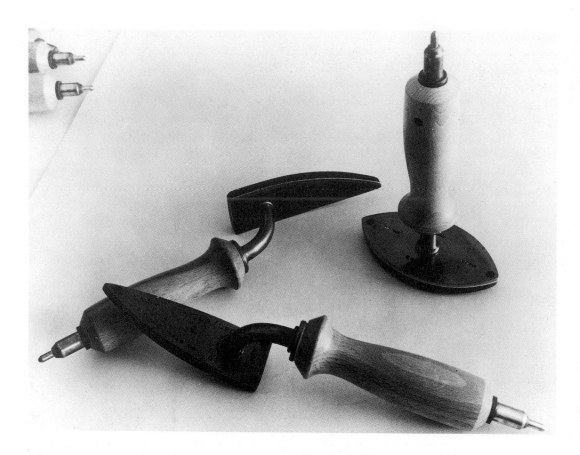

Left *Still Life with Tools,* nd, by Albert Renger-Patzsch. The precise forms of new realism were a source of stimulation as Germany reconstructed. (Staatliche Museen Preussischer Kulturbesitz, Kunstbibliothek mit Museum für Architektur, Modebild und Grafik-Design, West Berlin.)

Right *Kölnische Zeitung, Pressa,* 1928, by Werner Mantz, who applied Bauhaus ideas to his picture making. (San Francisco Museum of Modern Art, Mrs Ferdinand C Smith Fund Purchase. 80.1.9.)

made within living memory and so escaping history's potential for romance, we have one of the first sightings of fact transcending reality, of the photographer using a kind of realism relating only to this medium but employing forms familiar from everyday life. Where his predecessors relied on an amazement with fact in itself and his contemporaries with fact as the starting point for a visual adventure, Atget foretold a world where photographic realism might have a capability beyond history, telling of exotic distances or new ways of experiencing the familiar. He saw a way of making photographs that were at once firmly embedded in the real world and yet dependent on the camera for their very existence. His art gave meaning to the most ordinary items of life.

Atget's discovery was three-fold. One part was how photography could directly record a culture through objects – parks, architecture, street life – another how a photographer might express his or her own experience of that culture through selection. When some things are photographed, others neglected, what is pictured gains in importance as one questions the omissions. Why was this photographed but not that? (For instance, why did Atget not choose to photograph the Eiffel Tower?) The third was process – how photographing transformed what was in front of the camera into a 'photograph.' It was ideas of 'culture' through the camera and how it might be translated into political ideas that appealed to modernist Benjamin, 'experience' that invited avant-garde surrealists who loved photography's optical capacity for joining apparently random bits and pieces of the world, and 'process' that interested Atget. It was he who decided to make the pictures he did, it was his experience of the changing world that funnelled into photography.

Atget came into photography sometime around 1891. He was in his mid-thirties and had recently abandoned an unsatisfactory career as an actor. Photography seemed to offer the dual possibilities of working with a visual medium (he had tried painting) and making a living. He acquired a modest training and set up a business in Paris to supply artists with photographs. Photography was an established method of artists' gaining subject matter and Atget would supply them from stock or take pictures on commission. Such a livelihood, it seems, was satisfactory and he made a small reputation as well as his living. Then, around 1897 (the date is not firm as little of Atget's life is documented) he began a new initiative. His work previously had been somewhat random, but from it a pattern emerged that suggested a potential future and he resolved to concentrate on documenting Paris. Atget 'wanted to photograph everything' and Paris seemed just that – a great capital and world center of culture.

Atget's decision was a wise one. A market was growing for views of old Paris, remnants of the city that predated the modernization and rebuilding carried out by Baron Haussmann during the Second Empire. Haussmann's Paris was one of elaboration; imposing boulevards and grandly sweeping streets. Atget sought the medieval city, a place of times past, quiet corners and tradition. Even before the catastrophic events of World War I a sense of change had begun to filter through and it was felt necessary to preserve architecture, monuments, even street-life, the heartbeat of an ancient city suffering from what some believed to be terminal modernity. To record all this in photographs had precedent, going back to those early views of Rome, Greece and Egypt and a pictorial survey of France made in the 1850s for the Historic

Monuments Committee. Within an upsurge of change in Paris, an expanding population of workers needing housing and the streets almost daily growing more crowded, Atget found himself in the right place at the right time and with the right inclinations and his clients changed from artists to those who valued preservation. He prospered. First came the *amateurs de Vieux Paris*, collectors of prints, documents, drawings and now photographs of historic Paris. Later he was employed by government agencies: the Commission for Historic Monuments, the Bibliothèque Nationale, the Bibliothèque Historique de la Ville and even the Victoria and Albert Museum, London, commissioned prints.

Atget's project was intensive and his clients were pleased with the results. But like many of his generation, Atget found World War I a devastating experience. It robbed him of his livelihood and, when peace offered possibilities of a return to work, the retrospection that made his work so viable had given way to ideas of reconstruction. There was no place for a specialist in old Paris. In 1920 he sold a portion of his glass-plate collection to Les Monuments Historiques saying 'for more than twenty years I have been working alone and of my own initiative in all the old streets of Old Paris to make . . .

artistic documents of beautiful urban architecture from the sixteenth to the nineteenth centuries . . . Today this enormous artistic and documentary collection is finished; I can say I possess all of Old Paris. . .' The sale was made for 10,000 francs; it left Atget financially secure. And now in his seventies he began to photograph with a new energy. This time his subject matter was the countryside just outside Paris; he pictured trees, gardens, plants and parks. The war had changed his vision as well as subject matter and these photographs possess a more lyrical air, as if strict documentation of the past was no longer sufficient to address the future of an aging photographer. This phase lasted until 1926 when his common-law wife died. He had loved her dearly and her departure was the final blow. Made ill by grief and unable to photograph, Atget died a little over a year later.

At the time of his death Atget was all but forgotten. Old Paris had few remaining enthusiasts and most of Atget's photographs lay unlooked at in archives. Within a year, however, the work was to reappear in a new and very different context. In 1928 an exhibition, the *Premier Salon Indépendant de la Photographie*, opened to excited reviews. In it was a group of Atget prints, the first to be publicly exhibited. When

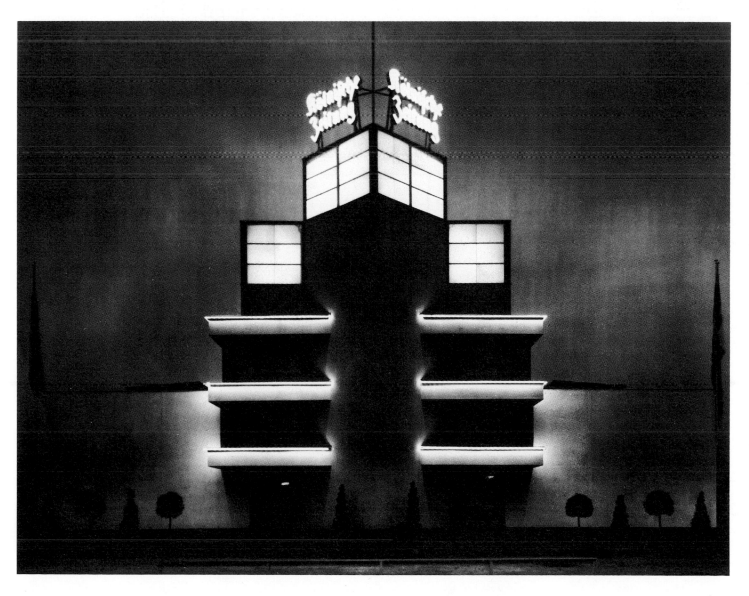

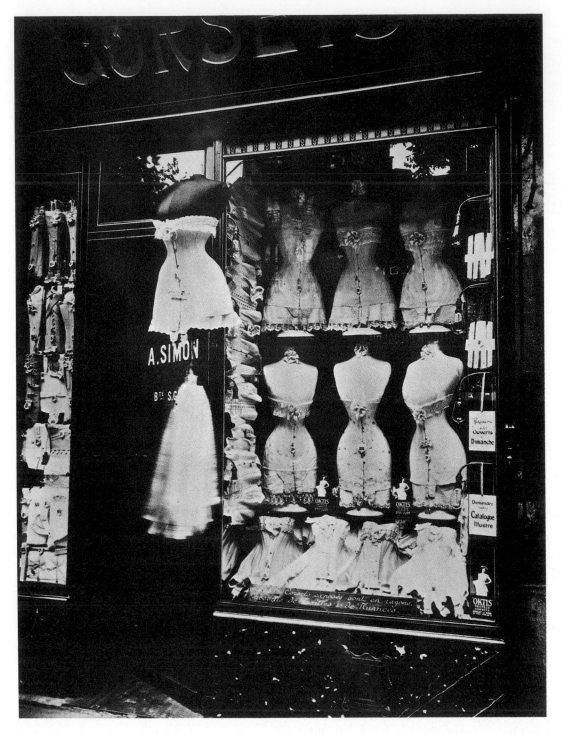

Left *Boulevard de Strasbourg, Corsets,* 1912, by Eugene Atget. This was part of Atget's collection which Berenice Abbott bought. (Private collection.)

Right *Paris,* nd, by Eugene Atget. (Victoria and Albert Museum.)

the show closed an American photographer living in Paris, Berenice Abbott, announced that she had bought the old man's collection. Abbott worked with Man Ray as his assistant in the same street as Atget lived, knew the old photographer and clearly saw a meaning in his work which went beyond its documentary value. For Abbott, who was to serve as Atget's photographic guardian for many years to come, his work marked an entirely new kind of photographic creativity, a form of expression that was 'so utterly new that some time must elapse before we conquer our surprise.' She wrote that in 1929. In the years from then to now, Atget's reputation advanced in fits and starts, culminating in a four-volume work published by the Museum of Modern Art, New York, between 1981 and 1985. This constitutes the most compre-

hensive work ever published on a single photographer and has served to raise Atget to the status of a twentieth-century photographic demigod. For a man who pursued a quiet but industrious life and wanted little more than 'to photograph everything' such adulation might seem curious. But, as mentioned earlier, paradox seems rampant when Atget is considered. With this in mind and the work aside, what caused (in historical terms) such elevation? One answer lies in influence. In 1971, writing on Walker Evans, an American modernist who stands as Atget's successor, John Szarkowski, Director of the Department of Photography at the Museum of Modern Art, New York, had this to say on Evans' record of the United States of the 1930s: 'It is difficult to know now with any certainty whether Evans recorded the America of

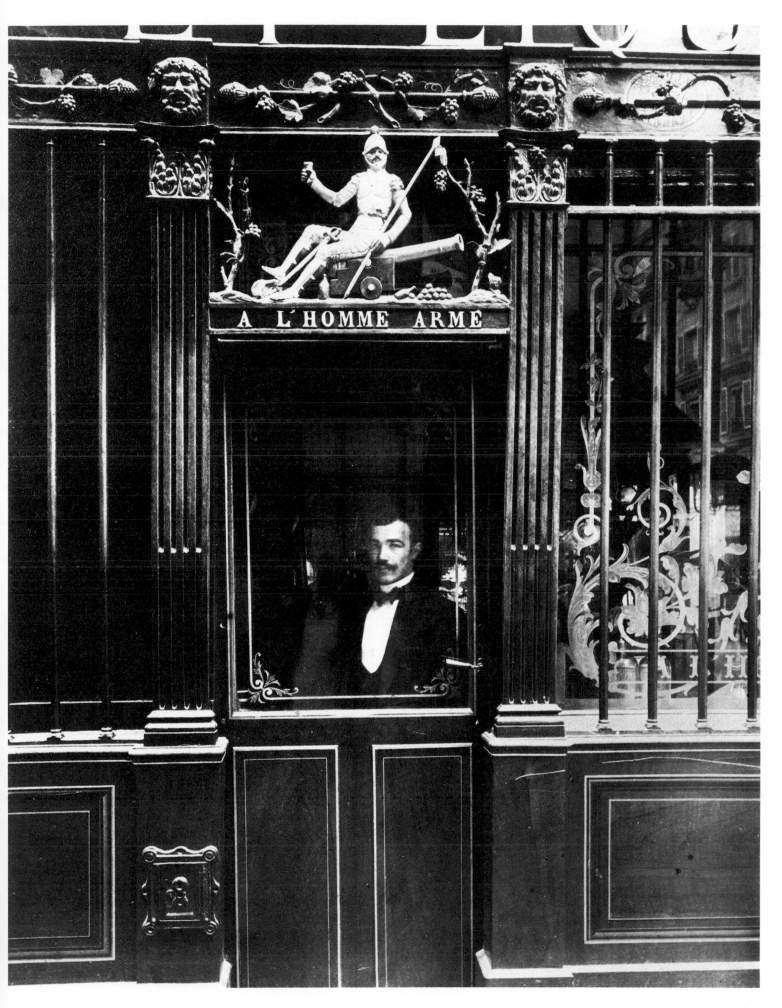

A L'HOMME ARME

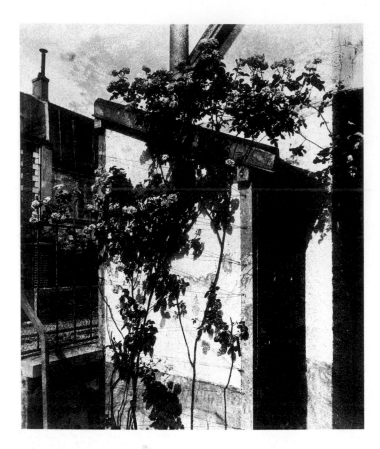

his youth, or invented it.' In other words, are documentary photographs the simple facsimiles they seem or do they somehow change what is in front of the camera? Are they machine-made replicas of what is known or individual creative acts of seeing? Can fact remain actual but become personal? Transformation was Atget's gift and one indirectly passed on to Walker Evans and others in the United States, who in turn altered understandings of the medium in their country. Similarly in Britain, Edwin Smith, who later involved himself in finding the same mystery in fact, brought ideas of a traditional England to the new vision offered by the camera. Picturing a culture with precise ways of seeing and a capability for going beyond the fact of the matter and making it a matter of fact were hallmarks of Atget's legacy. His work touched base at the root of photography's potential outside commerce and was to inform the future.

Walker Evans, born in Chicago in 1904, was a student at the Sorbonne during the last year of Atget's life. His subject was literature, he was going to be a writer, and it was not until 1928 when he had returned to the United States that he began to concern himself with photography. Almost immediately be began to make the kinds of picture that characterized his importance to photography. Like Atget's they were of common enough subjects – architecture, interiors, shop fronts, post offices, farm tools, billboards, gas stations, pool halls – urban and rural still-lifes that served to first present and then analyze a culture. Indeed, while it is inaccurate to assume that Evans took Atget's works as a model for his own, something he wrote on Atget in 1931 might apply equally to himself: 'His general note is lyrical understanding of the street, trained observation of it, special feeling for

patina, eye for revealing detail, over all of which is thrown a poetry which is not "the poetry of the street" or "the poetry of Paris" but the projection of Atget's person.'

Evans' fascination was for an idea of the United States that might be made plain through an accumulation of detail. Unlike Atget, who systematically catalogued old Paris, his was a more random collection of American particulars that might somehow add up to an American culture. Where Atget sought to preserve Evans was looking to discover – hoping to find some visible links between an American vernacular and the meaning of America.

It was frustration with writing that made Evans turn to photography and strong parallels can be drawn between his kind of picture making and certain literary forms. Evans said he wanted his work to be 'literate, authoritative, transcendent' and his photographs echo the writings of poets like Walt Whitman who used an accumulation of fact rather than more conventional symbolism to express the American experience. Fact was important, it spoke of democracy, egalitarianism, puritanism – the very core of an immigrant nation where people might feel pride at the freedom of plain talking. It is fact, too, that Evans began his photographic career in the period immediately before the Wall Street Crash of 1929. By 1931, when he was acquainted with the rudiments of photographic craft, America doubted itself and questioned the values of a regime which had the potential for crumbling like a house of cards. What better time to examine and perhaps reinforce the underlying values of an ordinary people with a

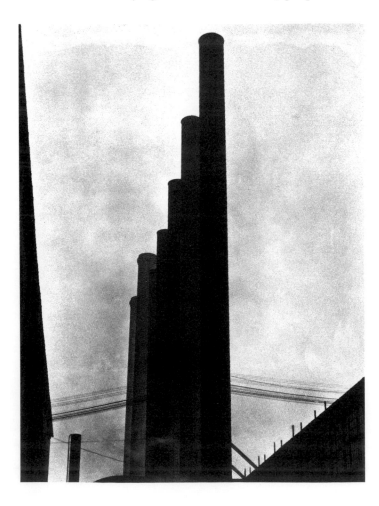

Far left *Rosier Grimpant,* 1910 or earlier, by Eugène Atget. An astonishing example of Atget's capacity to transform the everyday into an image both mysterious and explicit. (Collection, The Museum of Modern Art, New York. The Abbott-Levy Collection. Partial gift of Shirley C Burden.)

Below left *From an American Place, Looking North,* 1931, by Alfred Stieglitz, reflects the power of a city thrusting upward. (Courtesy, Museum of Fine Arts, Boston. Gift of Miss Georgia O'Keeffe.)

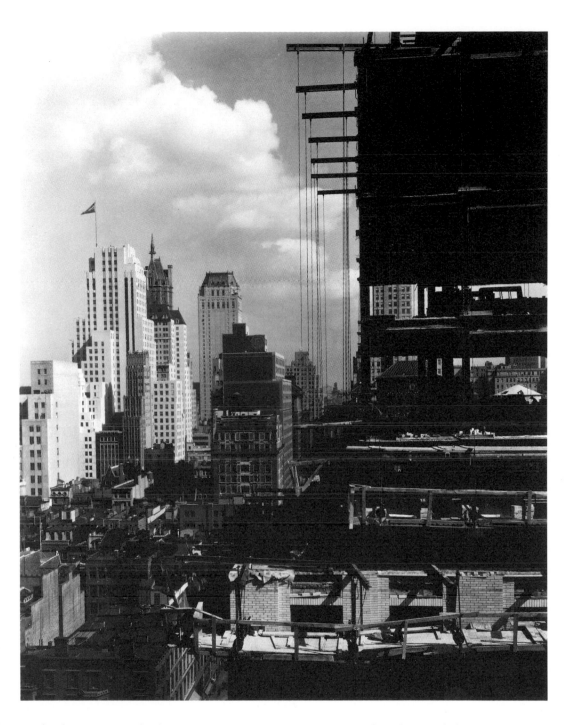

Right *Armco Steel, Ohio,* 1922, by Edward Weston. Associated with landscape, Weston also embraced modernism. (© Arizona Board of Regents, University of Arizona. Courtesy Center for Creative Photography.)

vision composed of positive facts? What better time to look at everyday items and find in them possibilities for redemption? As the stock market tumbled, some solace might be found in the trivialities that support day-to-day living. Not romantically – photography could penetrate further than an idealized view – but realistically. In the midst of individual, corporate and national chaos the world insisted on being allowed its way and Walker Evans set out to picture what was that way. It was an intuitative move; Evans trusted intuition, and he was not the only American photographer to begin a study of the importance of the everyday. Ralph Steiner was another, and so was Berenice Abbott, who began her career as a portraitist then moved into modernist documentary after discovering Atget. And Paul Strand's seeing vitality in the vernacular actually anticipates Evans' work but eventually became more diffuse. Painters also turned to the everyday;

Edward Hopper and Evans' friend Ben Shahn are just two who looked for a new vocabulary of images to locate within a world of change.

For photographers, however, it was Walker Evans who proved the most persuasive and he who introduced new icons and a different grammar into the language of the medium. He photographed things for what they were, but to succeeding generations they became symbol. Those same simple items of domestic use which Evans pictured so carefully they might be treasured museum pieces transferred their meaning when seen by those who thought America had been corrupted by consumerism. But before Walker Evans nobody really bothered with such minutiae as a useful way of explaining a consciousness. And after him, when his lessons in the importance of accumulating detail had been absorbed, gas stations, billboards and the bric-a-brac of small-town life

101

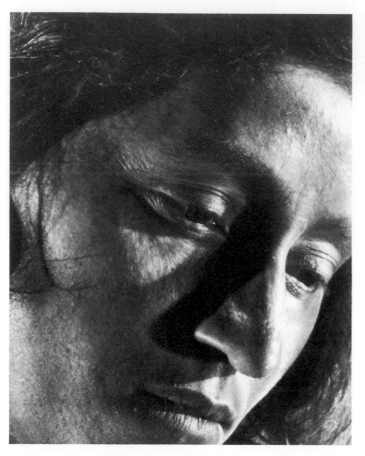

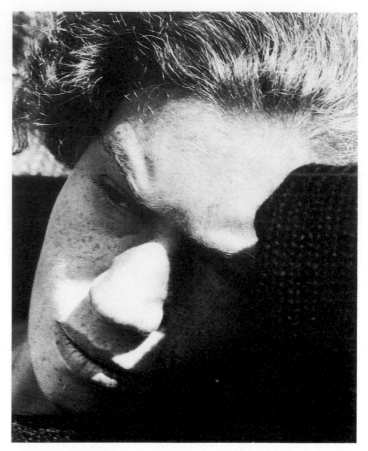

were used, sometimes thoughtlessly, as emblems of an America photographers found wanting. Like Atget in Europe it is difficult to conceive of American photography today without Walker Evans.

Evans' first years as a photographer were financially precarious. He tried advertising photography and found it distaste-

ful, then depended on occasional assignments. Evans was not alone in finding the 1930s tough – financial distress could be found everywhere as the Depression took its toll. Farms and farmers were particularly hard hit as prices for their produce fell, and many were forced to sell up at low prices or stand by, helpless, as banks and loan sharks took over their land when

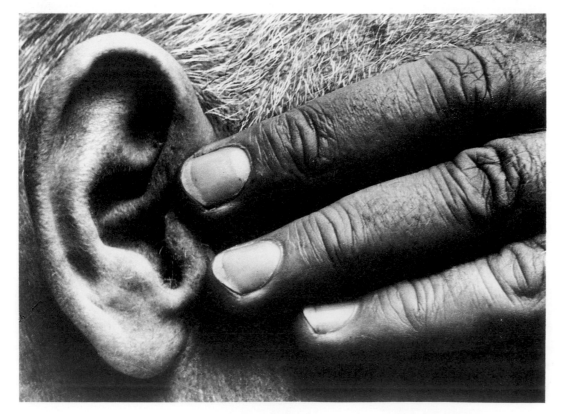

Above left *Portrait, c*1930, by Helmar Lerski is typical of new realism in portraiture. (International Museum of Photography at George Eastman House.)

Above *Etude d'Expression,* 1931, by Raoul Hausmann. (San Francisco Museum of Modern Art. Purchase.)

Left *Fingers and Ear,* 1929, by Brett Weston, was exhibited in the 'Film und Foto' exhibition in 1929 as exemplary of all that was new in American photography. (© 1986 Brett Weston; Courtesy Center for Creative Photography.)

Right *Portrait of a Woman,* 1929/ 1974, by Florence Henri. (San Francisco Museum of Modern Art. The Helen Crocker Russell and William H and Ethel W Crocker Family Funds Purchase.)

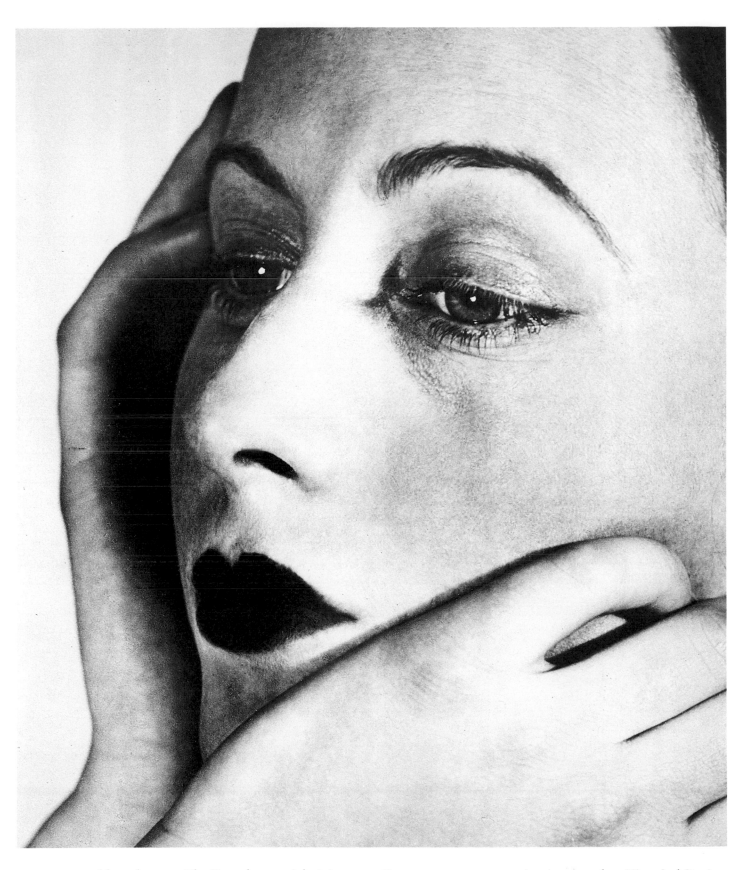

mortgages could not be met. The Resettlement Administration (RA), part of President Franklin D Roosevelt's 'New Deal,' was set up to combat this misery – farming, small-scale farming in particular, was an integral part of the American way of life and ways of preservation needed to be found. The Resettlement Administration mainly concerned itself with low-interest loans, land reclamation and similar schemes.

But as a government project it enjoyed an Historical Section and Walker Evans was invited to join this. The work of the RA (later renamed Farm Security Administration) remains one of the most ambitious photographic projects of the twentieth century (considered in greater detail in Chapter 6) but during the two years of his tenure Evans made some of the most powerful pictures of his whole career. Their context is

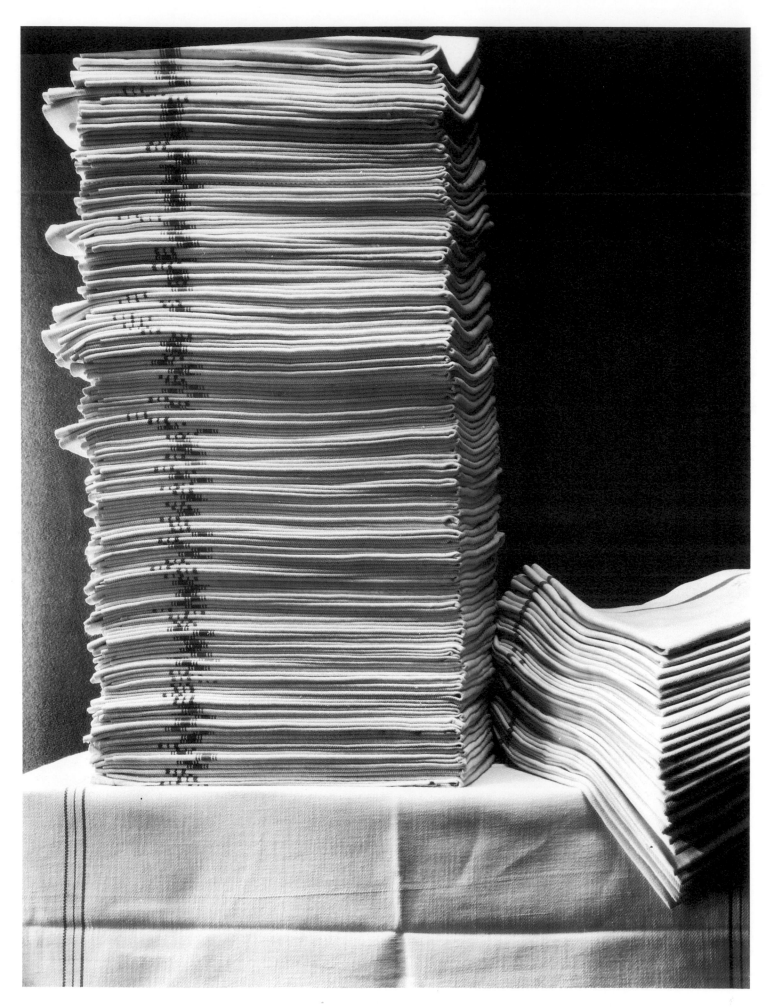

Left *Linens,* 1935, by Emanuel Sougez, a subscriber to new objectivity in France. (Bibliothèque Nationale, Paris.)

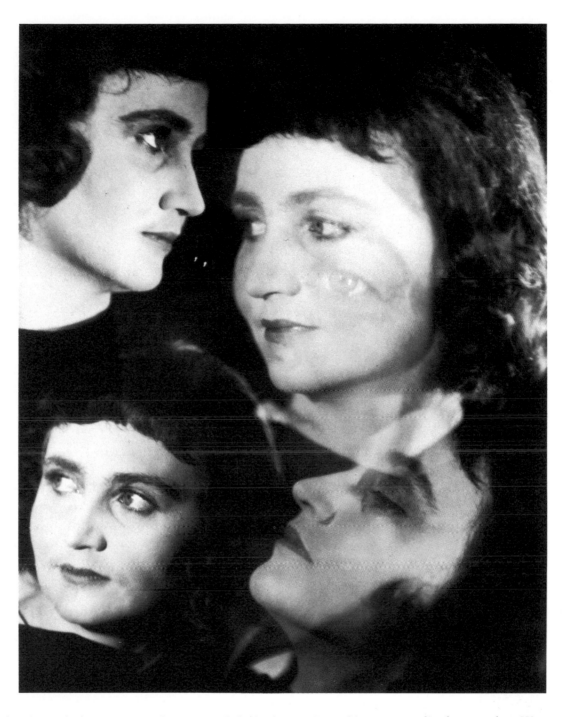

Right *Heads of Cynthia, My Sister, c* 1935, by Francis Bruguière, an early experimenter with photography beyond explicit representation. (© Francis Bruguière; courtesy Center for Creative Photography.)

one of factual documentation, but in truth they are examples of Evans doing what he was best at – distilling the American experience – when freed from day-to-day financial worries. Such wilfulness could not last, Evans was an independent beyond bureaucratic toleration, his pictures more descriptive than reforming and he was asked to leave the project when a budget reduction provided the opportunity. A year later, in 1938, Evans' work was exhibited at the Museum of Modern Art, New York, the first solo exhibition by a photographer as artist. With the exhibition came a book *Walker Evans: American Photographs.* In it, Lincoln Kirstein wrote, 'after looking at these pictures with all their clear, hideous and beautiful detail, their open insanity and pitiful grandeur, compare this vision of a continent as it is, not as it might be or as it was, with any other coherent vision that we have had since the war. What poet has said so much? What painter has shown so

much?' The key to Evans' importance lies here – when Kirstein writes of a 'coherent vision,' he means a vision that is coherently *American.* For all the useful ways in which we might compare Evans with Atget and the paradox of their seemingly plain photography, Evans was one of the first to pin down a uniquely American means of viewing the world. He was a pop artist before pop art existed; an appreciator of how forcefully a culture can manifest itself in the way it looks, what it regards and discards, what it makes, breaks and chooses to mend.

Evans continued to work, albeit at a slower pace, until his death in 1975. In 1941 *Let Us Now Praise Famous Men,* his collaboration with writer James Agee, was published. In 1943 he became a writer with *Time* magazine and two years later transferred to the same publisher's business journal, *Fortune,* as a writer and photographer. He stayed with *Fortune* until

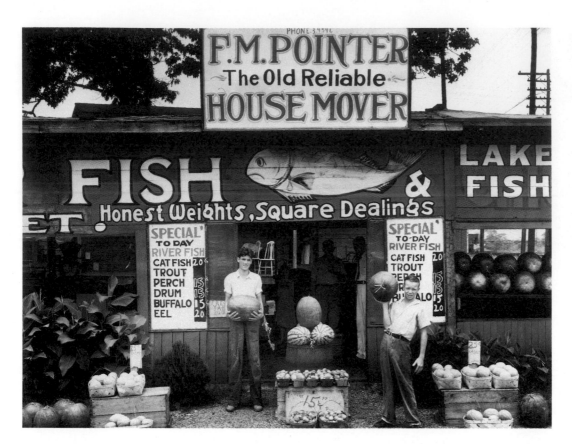

Left *Roadside Stand, Vicinity Birmingham, Alabama,* 1936, by Walker Evans, who revelled in photography's authenticity. (Library of Congress; courtesy Victoria and Albert Museum.)

Right *Highway Corner, Reedsville, West Virginia,* 1935, by Walker Evans. (Library of Congress; courtesy Victoria and Albert Museum.)

Below *Optical Parable,* 1931, by Manuel Alvarez Bravo. Bravo lent a sense of Mexican culture to international surrealism. (© Manuel Alvarez Bravo; courtesy Victoria and Albert Museum.)

1965, producing visual and verbal essays that show an intelligent mind in successful combat with an intractable medium. Throughout that 20-year low-profile period he also served a separate function as mentor to like-minded photographers. As we will see later some of the brightest of a new group of photographers took their leads from Walker Evans in the 1950s and 1960s – sought him out and learned valuable lessons in how to bring the tangibility of a recording medium to life's mysteries and resolve them in pictures that simultaneously ask and answer questions. After his retirement from *Fortune,* Evans was made Professor of Photography at Yale University – some indication at least of the importance felt by one generation for an older peer who showed America how photography can make the past ever present.

Walker Evans was not alone in his immersion in photographic modernism. In 1938, the year that Evans' show opened at the Museum of Modern Art, an American West Coast photographer, Edward Weston, was working in California, financed by the first-ever Guggenheim Fellowship grant to be given to a photographer. The Fellowship was a singular honor, given to a man at the height of his creative powers. Weston had begun his career as a commercial portraitist and had become known, also, for his personal work produced in the pictorialist style. Soft focus gave way to a sharper imagery in the early 1920s as he left metaphor and symbol to those of a more nineteenth-century disposition and became attuned to ideas of description. As he wrote in 1926 'once my aim was interpretation; now it is presentation.' In this Weston can be likened to Walker Evans and Paul Strand as a searcher for ways of discovering and recording the truth of twentieth-century America. Evans found his in the folk art

of billboards, country stores and the tender realities of everyday items which spoke of a particular set of values. Strand's concerns were more directly democratic, involved with making the ordinary heroic enough to become beautiful. Weston

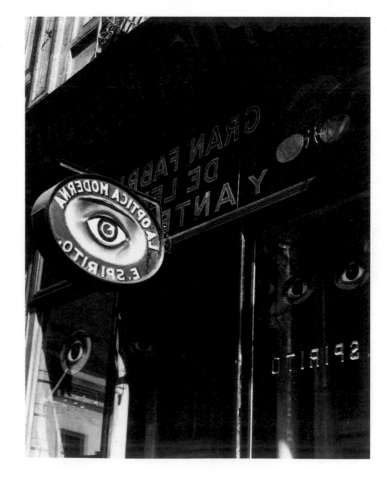

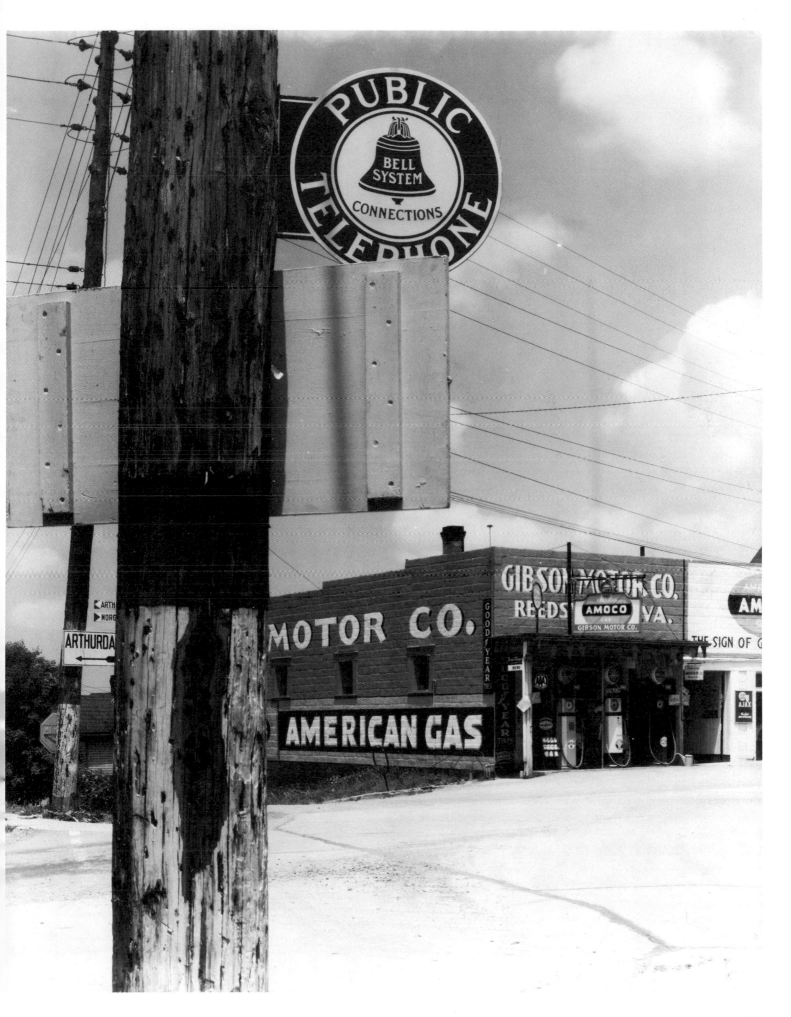

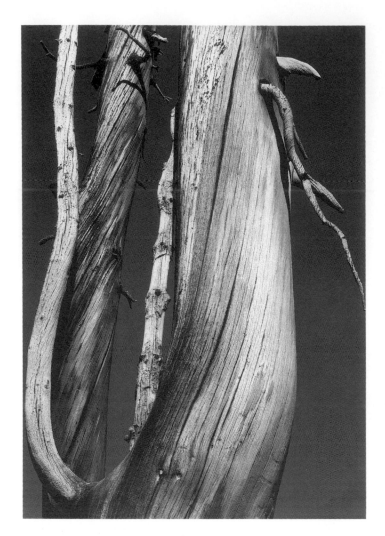

1931 that 'the conservative German writers deny emphatically that modern photography was born in Germany. They point out the *Camera Work*, the *Broom*, the photos of Paul Strand, the American commercial photography, as the strongest influences which corrupted German youth and made it depart from the sacred dogma of pictorialism. Outerbridge is one of the heaviest and earliest offenders and, as such, deserves our deep respect.' In common with some of his modernist colleagues in Europe, Outerbridge was no simple commercial photographer content to lend his technical skills to illustration, but an innovatory image maker whose concepts of modernity found a useful resting place in the expanding field of mass media.

Like a number of young photographers who emerged in the 1920s, Paul Outerbridge came to the medium deeply influenced by ideas of cubism. Photography, it seemed, could abstract details of the real world and re-present them in clean, clear-cut formal terms that avoided the sentimentality associated with pictorialism. Outerbridge, who had studied

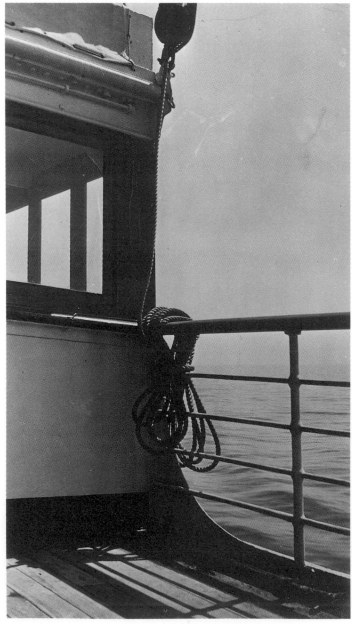

pursued liberty, and for this has become legend. Evans, the aristocrat, drew his viewers to an overlooked sense of worth in the commonplace. Strand, a democrat, was to make pictures that affirmed his belief in common man. And Weston took American concepts of liberty and became a photographic bohemian, photographing strong people and a strong country to emphasize the freedom of it all.

Like his colleagues, Weston felt the pull of newness. During a 1922 trip to New York where he hoped to show work to Alfred Stieglitz (still American photography's dominant father figure) he pictured factories in Ohio. Later he was to photograph Mexican radicals and celebrate avant-garde ideas of sexual freedom in sensuous nudes. He also made landscape pictures and still-lifes (discussed in Chapter 7). But Weston the open modernist, a photographer obsessed by notions of the new age – precision and detail – was sufficiently regarded internationally to stand as the United States' representative and selector for Germany's 'Film und Foto' exhibition in 1929. Among those chosen were Imogen Cunningham, who worked for a time as Weston's portrait assistant and Paul Outerbridge, an advertising photographer.

At a time when Weston was gearing himself up for his role as a purist beyond the reaches of commerce, his choice of Outerbridge as a representative of the 'new vision' might seem questionable. But a German critic, Dr M F Agha, put an ironic finger on the contemporary pulse when he wrote in

Far left *Dead Tree, Dog Lake, Yosemite National Park, California,* 1933, by Ansel Adams, perhaps best known of all landscape photographers. (Courtesy of the Trustees of the Ansel Adams Publishing Rights Trust. All Rights Reserved.)

Below left *Atlantic Voyage,* 1931, by Paul Nash, one of Britain's major mid-twentieth century painters. (Paul Nash Trust, Tate Gallery Archive.)

Right *Sun Baker,* 1937, by Max Dupain, Australia's principal modernist photographer (Art Gallery of New South Wales.)

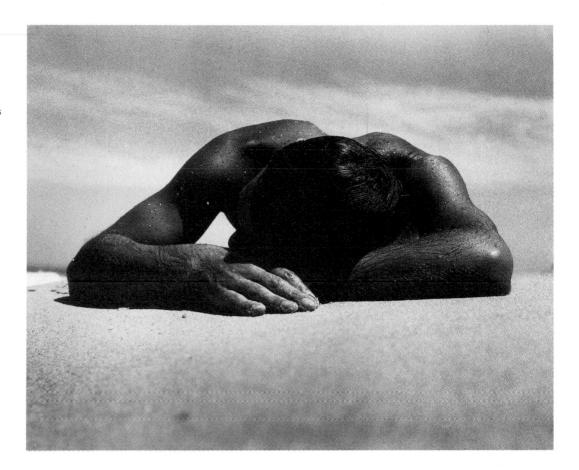

first at the Art Students League, New York, and later with Clarence H White (a photo-secessionist whose school was a hot-bed of modernism), favored studio work and the still life. His concern was for light, form, pattern and the geometry made possible by contrasting deeply cut shadows with angular highlights. The work was bold, sculptural and successful — while still a student his work was published in *Vanity Fair* magazine and by 1922, a year after he had begun to photograph, he was working commercially. Outerbridge's first assignment, to photograph a collar for the Ide Shirt Company, is a fine example of his personal style and the excitement modernist thinking was bringing to advertising. The *Ide Collar* is both functionally descriptive and visually abstract. Three years after it was taken Outerbridge found a copy, torn from *Vanity Fair* in which it was published, tacked to Marcel Duchamp's studio wall. He was in Paris, working for *Vogue* and meeting as many artists as he could.

On his European trip, which was to last four years, Outerbridge visited London. Like Paris, New York and Berlin, London was a center for modernist ideas and experiments, though modernism came later to Britain and was heavily influenced by France, Germany and the United States. As in Europe and the United States, two contexts existed for 'new photography' in Britain – cultural and commercial. A cultural reaction against pictorial soft focus and 'effect,' similar to that experienced in Europe and the United states, fuelled interest in photographic realism. The same concerns for sweeping away past debris were felt across the board as artists in many media looked to newness in literature, poetry, filmmaking, architecture and design to inform their work.

And in commerce, with advertising agencies growing in size and importance as new marketing techniques took hold, the newness intensified. Ideas of business were changing too – the United States' example of 'the corporation' questioned ideas of the comfortable family firm and some fresh way of presenting goods made for an expanding mass market was urgently needed. Borrowing from European and American concepts was seen as a sound idea and photographers like Noel Griggs came forward to lend visual dynamism to the notion of romance in industry, just as their German counterparts had made engineering 'romantic' and Americans like Charles Sheeler had turned the factory into a contemporary pantheon. Portrait photographers too, faced by competition from newly developed automatic techniques (forerunners of the still-viable Photome booths) which could 'mass produce' portraits, turned to new methods in order to maintain their business. Lighting was hurriedly borrowed from avant-garde film, and settings took on a more radical look. Howard Coster is an example of one who changed from conventional sittings to notions of surrealist fantasy in order to be 'original' at all costs.

Modernism, the movement that finally drew photography into the mainstream of a visual vanguard, was composed and confused, seen as clear and direct by some parties and open to the wildest experimentation by others. Between the wars it served to catapult photography from a form of simple painterly imitation to a medium of unique and recognizable complexity. As Moholy-Nagy expressed it in 1936 'the illiterate of the future will be ignorant of the camera and pen alike.' Modernism was photography's coming of age.

CHAPTER SIX

A Witness to the World

The Photographer as Commentator

For all their ambitions, all their desires to be seen keeping company with the avant-garde, artist-photographers remained a tiny group within the body photographic. It was, perhaps still is, photography's capacity for recording fact, giving evidence, presenting a document, that practitioners and their public valued most. Verisimilitude, that seeming truthfulness offered in a photograph, was the medium's first attraction – photographs had an authenticity missing from even the most detailed drawings. And, as the nineteenth century progressed and social reform became an active issue, photographs were pressed into service as transmitters of facts demanding public attention. As mass reproduction of photographs became possible through a primitive form of photolithography (1855), the woodburytype (1866), the collotype (1868) and finally halftone in the 1880s, it became clear to advocates of social change that while words worked, photographs carried an even more effective mix of hard fact and emotional backup. From a text the reader might know of the plight of London's orphans or the rat-infested squalor of New York's immigrant housing. With a picture they might see and believe. 'There is a terrible truthfulness about photography' wrote George Bernard Shaw.

By the turn of the century photographs of what an American magazine of the time called 'contemporaneous history' were regularly published in replacement of drawings, engravings or woodcuts – the staples of illustration. Ten years earlier the *British Journal of Photography* had called for a collection of photographs to be made illustrating 'the present state of the world' which would become 'most valuable a century hence.' That archive was never established but its very proposal serves to show enthusiasm for the importance of fact preserved through photographs. Similarly, an editorial in the *New York Times* in 1862, commenting on an exhibition of Civil War pictures made by Mathew Brady's team of photographers, displays a nineteenth-century view of photography's power to persuade: 'Mr Brady has done something to bring home to us the terrible reality and earnestness of war. If he has not brought bodies and laid them in our door-yards and along the streets, he has done something very like it.'

Until the advent of television as an overwhelming source of news, views, fact and opinion, the vivid clarity of what we now call 'documentary' was motivation for some of photography's most eloquent practitioners. They attempted and sometimes succeeded in setting fact against fiction, objectivity against subjectivity, developing meanwhile a visual rhetoric that at times changed world events. If artist photographers were able to pin down the butterflies of visual fancy, documentarians tried truth and matter of factness to explain the world. Like the philosopher Francis Bacon, they felt that the 'contemplation of things as they are, without

Left *Valley of the Shadow of Death*, 1855. Albumen print by Roger Fenton. Negative made in the Crimea during the first systematic reportage of war. (Victoria and Albert Museum.)

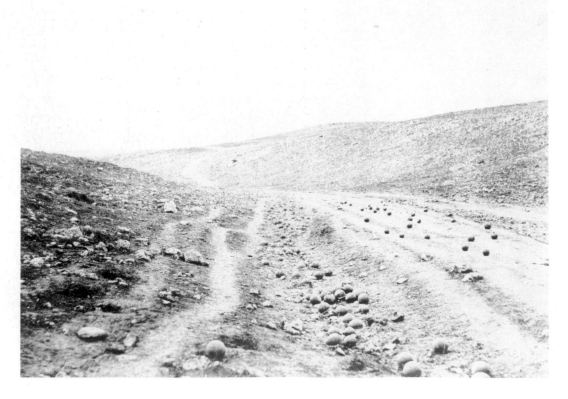

Right *Migrant Worker, Nipomo, California*, 1936, by Dorothea Lange, taken in the United States during the Depression. (Library of Congress.)

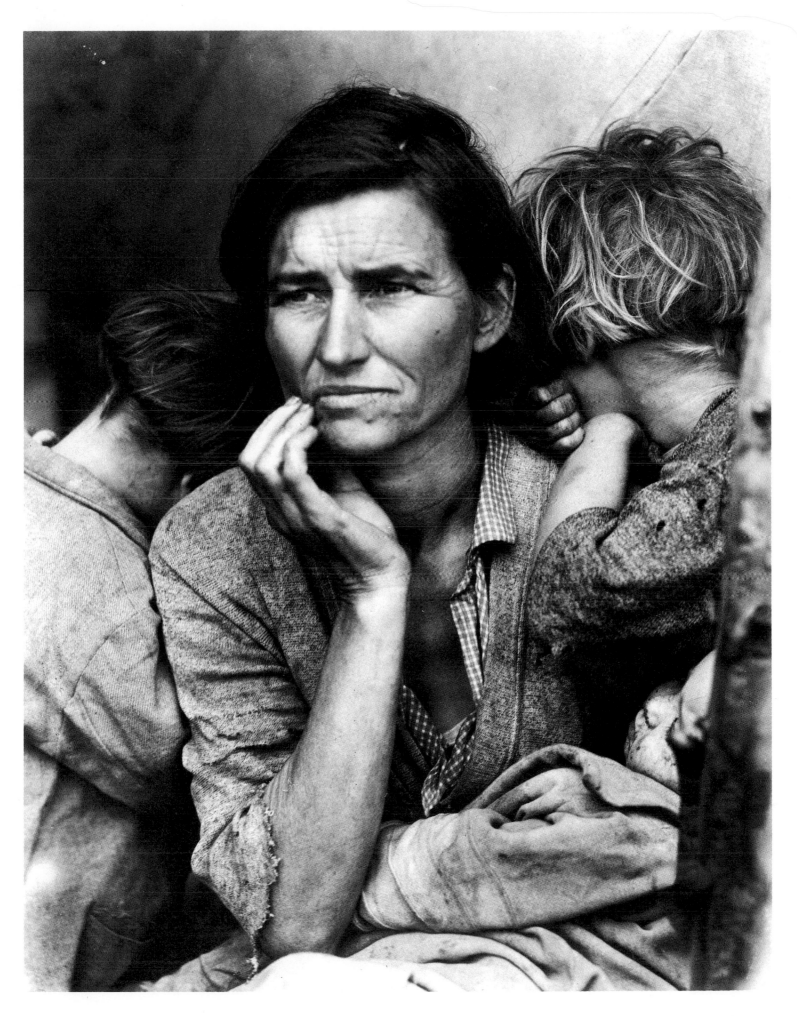

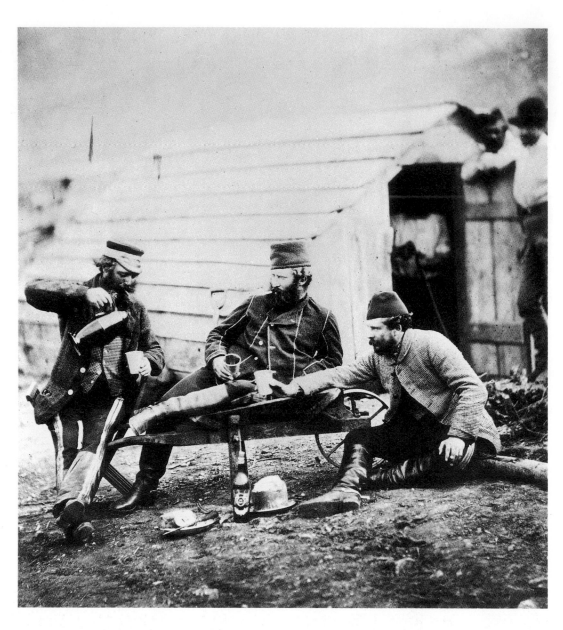

Right *Hardships in the Camp*, 1855.
Albumen print by Roger Fenton
from his Crimean War series.
(Victoria and Albert Museum.)

substitutions or imposture, without error or confusion, is in itself a nobler thing than a whole harvest of invention.'

'Documentary' is a difficult expression; all photographs that transcribe the external world are 'documents' of one sort or another. As Walker Evans observed 'it's a sophisticated and misleading word . . . not really clear.' For his own work (discussed in part in chapter 5), Evans thought 'documentary style' was a more appropriate phrase – he was intent on art and 'a document has use, whereas art is really useless.' This said, how do we then define photographs which record but simultaneously reach beyond simple fact? It is these that have separated themselves from the countless millions of camera images produced and stand as part of the medium's foundations and contemporary superstructure. No easy answer to the question exists; despite, or perhaps because of, its universal presence, photography resists easy categorization. One way out of the dilemma is to look at the reasons documentary pictures were taken as well as their content. Some photographs can then be seen as statements of appearance, others suggest ideas and meanings.

Before the 1880s, when art photography began to spread,

virtually all photographic images could be called documents. Some, however, had a purpose outside description. The earliest example of photography for propaganda and change lies in the partnership of D O Hill and Robert Adamson. The major body of their work (discussed in Chapter 1) was calotype portraits of Scottish notables but in 1845 they photographed the fisher-folk of Newhaven, a port on the Firth of Forth, near Edinburgh. It seems likely that these pictures were made in support of a fund-raising campaign organized by Reverend James Fairbairn to provide safer working conditions for local fishermen. Hill and Adamson's strongly composed and dramatically sunlit calotypes are hardly what we think of today as 'social documents,' but if, as is thought, Fairbairn used them to back his requests for aid, they were highly effective. He raised over £15,000 and used it to deck-in the dangerous open fishing boats and provide better tackle for their crews.

Wet collodion, invented in 1848, with its vastly improved rendering of detail, proved a more useful process for documentation than calotype. It was collodion that Roger Fenton used in the first systematic coverage of war; he journeyed to the Crimea in December 1854 to make photographs that might counter fears in Britain, created by reports in *The Times*, that its conflict with Russia had turned from a series of glorious campaigns into a messy bloodbath. Fenton, a rich amateur instrumental in founding the Photographic Society (see Chapter 3), then professional photographer enjoying Royal patronage, can hardly have been prepared for his brief career as a war photographer. Nevertheless it is for this work that Fenton is best remembered. He had been approached with the commission by Thomas Agnew, a Manchester print dealer who was working in conjunction with the British government. The War Office wanted support for their campaign and Agnew seized the commercial opportunity of satisfying a public presently discontent with published drawings. As one officer remarked on engravings depicting the Battle of Balaklava which appeared in the *Illustrated London News*, 'drawn in London, they are as unlike the reality as possible.' It was Fenton's expertise with collodion which won him the assignment 'to proceed to the Crimea, and take such a round of portraits, scenic and personal, as should illustrate as perfectly as possible the aspects of the campaign.' With letters of introduction from Prince Albert (a keen photographer and collector), he set out, arriving in the Black Sea port of Balaklava in March 1855 to experience for himself the rigors of warfare at the Siege of Sevastopol.

What Fenton witnessed amazed him. Balaklava Harbor seemed little short of a cesspool filled with rotting meat, the battlefields strewn with corpses like one he described as 'lying as if he had raised himself upon his elbow, the bare skull sticking up with still enough flesh left in the muscles to

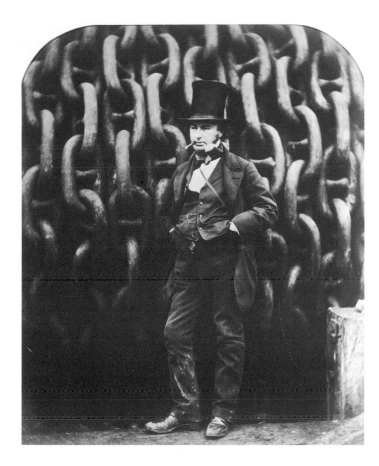

prevent it falling from the shoulders.' Fenton saw drunkeness among the troops, high living among officers, military mayhem, death and destruction. Curiously, none of this was photographed. The 300 or so pictures he exhibited in London

Above *Isambard Kingdom Brunel and the Launching Chains of the Great Eastern*, 1857. Albumen print by Robert Howlett that transforms record into an iconic image of Victorian greatness. (Victoria and Albert Museum.)

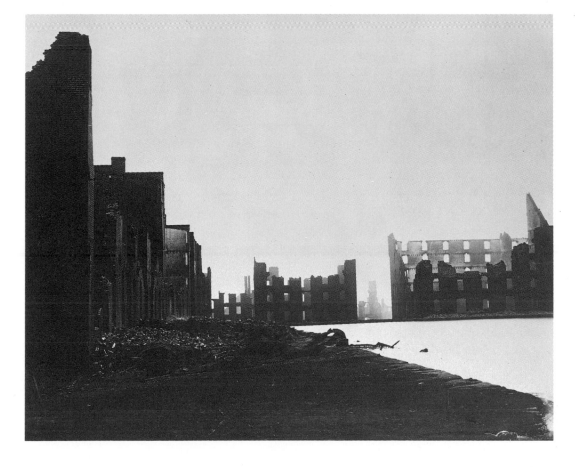

Left *Ruins of Richmond*, 1863–4. Albumen print by Mathew Brady. Chillingly evocative of the aftermath of war. (Collection, The Museum of Modern Art, New York. Purchase.)

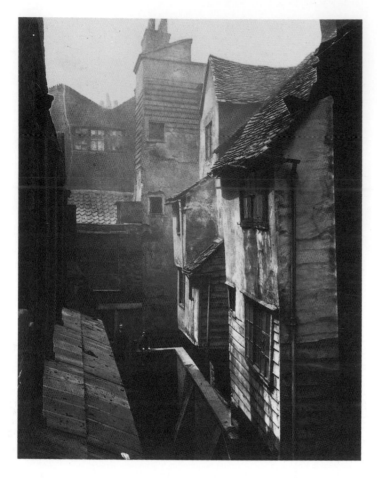

in September 1855 were those he had been commissioned to take, namely portraits and scenes. There were no action shots. Technical and physical constraints may account for this – collodion performed poorly in the heat of a Crimean summer and Fenton had not only broken several ribs in an accident when he first arrived but had also contracted cholera. Working conditions were also appalling – on one occasion, close to the battle front, the van he brought from England as a travelling darkroom had its roof blown off.

However, personal sensibilities are a more likely explanation for the lack of total coverage. Fenton was not asked to comment but report, and report in support of one anxious client – the British government – and a royal patron. It is likely that even without these moral restrictions the pictures would not have been different; they had no real precedent. So Fenton simply did the best he could. Some agreed with the review of Fenton's exhibition in *The Observer* which considered it unsatisfactory, partly because he made no attempt 'to photograph the armies in action.' However, some viewers paid more careful attention to Fenton's prints and bothered to interpret them, remarkable when one considers the Victorian notion of photography as fact unadorned by meaning. The *Photographic Journal* noted the 'terrible suggestions' of one of his pictures, untypically not a portrait but showing the cannonball-strewn aftermath of a battle at 'The Valley of the Shadow of Death' (that Inkerman ravine where 'The Six Hundred' of the British Light Brigade rode to mass destruction because of military ineptitude). And the *Literary Gazette*, reporting on Fenton's pictures of Balaklava Harbor (where he

photographed the war's background) detected the ironies of 'the quays everywhere covered with cattle for sustaining life, and piles of shot and shell for annihilating it.' Fenton's was a subtle document of a carelessly organized war; his portraits were filled with understatement – boy officers adopting military bravado to look like men, soldiers looking like ordinary Englishmen dressed for a part in some ghastly play and senior officers displaying 'character' sufficient to overcome the absurdity of their position. One of these offered Fenton 'his commission, medals and other advantages if I would only get him safe back to Pall Mall.' The Crimea was unpleasant beyond belief and Fenton's job was to report, make it truthful yet leave it publicly palatable.

War was ideal subject matter for nineteenth-century photographers – it brought the medium's ability to present evidence of man's actions to a public desperate for first-hand information and presented a new challenge to picture makers. Nowhere was this more true than in America in 1861 when Civil War broke out. 'A battle scene is a fine subject' said the *American Journal of Photography*'s editor, 'We hope to see a photograph of the next battle ... There will be little danger in the active duties for the photographer must be beyond the smell of gunpowder or his chemicals will not work.' His excitement is obvious but the suggestion of 'little danger' naive. Where Fenton had pictured war as somehow remote from killing, photographers of the American Civil War took on death and destruction as being as much a part of the scenario as portraits of generals, and devastation was shown head-on alongside the more homely aspects of camp life.

Pre-eminent among the Civil War's chroniclers was Mathew Brady, who almost lost his life at the battle of Bull Run in 1861 when his darkroom wagon was caught in cross fire. He was an extraordinary mix of entrepreneur and man with a mission. Established as a successful daguerreotype portraitist (he won a prize for this at London's Great Exhibition in 1851), Brady had developed the idea of dividing activities at his studios into individual functions. The client, probably persuaded by seeing a Brady portrait of Lincoln or some other worthy, would arrive at the handsomely furnished studio and be pictured by an 'operator.' Behind the scenes a battery of other workers took over the processing, finishing and mounting. Meanwhile Brady himself took care of business; he was an adroit publicist and charmed the leaders of New York and Washington society into his studio. When the war between the Union and Confederacy broke out Brady saw another photographic opportunity. This time it was as a reporter able to sell his works to a news-hungry public. Repeating his studio successes he raised $100,000 and organized a crew of photographers to cover the scenes of battle. Like Fenton in the Crimea they used collodion, coating their glass plates in horse-drawn vans (called a 'What is it?' wagon by the soldiers). They pictured 'the compassion of the hospital, the romance of the bivouac, the pomp and panoply of the field review – aye, even the cloud of conflict, the flash of the battery, the afterwreck and anguish of the hard-won field' as one report described it.

Brady's team included Timothy O'Sullivan, George Barnard and Alexander Gardner, all excellent photographers. There were others whose names are not recorded; Brady's policy was to mark each picture as his own. Between them this 'photographic corps' recorded the major battles of the war in over 7000 images, many as large as 20 x 16 inches. They present an evocation of destruction that ends with the Northern victory shown in the shattered buildings of Southern cities – silhouetted shards and ruins so elegantly composed they might be studio sets, except for their quality as reminders of the melancholies of human intervention.

Mathew Brady was not alone in recognizing opportunity in war photography. The military, particularly on the Union side, saw a propaganda value in documenting events, and this persuaded them to give photographers total access. Another, more sinister, use for photographic evidence emerged in Europe during the short but turbulent period of the Paris Commune in 1871. This socialist revolution, which began in reaction to the Franco-Prussian war and the Siege of Paris, enjoyed a brief success before being brutally suppressed by the French Government. In one week in May 40,000 Communards were killed and photographers were called to make grisly records of the dead street-fighters and executed revolutionaries. Some of the dead had met their end after being identified as Communards from photographs taken while they posed triumphantly before a vandalized statue of Emperor Napoleon I. Worse still, from a photographic point of view, was a scheme involving fakes showing apparent Communard atrocities pictured by a photographer called Appert. Once it was realized that truth and photography were no longer synonymous, that the medium might be subverted and used for distortion, its innocence was lost.

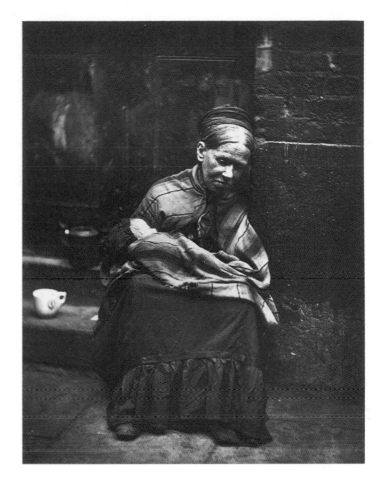

However, if photography had fallen from grace, there were few takers for its new potential and the pleasant odour of documentary purity survived to fan the fires of social change. Paris was but one city where industrialization had brought a new and restless spirit. A few years before the Paris

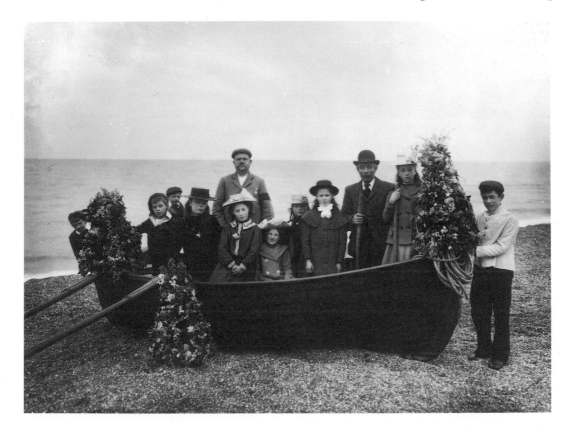

Above 'The Crawlers' from *Street Life in London*, 1877-8, an early but effective example of social documentary. Woodburytype by John Thomson. (Victoria and Albert Museum.)

Opposite *Old Houses in Bermondsey Street, c*1875, a carbon print by Henry Dixon. (Victoria and Albert Museum.)

Left *Garland Day at Abbotsbury*, 1903, by Sir Benjamin Stone, a Member of Parliament who made photographing disappearing festivals and customs a personal project. (Reproduced by permission of Birmingham Public Libraries.)

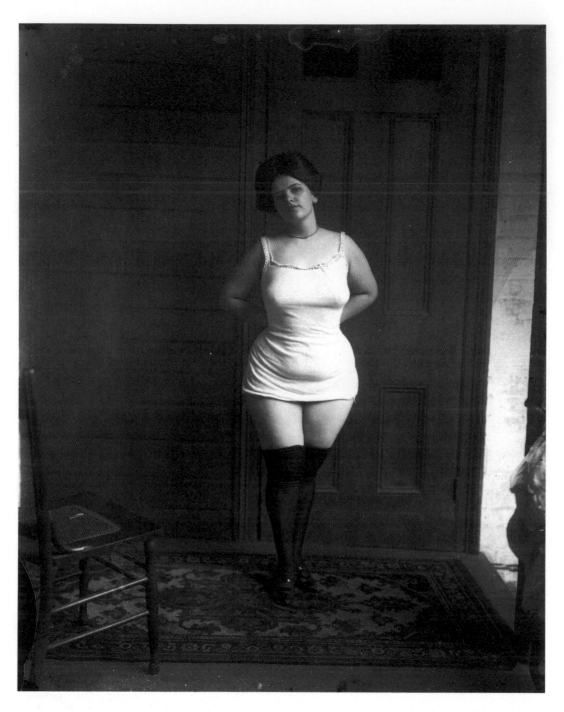

Left *Prostitute, New Orleans, c* 1912. Contemporary print by Lee Friedlander from a negative by E J Bellocq. Otherwise a commercial photographer, Bellocq is remembered for his portraits that bring sensitivity to authenticity. (Courtesy Lee Friedlander.)

Commune Karl Marx had been in London working on *Das Kapital*, his critique of the new order. And while few in England would agree with his solutions to problems of change in society, it was becoming painfully obvious that a great divide separated those caught up in the gains of industry and empire from those too small for the mesh of plenty's net. Slums proliferated, along with drunkeness and disease. One sector of Victorian morality deemed this distasteful and while the golden age of pornography and child prostitution boomed, organizations like the Salvation Army were founded. Their aim was to redeem poverty-stricken sinners, return them to god and thus save them from themselves. While Marx wrote of labor as the basis of an evenly distributed national wealth, those persuaded by capitalism's obvious attractions saw city squalor as a sign of a departure from Christian right. Christianity met commerce somewhere

down the line and slum clearances began. With them came photographic documentation. At first the motive for making records was more romantic/historic than reformist – ancient city centers at bursting point were being torn down and what better medium than photography to preserve the past and show the future how life might have been but for progress?

With Thomas Annan's work in Glasgow in 1868 the style changed. Annan's photographs were commissioned by the Glasgow Improvement Trust and side-stepped nostalgia in favor of optical accuracy. His slum pictures, of buildings rather than people, are directly constructed and reek of dank decay. Equally powerful and similarly involved in the web strung between record and reform were John Thomson's pictures *Street Life in London*. When he returned from China (see Chapter 3), Thomson set about documenting the downside of London in the company of writer Adolphe Smith.

Their collaboration was published between 1876 and 1877 as a partwork, the photographs (reproduced in woodburytype) supplemented by Smith's sometimes sensationalist reports of working-class life. *Street Life in London* was designed to arouse middle-class sympathy and borrowed something of the style of Henry Mayhew's book *London Labour and London Poor* (1850). Mayhew's book had been illustrated with wood engravings made from daguerreotypes by Richard Beard; Thomson and Smith looked to the authenticity of wood-burytypes – with their facsimile feel – in the hope that their report would squash any accusations of underrating or ex-aggerating the situation. But for all their noble intentions they were still on-lookers, strangers down dark alleys, and their readers – still wondering at Charles Darwin's ideas of evolution – were treated to a believable glimpse into what they thought might prove to be a human sub-species. Physi-cally they were like themselves but somehow lacking in the spiritual means to join in prosperity. Poverty was God's reward for sin.

Thomson's investigations were the outcome of his natural curiosity, the same curiosity that had taken him East. The plight of London's poor certainly stirred humanitarian senses within him, but as *Street Life in London*'s preface pointed out, he and Smith were interested in 'true *types*,' not individuals, nor cause and effect. Christian ethics, identifying improve-ment in social conditions as a 'good work' for the advan-taged, seemed to find general evidence more useful (or

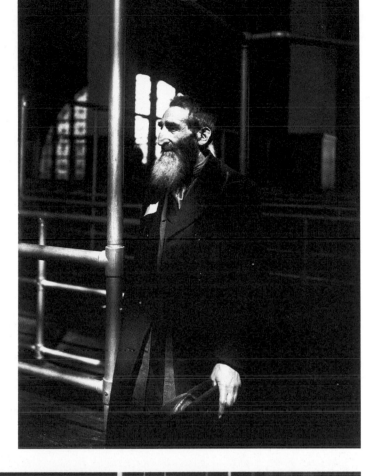

Above right *Elderly Jewish Immigrant, Ellis Island, New York,* 1905, by Lewis Hine, a photographer of social conviction whose work changed laws. (International Museum of Photography at George Eastman House.)

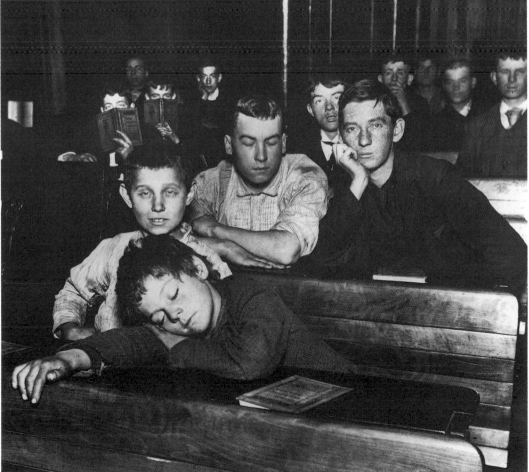

Right *Nightschool in the Seventh Avenue Lodging House,* nd, by Jacob A Riis. Riis used photography as a weapon in his fight to improve New York slums. (Jacob A Riis Collection, Museum of the City of New York.)

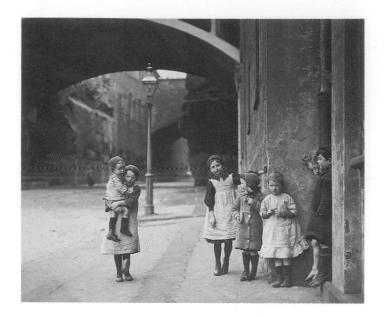

palatable) than specific fact. Dr Thomas Barnado, whose founding work for children continues to this day, was one so moved. Barnado set up a Home for Working and Destitute Lads and employed photographers (one was Oscar Rejlander, see Chapter 3) to show before and after scenes which were sold to well-wishers. These pictures came in pairs showing transformation – a ragged semi-beggar child would be pictured in defeat then re-presented clean and wholesome 'Out delivering Brush Orders' or 'Going to Sunday School.' As a primitive public-relations exercise it now seems obviously cosmetic, but it was effective. From open-ended comment on 'types,' photography was starting to be seen as part of a specific arena of social change.

A swing from nostalgia and romance to positive reform can be seen clearly in works by Jacob Riis, a Danish emigrant to the United States who arrived in 1870. Riis became a reporter in New York, first stop for many who fled poverty in Europe and sought a second chance. They imagined jobs but found instead a nation still reeling from the economic effects of the Civil War. Pressed into tenements, working (if at all) in sweatshops, their existence was as miserable as anything seen by Thomson in London. The popular sentiment of their hosts was that they had 'brought it upon themselves' and Riis looked to ways of proving this otherwise – he wanted a better future for new Americans caught in a downward spiral. When his war of words in the New York *Tribune* and later for Associated Press failed to stir official conscience, he turned to public speaking, illustrating his talks with lantern slides he made himself. Where Thomson used a visual elegance and Barnado a public-relations strategy, Riis looked to gut reactions. He photographed directly, often crudely, and made raw and powerful pictures. Unlike most of his contemporaries, his knowledge of the craft was sketchy, but Riis realized intuitively that a method of making flash pictures, announced in 1887, was perfect for his excursions into the dingy rooms and cellars serving as home for thousands of new arrivals. Riis wanted more than to expose the wretched lifestyles of his subjects – he sought change. As he said

himself, his pictures were to show 'as no mere description could, the misery and vice' and to 'suggest the direction in which good might be done.' As it was, the good he hoped for could only be made clear in his texts – Riis's pictures alone are grimly detailed tales of human woe. *How the Other half Lives*, a book of words and pictures, was published in 1890.

Jacob Riis hoped for a better America, his successor as a photographic reformer, Lewis Hine, tried to show where that land might be found. 'I wanted to show,' said Hine, 'the things that had to be corrected. I wanted to show the things that had to be appreciated.' The individuals he portrayed, at work in factories and mines, on the streets and in their homes, presented a positive sense of their spiritual worth as human beings. No matter the often depressing background, Hine found children to be angels, pit workers graceful in their grimy labors and families a bulwark against tenement hardship. Trained as a sociologist, Hine worked as a teacher at the Ethical Culture School in New York City (one of his students was Paul Strand, see Chapters 5 and 7). Ethical Culture was a strongly humanist religion and its precepts of human dignity informed Hine's photography. He began using the camera in 1903 as a teaching aid and by 1906 was freelancing for the National Child Labor Committee. The Committee had been established to end exploitation and Hine now resigned from teaching and, calling himself a 'social photographer,' travelled more than 50,000 miles in search of images. His goal was to show America's future, children, being kept from their education and forced to work long

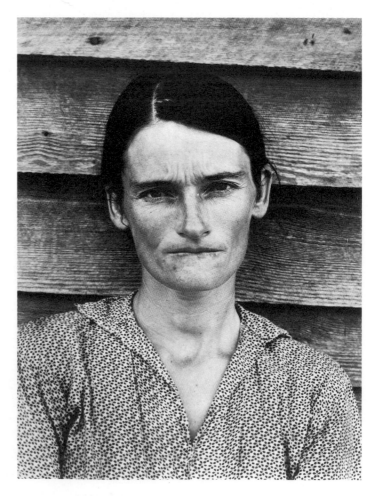

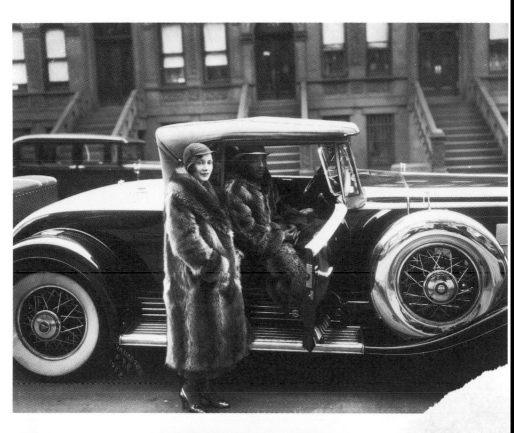

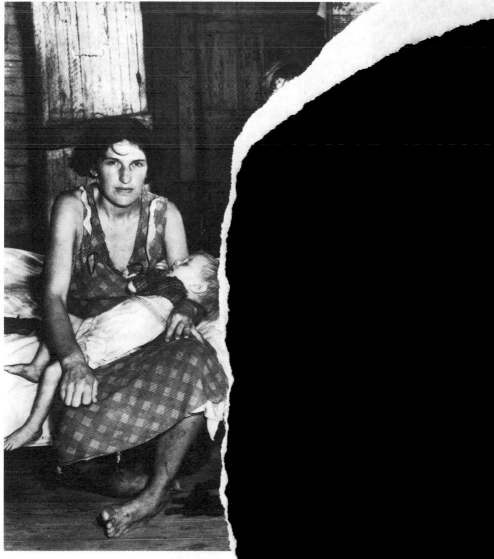

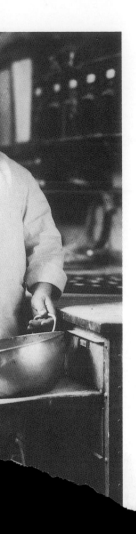

hours for low pay in mills, mines, canning works and farms. Hine's style was direct, confrontational, but warm. Where Riis looked for gut reaction Hine was more a man of the heart, using tenderness and human worth as a visual contradiction to the indignation poor housing and sweatshop labor might induce. His was a worthwhile and persuasive strategy; child labor laws were eventually introduced and Hine himself, considered a success, was able to find other work in similar fields.

In 1918 the American Red Cross made Hine a Captain and sent him to Europe to photograph their relief mission in France and the Balkans. When he returned the following year Hine felt at the peak of his powers. His work was known and respected; beyond the institutions for whom he worked a broader public had emerged. As the *Literary Digest* wrote in comment on an exhibition in the early 1920s, 'In his pursuits as a sociological investigator and recorder, Mr Hine had, whether consciously or not, employed his instincts as an artist.' He began a series of 'work projects,' trying to show workers as positive and individual contributors to new industrialization and its challenges. Man and machine were shown in compositional harmony – the one a hero with 'brains and toil,' the other a symbol of strength and monumentality. From this came a commission to photograph the Empire State Building in construction – America's most potent symbol of mastery and an edifice reaching higher than any man had built before. Hine pictured its progress from level to ever-higher level, compiled in his book *Men at Work* (1932). He wrote in the introduction that they were ... of courage, skill, daring and imagination.' After this his ... to falter – he was a respected pioneer but others, ... now caught in the Depression, came forward

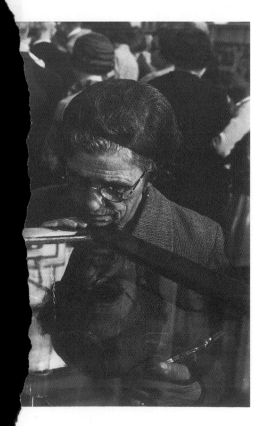

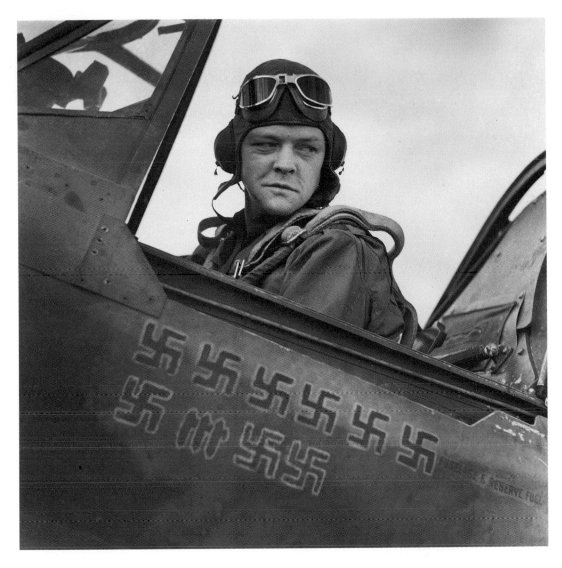

Left *English Fighter Pilot,* 1941, by Robert Capa, a Hungarian-born war photographer who began in Berlin, covered the Spanish Civil War (1933) and lost his life in Indochina (1954). (© Robert Capa/ Magnum; courtesy John Hillelson Agency.)

with similar concerns for humanism and egalitarianism but more specific intent. Where Hine had generalized the 'productive' spirit of man and had wanted to 'interpret' industry, a new group doubted. Industry and machine-age economics were crumbling as the stock market slid – new initiatives were needed if human worth and fulfilment were to be preserved.

In the summer of 1935 Roy Stryker, a young economics teacher at Columbia University, was called to Washington and given the brief of directing an Historical Section of the newly formed Resettlement Administration (RA). Stryker previously had been responsible for picture research for the textbook *American Economic Life and the Means of its Improvement* (1925). He knew the field and how words and pictures could be brought together effectively. The RA, part of President Roosevelt's 'New Deal' for the United States, was aimed at helping small farmers; hit as hard as the riveters, steelworkers and stonemasons who constructed the Empire State Building, farmers were desperate. Their livelihood had always been precarious but during the Depression crop failures, land erosion and dispossession from their farms were forcing a rapid exchange from a cornerstone position in the American ideal to the vagaries of a migrant worker's lot. The RA was set up to make low-interest loans, promote more

efficient farming methods and give aid to migrants who travelled from town to town in search of work. Stryker, employed to organize a record of what the government was doing to alleviate such poverty, decided photography was the key. He knew of Lewis Hine but thought his work too old-fashioned for this task.

The South suffered most; 'Humanity Hits Bottom in the Deep South' stated a 1937 magazine headline. It was to document this distress that Stryker sent the department's first photographer – Arthur Rothstein. Others were to join him in what was to become photography's greatest documentary project – a massive portrait of an unhappy nation. He was followed by Theo Jung, Ben Shahn, Walker Evans, Dorothea Lange, Carl Mydans, Russell Lee, Marion Post Wolcott, Jack Delano, John Vachon and finally John Collier Jnr. For each Stryker assembled a 'shooting script' from which he hoped a detailed image of America in distress would emerge. They were a diverse but highly talented crew: Jung retired quickly; Rothstein was a solid, reliable company man; Shahn an unemployed painter turned photographer; Evans a wilful individualist; Lange a motivated humanist; Mydans a calculating journalist and so on. Each contributed their own ideas to the project (known from 1937 as the FSA or Farm Security Administration) and produced photographs charged with the

121

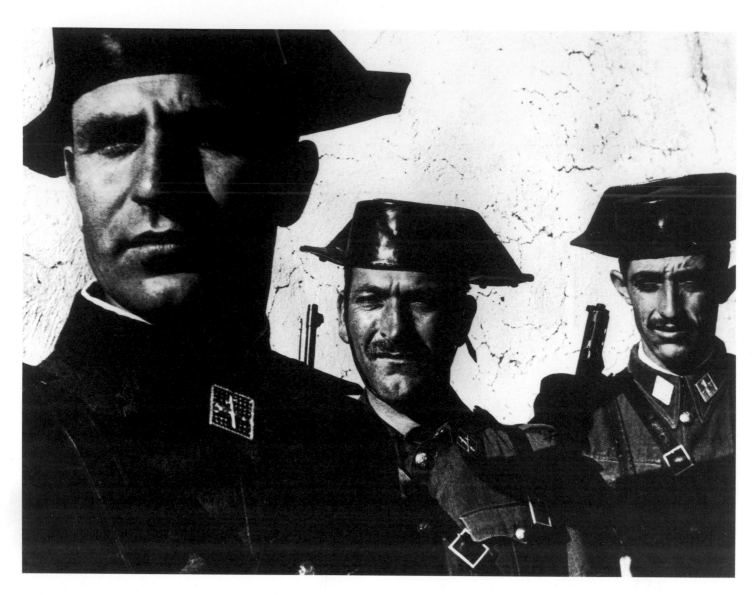

high voltage of a nation in trouble. Their pictures were for history (and so remain – in America's Library of Congress) and thus avoided overt sensationalism, but were soon used beyond their immediate utility as archive and illustration to government publications. Some, like those made by Shahn and Rothstein, appeared in newly emerging picture magazines; others, like Lange's portrait of an Okie madonna mother with wide-eyed child pulling on her breast, found their way to book jackets (in this case John Steinbeck's novel *Their Blood is Strong*). The FSA's Information Division was a government project made bold by those who worked for it, seen to succeed in its own time and later as an unprecedented record of the United States in a critical era. It is a perfect example of how photography can capture, hold and finally mold national consciousness. From Lange's compassionate tales of West Coast breadlines to Evans's richly detailed visual audit of ordinary life in the deep South, the FSA project wrote concepts of documentary photography large in people's minds as a means of examining society.

With changes of personel the project lasted until 1942, when it became absorbed into the Office of War Information. But documentary was not confined to the United States though during this period nothing of similar scale was under-

taken in Europe or Australasia, and Africa, Asia, China and the Middle and Far East were still culturally (in most cases actually) colonized. In Germany August Sander was undertaking an ambitious project to document his peoples according to type – class, trade, profession and so on – which resulted in a powerful but generally hidden body of work that has only recently been open to inspection. In Germany, too, picture magazines were growing alongside improvements in reproduction and this provided a public platform for 'human interest' photography. Wide-ranging in content, these pictures were made possible in part by developments first in large-aperture lenses (the Ermanox, introduced in 1924 had an f2 then an f1.5 lens and was sold under the banner 'what you can *see* you can *photograph*') then of 'miniature' cameras using 35mm film (first was the Leica which also came on to the market in 1924). Two magazines in particular led the field: the *Münchner Illustrierte Presse* and the *Berliner Illustrierte Zeitung*. The latter had used photographs since the 1890s but these two magazines, spurred on by commercial rivalry, refined a new form, the 'picture story,' and helped develop the area of photography we now call photojournalism. Pictures, edited to form a narrative and designed to entertain and inform, were used with a minimum of words to bring the

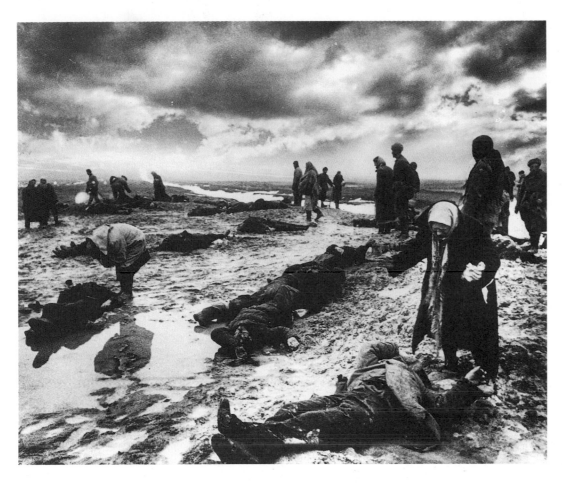

world to a magazine buyer's door. Paris nightlife, Berlin lowlife, political intrigues, life on the farm, the circus, sport and travel all appeared. Everyday images were given an exotic tinge: new and faster shutter speeds halted action at a gestural climax; small cameras revealed private lives in candid pictures of politicos and diplomats at work; far distances were brought close to home in reports from the Pacific, Africa and India. They were heady days. In Germany Erich Salomon, Tim Gidal, Felix Man, Wolfgang Weber, Kurt Hübschmann, Alfred Eisenstaedt, Otto Umbo and Martin Munkacsi were among the best. In France André Kertész and Brassaï (Hungarian emigrés like Munkacsi) ignored the drama of politics and prowled the streets in search of intimacies snatched from polarized, hidden worlds. Prostitutes and the monastic life were all part of their repertoire.

National Socialism brought this era to an end. When Hitler came to power in Germany in 1933 fear drove many who had ascended in the previous decade to live elsewhere. Photographers, picture editors and journalists left en masse; fear of life for Jews and fear for independence for Gentiles created an exodus. They hurried to Britain, to the United States and to France.

Stefan Lorant (another Hungarian), editor of *Münchner Illustrierte,* arrived in Britain in 1934, helped found a new picture magazine, *Weekly Illustrated,* and later edited *Picture Post.* Gidal, Hübschmann (now calling himself Hutton) and Man joined him. Salomon went to Holland, eventually to die in Auschwitz, Eisenstaedt and Munkacsi chose the United States where they found work with *Life.* A magazine based

on the German model and founded by Henry Luce in 1936, *Life* followed *Time* and *Fortune* to success then legend.

Equally legendary was Britain's *Picture Post.* Published by Edward Hutton it lasted until 1957. Among the young photographers to work for *Picture Post* were Bill Brandt (see Chapter 7), Bert Hardy and Thurston Hopkins. This magazine's thrust was towards society and changing values. Similarly *Life* was first directed towards current issues – its first

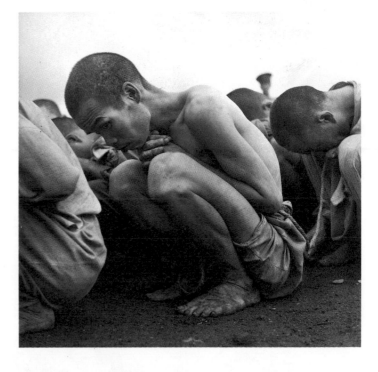

123

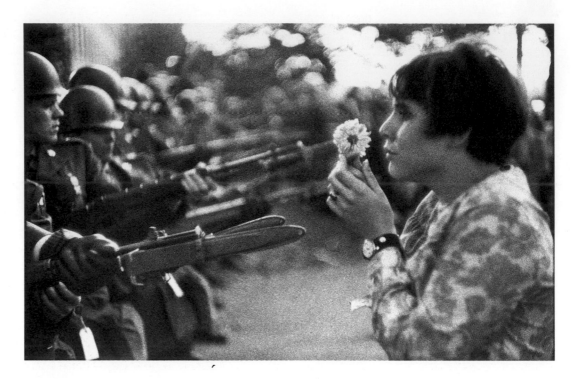

Right *Anti-Vietnam Demonstration, Washington,* 1967, by Marc Riboud; a symbol of dissent preceding the youth revolution. (© Marc Riboud/Magnum; courtesy John Hillelson Agency.)

cover, of Fort Peck dam, was by Margaret Bourke-White who used journalistic ethics to expose the United States in ways denied FSA photographers in government employ. Change, exchange of ideas and rapid shifts in style marked the magazine's movement from passive but pictorially vital commentary to propaganda. Photography's objectivity still held sway and some photographers hoped that picturing social ills might alter balances in aid of those whom fortune did not favor.

The 1930s was a troubled era. As Hitler began his reconstruction of a Germany wrecked by inflation, France fell into a period of strikes, demonstrations and demands for govern-

ment by a Popular Front. In Spain pro- and anti-Fascist faction quarrels grew into a civil war, while in Britain rising unemployment spelt out bitter divisions between those who had and those who had not. Where early photojournalists had looked to celebrating the ordinary, making it 'larger than life' or making candid pictures of hidden worlds, younger photographers of this period felt themselves to be participators in the politics and conscience of their times. Young men like Robert Capa and Chim Seymour, Hungarian and Polish respectively and both working from Paris, saw 'human interest' invested in the individual and made photographs requiring the viewer to share in the experiences of that

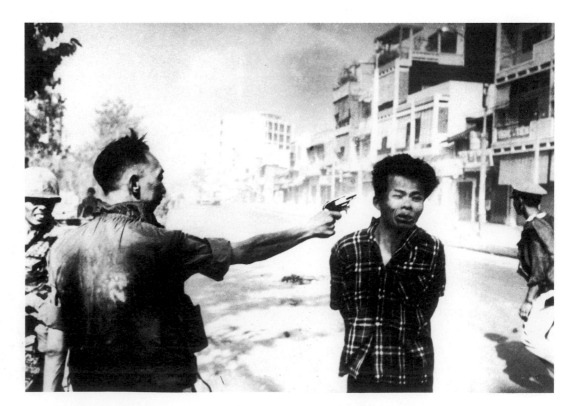

Right *Saigon, Vietnam,* 1 February 1968. This photograph by Eddie Adams of a Vietcong officer assassinated by a brigadier general stands as one of the most memorable images of the Vietnam war. (Associated Press.)

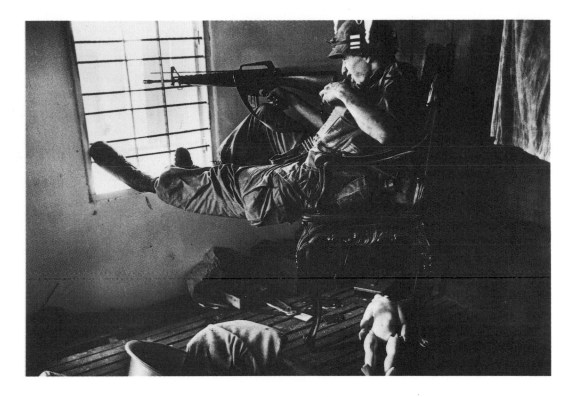

Right *Vietnam,* nd, by Philip Jones Griffiths who compiled the most astute, intelligent coverage of a war yet seen. (© Philip Jones Griffiths/ Magnum; courtesy John Hillelson Agency.)

Below *Biafran Mother and Child,* 1969, by Don McCullin. He said, 'I found a woman feeding her baby, the breasts were old and empty.' (© Don McCullin; courtesy Victoria and Albert Museum.)

particular human being. It was a new kind of image making, dependent on intimacy, fellow feeling, compassion, outrage, intelligence and the heroism seen to surface as men, women and children coped with assaults on human values.

When World War II broke out in 1939, photojournalists were well prepared to record and tell its awful tales: narrative styles had been developed – the 'picture story' was understood; heroism and human suffering as counterparts to conflict were known as a genre; and the value of visual communication appreciated as a means of information and propaganda. On all sides picture magazines flourished – *Life, Picture Post, Parade, Parada, Images, Signal* and *Soviet War Weekly* from the United States, Britain, Poland, France, Germany and Russia used pictures by Robert Capa, Leonard McCombe, Bela Zola, Tim Gidal, Harold Lechenpurg, Dmitri Baltermans and many others. Their stories were of triumph in tragedy, human sorrow and resilience.

After the war photojournalists found a new and different outlet for their talents. The Western world wanted reassurance, renewal, a future. And while Japan tried to come to terms with postnuclear devastation and Germany with Allied control, a group of photographers saw fresh opportunities in moving out of direct magazine employment and into a more ambitious role as a co-operative agency offering world coverage and picture stories of their own devising. Made bold by the praise their war work received in *Time* and *Life*, Robert Capa and George Rodger (who had met as colleagues covering European battles and frequently discussed a photography beyond editorial sanction) were joined in 1947 by Henri Cartier-Bresson, Bill Vandivert and Chim Seymour. They gave themselves a champagne title, Magnum, and resolved to interpret the world as they, not a desk-bound editor, saw it.

Capa had begun his career in Berlin in 1931 working with Dephot, an early picture agency. Based in Paris from 1933, he

covered the Spanish Civil War, the Japanese attack on China in 1938, then the war in Europe and the foundation of Israel. Rodger had freelanced precariously in London before the

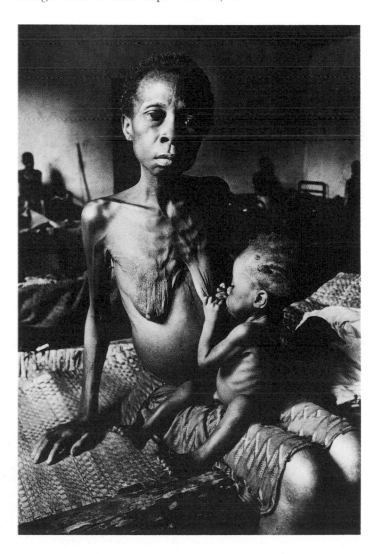

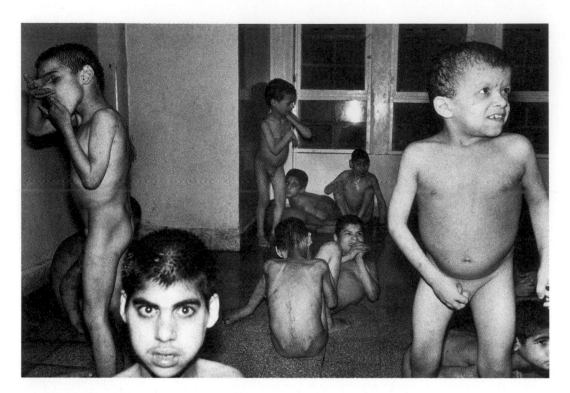

Left *Children in a mental hospital after their dormitory was destroyed by Israeli shooting, Beirut, Lebanon, 1982,* by Chris Steele-Perkins. (© Chris Steele-Perkins; courtesy Magnum Photos Ltd.)

Right *Blind boy, 1961,* by Charles Harbutt. (Archive Pictures Inc.)

Below *Tomoko in Her Bath, Minamata, Japan, 1972,* by W Eugene Smith, from an extensive project on mercury pollution and its effect on a Japanese town. (© 1975 Aileen & W Eugene Smith; Black Star.)

war, then become a photoreporter for *Life*, first offering stories on how Britain needed and used American aid then 'chasing the war for 75,000 miles by sea, land and air.' He went to Burma, Africa, Italy and France, ending the war by photographing liberated concentration camps. Vandivert had worked for *Time* and left Magnum almost as soon as he joined. Seymour had also photographed the Spanish Civil War, and he and Capa had shared a darkroom. He was in Mexico when World War II broke out, went to the United States, became a citizen and served in photoreconnaissance in

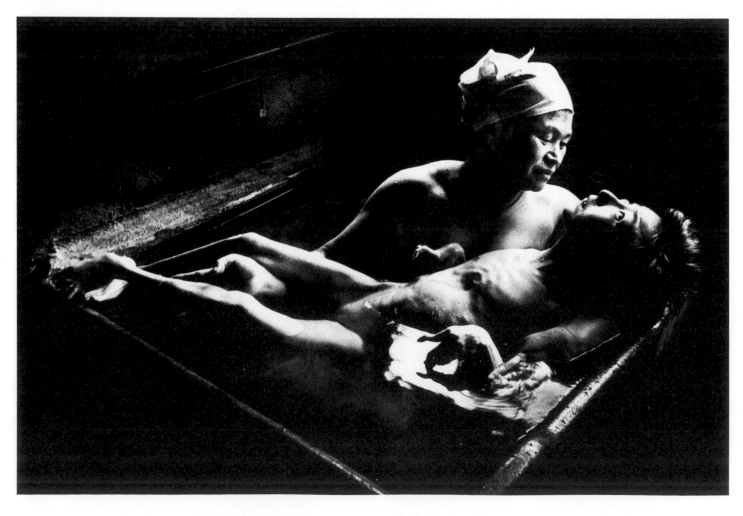

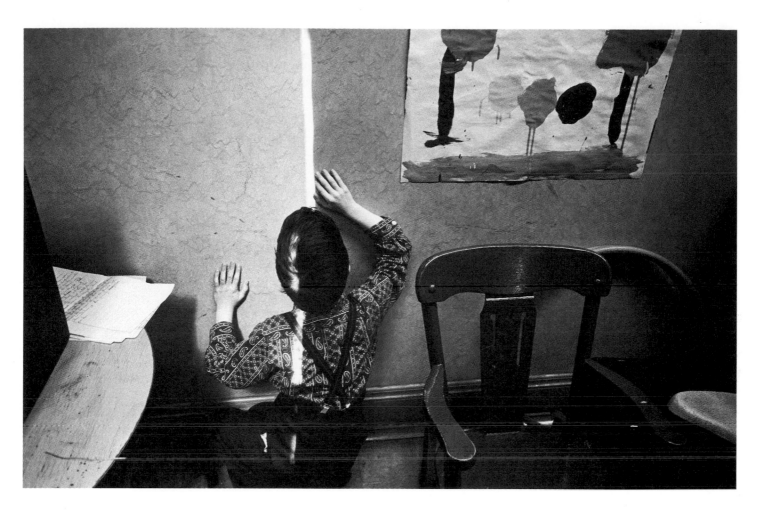

the US Army. When the war ended he returned to Europe for UNICEF to photograph children in the aftermath. Cartier-Bresson, French and now the best known of Magnum's founders, had been excited both by filmmaking and by the photographs of Man Ray and Atget, learned from the work of Kertész and become a prisoner of the German Army of Occupation in 1940. In 1943 he escaped and joined the French resistance, eventually working for the US Office of War Information. Magnum wanted to marry independence with sound marketing; they hoped to create a journalistic niche involving finding, photographing and selling stories of the highest quality. They would be free but work together. With offices in Paris and New York, their first joint project, proposed by Capa, was 'People are People the World Over,' an affirmation of family life across the globe.

The benign concepts behind 'People are People' were perfect for a world in reconstruction where global unity seemed a worthwhile goal. Those same concepts led to 'The Family of Man,' a major exhibition at the Museum of Modern Art, New York, directed by Edward Steichen which began in 1955. Steichen and many of his colleagues believed that photographers had the new role of explaining 'man to his fellow man and to himself.' But by the time the show opened Capa had died, victim of a landmine in Indo-China (soon to become Vietnam). In 1956 Seymour also was killed, in the confusion surrounding the end of the Suez Crisis. Other, newer, Magnum recruits also were to meet extreme ends while trying to reconcile man with his fellow man – Werner

Bischof, for example, a Swiss who had worked for *Picture Post* and came to Magnum in 1949, died while on assignment in Peru. But Magnum's strength remained; it lay in harnessing the skills of photographers sufficiently gifted and intelligent to inspire editorial confidence in their abilities to find stories. Some, like Cartier-Bresson, acquired the status of artist, others were content with the reporter's role, but all were committed to ideas of individual vision and a personal point of view.

Individualism, the notion of photographers making 'personal' pictures, was an important concept to postwar journalist-photographers. They were growing restless at their status as 'illustrators' and ever more conscious of how decision makers in image selection, juxtaposition and size could affect public reaction and reading of their work. Magnum wanted freedom for its members to suggest, shoot and edit stories; Henri Cartier-Bresson once said that he respected 'reality more than editors.'

Outside the co-operative some photographers felt the same way. Most famous, or notorious, was W Eugene Smith, an ambitious young photographer who joined the staff of *Life* magazine in 1939. Smith's career epitomized photography's ideas of the journalist as hero and truth teller – his was a world of struggle but no compromise and he resigned from *Life* in 1955 in dispute over their use of his material. He described himself as a 'photographer-artist working in journalism' and produced some of the most memorable picture stories of the postwar years. Smith's view was that the photographer must

Right By Eugene Richards from his book *Exploding Into Life* (1986), a collaboration with Dorothea Lynch. (© Eugene Richards/Magnum; courtesy John Hillelson Agency.)

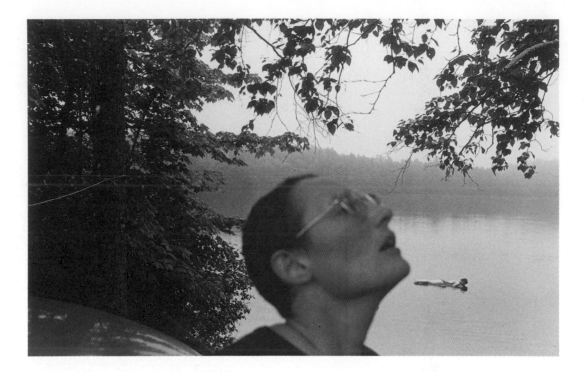

Below *Falkland Road, Bombay, India*, nd, by Mary Ellen Mark, from *Falkland Road*, her book on Bombay's red light district. (Archive Pictures Inc.)

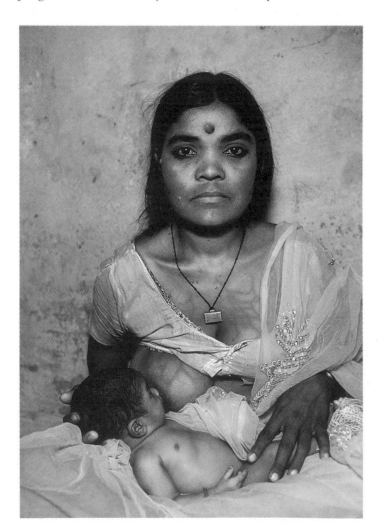

'bear the responsibility for his work and its effect ... But because he does not wish to offend the editors who pay him his bread money, the photographer frequently tries to make his story conform to someone else's shortsighted or warped judgment.' Smith's essays were wide in scope, from combat photographs during World War II to an exosé of the effects of industrial pollution in the Japanese town of Minamata. His stance was always moral, his mood compassionate, and his working methods rigorous. For one essay on the city of Pittsburgh begun in 1955, he made nearly 10,000 pictures over a period of two years. 'Pittsburgh' in its finished form as published in *Popular Photography* ran to 37 pages and covered the community in its entirety. His talent was for contrasts – using the somber end of the black-and-white spectrum for its emotional value he would show dignity in distress, human warmth as a force to counter evil and the human condition as a repository of noble thoughts and feelings. Such dramas, played out on the pages of magazines, gave Smith a rare status among his colleagues. The puritan undertones of his philosophy, his struggles to retain his integrity and his powerful (if melodramatic) vision were all held as models for the committed photographer. He was seen as a champion who fought first for human causes then for photographer's rights; he was revered, emulated and called 'the greatest photojournalist of all time.'

Smith worked for *Life* during its most impressive years, when, with its rival *Look*, picture magazines were a major medium of communication within the United States. In Britain *Picture Post* was going strong, selling well over a million copies weekly. Unlike European equivalents now, which tend towards hard news, they concentrated on features. Social issues were important to *Picture Post*. 'Is There a British Colour Bar?' asked a 1949 headline, and answered it positively in words but mainly pictures. *Life* looked more towards stability and affirmations of the American way of life. 'Sunday in Missouri,' pictures by Ralph Morse and Cornell Capa (Robert's brother) idealized small-town values. The calm on both sides of the Atlantic was shattered, momentarily, with the war in Korea. For *Picture Post*, Korea was a decisive issue. A report sent by James Cameron with

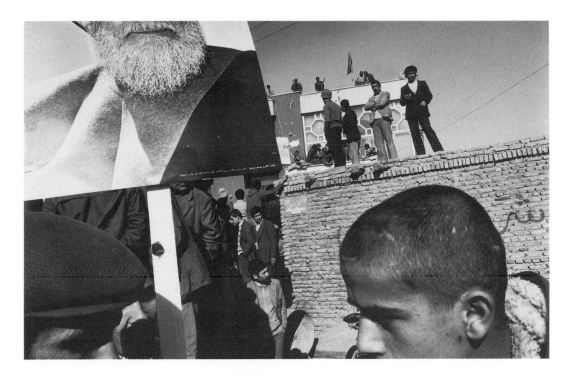

Right *Iran,* 1979, by Gilles Peress, cover of *Telex Iran,* an innovatory French book of new-style photojournalism. (© Gilles Peress/ Magnum; courtesy John Hillelson Agency.)

pictures by Bert Hardy pointed to improper treatment of North Korean prisoners by the South. Edward Hulton, the magazine's proprietor, fearing accusations of being pro-Communist, suppressed it and sacked the editor, Tom Hopkinson. With his departure *Picture Post* went into terminal decline and ceased publication in 1957. *Life* and *Look* lasted longer, until 1972, though both have since had occasional short-lived revivals. Competition from television and subsequent falls in advertising revenue were the official reasons for their demise.

Before its departure, *Life* in particular gave extraordinary coverage to the war in Vietnam, a conflict described by some as 'the first media war.' But despite the many pages devoted to pictures of dead, dying and wounded and the unparalleled access given to photographers and television cameramen by 'US military advisors,' the most memorable analytical pictures of Vietnam's troubled fortunes seen in the West appeared in books. The magazine's problem was what W Eugene Smith had called 'warped judgment' – processing images through a hundred New York City newsdesks with claims and counterclaims being hurried through telex and wire-photo machines left little time for the views of actual witnesses to be compared with overt propaganda. What left the camera as clear evidence of ineptitude, poor military tactics or unnecessary brutality might emerge in print as a triumph, albeit within human tragedy. However photographers like Don McCullin who were experienced in the field of man's inhumanity to man made unequivocal statements of disgust at war which no magazine caption could mollify. Others retrieved those pictures sent from the front then syndicated to publications around the world and worked them into a personal, eye-witness statement. *Vietnam Inc.*, a book by Philip Jones Griffiths who spent three years in the war zone, is the most direct, concise visual indictment of war as folly ever made. *Face of North Vietnam* by Marc Riboud,

which attempted to personalize an unknown enemy, is similarly powerful. Ironically, McCullin is English, Jones Griffiths Welsh, and Riboud French. American publishing houses produced both books intact, despite their condemnation of the United States' conduct.

As television gained more and more attention in the hard news and documentary area, photojournalists looked increasingly towards books as an outlet. W Eugene Smith's *Minamata* (1975), his account of Japanese industrial pollution, was published in this way, as were several other notable volumes including *East 100th Street* (1970) by Bruce Davidson, *Black in White America* (1968) by Leonard Freed, *Conversations with the Dead* (1971) by Danny Lyon, *House of Bondage* (1968) by Ernest Cole and *America in Crisis* (1969) edited by Charles Harbutt. All these dealt with the grimness of contemporary life and struggle. Optimism had given way to bleakness. Davidson pictured 'the worst block in Harlem,' Freed the fight for civil rights, Lyon the troubled lives of prisoners in a Texas State penitentiary and Cole the marginalized lives of black South Africans. Making these and books like them required a move from magazine-style presentation with interlocking images, a short narrative, lead pictures, scene setters and so on to a more complex marriage between images and text. Adjustment was uneasy, but by the 1980s the switch is almost complete. *Falkland Road: Prostitutes of Bombay* (1981) on the lives of prostitutes by Mary Ellen Mark is an example, as are *Nicaragua: War in South America* June 79-July 79 (1981) by Susan Meiselas, *Survival Programmes: Britain's Inner City Problems* 1982 by Chris Steele-Perkins, Paul Trevor and Nick Battye, and *Telex Iran* (1983) an account of Islamic revolution by Gilles Peress. Increasingly personal and political, these works represent the furthest the photographic journalist has gone from the days of illustrating editorial ideas. They demonstrate too, how vital still photography remains in a world of accelerating change.

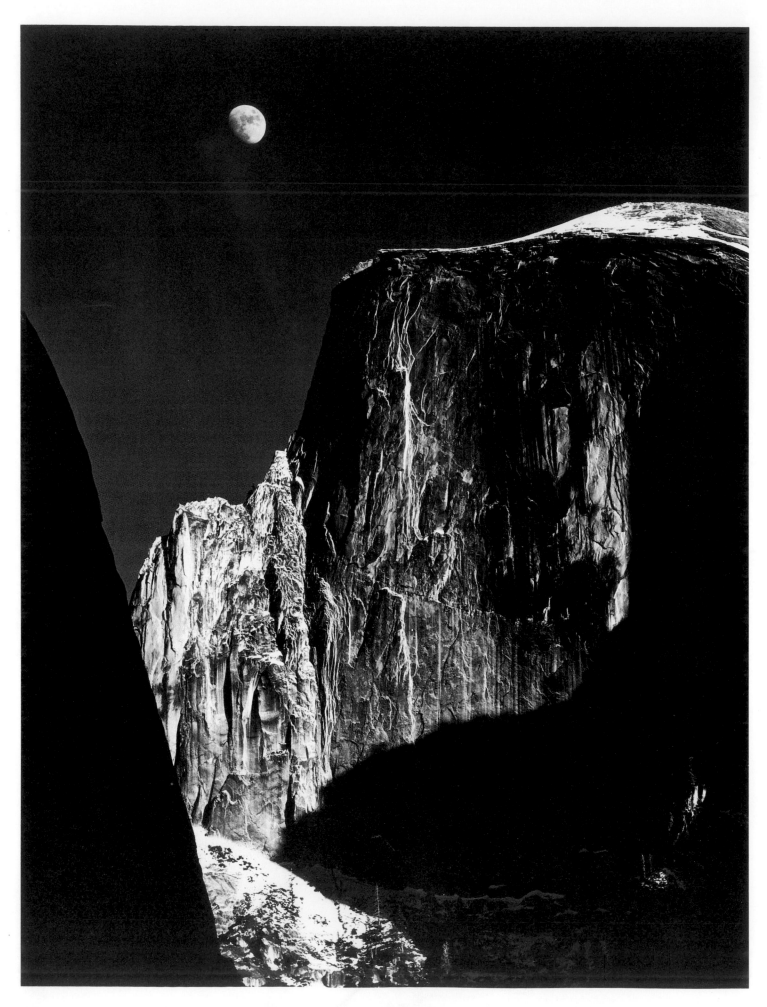

CHAPTER SEVEN

The Rage to See

Formalism and the Photographer

Crucial to ideas of documentary and journalistic photographers was a concept of 'recording,' making direct and generally unequivocal statements of specifics. As they prowled through slums, trod battlefields and sought out social injustice, place and time were of the essence. The reverse was true for picture makers working towards a consciously aesthetic end. Artists in photography – at least those working from the close of World War I until the early 1970s – were attempting to invest their works with timelessness, to transcend any 'sense of place' and reduce their pictures to formal issues. After pictorialism's European flowering, the lush, textured and sweeping impressions of photography as a painterly art took hold in the United States but its ascendency within the avant-garde was short lived. There was a quality to the visual understanding of the new nation still trying to find substance in its own tenuous roots that demanded something other than a photo-technical reconstruction of the swirls and blurs of European culture. A new art in a cosmopolitan culture wanted something expressive of the American spirit – something homespun which would stand fast against all the Old World could throw at it. The United States believed in actuality, fact, frontier possibility and it was this that caused a divide between the photographic art of Europe and the United States. This was the establishment of a photography based first on how things looked, their shape and form, then their meaning, real and metaphoric. While European photographers turned to postwar society in transition for their subject matter, American artists looked towards some sense of finding a universal (or at least Pan-American) spirit in their life and landscape. Formalist photography, for this is what the search became, rose out of the desire for an art showing the American experience as a combination of utility and individuality, reality and mythology, culture and what the writer and poet Walt Whitman called a 'grand race of mechanics, work people and commonality.' Photography was machine based, had democratic potential as it could be used by all and in its clarity and sharpness embodied the puritan foundations of the New World.

Alfred Stieglitz was the energy behind the move towards a new American photography. He was concerned for the spirit of things, which influenced not only his work as a pictorialist (see Chapter 3), but also the exhibitions he organized at *291* (1905-17), the Intimate Gallery (1925-9) and An American Place (1929-46), and finally his editorship of *Camera Work*. Stieglitz's personal style evolved during his career from prize-winning 'spontaneous' pictures of the 1880s (see Chapter 3), through pictorialism, an extended series of portraits of painter Georgia O'Keeffe, who became his wife, and 'Equivalents,' photographs of clouds designed as records of something available to all ('no tax as yet on them free' he wrote in

Left *Moon and Half Dome, Yosemite National Park,* 1960, by Ansel Adams. (Courtesy of the Trustees of the Ansel Adams Publishing Rights Trust. All Rights Reserved.)

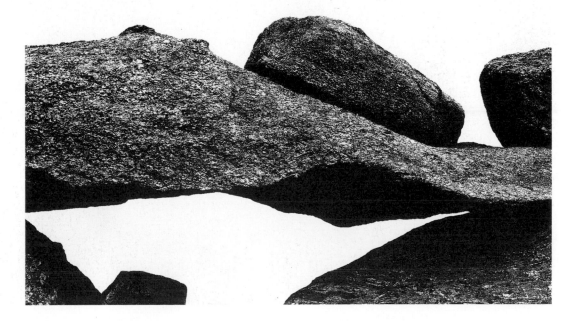

Right *Rocks, Martha's Vineyard,* 1954, by Aaron Siskind, whose transition from documentary photography can be likened to painting's move from a figurative to an expressionist style. (© Aaron Siskind.)

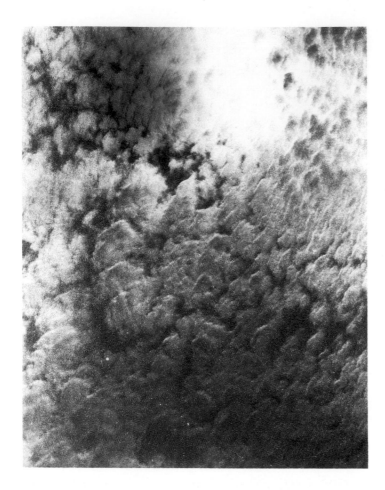

take up the idea of photography as art. And while his subject matter changed over the years, his central ideas remained the same – 'Underlying all,' he wrote in 1942, 'is a natural law and on this natural law rests the hope of mankind.'

Stieglitz encouraged acolytes and attacked detractors. One of the former was Paul Strand, a young man introduced to the atmosphere of photography via a train of events that typifies both the assertiveness of new American photography and its mixed origins. Strand was introduced to photography in 1907 by Lewis Hine (see Chapter 6), one of Strand's teachers at the Ethical Culture School. Hine prompted him to visit *291*, meet Stieglitz and become absorbed in the exciting milieu that surrounded this outpost of the visual avant-garde. Strand's first pictures (see Chapter 5) were taken in the streets of New York, but these quickly gave way to a more contemplative photography that echoed his attitude towards the role of the artist as a 'researcher using materials and techniques to dig into the truth and meaning of the world.' Like Stieglitz, whom he admired deeply, he sensed that natural laws and truth were intertwined, and like Hine he had an implicit belief in the essential nobility of man. 'Photography is only a new road from a different direction,' he wrote in 1917, 'but moving toward the common goal which is life.' Strand looked to the commonplace for his subject matter, seeking a purity of form that would stand for the social idealism taught by the Ethical Culture society. It was a peculiarly American ideal, bringing egalitarianism and sexual purity to individual sanctity; and Strand's photographs, whether of plant forms, architecture or people, assert morality and interior spirit. His plants are clear and clean affirmations of nature as a primal force, his people are heroic, strong and dignified and his

1923) but functioning as metaphors, signs of life to be interpreted. Stieglitz's clouds were equivalent to the human spirit. Alfred Stieglitz was something between a preacher, high priest, prophet and shaman who urged all willing to listen to

Above *Equivalent,* 1972, by Alfred Stieglitz. (Estate of Alfred Stieglitz; courtesy Victoria and Albert Museum.)

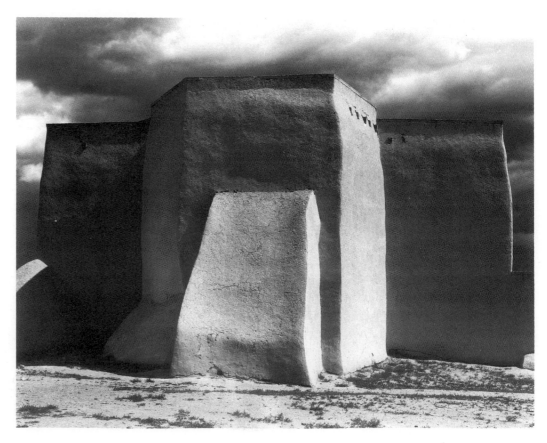

Right *Ranchos de Taos, New Mexico,* 1932, by Paul Strand. (Copyright © 1971, Aperture Foundation, Paul Strand Archive.)

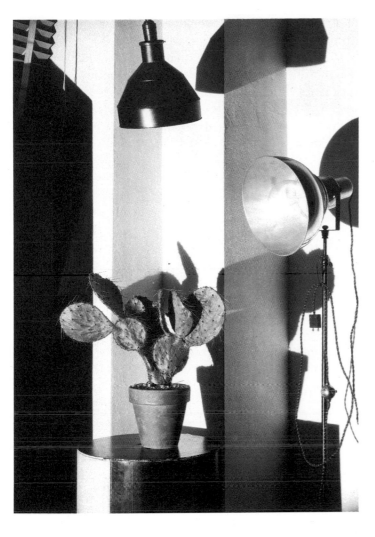

Above *Cactus and Photographer's Lamp, New York*, 1931, by Charles Sheeler, a painter who embraced concepts of modernist photography. (Collection, The Museum of Modern Art, New York. Gift of Samuel Kootz.)

buildings eulogize puritan simplicity. Like Stieglitz, Strand believed in what has been termed 'straight' photography, that is, the unmanipulated image, and in his understanding of objectivity, he wanted to see directly and respond with humanism. He was also adamant that the essentials marking photography apart from other media should be recognized. 'The photographer's problem,' he wrote in 1917, 'is to see clearly the limitations and at the same time the potential qualities of his medium, for it is precisely here that honesty no less than intensity of vision is the pre-requisite of a living expression. This means a real respect for the thing in front of him.' And in 1948 he continued 'It is my conviction that the sense of weight and air in a picture are above all important. A photograph like other graphic arts is two dimensional in actuality but it must give the illusion of third dimension . . . allow the spectator to move into it.' The latter comment was written to a young photographer and published in *Photo Notes*, the newsletter of a New York group bound together by common concerns for photography and a social motivation. The Film and Photo League, the group's first title, had emerged in 1934 as a left-wing organization which soon split into factions. The Photo League, for still photographers, was formed in 1936 as the original organization collapsed and Strand was something of a hero to its members. He had become a filmmaker while retaining his interest in still photography and his form of socialism, based on what Whitman had called 'commonality' years earlier, was an embodiment of the old-style American Dream. The dream was never realized. Disgusted by the rise of right-wing conservatism embodied in Senator McCarthy's notorious witch-hunt for people involved in 'Un-American Activities,' Strand left his

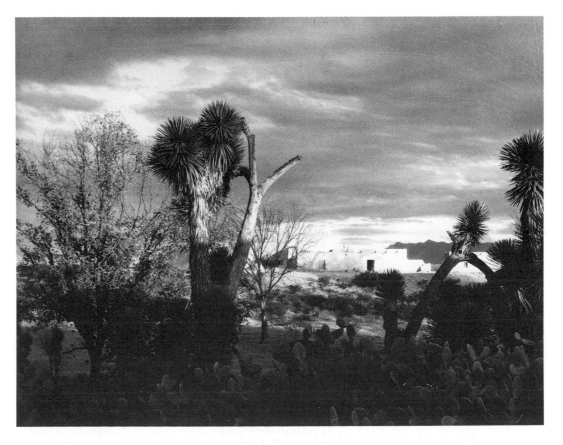

Right *Near Saltillo, Mexico*, 1932, by Paul Strand. (Copyright © 1940, Aperture Foundation, Paul Strand Archive.)

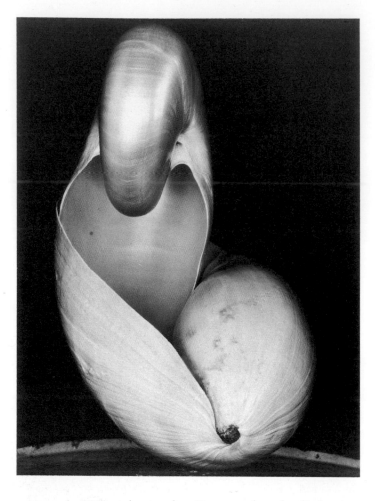

country in 1949 and moved to France, where he died many photographs the richer in 1976. His move may have been hasty, the Ku Klux Klan were indicted alongside subversive

photographers as 'disloyal' to their nation, but it was to be complete and final.

If Paul Strand was committed to 'commonality' and visions of the American experience as a form of freedom, his colleagues in the move towards a photography based on twentieth-century aesthetics were equal in their ardor. Stieglitz ultimately looked to photography as a way of representing ecstasy, indeed he once remarked that for him making a photograph was synonymous with making love. His ecstasy however was spiritual rather than orgasmic. No less a searcher for ecstatic moments was Edward Weston, who approached the world as a source of objects that might give of themselves profoundly when photographed. He once wrote that his pictures 'should be the thing itself and yet more than the thing.'

Born in 1886 Weston was four years Strand's senior. He began his career as a studio portraitist and found time to make highly acclaimed pictorialist pictures as a relief from the daily round of commerce. In 1922 on a trip to meet Stieglitz, Strand and Charles Sheeler (a painter and photographer) he abandoned the soft-focus works tinged with romance that established his reputation and turned to sharply defined straight photographs in the literal, modernist manner. Soon after he abandoned his California studio and travelled to Mexico to live with Tina Modotti, adopting a bohemian lifestyle and living among artists and intellectuals. Weston's move, made at a time when Mexico's cultural life was flowering as never before, enabled him to assess the leap he had made from pictorialist to realist. He kept a Day Book, a journal of his thoughts, ideals, struggles and triumphs and was able to write in 1923 that the camera 'should be used for a

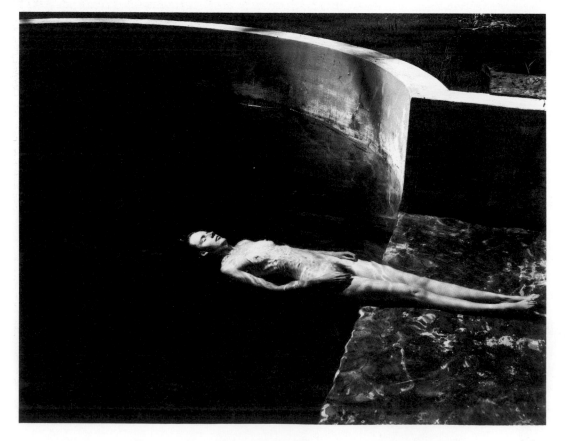

Above left *Two Shells,* 1927, by Edward Weston. (San Francisco Museum of Modern Art, Albert M Bender Collection, Bequest of Albert M Bender. Photo source: Ben Blackwell. 41.2995.)

Left *Nude Floating,* 1939, by Edward Weston. (© 1981 Arizona Board of Regents, University of Arizona. Courtesy Center for Creative Photography.)

Right *Moonrise, Hernandez, New Mexico,* 1941, by Ansel Adams, the most acclaimed twentieth-century landscape photograph. (Courtesy of the Trustees of the Ansel Adams Publishing Rights Trust. All Rights Reserved.)

recording of *life*, for rendering the very substance and quintessence of the *thing itself*, whether it be polished steel or palpitating flesh ... I feel definite in my belief that the approach to photography is through realism.' Weston's Mexican period lasted four years. Smelling revolution in the air, he returned to California, his vision matured and mind set on 'pure photography' as the means through which he might express life.

Weston's homecoming eventually led to Carmel, a village by the Pacific, and there in 1929 he began a most productive period. He photographed daily, obsessively – still lifes, nudes, landscapes, portraits. In each form was invested a sensuous, sculptural delight in transforming subjects through the camera. As Weston developed an aesthetic based on exploiting his own and the medium's capabilities of presenting the natural world, he wanted it seen as freshly found. Reiterating remarks made 20 years earlier, in 1942 Weston wrote: 'An intuitive knowledge of composition in terms of the capacities of his process enables the photographer to record his subject at the moment of deepest perception; to capture the fleeting instant when the light or a landscape, the form of a

cloud, the gesture of a hand, or the expression of a face momentarily presents a profound revelation of life.' The 'life' to which he so often referred and wished to capture and hold through photography was not to be found in the day-to-day routine of simply living because 'the camera lens sees too clearly to be used successfully for recording the superficial.' No, Weston's 'life' resided in the imagination. Stieglitz had found ecstasy in images that might call up interior feeling, Weston wanted something similar – but his pictures had to be firstly 'the thing itself' (in which Stieglitz had small interest) they needed physicality, then to be 'more than the thing.' 'More than' existed in Weston's hidden hopes for his art. During his life he resisted any interpretation of works from this period as anything other than views of what they appeared to be but time reveals them as first darkly then sexually expressive of a restless, at times turbulent, mind. He was trying to reconcile modernist objectivity with interior forces somewhat beyond the puritan American 'spirit.'

This work was enormously successful, in the low-key way an artist using photography might find acclaim. It was Weston, with Steichen, who selected the United States'

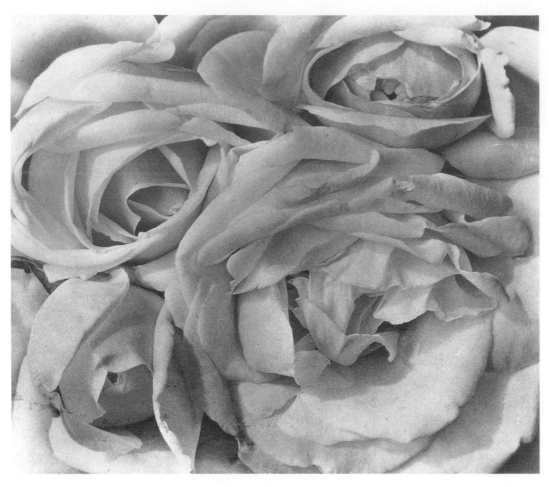

Left *Roses, Mexico,* 1924. Platinum print by Tina Modotti, who lived and worked with Edward Weston. (Collection, The Museum of Modern Art, New York. Gift of Edward Weston.)

Right Outside the conventions of the straight print lay myriad possibilities. This is a solarized (partially reversed) portrait. *Dora Maar* by Man Ray, 1936. (Copyright © Juliet Man Ray.)

contribution to the 1929 exhibition 'Film und Foto' in Germany (see Chapter 5), and Weston who was selected to be the first photographer to receive a John Simon Guggenheim Memorial Fellowship in 1937. The award was financially valuable – it gave Weston a period in which to work without direct money worries – and served as a kind of accolade. At

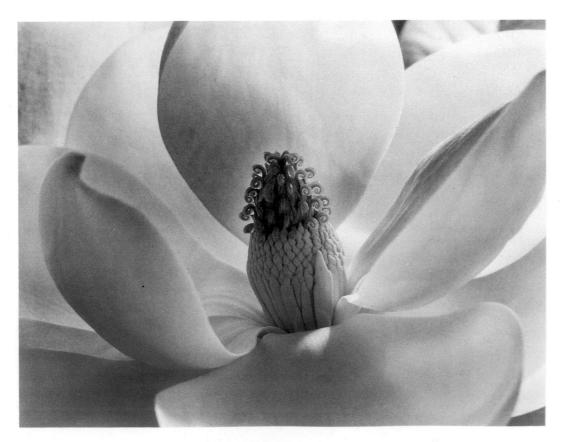

Left *Magnolia Blossom,* 1925, by Imogen Cunningham, later to be part of Group f64, a society of West Coast photographers including Edward Weston and Ansel Adams. (San Francisco Museum of Modern Art; The Henry Swift Collection; Gift of Florence Alston Swift. Photo source: P Galgiani. 63.19.112.)

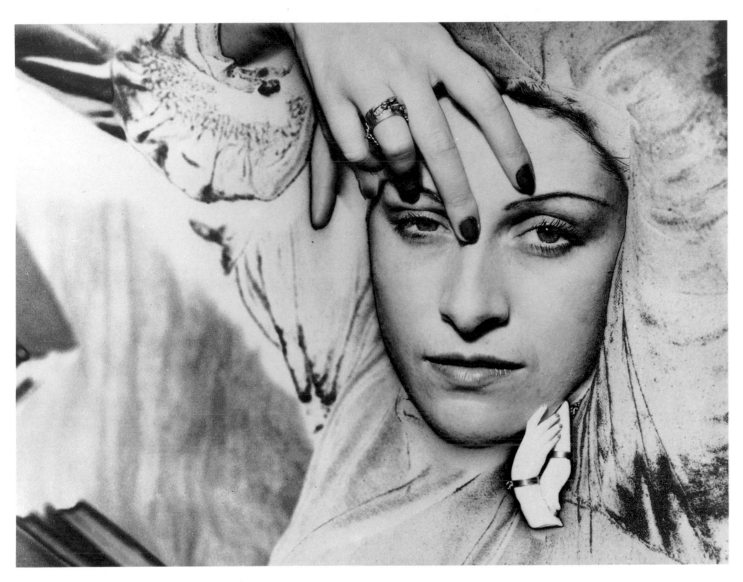

last photography was deemed as worthy as the more tradi-tional media considered within the orbit of Guggenheim's grace. The Fellowship was continued in 1938 and these two years marked a further maturity in Weston's vision. Some of the pictures taken during this period, including landscapes with a curiously contemporary feel, were published in *California and the West*, a book published in 1940. He concentrated then and for the next few years on the land, tying into the pictures a brilliantly descriptive sense of America. Like Strand, Weston came to find his country falling short of the ideal and for every vista of curvacious, undulating sand dunes and a discovered natural beauty (Weston avoided the pic-turesque), one could be found that spoke of decay and disin-tegration. His was an art now dependent on polarization: optimism and life (the landscape) versus pessimism and death (the thoughtless hand of man). In 1941 he had worked on photographs to supplement a new edition of Walt Whitman's most famous work, *Leaves of Grass*, and he seemed to have joined Whitman in insisting on a nation that loved 'the earth and the sun and the animals.' The grim alternative – a desolate and abandoned land littered with man's lunacies spelled out in decaying cars and houses – was photographed with cold detachment. Weston's last significant works were made in

1948 on Point Lobos, a coastal area of dramatic landscape near his Carmel home. From that point on Parkinson's disease made it increasingly difficult for him to carry his equipment and his attentions turned to printing his life's work. Over the following years the disease gradually worsened and he died on New Year's Day 1958.

As early as 1922, when he switched from a pictorial style to the precise forms of realism, Weston evolved a technique that matched his aesthetic concerns. Working with a view camera he stressed the importance of 'previsualizing' the final result, controlling tones and textures through exposures and de-velopment. 'I see the finished platinum print on the ground glass in all its desired qualities before my exposure' he said in a lecture given that year to the members of the Southern Cali-fornia Camera Club.

Previsualization was to be advanced to a finely tuned and scientific means of technical/aesthetic control by Ansel Adams, a fellow West Coast photographer who met Weston first in 1927 and later became his close friend. Adams had begun his professional life as a pianist of some talent, and became interested in photography and exploring the trails of Yosemite Valley in the Sierra Mountains almost simul-taneously. He was 14 years old then, and photography vied

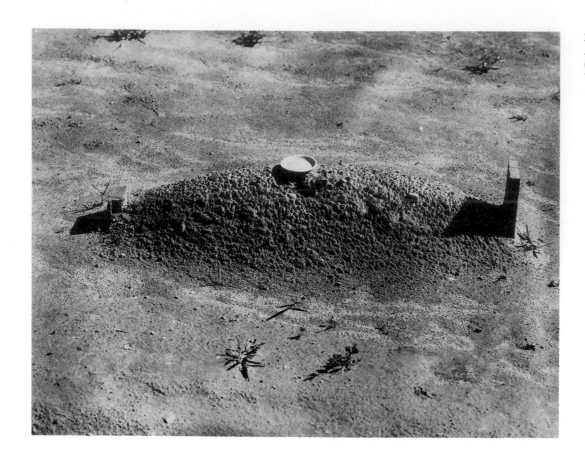

with music and the outdoor life until 1930. By chance Adams met Paul Strand in Taos, New Mexico, and Strand's work convinced him that photography in the direct, precise, penetrating manner which Strand used could make music more compelling than that which Adams could produce from the piano. His choice proved a wise one; a young concert pianist would have been given short shrift in the Depression.

As the economy improved Adams went on to develop a flourishing photographic business. Commerce aside, Adams' concern was for a photographic art. In 1932 he joined Edward Weston, Imogen Cunningham, Willard Van Dyke and several others in the f64 group of photographers who shared a distaste for still rampant pictorialism and wanted 'pure form.' In 1933 he opened the Ansel Adams Gallery in San Francisco;

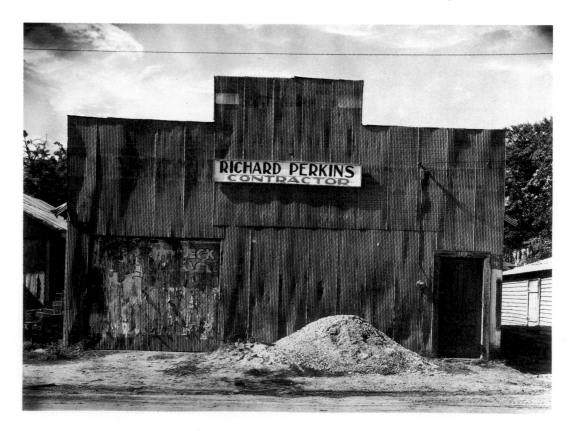

Right *Tin Building, Moundville, Alabama*, 1936, by Walker Evans. (© Estate of Walker Evans; courtesy Victoria and Albert Museum.)

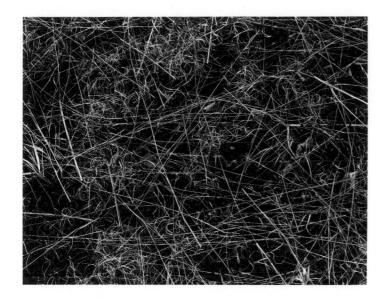

in 1940 (by now a well-known and highly respected figure) he helped set up a Department of Photography at the Museum of Modern Art, New York; in 1946 he founded the first Photography Department at the California School of Fine Arts; and in 1967 he became the first President of The Friends of Photography, a Carmel-based center of exhibitions, publications and photographic workshops.

Adams' art was in the puritan vein – purity of vision met purity of technique in works that were above all useful. Like Shaker furniture, many of his pictures were simple, elegant, utilitarian and ordained. Man seems quiet in the presence of majesty. Adams was a passionate conservationist and his works often display a reverence for nature. In some the reverence reached epic proportions – his boyhood trips to Yosemite had led to a love of the American wilderness and a battle to retain it for future generations. Adams looked for pictures that spoke of the eternal verities he saw symbolized in mountains, forests, streams and deserts. In others a forced heroism becomes so rampant that the work declines into handsome but decorative 'views.'

Technique and technology were a part of Adams' personal landscape. By 1942 he had developed previsualization into a defined and repeatable means of formal control called the 'Zone System.' This method of adjusting exposure and development allowed photographers to replace the intuition Weston used with measurable and controllable values that were expressive and subjective rather than actual. Through precise craft, shadows, highlights, sky and midtones could be predetermined to allow personal interpretation – it was the realization of the pictorialist dream (to have a painter's finesse) and the precisionist desire to celebrate technology.

In later life Adams, who died in 1984, was the most publicly recognized photographer as artist the United States has ever seen. Featured on the front cover of *Time* magazine, interviewed by *Playboy*, his was a success story that has yet to be equalled. Prices for his finely crafted prints eventually soared, touching a world record of $71,500 for a large-scale version of *Moonrise, Hernandez, New Mexico*, perhaps his most celebrated work. To an extent this acclaim served to obscure realities surrounding Adams' work as a photographer. As success brought acclaim and financial rewards it also brought a mixture of self- and imposed selectivity to his works. Adams spawned an industry so anxious for his welfare that many outstanding, sometimes radical, photographers were ignored in favor of Adams' directly accessible monuments to an heroic landscape which so stirred the spirits of collectors. He has yet to be seen fully as the sometimes complex visualist

Above *Providence, c* 1962 by Harry Callahan. (Copyright: Harry Callahan. Courtesy: Pace/MacGill Gallery.)

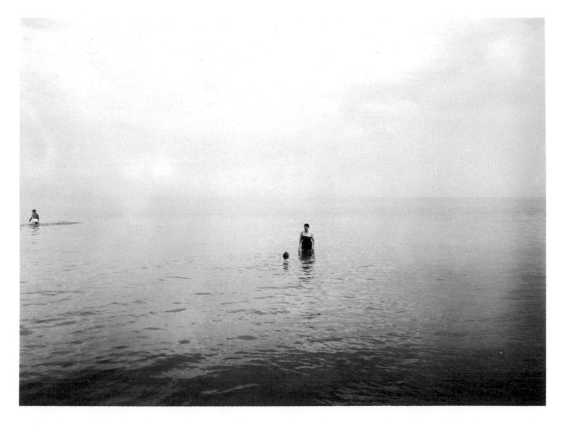

Right *Lake Michigan,* 1953, by Harry Callahan. Now seen as a twentieth-century master, Callahan has been described as an artist without peer. (Copyright: Harry Callahan. Courtesy: Pace/MacGill Gallery.)

Right *Arizona Landscape,* 1945, by Frederick Sommer, who added philosophic concepts to an acute visual sense. (© 1986 Frederick Sommer. Courtesy Center for Creative Photography.)

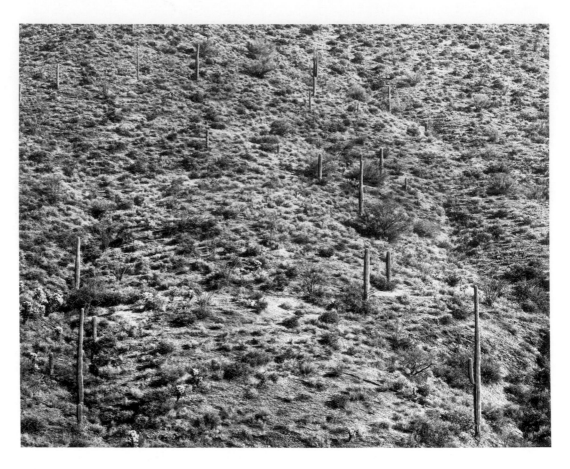

Below *Homage to F.K., Rome 162,* 1973, by Aaron Siskind. (© Aaron Siskind.)

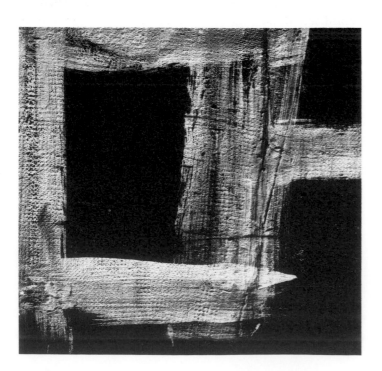

occasional glimpses of the less-well-known works suggest.

Strand, Weston and Adams formed a kind of trio in the 1930s and 1940s – each had been deeply affected by Stieglitz and each struggled to find some interior sign of the truth of the United States in its land and people. In terms of influence the trio became a quartet – to Strand the humanist, Weston the sensual realist and Adams the land lover must be added Walker Evans, who put down the American experience in terms as far removed from his peers' spirituality as he could manage. Evans' work has already been considered (see Chapters 5 and 6) but his approach was a subtle one and can be fitted into several categories. But how can a supposed documentary photographer, whose work implies a record of time and place, be cast in the role of formalist? An heroic peasant worker, as photographed by Paul Strand, may carry his or her dignity intact through decades – it is dignity that is of the essence. Similarly Edward Weston's recognition of how a shell might become more than a mollusc's discarded shelter stands outside time, as does the drama of a primal Adams' landscape. For Evans a new term is necessary. In his most productive period during the 1930s he photographed that time specifically, but with a view to how a picture might look and what the looking might mean. More than an impartial record of life's structures his works became a vibrant art. Written in a vernacular vocabulary and full of signs of place and time the works are finally about the act of looking. As records they recede to become simple, if beautiful, circumstantial evidence. As formal constructions, however, they transcend fact. As Lincoln Kirstein succinctly pointed out, the works have 'intention, logic, continuity, climax, sense and perfection.'

Almost simultaneous with the quartet's radical activities in the field came pressures from a vocal minority to see photography accorded more respect within the art world. Stieglitz had been an almost-lone voice in demanding that photography be treated on equal terms with the other visual arts, and his successes were largely self-generated. Between the wars a few like-minded individuals, generally gallery owners such as Julian Levy, tried integrating photography into a broader

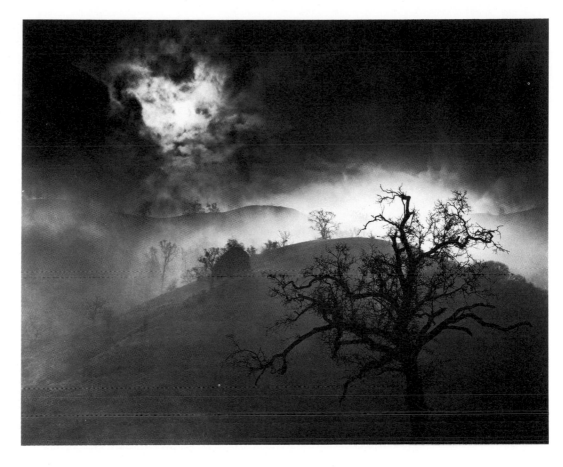

Right *Stark Tree,* 1956, by Wynn Bullock, a seeker for new symbols in the land. (Courtesy The Wynn & Edna Bullock Trust.)

Below *Ritual Branch, Frost on Window,* 1958, by Minor White from the sequence *The Sound of One Hand Clapping,* 1959. (Courtesy The Art Museum, Princeton University, The Minor White Archive. Copyright © 1982 the Trustees of Princeton University.)

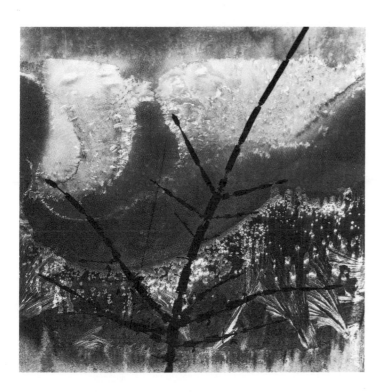

scenario but relatively little happened to inform or excite the American public about photography's internal debates and ferments. But in 1937 a small event took place that was to have a huge impact on art photography. A young art historian, Beaumont Newhall, who had been successfully dodging the Depression, was given the job of organizing an exhibition at the Museum of Modern Art, New York, where he worked as librarian. The museum, founded in 1929, was proposing a

retrospective of photography's first 100 years and Newhall, who had a strong interest in the subject, seemed a natural choice as curator. The show was the success photographers like Ansel Adams had predicted and the museum decided to go further with photography; in 1940 Newhall was made director of the newly formed Department of Photography. It was a signal move. The first one-person show, by Walker Evans, took place a year later. Adams was accorded similar treatment in 1944, Strand in 1945 and Weston in 1946. Outside the obviously compelling magazine reportage made in World War II, photography seemed to be gaining ground as an expressive medium to rank with anything made in two dimensions. Such freedoms as persistence wins were gradually to perculate throughout the American photographic community, and then the Western World.

The medium's move into the museum was an outward sign of broader recognition for photography as an aesthetic pursuit. But it was short lived. Formalism had to contend with social documentary and photojournalism and Newhall's immediate successor as director preferred the latter as a more public photography. Seeds had been sown, however, and changes began to occur. With the United States entering a period of postwar economic growth and political conservativeness the door to non-utilitarian kinds of photography seemed slightly ajar. Returning servicemen and women were able to take up the GI Bill of Rights, giving them access to free education, and significant numbers chose art. Personal expression seemed an appropriate reaction to the formality of military life and reaching for interior concerns a suitable antidote to the rigors of war.

141

Indicative of the shifts in consciousness and postwar change is the early career of Aaron Siskind. Siskind, a New York school teacher, who joined the Photo League in 1930 and began working on documentary projects including The Harlem Document, the League's most ambitious undertaking. Siskind hated social injustice and was pleased to be involved in the most dynamic group in New York, but his work had formal leanings which troubled the League's more politically motivated members and in 1941 he resigned. Confusion and low output followed but in 1943 the formalism which had so disenchanted his Photo League comrades began to take on a new and more serious appearance. Alongside avant-garde painters such as Franz Kline, William de Kooning and Barnet Newman, Siskind began examining an aesthetic based on flat planes. Instead of trying to re-create the three-dimensional world when using only two dimensions he turned his attentions to how a flatness might work on its own accord. He wanted to make a photograph 'an altogether new object, complete and self-contained, whose basic condition is order.' Siskind's departure from photographic conventions was not well received by the photographic community. Here was a star turn from the Photo League, an accomplished documentary photographer, making outrageous statements such as: 'the essentially illustrative nature of most documentary photography, and the worship of nature *per se* in our best nature photography is not enough to satisfy the man of today, compounded as he is of Christ, Freud and Marx. The interior drama is the meaning of the exterior event.' But as Strand, Weston and Adams had been attempting to define spirit in the American experience, so Evans and

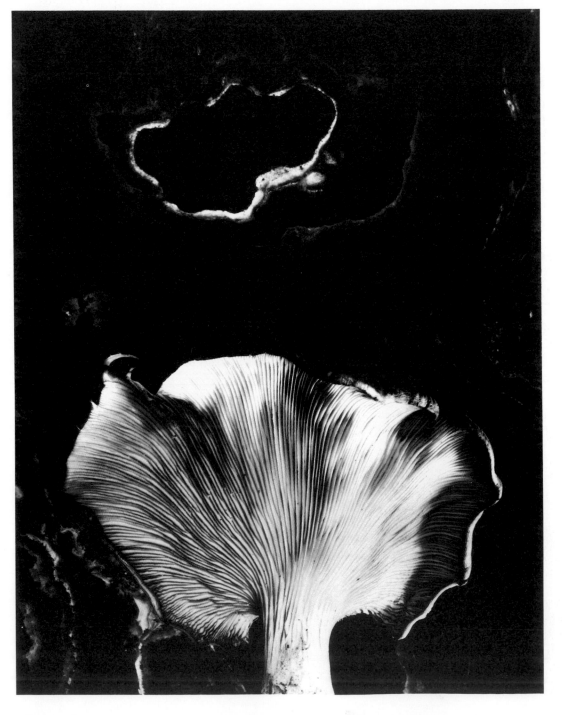

Left *Fungus, Ipswich, Massachusetts,* 1962, by Paul Caponigro. (© Paul Caponigro; courtesy Victoria and Albert Museum.)

Right *Ekstasis, Martha Graham,* 1935, by Barbara Morgan. (© Barbara Morgan.)

Above right *Stonehenge* from 'Stonehenge Portfolio,' 1967-72 by Paul Caponigro. (Copyright Paul Caponigro; courtesy Victoria and Albert Museum.)

now Siskind were, in their different ways, trying to pinpoint culture, and disapproval was insufficient motive to stop this wave of new photography.

Siskind gave up school mastering in 1949 and might have been forced into economic retirement as an artist had it not been for the postwar learning boom. The flood of GIs into higher education gave a fresh lease to existing schools, prompted new ones, and photography was carried along. In Chicago the Institute of Design had come into being as Bauhaus artists fled from Germany. It was modelled on modernist concepts and directed by Laszlo Moholy-Nagy (see Chapter 5). In 1946 a photographer, Harry Callahan, began teaching there. By 1949 he was Head of Department and in 1951 Siskind was invited to join him.

Callahan was a surprising but prescient choice as head of photography in the new Bauhaus. A quiet man, self-taught and not given to unnecessary theory he nevertheless had, and has, a capacity for joining ideas. Seen in retrospect his pictures are a fusion of European structures and American personality. He was open to experimentation (external and European), and biography (internal and American). And he explored both avenues. As Siskind sought a new meaning from the abstract but elegant calligraphy of decay, so Callahan looked to fresh meanings in the everyday. He started working life as an engineer, began to photograph in 1938 and was impressed by the importance given to works by Stieglitz, Adams and Weston. By 1946 when he went to the Institute of Design, the various kinds of photography Callahan would

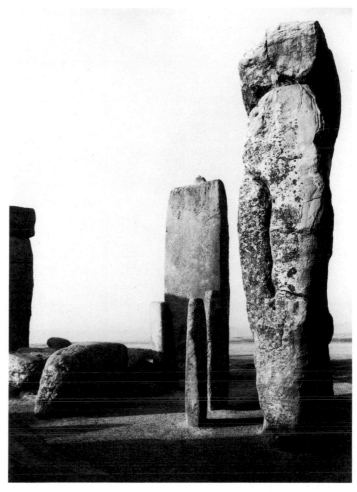

practice for the next four decades – landscape, cityscape, family portraits and experimental – were fully formed and his contact with students served to stimulate and enrich the work. He would isolate the graceful curves of something as minimal as a blade of grass and instil in it sculptural monumentality; snatch a sun-strewn moment from the city street and present it as tense, ambiguous, frightening; photograph his wife Eleanor as the Mother of all Creation; or collage a thousand photographic fragments into a complex criss-cross web of forms.

Callahan's *oeuvre* is broader than any of his contemporaries but each area is linked to the other by the forces of his way of seeing. In one of his rare written pronouncements on photography (in 1962) he made his position clear: 'It's the subject matter that counts. I'm interested in revealing the subject in a new way to intensify it. A photo is able to capture a moment that people can't always see.' This statement, like Callahan's photographs, is direct but deceptive in its simplicity. The photographer's job, as Callahan perceives it, is not to deal in generalities but particulars. Subject matter begins and ends the debate and it is what was seen and photographed that must be looked at. *How* the photographing reveals the subject is another matter, and where simplicity ends. For all their physicality and cool elegance, his images have under-layers of metaphorical and metaphysical intent – almost as if Callahan is asking (and answering) how the world works. Each, in different ways, taps into an idea fundamental to existence:

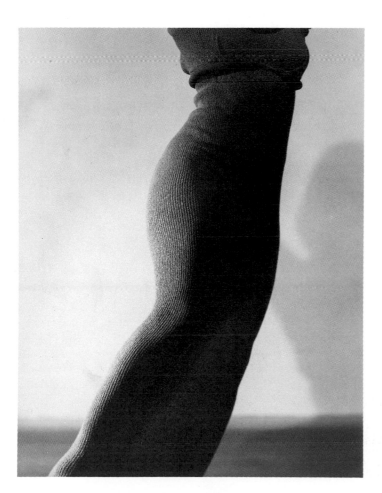

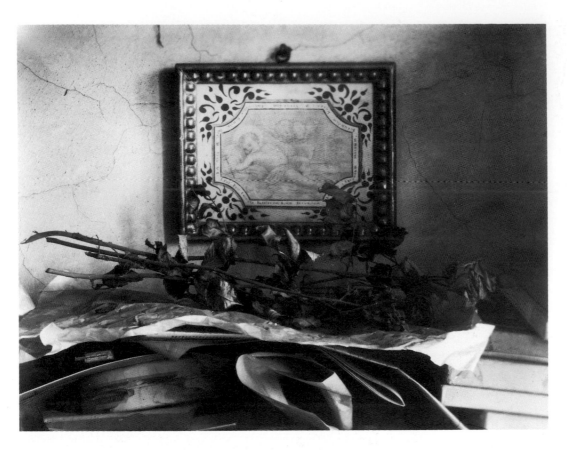

Left *Still Life c* 1936, by Josef Sudek, an Eastern European classic artist-photographer who equalled Steiglitz in intensity and Weston in vision. (Private collection.)

relationships – humankind with itself, with others, with nature, with time, with creation. Philosophers have contemplated infinity; Harry Callaghan tried to photograph it.

Callahan and Siskind formed a good teaching partnership and helped establish the notion of photographer-artists supporting themselves in this way. Another following a similar route was Minor White. Intense, at times mystical, he spawned a school of followers. His charisma was such that after his death in 1976 White's school literally vanished – unable to sustain itself without the guru. That said, Minor White brought Stieglitz's ideas of the 'equivalent,' photographs as metaphors, to a new generation and developed the concept. His extensions came from Zen and meditation, the philosophies of Gurdjieff, Gestalt psychology and ideas best expressed in White's own words 'be still with yourself until the object of your attentions affirms your presence . . . when the image mirrors the man and the man mirrors the subject, something might take over.' White was at the apex of his career, teaching at Massachusetts Institute of Technology and greatly admired during the freewheeling 1960s when such unlikely aphorisms seemed plausible, attractive even. But his photographic concerns were of a more lasting quality than a dip into hippy history might suggest.

His pictures, when removed from the cathedral-like context in which they were placed, resonate beyond the counterculture titles White imposed on them. Sequences of pictures, for example *The Sound of One Hand Clapping*, are made conspicuous by their visual strength and beauty. White would often photograph very close to things, disguising the origins of a rock form or ice-patterned window and presenting instead an other-worldly image, a duality suggestive of hell

fires and heavenly redemption, pain and pleasure. He shared Stieglitz's wishes for ecstasy but seemed ever mindful of the price to be paid for such a glimpse of earthly bliss.

His background was coincident with photography's departure from self-assigned functionalism. Self-taught, as were most at the time, he worked with Beaumont Newhall at the Museum of Modern Art, New York, in 1945, then became a teacher in California.

In 1952 White was party to a decisive event in formalist photography's growth – the foundation of a quarterly magazine dedicated to the new photographer. '*Aperture* is intended to be a mature journal,' the manifesto read, 'in which photographers can talk straight to each other . . . We, who have founded this journal, invite others to use *Aperture* as a common ground for the advancement of photography.' It was signed by White, Dorothea Lange, Ansel Adams, Beaumont and Nancy Newhall, Dody Warren, Ernest Lonie, Melton Ferris and Barbara Morgan. The group chose Minor White as editor and he proceeded with the first serious magazine American photography had witnessed since the demise of *Camera Work*. White, however, seemed at odds with the others almost from the beginning and by issue seven they voted to cease publication. At this point White found new backing and continued to develop the magazine. His concern, as rapidly became clear, was for photography as a means of spiritual and psychological revelation. It was a contemplative art. Subject matter was of small importance – one should read into photographs, not out from them. And subjects such as *Octave of Prayer* and *Be-ing Without Clothes* point to White's concerns. Alongside the magazine he continued teaching, giving workshops, and writing; he was one of photography's most able, persistent and persuasive voices. The visions of three photographers dominated photography in the United States during the 1950s and early 1960s: W Eugene Smith, the committed photojournalist (see Chapter 5); Robert Frank, the streetwise rebel (see Chapter 9); and Minor White, the mystic formalist.

White's incandescent influence faded on his deathbed, but his ideas – and those of Stieglitz – can be seen kept alive in work by Paul Caponigro. Caponigro, who studied with White and came to share White's interests in Gurdjieff's philosophy, is representative (as any one photographer can be) of an American romantic concept of the land. As the poet Rilke proposed, through art, landscape and man can find one another. Of the union, Caponigro wrote: 'I was exploring two separate worlds. Somehow I must unite the two. Through the use of the camera, I must try to express and make visible the forces moving in and through nature . . . My concern was to maintain a freedom which alone could permit contact with the greater dimension – the landscape behind the landscape.'

Jerry Uelsmann, another who had studied with White, took up the psychological emphasis that formed one part of the mentor's philosophy. Uelsmann developed 'post-visualization' (deciding after, not before an exposure) and took up nineteenth-century ideas of combination printing – making pictures from several negatives. Images with titles such as *Small Words Where I Met Myself* (1967) display the residue of White's emphasis on private visions: photography as a medium of internal, personal discovery. In later years and with greater confidence, Uelsmann managed to introduce a

playful part into his synthetic universe but his underlying seriousness is beyond doubt; 'the mind knows more than the eye and camera can see' he said in 1967 and went on to prove it personally.

Minor White, his peers and their students formed part of a rapid growth in photographic education in the United States. Boosted at first by GIs returning from World War II, then given an unexpected fillip by the war in Vietnam (many young men went to college to avoid the draft), it took a generation of self-taught enthusiasts who formed the vanguard and placed them squarely in front of young would-be's. John Szarkowski, who assumed the director's mantle at the Museum of Modern Art, New York, in 1962 (his predecessor was Edward Steichen, see Chapter 3), summed up this change in photography's fortunes most succinctly in 'Mirrors and Windows,' a catalogue published in 1978: 'An intuitive recognition that photography was ceasing to be a specialized craft (like stone carving), and becoming a universal system of notation (like writing), perhaps made it easier for educators to believe that it did fit within the proper boundaries of liberal education.' Chicago, Rochester, New York, San Francisco and Los Angeles were centers from which the word of photography's respectability spread like ripples.

Meanwhile photographic formalism was gaining footholds in nations outside the United States. Ironically, because it stemmed from overtly self-contained notions of humanism and used reportage as its basis, 'The Family of Man' – an exhibition first seen in 1955, was partially responsible. As it travelled around the world – to be viewed in the end by some nine million visitors – it caught the imagination of significant

Right *Untitled, 1982,* by Jerry N Uelsmann. (©Jerry N Uelsmann.)

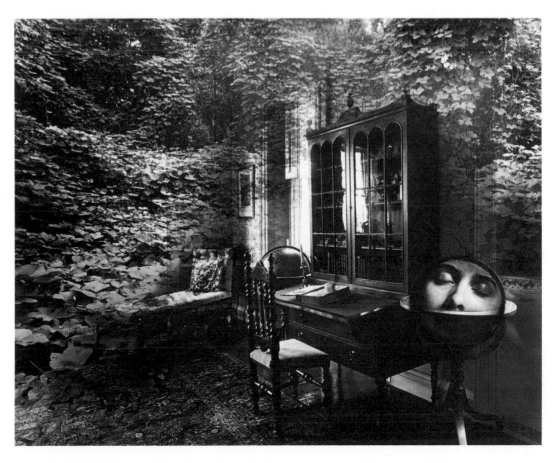

numbers of photographers. They yearned for their medium to be seen outside commerce and function and this 503-picture exhibition suggested it might be possible. But even without 'The Family of Man' photographers in Britain, Europe and Australasia had been working towards a form of image making that ignored reportage's insistence on time and place and rested instead on individual sensibility.

In Western Europe the idea of personal expression and photography outside a commercial context moved at a slower pace in the postwar years. Aside from the bombing of Pearl Harbor, Hawaii, the United States was physically untouched by its participation in World War II; Europe had to reconstruct its shattered buildings and economies, which absorbed most national energies. In Germany a culture too had been

shattered under Hitler's regime. The avant-garde had left or was suppressed and the five years following the war's end were bleak. Bauhaus excitement in experimentation and integration were virtually unknown to Germany's post-1945 generation, but a desire for some sense of change, a re-birth, was strong. They surfaced in the work of Otto Steinert, a Doctor of Medicine turned photographer and teacher who founded Fotoform, a group of radical young photographers in 1949. Fotoform gave way to a larger, international group, the 'subjective photographers,' Steinert's title for those who corresponded to his view of 'humanized and individualized photography.' Steinert was a progressive photographer and energetic activist on behalf of the medium. In 1955 he organized an exhibition with subjective photography as its title. In

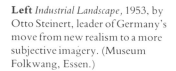

Left *Industrial Landscape,* 1953, by Otto Steinert, leader of Germany's move from new realism to a more subjective imagery. (Museum Folkwang, Essen.)

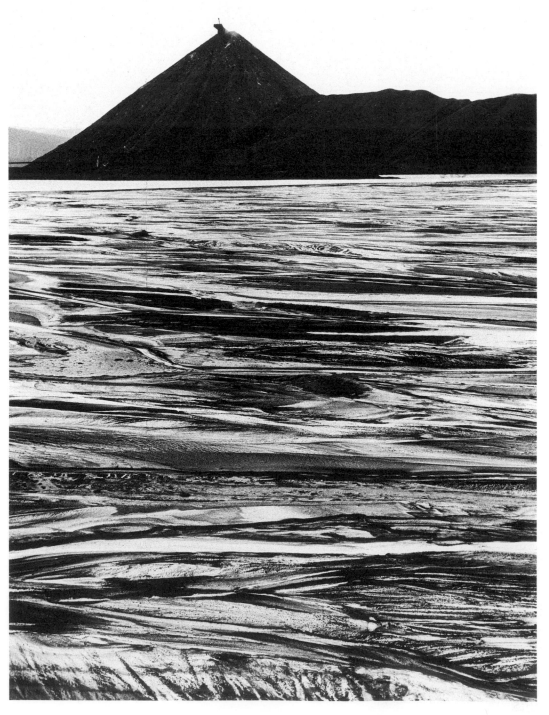

Right *Nude,* 1958, by Bill Brandt, Britain's most influential twentieth century photographer whose work touched three generations. (Courtesy Noya Brandt/Victoria and Albert Museum.)

Above right *Snickert, Halifax,* 1937, by Bill Brandt. (Courtesy Noya Brandt/Victoria and Albert Museum.)

Above far right *West Wycombe Park, c*1945, by Bill Brandt. (Courtesy Noya Brandt/Victoria and Albert Museum.)

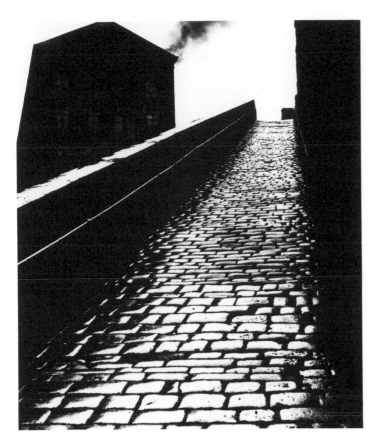

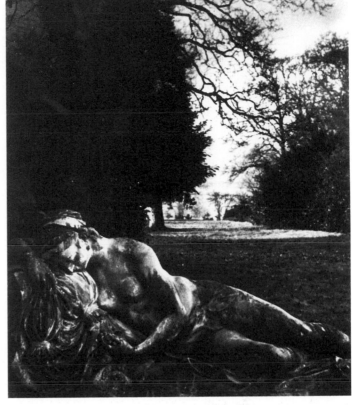

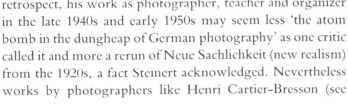

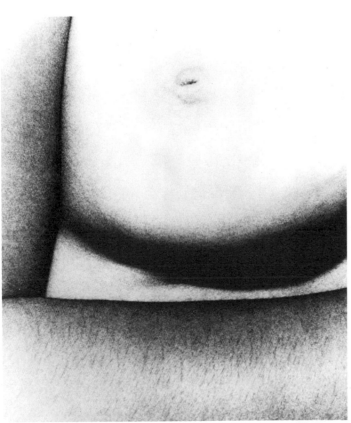

retrospect, his work as photographer, teacher and organizer in the late 1940s and early 1950s may seem less 'the atom bomb in the dungheap of German photography' as one critic called it and more a rerun of Neue Sachlichkeit (new realism) from the 1920s, a fact Steinert acknowledged. Nevertheless works by photographers like Henri Cartier-Bresson (see

Chapter 5), from France, Rune Hassner from Sweden, Wolf Suchitzky from England and Jacob Tuggener from Switzerland gave 'subjective photography' a credence that supported Steinert's view of a medium 'which embraces all areas of personal photographic creation from the abstract program to the visually composed reportage.'

Eastern Europe was in a different position after the war. Confusion reigned as the Allies divided up countries once occupied by Germany and the Soviet Union saw territorial expansion as fair compensation for their involvement in the conflict. When the dust settled it was clear that the old order had changed under socialism. Many of Hungary's most able photographers had left before the war – Kertész, Brassaï, the brothers Capa, Moholy-Nagy, Munkacsi. Those who were left had to develop a new kind of image making, celebratory of socialism if it was realist or highly graphic if self-expression was involved.

Much the same was true in Czechoslovakia, though there a more defined sense of tradition prevailed. Avant-garde Czech photographers had been influenced by cubism, surrealism and Russian constructivism during the 1920s and 1930s and developed a strong national style. Several outstanding figures emerged, of whom Josef Sudek became best known. Sudek died aged 80 in 1976 after a long career. His work – still lifes, panoramas and nature studies – combines absolute adherence to straight photography in the manner of American purists with a strong sense of soulful lyricism.

Britain too was in a different position. After the flurries of photography as art in the nineteenth century, the notion of a purely expressive medium seemed relegated to a band of amateur enthusiasts who were bent on nothing more than

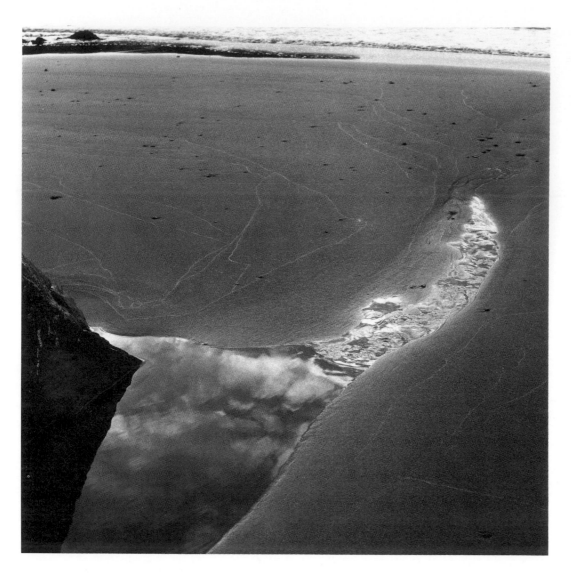

Left *Pembrokeshire,* 1964, by Raymond Moore, a painter-turned-photographer who now stands as Britain's major photographer. (© Raymond Moore.)

Right *Flooded Tree, Derwentwater,* from Cumbrian 'Presences' series, 1981, by Fay Godwin. Successful as a published photographer, Godwin has combined acute sensitivity with popular accessibility. (© Fay Godwin.)

maintaining the status quo for pictorialism. More progressive picture makers found their way into commerce and populist culture. As late as 1960 the guardians of what passed for pure photography were contentedly proclaiming in the foreword to an exhibition catalogue that 'viewers will be able to see the continuing tradition of pictorial photography, which continues largely unruffled by modern movements.' As Ralph Waldo Emerson pointed out in 1856, 'The bias of the nation is a passion of utility . . . The English mind turns every abstraction it can receive into a portable utensil.' Small wonder, then, that photography of the kind practiced in the United States or Europe received little attention in Britain. The British looked to utility first, then 'atmosphere' and had not time for the piercing clarity of straight formalism.

The postwar years marked a change, though this was slow in coming. Bryn Campbell, then Editor of a magazine called *Cameras,* wrote, '1961 will be an extraordinary year as far as British photography is concerned. In May Bodley Head will be publishing a book of photographs by Bill Brandt (*Perspective of Nudes*). In October Collins will be publishing a book by Michael Peto (*The Dancer's World*). Nothing extraordinary about that you may think unless you realise that these two books by the greatest of British photographers are the only works of this quality to be published in this country since the

War.' Peto, sadly, was to die before he could be lionized, but Brandt, who continued photographing almost up to his death in 1983, had a marked effect on the medium.

Brandt had taken up photography in 1928, worked briefly with Man Ray in Paris, then in London, largely on his own account. His early works were cast in the reportage mold, though tinged with surrealism. In 1936 *The English at Home* was published, a book which compared and contrasted the social classes, and in 1938 *A Night in London* appeared, commissioned as a journey into the city's secrets to follow-up Brassaï's *Paris du Nuit*. Brandt also worked for magazines (*Lilliput, Weekly Illustrated* and *Picture Post*), then for the Home Office, recording life in wartime airraid shelters, and the National Buildings Record who needed photographs of important buildings so that they might be rebuilt in the event of bomb damage. Thus far in his career he had corresponded to Emerson's dictum 'passion of utility' – with the exception of his first pictures, all Brandt's work was produced on commission with some specific purpose in mind.

The end of the war spelled change. 'Documentary photography had become fashionable. Everybody was doing it,' Brandt wrote later, 'Besides my main theme of the past few years had disappeared. England was no longer a country of marked social contrast.' Well before war's end Brandt was recognized as a photographer of very individual vision. 'He wasn't interested in anything that didn't lend itself to mystery,' commented Tom Hopkinson, editor of *Picture Post*. However, 1945 was to mark a new departure into the photography which accorded him world recognition. Brandt was asked by *The Saturday Book*, a whimsical blend of poetry, prose and pictures, to produce some nude studies. He had photographed nudes before (*Lilliput* published one in 1942) but for this project another possibility arose. His friend Peter Rose Pulham had persuaded him to buy a Kodak wide-angle camera. The camera took in an enormous 110-degree view, gave little clue to how things would appear and distorted perspectives. Brandt was delighted. Here was a tool that could be used to change vision, to leave the convention of human senses behind and allow a man to see more 'like a mouse, a fish or a fly.' The pictures were extraordinary – dislocations of space and time, they became experiences of form at its most sculptural underpinned with a disturbing sense of psychodrama. These pictures, published as *Perspective of Nudes* in 1961, aroused controversy. In Britain some photographers were enthusiastic about the work, witness Bryn Campbell's remarks; they seemed to herald a real departure from functionalism. In France they were embraced as exciting extensions of surrealism. In the United States *Popular Photography* magazine arranged a symposium review headed 'Art, Pornography or Simply Shocking' while John Szarkowski at the Museum of Modern Art said in photography 'only Edward Weston had made nudes of equal power.'

Function, though, remained dominant in Britain. While Brandt was elevated to the world league of 'masters' it was principally fashion photographers who took their cue from his spatial ambiguities, and fashion photographers too who first adopted Brandt's high-contrast style of black-and-white printing. Poetry and sub-surface mystery – the other qualities his work holds – was left to those who would be artists. Britain's primary concern remains in documentary (see Chapters 7 and 9) but formalism was given strong emphasis by Norman Hall, editor of *Photography* magazine during the mid-1950s and into the early 1960s. Although many of the best young photojournalists of that period were given first breaks by Hall, his thrust was towards photography in its fine sense. A progressive, Hall was also an internationalist who put Weston, Adams, Stieglitz, Steinert and many other leading Europeans and Americans before his readers. It helped change the climate, indeed re-created a climate where photographers disinterested in directly picturing society felt their work might have some worth. One such, in fact the only photographer aside from Brandt who might claim parity with his American peers in this field, is Raymond Moore.

Moore's claims to formalist attention rest on a body of work, still unfinished, that began in 1956. The pictures might be likened in sensibility to Harry Callahan's, except that Moore refuses to isolate the things of everyday and insists on weaving them into his pictures, or Minor White's because he shares the Zen concern for one-ness, or be-ing. But White looked to a celestial photography and Moore is earthly,

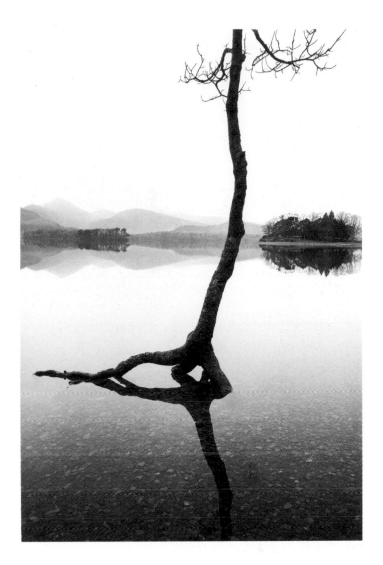

finding his stars twinkling in places we all inhabit. His work is clearly British but of a quality and kind only possible in the more benign era beginning in Britain in the 1960s when artist-photographers began demanding admittance to the realms of those who should be seen. Like Brandt, Raymond Moore 'invented' a unique visual language that has slipped into British photographic parlance. As the poet Jonathan Williams put it 'he likes to shoot "what is there". The point is: what is there also includes what isn't there – except at this one, most luminous moment in the history of seeing.'

The rage to see, to make a recording medium bow to the will and desire of its operator and transcend its mechanical origins, did not stop at the end of the 1960s. Nor is it confined to those classified here simply as 'formalists.' Increased educational opportunities changed photography's face in a way Alfred Stieglitz could not have dreamed of and the medium's shape altered as a result. Increasing public knowledge, particularly in the 1970s, also contributed to change. After 50 years of pressure, museums, art galleries, mass-market book and magazine publishers all began to take photography very seriously. Such industry created workers, some taking off from where others began, some trying new and photographically radical departures. But conscious formalism, a knowing wish to make a *photograph* rather than record a time or hold a memory, is still a prime force today.

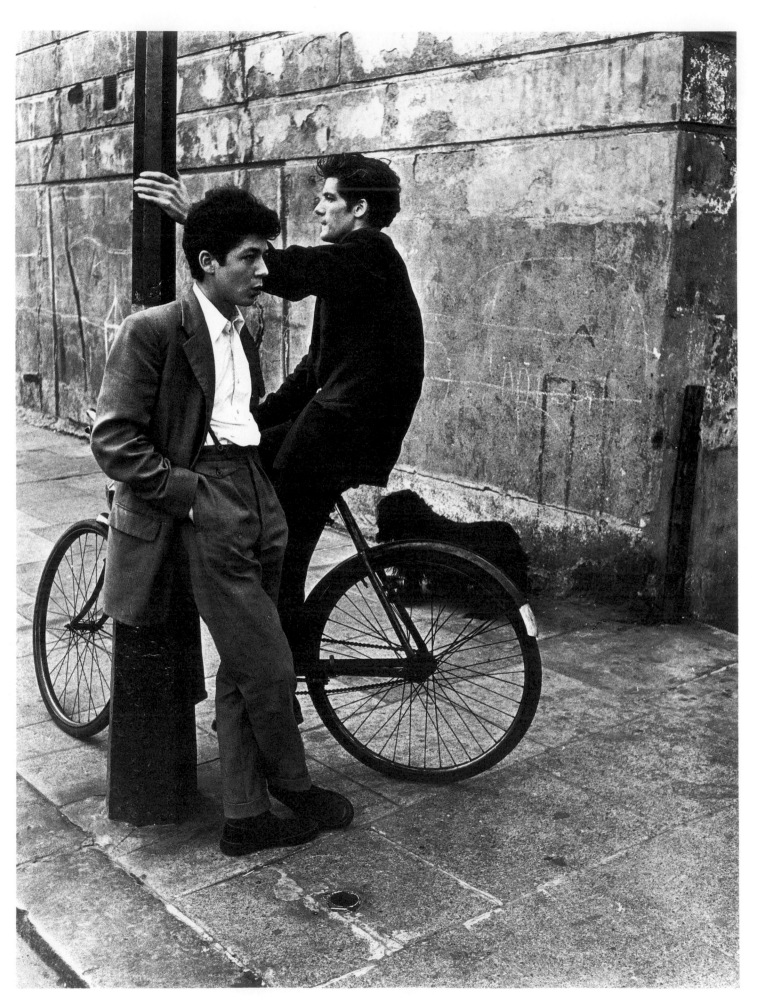

CHAPTER EIGHT

The Decisive Moment

The Street as Studio

At the close of World War II photographers considering themselves serious about their medium could be classified, loosely, in one of two groups: public and private. The first looked mainly to the city as subject and mass-circulation magazines as outlets for their works, the second preferred nature and rural climes and saw exhibitions then (perhaps) small-run books as a goal for what they did. 'Public' photographers were witness to events of the day and cast themselves in the role of interpreter. 'Private' photographers, who were intent on art, tried to portray 'experience,' find 'universality' – some even aimed at picturing the 'cosmos.' We might usefully exchange ideas of public and private for 'exterior' and 'interior.' The latter group made few if any concessions to demands other than their own.

Such a division is crude and not wholly accurate. But in its very lack of exactness lies much of recent photography's vigor. Cross-overs and confusions occurred. Photographers with essentially private concerns like Bill Brandt could often be found in the public arena and vice versa (witness, say, W Eugene Smith). However, the divide was evident in a broad sense by the 1920s and became ever more complex in the decades following the end of World War II. So where did the work of the photographer as public artisan end and the photographer as private artist begin? And was there in actual terms any difference in the images produced? After all, a photograph is just that, a representation of things before the camera. Some saw differently, some thought differently.

Representation is one thing, what gets represented is another as has been seen. The period from 1945 saw photographs of a new kind being made – their genesis was public, in the mass market world of magazines, and their apogee private, in the more reserved arena of galleries and museums.

The formation of Magnum Photos Inc in 1947 was one of the first sightings of photographers in the strict area of commerce questioning an inherent wisdom from those who employed them. One photo magazine headline announced the beginnings of this photographer-owned co-operative as a 'new deal for photographers.' Magnum was 'tired of having pictures not used or misused ... Photographers will retain control over their work, and pictures will be sold on the understanding that they cannot be reslanted or miscaptioned.' Magnum's founders (see Chapter 6) were conscious of how far removed a magazine's picture editor was from the reality they confronted, how filled with editorial preconceptions and how lacking in respect for a photographer's intelligence and integrity. But while they and other photojournalists were trying to become an authoritative part of the process through which the wide world might be contained in a six-page magazine spread, concepts of editorializing had spread. The few institutions promoting photography as contemporary art, such as the Museum of Modern Art, New York, seemed to take on extensions of magazine ideas. As one observer of a 1945 exhibition noted 'some of the photographs resemble presentations for a magazine, bled over the

Left Body language and the interplay of gestures formed part of the visual vocabulary of street photographers. *Southam Street, North Kensington, London*, 1956, photographed by Roger Mayne. (© Roger Mayne.)

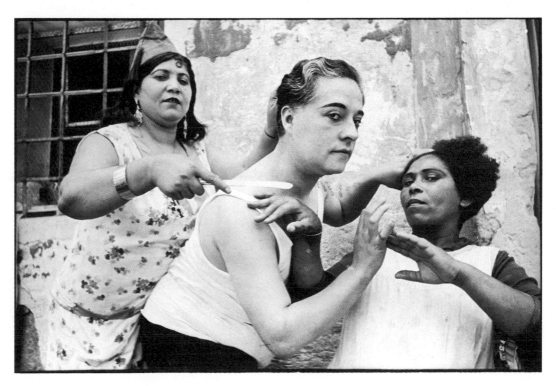

Right *Alicante, Spain,* 1933, by Henri Cartier-Bresson. He coined the term the 'decisive moment,' the fractional period when all elements in a photograph work in harmony. (© Henri Cartier-Bresson/ Magnum; courtesy John Hillelson Agency.)

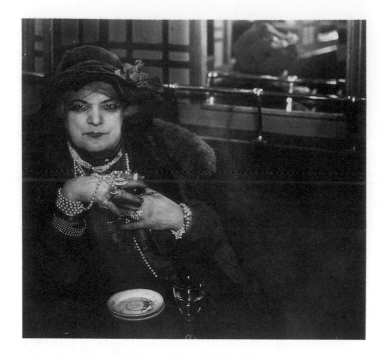

edges according to current custom. You almost expect . . . to read . . . the word LIFE. This kind of display makes good advertising but I doubt if it makes Cartier-Bresson's photographs any more astonishing than they are.'

Cartier-Bresson, one of Magnum's founders, was one of those rare photographers whose pictures seem equally fitting in museum or magazine. He worked within the well-defined concept of 'human interest' but brought to each image a compositional choreography, sense of timing and feeling for inherent culture that promoted responses like 'astonishing' when his photographs were seen. Cartier-Bresson began photographing seriously in 1930. He was caught by the fever of surrealism that swept avant-garde Paris and wanted to make pictures like those by Atget. Using a wooden camera on a tripod he quickly found picture making exciting but the results too static. Following a trip to Africa in 1931, Cartier-Bresson discovered the newly introduced Leica camera; small, unobtrusive and quick to use, it became (in his words) 'an extension of my eye.' From this enthusiasm, this desire 'to "trap" life – to preserve life in the act of living' came a succession of memorable images that spawned a whole school of photography. Bringing the possibilities of chance juxtaposition to his appreciation for the surrealist impulse, Cartier-Bresson evolved a concept he called 'the decisive moment' – an interplay between form and content caught at its revealing climax.

Cartier-Bresson photographed worldwide, but his primary lessons were learned in Paris; from photographers like Munkacsi, Brassaï and especially Kertész. During the 1930s Europe was in political turmoil, each day seemed uncertain, new and different. The countryside and rural life represented tradition, the city was where the pulse of newness could be felt and it was in the streets of Paris that Kertész worked on his sense of a photography that might evoke life by seeming to be a part of it. Kertész dealt in details – a gesture here, a glance there, chance meetings and the paradoxical side of the daily round. With pictures such as these as a stimulant, Cartier-Bresson went on to define his own style; it shares Kertész's love of the moment, but often departs into a more complex formal structure. 'To take photographs' he once wrote 'means to recognize – simultaneously and within a fraction of a second – both the fact itself and the rigorous organization of visually perceived forms that give it meaning. It is putting one's head, one's eye and one's heart on the same axis.' Cartier-Bresson travelled, producing reports on Europe, Asia, Africa, China, Russia and America, but his most telling works are those of France where all his skills in picture making are allied to a deeply felt sense of French culture and how it can be summoned up in a still photograph. Hands are shaken, bread broken, wine carefully carried and hopefully poured, conversations take place and children allowed their innocence.

Cartier-Bresson's France is a place of moments seized from the flux and flow of life as seen by an acute observer. Robert Doisneau, four years his junior, and another long-time recorder of French culture, relies less on form and geometry and more on humor to convey his sense of nation. Doisneau's early photography, part self-assigned, part industrial and commercial, was interrupted by World War II. After the Liberation of Paris he resolved to stick to the streets where he might find the tragi-comic events that made life, for him, so interesting. Where Cartier-Bresson could be likened to one of the grand school of Japanese filmmakers such as Kurosawa, Doisneau is more in the mold of Jacques Tati or Charlie Chaplin, using potential failure to point at society's idiocies

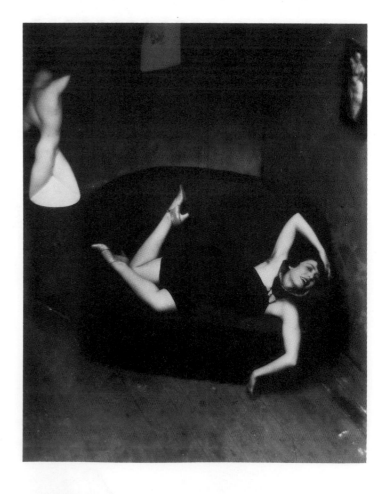

Far left *Bijou Montmartre, c* 1932 by Brassaï, a crucial contributor to changing trends in Europe in the 1930s. (© Gilberte Brassai 1987.)

Below left *Satiric Dancer,* 1926, by André Kertész. Kertész was hailed by the younger Cartier-Bresson. 'How much we all owe him' was the comment. (© Estate of André Kertész, all rights reserved; courtesy Victoria and Albert Museum.)

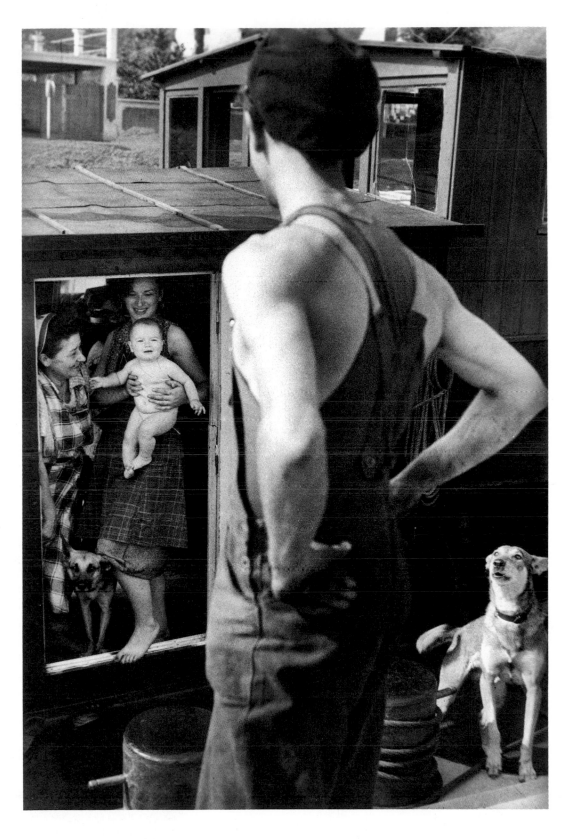

Right *Bank of the Seine,* 1953, by Henri Cartier-Bresson, most influential of street photographers. (© Henri Cartier-Bresson/ Magnum; courtesy John Hillelson Agency.)

and humor as a sign of our capacity to rise above impositions. He once said he works 'more in everyday chronicals and with "smallness."' That 'smallness,' life's little quirks and graces within which pleasure might be found, seemed reserved for postwar optimism. As Robert Doisneau wandered the streets of Paris in search of celebrations of ordinariness – a wife's disapproving glance at her husband, a stout, plodding farmer's wife watching seven cats perform a feline ballet or a monkey assert dignity in the face of human mockery –

another kind of life was beginning. In Europe it had its roots in the rise of existentialism and a retreat from middle-class values. In the United States it came from the 'Beats,' who had borrowed a sense of youthful disaffection from Europe, infused it with jazz and were beginning to create a counterculture. Where Doisneau and others in France like Ronis, Boubat and Izis identified with their subjects and sought to show the warm endurance of human spirit, younger photographers began to walk mean streets.

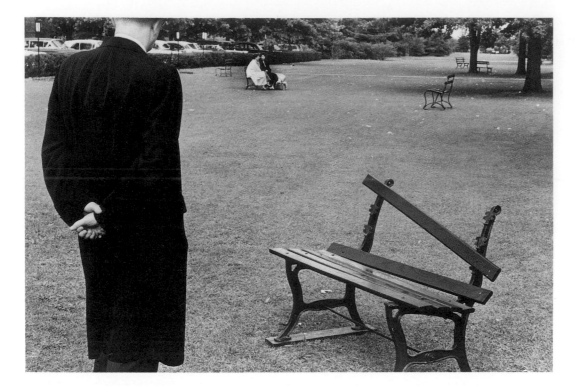

Both generations had witnessed the war – for one its end was proof of mankind's essential reason, for the other, with an adolescence spent surrounded by war's traumas, it marked nothing more than a temporary cessation in hostilities. Recoiling angrily at the seemingly mindless behavior of their elders who had born them into a painful world made yet more ghastly by knowledge of the atomic bomb, they took sides. As the photographers of 'human interest' had wished to step inside the scenes they photographed, and carry viewers with them, these newer picture makers stood outside. The novelist Colin Wilson summed-up the outsider's relationship to others in society: 'they [society] keep up a pretence, to themselves; their respectability, their philosophy, their religion, are all attempts to gloss over, to make look civilized and rational something that is savage, unorganized, irrational. He is an Outsider because he stands for Truth.' In photography's case the savagery took new form as iconoclasm. Where the older generation looked for hope in simple human interchanges, those younger worked through alienation and found ways out of ideas of 'human familyhood.'

The drift past the genialities and optimism found in humanistic photography towards a darker view of the world began in Europe, particularly Paris. There converged young men like Christer Strömholm from Sweden, Ed Van Der Elsken from Holland, William Klein from New York and Robert Frank from Zurich. They arrived and departed at different times, had no contact with each other but shared a sense in common of a restless search for 'the true blue song of man.' They were angry outsiders and bent on nothing less than putting down their full 'experience' on film. Like the existentialists who dominated Paris's intellectual avant-garde they were attempting to locate a sense of personal identity – waiting and watching the world go by to see where and if they fitted in. Of the four, history has accorded Frank prime

place, though at the time he was considered little more than an unsuccessful fashion photographer.

Frank left Paris for New York in 1947. He was 23 and looking to escape the inevitabilities of European tradition. New York offered a kinder cultural climate than Paris and Frank fell in with Alexey Brodovitch, the radical art director of *Harper's Bazaar*. He also found his way into New York's avant-garde. Fashion gave way to reportage, but despite his success within photographic circles – his friendship with Walker Evans and Edward Steichen for example or a declined invitation to join Magnum – Frank's life was not easy. His ambitions as a photographer were matched by a fierce sense of individuality and a stance outside the corporate world of institutions and magazine publishing. Nevertheless he shot pictures for *Life*, *Look*, *Fortune* and *McCalls*, and undertook advertising assignments even though he generally hated the experience, 'I wanted to follow my own intuition and do it

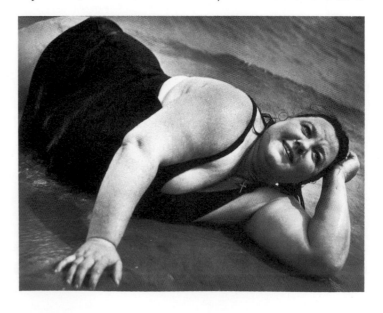

my way and not make any concession – not make a *Life* story . . . I hated those goddamned stories with a beginning and an end.' At *Harpers Bazaar* he met Louis Faurer, another fashion photographer who shared a love of the loose, elliptical possibilities found in street life which could be totted-up as points against the mythic America. *Life* represented materialism – trash and trivia was the found reality and Faurer and Frank thought it wonderful. In 1955, with help from Walker Evans, he received a Guggenheim Fellowship to photograph the United States: 'a town at night, a parking lot, a supermarket, a highway . . . advertising, neon lights, the faces of the leaders and the faces of the followers, gas tanks and post offices and backyards.' His odyssey lasted two years and was to reveal the United States as a helpless, hopeless catalogue of human ephemera. The process of cataloguing, learned from Evans, was turned sideways. Both photographers were determined to bring what was ignored or overlooked to public attention, but where Evans saw proudly such signs of a native culture as could be found in roadside vernacular, Frank discovered them seedy and dishevelled. 'What are you doing here? Are you from New York?' asked a group of boys outside a Mississippi High School in 1955. 'I'm just taking pictures,' Frank replied, 'For myself – just to see.' 'He must be a communist' was the retort 'he looks like one. Why don't you go to the other side of town and watch the niggers play?' Where Evans found pride, Frank saw desolation; in the decade and a half which separated their work the American dream had collapsed into a vision of thoughtless ritual fabricated in aimlessness – a perfect match for existentialism or the voice of Beat poets. 'What kind of sordid business are you on now?' asked Allen Ginsberg of his country in *On the Road* by Jack Kerouac 'I mean, man, wither goest thou?' He continues later in a poem

America I've given you all and now I'm nothing.
America two dollars and twenty seven cents January 17, 1956
America . . .
Are you being sinister or is this some form of practical joke? . . .
I'm addressing you.
Are you going to let your emotional life be run by Time Magazine? . . .
America how can I write a holy litany in your silly mood? . . .
America this is quite serious.
America this is the impression I get from looking in the television set.
America is this correct? . . .

Ginsberg wrote in religious terms which echoed some of the symbols in Frank's pictures: shrouded cars, roadside crosses – others were everyday items like the American flag, juke boxes and the road. Jack Kerouac supplied an introduction to the American edition of Frank's book *The Americans* which came from the pictures made on a criss-cross journey between the Atlantic and Pacific coasts: 'Anybody doesnt like these pictures dont like potry, see? Anybody dont like potry go home see Television shots of big hatted cowboys being

tolerated by kind horses. Robert Frank, Swiss, unobtrusive, nice, with that little camera that he raises and snaps with one hand he sucked a sad poem right out of America on to film, taking rank among the tragic poets of the world.' Tragedy indeed was part of Frank's seeing, but there was tenderness too. His was a sweet and sour world, as he said himself, talking of his exclusive use of monochrome, 'black and white is the vision of hope and despair.'

The Americans was rejected; it was seen as nihilistic, as was Robert Frank himself, called by one critic of the book 'a joyless man who hates the country of his adoption.' Confused by the subject matter and bewildered by his strange way of seeing, most people retreated from his downbeat view. By the mid-1960s his cries of outrage began to make perfect sense and his book became a bible to the young photographers then mourning America's lost spirituality. By then, ever the outsider, Frank had gone on to make underground films, but the 82 images composing *The Americans* lived on to influence future generations of photographers.

Part of Frank's approach was a seeming disregard for the niceties of technique. 'If a photographer wants to be an artist,' he wrote in 1958, 'his thoughts cannot be developed overnight at the corner drug store.' He evolved a casual style and used a gritty graininess to support his sense of irony, melancholy and detachment. Others were beginning to do the same, lending their pictures an authentic smell of the streets. Helen Levitt was one – she used all the structured rhythms Cartier-Bresson had reserved for his pictures of France to

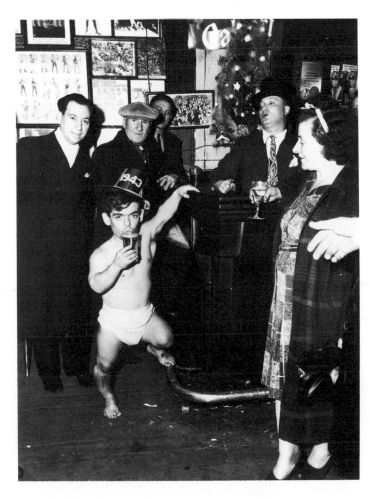

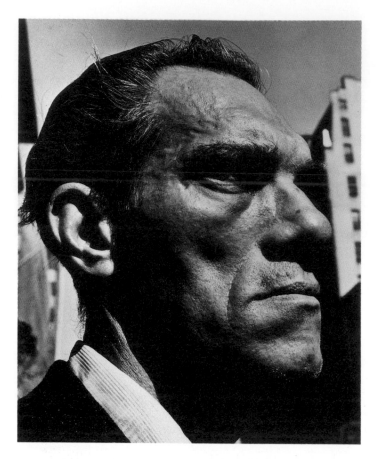

transform New York into a stage on which life's choreography could be observed, capturing grace and elegance within the most unlikely backgrounds – William Klein was another. He returned to his native New York from Paris determined to see the city with the freshness of a stranger, but his point of departure was different from Frank's. Frank knew 'the rules' and set about breaking them; Klein, trained as a painter, had less interest in photographic iconoclasm and more in finding ways of saying what was needed to show New York City as an experience. In 1956, two years ahead of Frank, he published *Life is Good and Good for You in New York; Trance Witness Reveals*, (the title is a parody of a headline from the *Daily News*). No less personal a work than Robert Frank's, it exchanged the former's sense of space and scale, sadness and hope for the brashness of a one-to-one confrontation with bright lights and a big city. Spattered with slogans, peopled by those propelled by a kind of madness, Klein's New York is a kaleidoscope of raw, aggressive energy. Billboards meet street graphics and clash with a nervy, streetwise human sideshow. His was an audacious mixture of pop art before the term was known, an abrasive abusive social realism and satiric documentary with images falling from the pages like a stream-of-consciousness visit to the underworld. In contrast to *The Americans*, whose American edition was remaindered, *New York*, also first published in Paris, was a comparative success and Klein's style became marketable. He turned to fashion, shocking and dazzling art directors, then to filmmaking, photographing for the books *Rome* in 1959 and

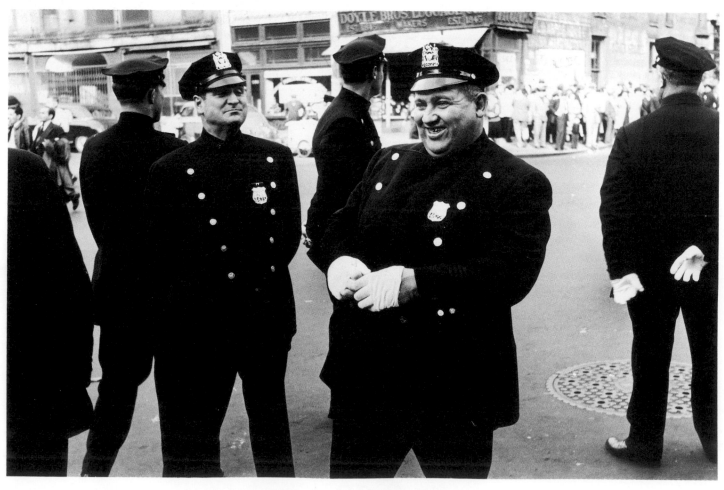

Tokyo and *Moscow* in 1964 meanwhile. All use a boldness of direct confrontation but none quite touch the same raw nerve exposed in *New York*.

Despite promises of newness offered by the Festival of Britain in 1951 and the 'New Elizabethan' age which was said to dawn as Elizabeth II ascended the throne in 1953, Britain seemed to sit out the 1950s as far as self-motivated, self-directed street photography was concerned. Streetlife was not a part of Britain's way of social interchange except in inner-city areas which were thought of, then, as slums. A

sense of class division kept most amateur photographers clinging to the sleepy comforts of pictorialism's past and kept professionals in the security of their studios. News photographers dealt in stereotypes and something approaching the verve of commercial photography on continental Europe or the United States was restricted to an occasional sighting on the pages of *Picture Post*. There Bert Hardy managed to infuse some sense of vital everydayness into the weight given stage-managed stories. *Picture Post* however was nearing the end of its life (it closed in 1957). Eventually Britain's most talented

Far left Untitled, Fifth Avenue, New York City, *c*1959, by Leon Levinstein, a seeker of moments that spelled out city tensions. (© Leon Levinstein.)

Below left *May Day, New York,* 1948, by Dan Weiner. Weiner was a humanist who sought a gentle humor. (Courtesy Sandra Weiner.)

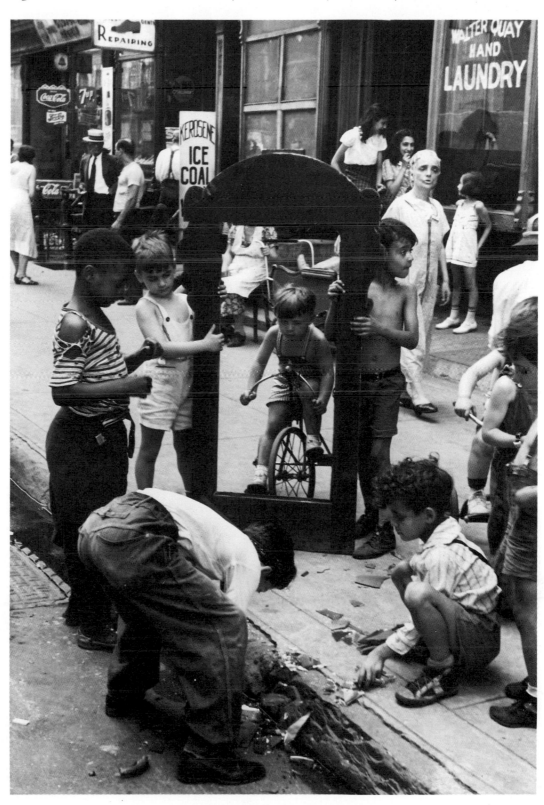

Right Untitled, New York, *c*1942, by Helen Levitt who invented her city as a backdrop to a continuing ballet. (© Helen Levitt.)

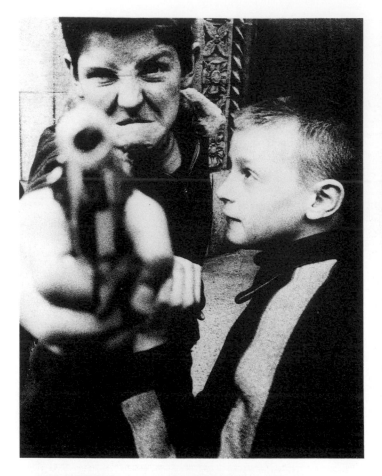

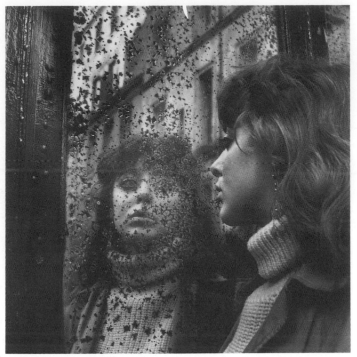

Above *St Germain des Prés*, Paris, 1950, by Ed Van Der Elsken, (© Ed Van Der Elsken.)

Below *Les Animaux Supérieurs*, 1954, by Robert Doisneau whose studio was the streets of Paris. (Photo Doisneau–Rapho.)

Left *Mini Gang, Amsterdam Avenue*, 1955, by William Klein. (© William Klein.)

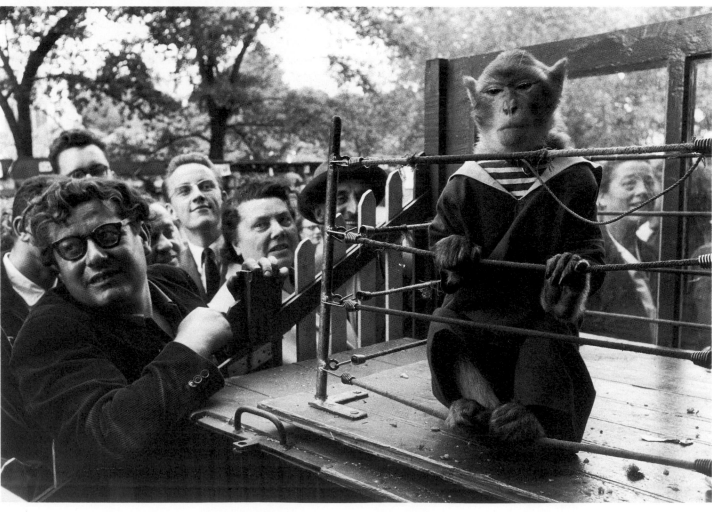

Right *Dance, Brooklyn*, 1954, by William Klein. A painter-turned-photographer, Klein broke photography's rules and so questioned convention. (© William Klein.)

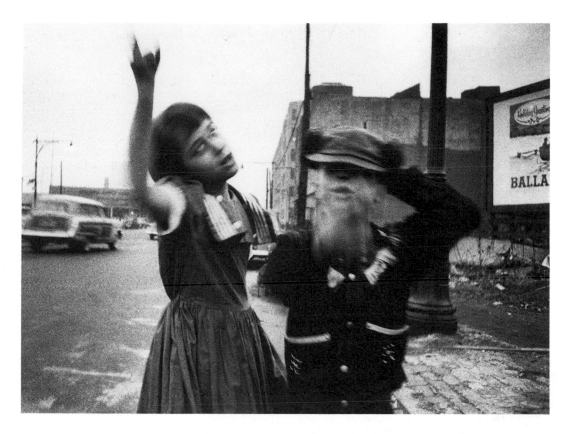

young photographers – the rough equivalents of Frank, Klein, Strömholm and Van Der Elsken – were to make their mark in mainstream media, emerging newly in color supplements or the rash of magazines to appear in the late 1950s and early 1960s. David Hurn, Don McCullin, John Bulmer, Patrick Ward, Philip Jones Griffiths were all swept into the world of commerce which Frank and his 'outsider' counterparts rejected.

One exception was Roger Mayne. No less a professional than the others (his first story was published in *Picture Post* in

1951 when Mayne was 22), he nevertheless had a concern for photography as medium of personal expression; he wanted to make a new kind of picture and see the world in photographic terms. Between 1956 and 1961 he photographed frequently in Southam Street, a London street where inner-city people acted out their lives. Boys learned to smoke, surreptitiously, young men to look macho, girls to give a quick, knowing eye-glance and women to pass the time of day. Brought together, these pictures seem no less street-theater than Klein's view of New Yorkers but somehow appear more

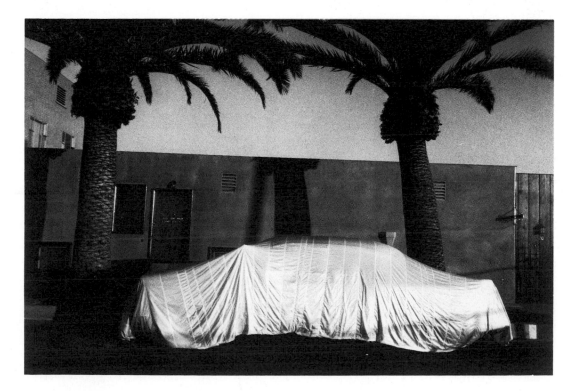

Right *Covered Car, Long Beach, California*, 1955-6, by Robert Frank, whose sometimes bleak view of American society influenced a generation of photographers. (© The Art Institute of Chicago. All Rights Reserved.)

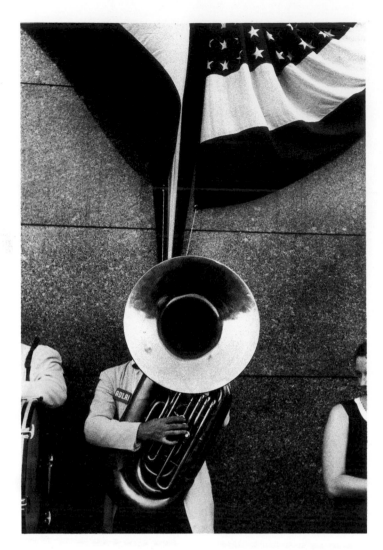

seems as if he photographed people discovering themselves, and discovered himself in the process. Sad to say, years of indifference to Mayne's very obvious gifts led him to a less public picture making, but at the time when his Southam Street project was first underway, such freshness in photography was received with excitement. 'The vitality of the working-class streets in London is powerfully reflected in the work of a young photographer' ran a caption when the *Observer* featured four of Mayne's pictures on its front cover in 1956. It was a liberally inclined paper and such championing brought rebuttle from the Right. *The Daily Telegraph*, appealing to a more conservative element, satirized the 'Observer Man' – 'Sensitive himself to a degree, he envies the working classes their lack of sensitivity. He likes photographs of handsome, uncomplicated proletarians illustrating what purported to be "the vitality of the working-class streets of London". As his portrait takes shape, it begins to look rather like a mild and well-adjusted version of Colin Wilson's *Outsider.*'

Mayne was on the edge of what turned into the Swinging Sixties, when the austerity of postwar Britain finally gave way to some exuberance. The term was a curious one, media manufactured on the back of a need for glitter to be injected into drab lives, but in magazine terms it worked. It was carried off by proxy into publications like *Topic*, *Queen*, *Town* and *Time and Tide* who (alongside more established titles such as *Vogue*) told a story of the British phoenix rising from the ashes of World War II. And suddenly photographers joined the models, hairdressers, designers and art directors as leaders of an exciting, excited new world. Britain no longer needed the *Picture Post* version of a romanticized 'Foggy London Town' where cliché replaced 'seeing' or 'feeling.' It could use 'style' instead. Some image makers resisted, most succumbed to the myths of high living photography offered.

authentic. Brashness, anger, sorrow and pity – American hallmarks – seem replaced with longing by Mayne, the outsider, looking at something of which he cannot be a part. It

Above *Political Rally, Chicago,* 1956, by Robert Frank. (© The Art Institute of Chicago. All rights Reserved.)

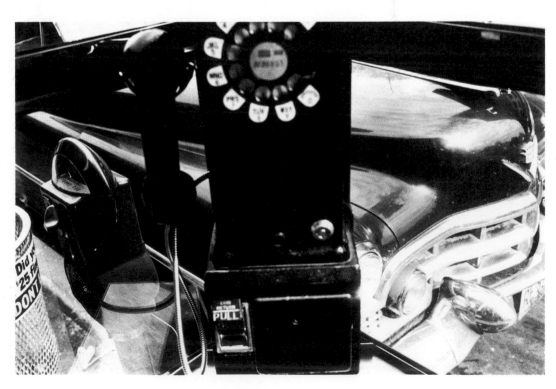

Right *New York City,* 1963, by Lee Friedlander, a re-inventor of the syntax of photography's visual grammar. (© Lee Friedlander.)

In the United States matters were different. Magazines bred a certain glamour but outside the fashion field photography's aura was rather static. If one was concerned the only decent thing to do was be a photojournalist. Young photographers, inspired by Frank's nonconformity and W Eugene Smith's insistence on the photographer as a self-assigned carrier of integrity's torch, were becoming impatient. They wanted more than the bland editorializing offered by *Life*, *Look*, *Colliers* or the other magazines to whom they looked for a living. Such desires were partly parallelled by a growth in opportunities for non-commercial photographers' work to be seen in other contexts. The Museum of Modern Art (MOMA) had pioneered the field, but other institutions in the early 1960s were fast on its heels. In 1966 the Rose Art Museum at Brandeis University mounted an exhibition called 'Twelve Photographers of the American Social Landscape.' Included were two photographers – Garry Winogrand and Lee Friedlander (who coined the term 'Social Landscape') – who were shown again together that same year – this time in company with Bruce Davidson, Danny Lyon and Duane Michals in a show curated by Nathan Lyons at George Eastman House in Rochester, 'Toward a Social Landscape.' In 1967 the two were coupled with Diane Arbus in 'New Documents' a MOMA exhibition. It began to seem as if a non-commercial photographer could practice in the manner of a painter – full time and with professionalism.

The shows, particularly 'New Documents' rocked the photographic establishment in much the same fashion as *The Americans* by Frank. John Szarkowski, successor to Steichen at MOMA, addressed 'newness' in his catalogue introduction: 'In the past decade a new generation of photographers

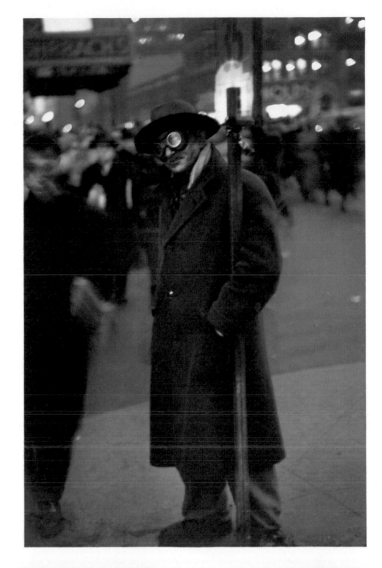

Above right *Goggle-Eyed Man*, 1947, by Louis Faurer, a photomagician who conjured angels and demons from New York streets. (Private collection.)

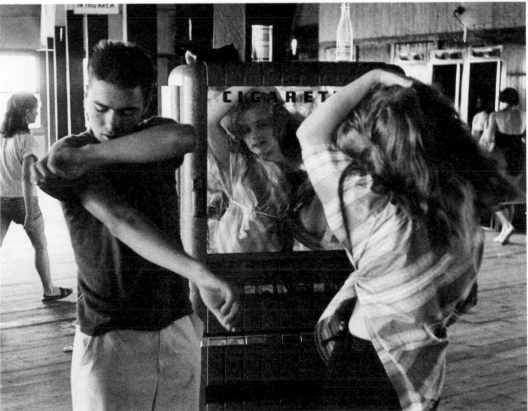

Right From the essay 'Brooklyn Gang,' 1959, by Bruce Davidson. At once evocative and accurate, Davidson's work is at the heart of the reportage tradition. (© Bruce Davidson/Magnum; courtesy John Hillelson Agency.)

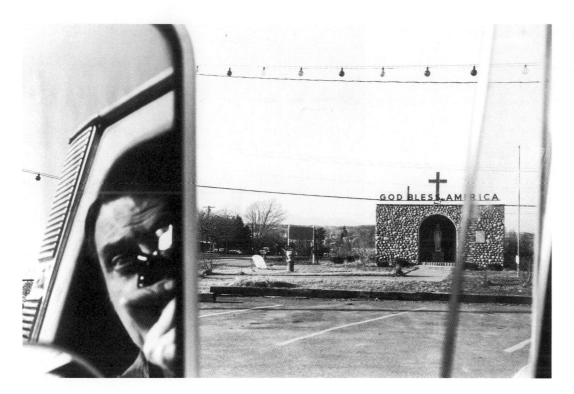

Left *Route 9 W, New York,* 1969, by Lee Friedlander. (ⓒ Lee Friedlander; courtesy Zabriskie Gallery Inc., NY.)

Below *Los Angeles,* 1964, by Garry Winogrand, who photographed to see what the world looked like as a photograph. (Courtesy Fraenkel Gallery, San Francisco and the Garry Winogrand Estate.)

has directed the documentary approach towards more personal ends. Their aim has been not to reform life, but to know it. Their work betrays a sympathy – almost an affection – for the imperfections and the frailities of society. They like the real world, in spite of its terrors, as the source of all wonder and fascination and value – no less precious for being irrational.' A photographer's job as then perceived was not to condone irrationality or use the camera to 'know life.' Truth came in thoughtfully composed, well-lit, easy to digest packages, not the complex somewhat crazy, slightly disjointed

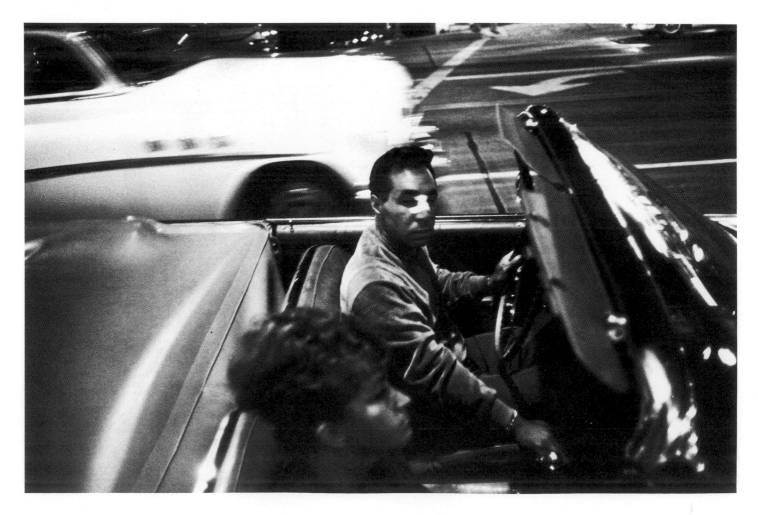

fragments of street intelligence now appearing on the walls of the United States' premier art institution.

Arbus, Friedlander and Winogrand as visionaries of a new way of photographing shared a common heritage. Instead of entering photography through an apprenticeship or being self-taught, they studied: Arbus with Lisette Model; Friedlander with Edward Kaminski; and Winogrand with Alexey Brodovitch. As well as working 'privately,' for themselves, each was a commercial photographer – Arbus worked in fashion photography, Friedlander worked for magazines and record companies and Winogrand was a photojournalist turned advertising photographer. Each can be seen as relating to, though overthrowing, a known genre. Arbus might be likened to August Sander, photographing 'types'; Friedlander to Atget, photographing a culture; and Winogrand to Cartier-Bresson, using the camera to capture and mold a multitude of human interactions into some visual coherence. The trio's mark on photography, like Robert Frank's, was decisive.

The trio successfully challenged existing notions of what a photograph should look like, what it could contain and what

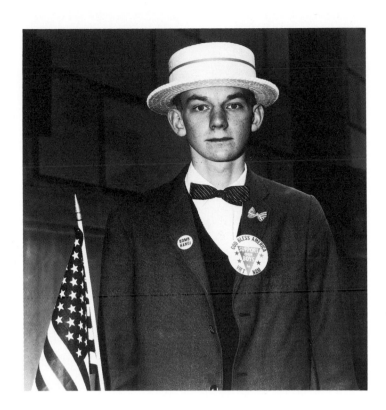

Above *Boy with a straw hat waiting to march in a pro-war parade, New York City,* 1967, by Diane Arbus. With Friedlander and Winogrand, Arbus turned photography on its head in the 1960s. (Copyright © Estate of Diane Arbus 1967.)

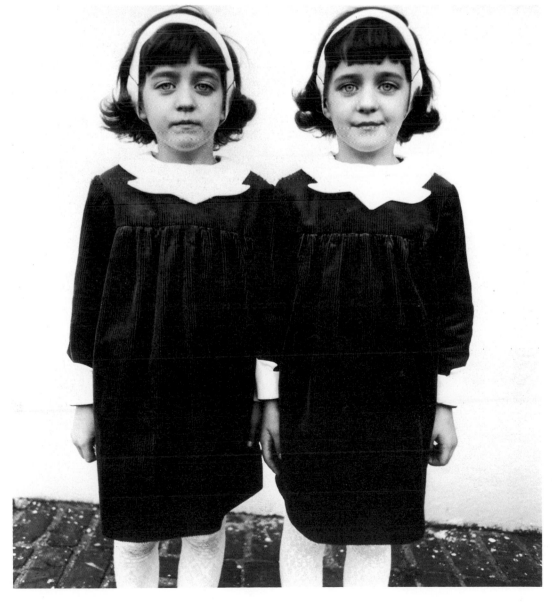

Left *Identical Twins, Roselle, New Jersey,* 1967, by Diane Arbus. (Copyright © Estate of Diane Arbus 1967.)

163

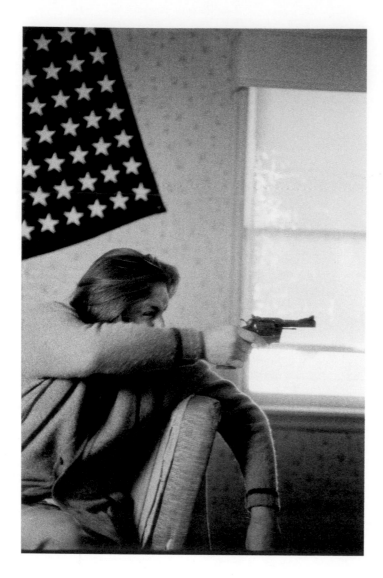

Above *Man with gun and flag* from the book *Tulsa*, 1971, by Larry Clark, a view from the underside of US society that shocked Middle America. (© Larry Clark.)

it might mean. Gone was what Walker Evans had called 'all the woolly, successful "photo-sentiments" about human-family hood [and] the mindless pictorial salestalk around fashionable, guilty, and therefore bogus heartfeeling.' In its place came an astringent, astonishing, eccentric and personal view of the United States informed by the discovery that photographs do not simply contain discrete portions of the world – it transforms them. As photographers of a 'social landscape' they were not simply replacing Ansel Adams' views of Yosemite with pictures of a manmade environment. Their 'landscape' was one of concept, where what was photographed took on a lesser role when set against the fact of how it looked as a photograph. The works of Arbus, Friedlander and Winogrand presented the world anew and forced viewers to step outside the seeing habits of a lifetime. Arbus drew attention to how the average American might seem when subjected to photography's undiscriminating record, how bizarre were the rituals of Middle America and how divided was society. Winogrand imposed a personal sense of order over the mayhem of street life, picking up on chance juxtapositions and redefining Cartier-Bresson's 'decisive moment' to include a sense of how far one might push the rectangular form of a 35mm frame and still retain clarity. Friedlander, who is now seen to rank with that tiny handful of photographers who represent a pinnacle in the medium's development in the twentieth century took the idea of documentary apart and reassembled it according to a new system of seeing. Placing the visual chaos of 1960s city life against a complex but internally ordered sense of description, he made pictures that were at once idiosyncratic, beautiful and illusive. In linking together discontinuous fragments of the urban scene he maintained a sense of ambiguity that seems at odds with the idea of a 'document.' Friedlander played with photography's impartiality, layering his pictures so that

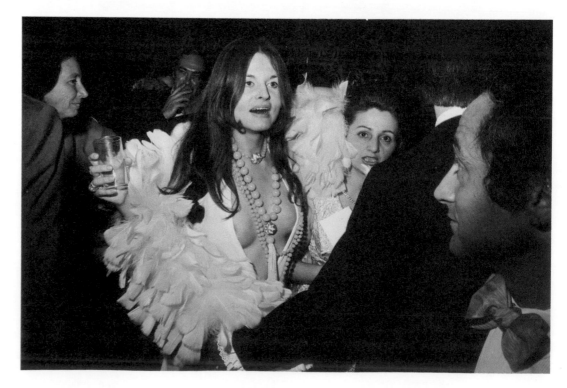

Right *Centennial Ball, Metropolitan Museum,* 1969, by Garry Winogrand. (Courtesy Fraenkel Gallery, San Francisco and the Garry Winogrand Estate.)

Right *Scanno,* 1963, by Mario Giacomelli, poetic, impressionistic, but still truthful. (© Mario Giacomelli; courtesy Victoria and Albert Museum.)

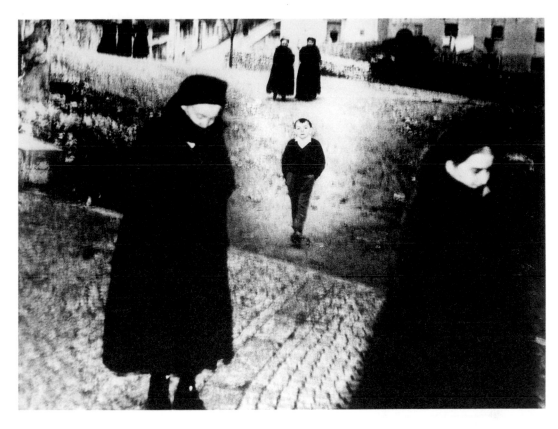

Below *Uptown Chicago,* 1965, by Danny Lyon, whose personal view of society was made from the inside. (© Danny Lyon/Magnum; courtesy John Hillelson Agency.)

background and foreground gained equal weight and structuring them according to a new and personal syntax. For all their clear authenticity and authority as statements of fact,

how we see the subject *now* is the photographer's invention.

None of this trio was much given to publicly commenting on their views on the medium, but in Arbus's statement 'I

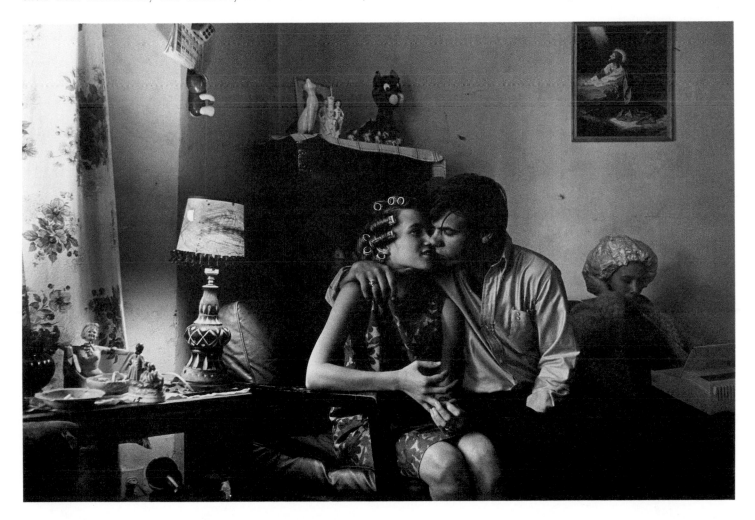

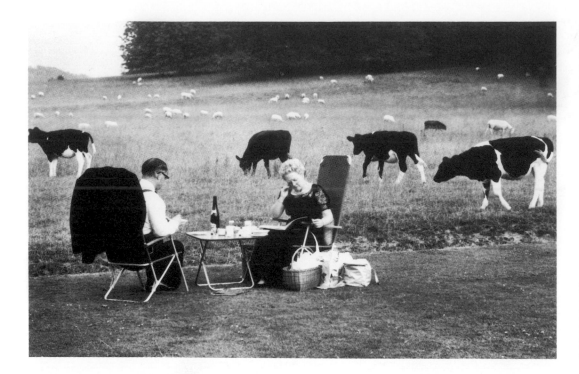

Left *Glyndebourne*, 1968, by Tony Ray-Jones among the most influential of British photographers in the 1960s. (Courtesy Anna Ray-Jones and Victoria and Albert Museum.)

Below *Sleeping Pilgrim, Levoča, Czechoslovakia*, 1968, by Markéta Luskáčova. Only through constant respect for her subjects could the photographer picture with such intimacy. (© Markéta Luskáčova.)

really believe there are things which nobody would see unless I photographed them,' Winogrand's 'I photograph to find out what something will look like photographed,' and Friedlander's 'the pleasures of good photographs are the pleasures of good photographs, whatever the particulars of their makeup,' we have three statements which express the broad concepts of social landscape as it came to be practiced during the 1960s and 1970s – a photography based less on judgmental views of society or an unravelling of the human condition and more on the act of photographing itself.

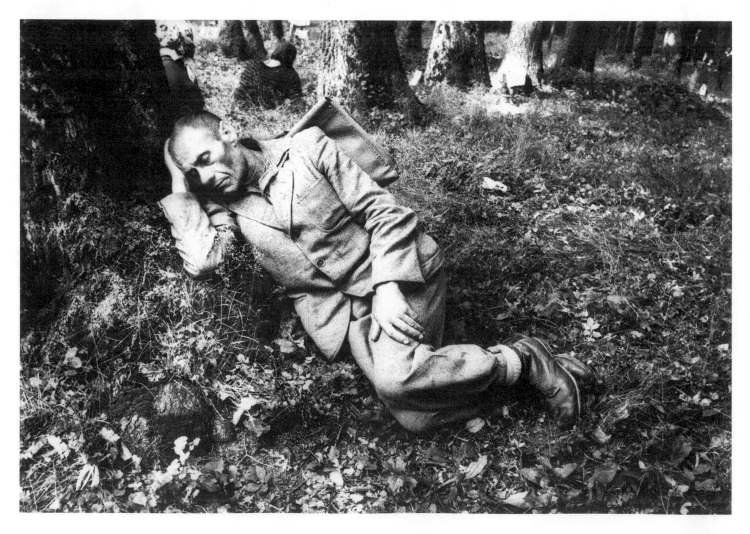

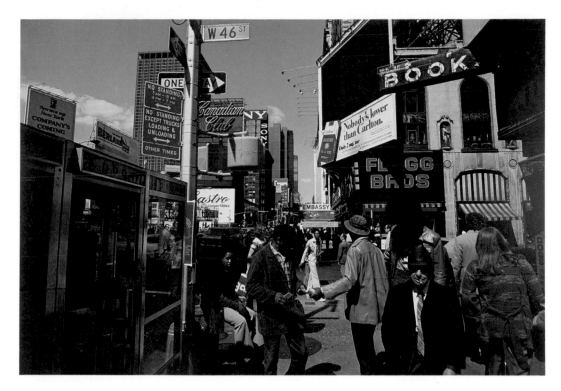

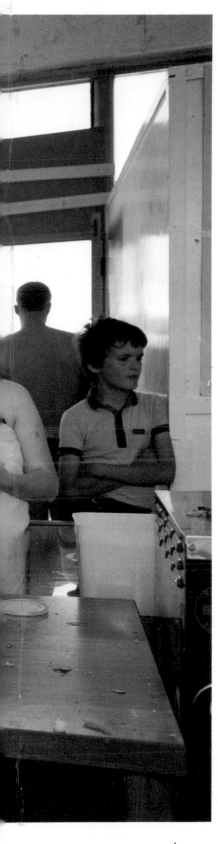

In Europe, where defining ideas of photographic expression remained more or less in a functional mode, there was less inclination to detach picture making from its relationship with commerce. Robert Frank's *The Americans*, first published by Robert Delpire in Paris in 1958, was tucked into a series *Encyclopedie Essentielle* which made a strong marriage between words and pictures. Packaged as a kind of popular

Above *Broadway and West 46th Street, New York City*, 1976, by Joel Meyerowitz. Jarring colors create a heightened street sense. (© Joel Meyerowitz.)

Below *South Bank*, 1983, by Graham Smith. (© Graham Smith.)

Above *Lido Cafe, New Brighton*, 1985, by Martin Parr. 'New color' brought to an old tradition adds valuable information. (© Martin Parr.)

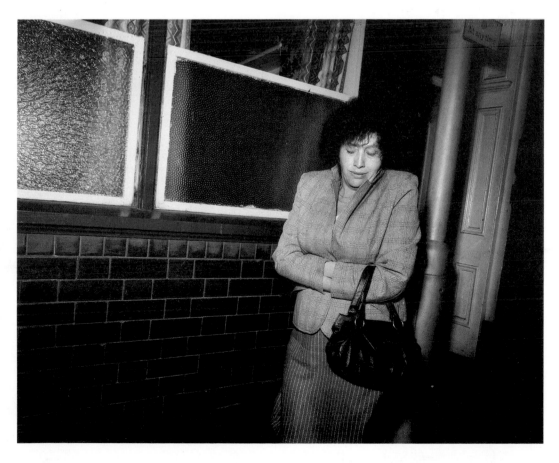

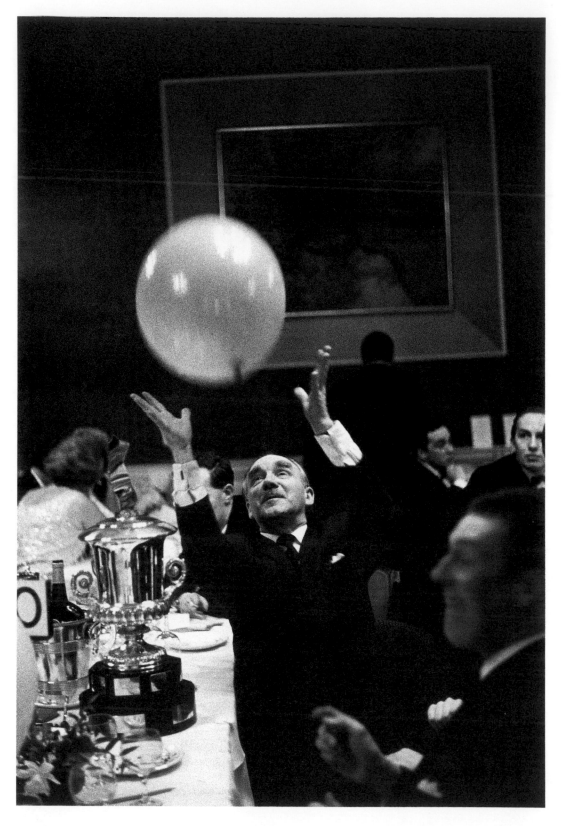

Left *MG Car Owners Ball, Edinburgh,* 1967, by David Hurn, who uses moments such as these to tell timeless tales. (© David Hurn/ Magnum.)

Right *'Bever' Skinningrove, Co. Cleveland,* nd, by Chris Killip. As the 1980s progress, photographers find new ways to present truth, authenticity and the human condition. (© Chris Killip.)

social science it slid quite reasonably into a publishing world that accommodated books by Cartier-Bresson on Russia or Brassaï on Spain. In many ways these books were exemplary. They took photography out of its habitually condensed and abbreviated presentation in magazines, and gave space for visual ideas to develop. But such works remained rare. In the late 1960s, however, came some sightings of a change in attitude – in one part because young photographers were naturally reacting against art-directed classicism, in another

because messages filtered through to Europe of the more exciting possibilities opening up in the United States.

In Britain the chief prophet was Tony Ray-Jones. His work was like no other in content or kind – being a rich fusion of American and European visual influences brought to an essentially British understanding of eccentricity and whimsy. A graphic designer turned photographer, Ray-Jones became caught up in the excitement and stimulation he found when he went to the United States in 1960. Photography was a live issue there in a way quite unknown in Britain and he fell under the spell of photographers like Frank and Winogrand and the legendary art director Brodovitch. He returned to Britain in 1966, an established magazine photographer, with strong desires to pursue a more personal kind of image making than most magazines would tolerate. Following leads from his American experiences, he mapped out a major project, 'The English at Leisure,' bought a camper van to use as a temporary home and set about travelling the country. His search was for old customs, social events and seaside gatherings that brought together the surreal humor and gentle pathos he found so particularly English. As the work began to be seen, primarily in little photographic magazines like *Album* and *Creative Camera*, Ray-Jones' voice became authoritative among young photographers. On the edge of a period when their medium was struggling to be viewed as something more than illustration, he became champion to a small but growing group demanding recognition from the art world. 'Photography for me is an exciting and personal way of reacting to and commenting on one's environment,' Ray-Jones wrote, 'and I feel that it is perhaps a great pity that more

people don't consider it as a medium of self-expression instead of selling themselves to the commercial world of journalism and advertising.' Such words, coupled with his increasingly complex, structured pictures, were music to the ears of young photographers. He wrote this in 1968 when it seemed that the young had inherited the earth and could overthrow the existing order by charm and individual energy alone.

Sadly, Ray-Jones died from leukemia in 1972, but his wish for a photography without compromise touched the generation to follow. His mentor, Brodovitch, had written some years earlier that 'the photographer, if he is to maintain his integrity, must be responsible to himself, he must seek a public which will accept his vision, rather than pervert his vision to fit that public.' This was Ray-Jones' guiding principle, passed on to photographers already seeing careers outside the world of magazines. As had happened a decade earlier in the United States, it was beginning to seem possible for the photographer to function independently, as an individual, with all the personality, wilfulness and grace of an artist. By 1970 the stage was set for photography's ascendency.

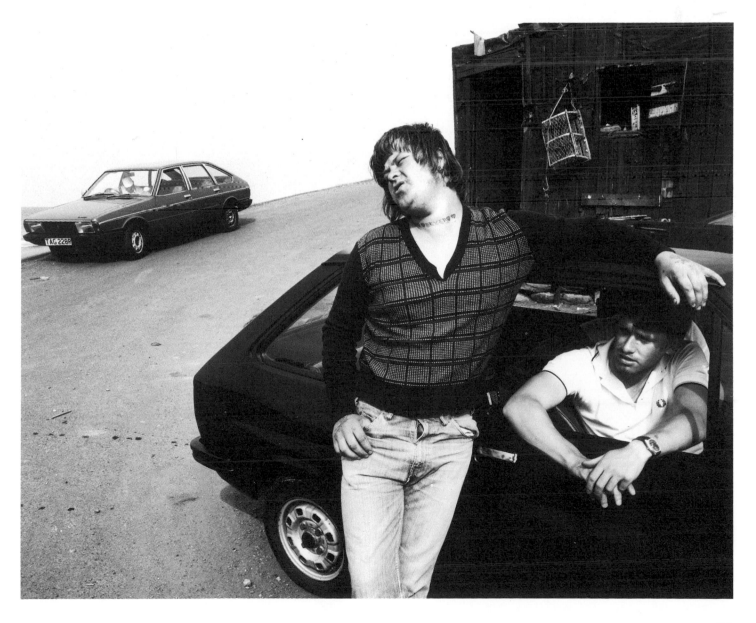

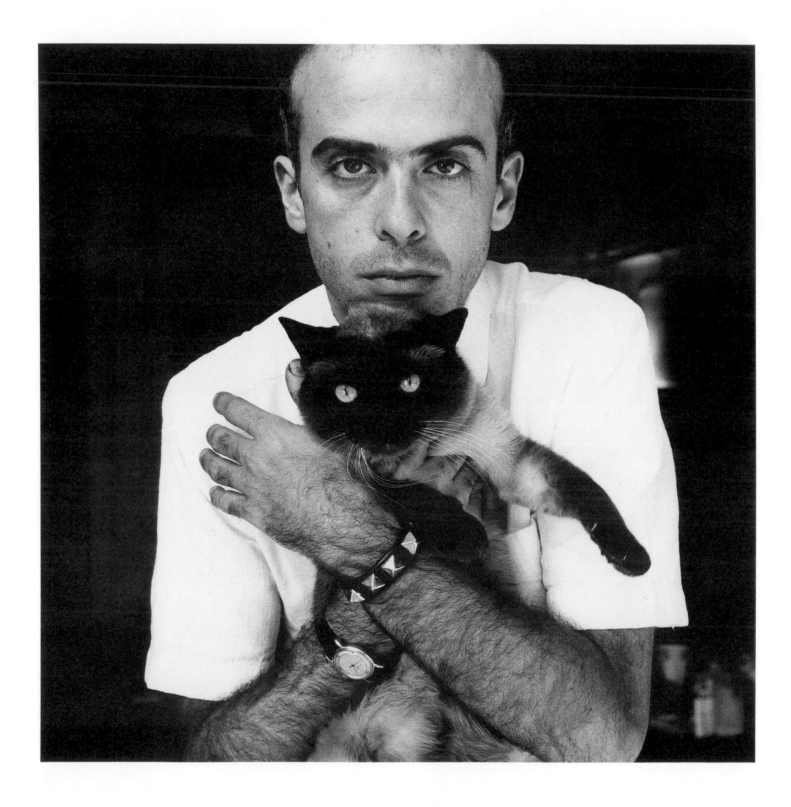

Above *Francesco Clemente*, 1984, by David Bailey, whose portraits first attracted attention in the 1960s. (© David Bailey.)

Right *Jean Shrimpton, Egypt*, 1973, by David Bailey for *Vogue*. For many Bailey and Shrimpton's personal and professional relationship epitomized 'swinging London.' (© David Bailey.)

CHAPTER NINE

The Selling Image

Fashion, Design and Art Direction

In view of the way it has affected twentieth-century life, it seems strange, though not altogether surprising, that no one has published a thorough historical survey of advertising photography. Despite the sociological value of such a study, the problem for writers on photography seems to be that the intervention of designers and art directors on the unsullied vision of the photographer has rendered the resulting image tainted and impure as a photograph, and therefore unworthy of serious consideration. It would be unrealistic to pretend that more than a small percentage of commercial photographs might repay the closer investigation we have begun here: but equally it is short-sighted to consign even the best of such work to oblivion – as though it should be seen exclusively in terms of morally and intellectually bankrupt consumer capitalism.

Many great photographers have sought financial support by undertaking paid commissions at some point in their careers, and we are unlikely to reach any accurate and well-rounded conclusions regarding their contribution to the medium if we overlook this. The list of famous names who worked frequently for magazines is endless, but Brassaï, Man Ray, Walker Evans, André Kertész, Henri Cartier-Bresson, Robert Frank and Diane Arbus serve as examples. For them and many others working to a brief, whether for editorial or advertising purposes, has involved an irreconcilable dichotomy between commerce – bread and butter – and 'personal' work. In other cases the situation is not so clear cut. Take the example of Walker Evans; some of whose most celebrated photographs were taken on commission for the Farm Security Administration and later for *Fortune* magazine. They now sit happily on the walls of museums and art galleries throughout the world. The recent publication of the book *Diane Arbus: Magazine Work* was partially intended as a corrective to the notion that she was solely a photographer of human oddities: it also made clear that working for magazines rarely involved her in any compromise of a highly individualistic stance as a photographer.

Nevertheless photography critics have generally found it convenient to approach an individual's *oeuvre* by consciously avoiding any more than a fleeting acknowledgment to his or

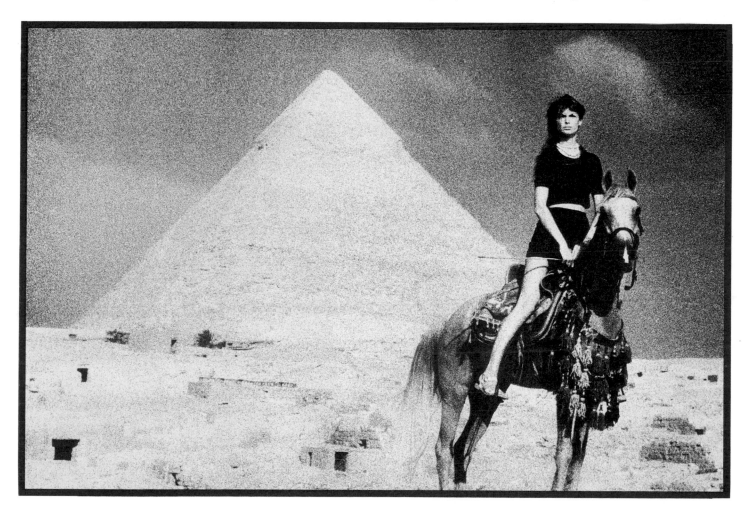

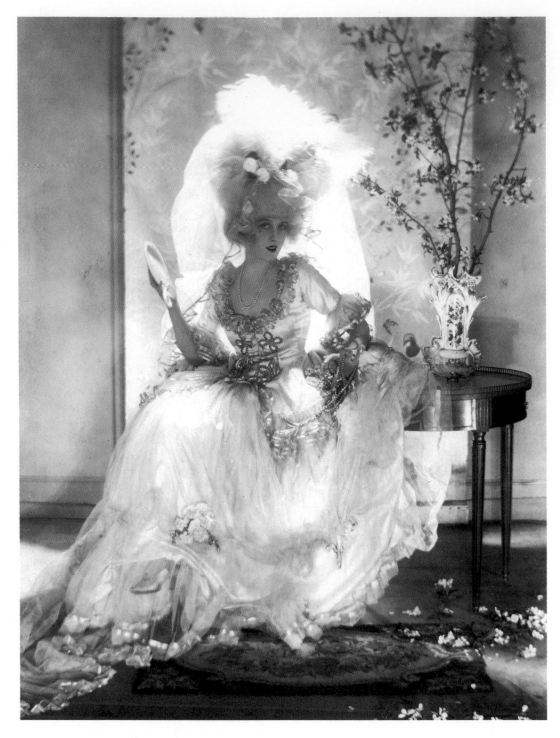

her commissioned work. The tendency is to promote hard and fast categorization, but it could be argued that it is both more illuminating for the medium, and more honest, not to dismiss commercial photography so lightly.

When mass-market magazine methods brought a boom in advertising photography early in the twentieth century many of the leading creative photographers quite happily embraced this new challenge. The advent of the Leica camera in the 1920s similarly gave birth to a new school of news and reportage photographers working for magazines. They brought personal vision to public concerns.

The arrival of fresh – but commercially linked – areas of expression for photographers presents this continuing dilemma quite neatly. A comparison between Edward Steichen and Alfred Stieglitz illustrates the point. The two men had met in 1900, by which time both were leading practitioners of pictorial photography. By 1920 they had both rejected the painterly deceits of pictorialism in favor of a sharp-focus approach which relied for its power on inherently photographic methods and principles. Subsequently the paths they chose were markedly different. Stieglitz continued to pursue photography in a wholly personal and private manner. Steichen, however, was persuaded in 1923 by the publisher Condé Nast, to work under contract for *Vogue* and *Vanity Fair.* Now there seems little evidence in the earlier work of these men to suggest that Stieglitz is a superior photographer to Steichen: Steichen's *Flatiron Building* (1905) is hardly a lesser milestone of early-twentieth-century photography than, for example, Stieglitz's *The Steerage* (1907). In the opinion of most commentators though, Steichen's 'selling out' to Condé Nast in 1923 signalled virtually the termination of his career as a serious photographer.

Such easy dismissal of such distasteful applications of photography continues today. In *American Photography* (1984) Jonathan Green clearly believes Lee Friedlander (see Chapter 9) to be a major artist – he gets about ten pages to Irving Penn's one line. But how does such a view incorporate the fact that Friedlander's nudes of pop-star Madonna were published recently in *Playboy*. Friedlander took these photographs some years ago, for a personal project and involving no concession to the popular taste of *Playboy*. After Madonna's rise to fame the photographs were obviously at a premium, and Friedlander sold *Playboy* the rights for 'a considerable sum.' Presumably Green would not argue that

retrospective payment had lessened the photographs in any way, but this instance does serve to emphasize that perhaps the boundaries between art and commercialism are often more blurred than purist critics would care to admit. And of course there are few photographer-artists who would decline the sale of their work to a dealer or collector from the walls of a gallery.

I first saw Friedlander's photographs in an American edition of a fashion magazine – *Harper's Bazaar* – in 1963. The person who had commissioned these shots, art director Marvin Israel, had already published Friedlander in 1961. Likewise Israel was responsible for introducing Diane Arbus to a largely uninformed public. Unless we insist that art galleries and coffee-table format books are the only true homes for photographs it seems a matter of regret that opportunities for great photographers to be published in magazines are so few

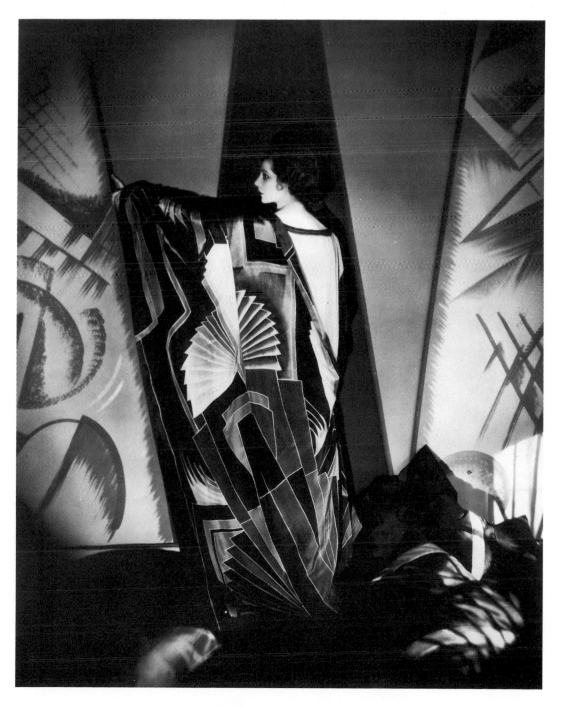

Right *Art Deco Gown*, 1925, photographed in the apartment of Nina Price for American *Vogue* by Edward Steichen. Steichen, De Meyer's successor at *Vogue*, introduced ideas of modernism to contemporary fashion photography. (Courtesy American *Vogue*. Copyright © 1925, renewed 1953, by The Condé Nast Publications Inc.)

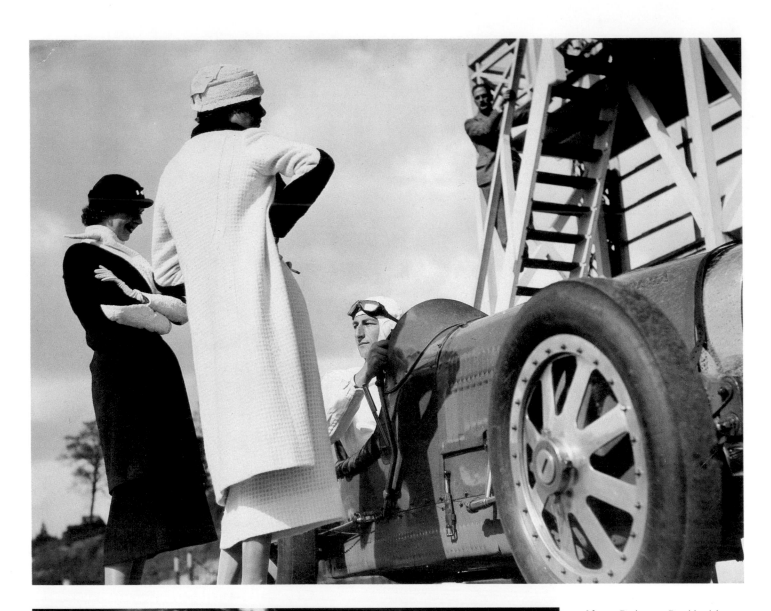

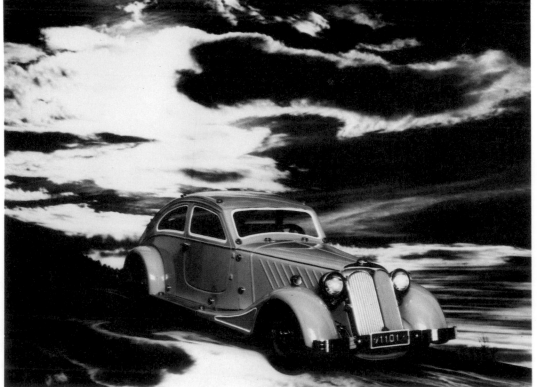

Above *Burberry at Brooklands* by Shaw Wildman for Matita Fashions, 1932/3. An early example of fashion in the realist manner. (Courtesy Sally Osborne.)

Left A constructed fantasy for Standard Cars by John Havinden, 1936/7. (Courtesy John Havinden.)

Far right, top *Coming . . . Parma Blue,* 1944, pictured for American *Vogue* by John Rawlings, who had directed *Vogue*'s first London studio. (Courtesy of the Edward C. Blum Design Laboratory, New York.)

Right Untitled swimwear photograph by George Hoyningen-Huené for American *Vogue,* 1930. (Courtesy American *Vogue.* Copyright © 1930, renewed 1958, by The Condé Nast Publications Inc.)

Opposite right *Lucile Brokaw, Long Island, NY,* by Martin Munkacsi for *Harper's Bazaar,* 1933. (Courtesy Joan Munkacsi.)

today. Rather than be worried at the prospect of 'pure photographers' being art-directed we might equally mourn the loss of great art directors, such as Israel or his renowned predecessor Alexey Brodovitch. The absence of such figures today, with a commitment to exciting and innovative photography, has resulted in the loss of an important forum for many fine photographers.

In Britain, advertising photography only slowly gained acceptance. A writer in the *British Journal of Photography* in 1904 noted that still 'we see little in the way of half-tone blocks.' With the decline of British industry in the 1920s, however, manufacturers increasingly sought the aid of advertising to sell their products, which in turn brought about a revolution in the application of photography to advertising techniques. As mentioned in chapter 5, advertising photography became one of the principle media by which the German 'new objectivity' was channelled into Britain. In Germany Hugo Erfurth, Albert Renger-Patzsch and Hans Finsler had already been enlisted into the ranks of advertising photographers. They were emulated in Britain by Walter Nurnberg (a German emigré), John Havinden, Barbara Ker-Seymer and Noel Griggs, who first brought a modernist sensibility to British photography.

Fashion photography represents a slightly different, rather specialized case. Or at least the editorial photographs taken for magazines, which, at least in theory, offer the photographer a greater degree of freedom of expression. It is certainly true, especially in the United States, that the most imaginative commercial photographers have often moved

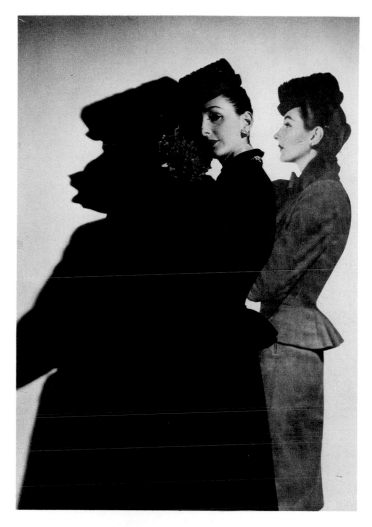

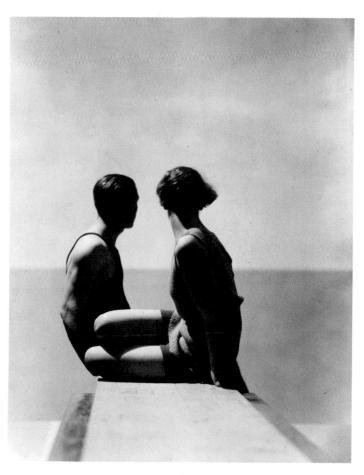

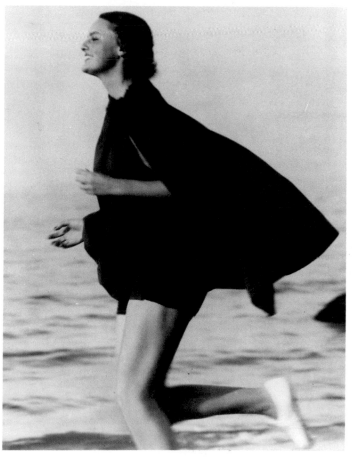

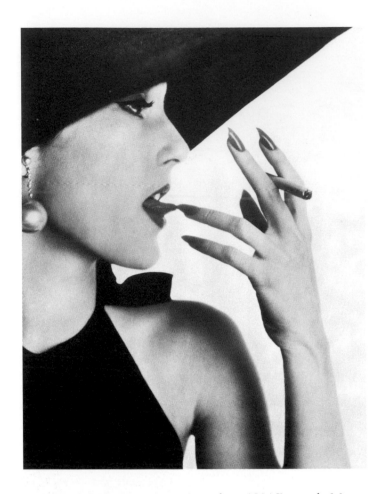

towards fashion magazines. As early as 1914 Baron de Meyer had become the first contract photographer for *Vogue*. His dreamy, evanescent lighting and Whistlerian poses worked well within the rather rigid black-bordered layouts of the

magazine, and his social connections in smart society were added bait for his *Vogue* employers. After World War I however the Edwardian milieu in which De Meyer had flourished rapidly became an anachronism, and his pictorial photographic style was soon equally outmoded. He was replaced at *Vogue* by Steichen in 1923, though the presentation of the magazine itself showed little change until the 1930s. The chief agent for hauling *Vogue* into the modern age was the arrival of a Turkish art director, Mehemed Fehmy Agha, in 1929. Dr Agha transformed the page layouts, using photographs in a much more graphic and powerful way. He also had strong opinions on the type of photograph which could best illustrate fashion. Until the 1930s fashion photographs were almost exclusively posed, theatrical and artificially lit in the studio. Agha would have no truck with this approach. Writing in 1944 he likened such efforts to the artifice of the Victorian photographer H P Robinson: 'Instead of recording the outside world they create their own universe in the studio, just as Robinson did; a world full of flowers, gilded carvings, baroque statuary and Powers girls in hieratic poses . . . it is a cross between stagecraft, interior decoration, ballet and society portrait painting done by camera.' Agha advocated instead what he termed straight photography: the argument oddly parallels the debate over naturalism between the supporters of Emerson and of Robinson in the nineteenth century: 'Fashion snapshot, on the other hand – the informal, lively reporting on sartorial doings of today, against a background of real landscapes outdoors, real restaurants, apartments, ballrooms indoors – is a field where some of the best straight photographic work is being done, often by people who also have made their mark in photojournalism.'

Above *Woman with Tobacco on the tip of her tongue* by Irving Penn for American *Vogue*, 1951. Using elegance, restraint and precise formality, Penn exchanged the direct depiction of fashion for the ideas clothes could conjour. (Courtesy American *Vogue*. Copyright © 1951, renewed 1979, by The Condé Nast Publications Inc.)

Right *Hat Check Girl*, 1937, by Cecil Beaton. Hovering between stylized fashion and a documentary image of 'style,' this picture hints at a fashion interest in surrealism in the 1930s. (Sotheby's London.)

Far right *Dovima with Elephants*, Evening dress by Dior, Cirque d'Hiver, Paris, France, August 1955, by Richard Avedon. With Penn, Avedon dominated postwar fashion photography for American magazines, creating a sophisticated style consistently conveying the mood of the moment. (Photograph by Richard Avedon. Copyright © by Richard Avedon Inc. All rights reserved.)

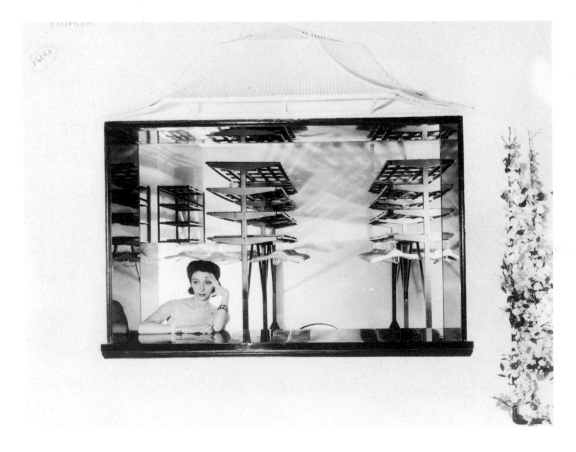

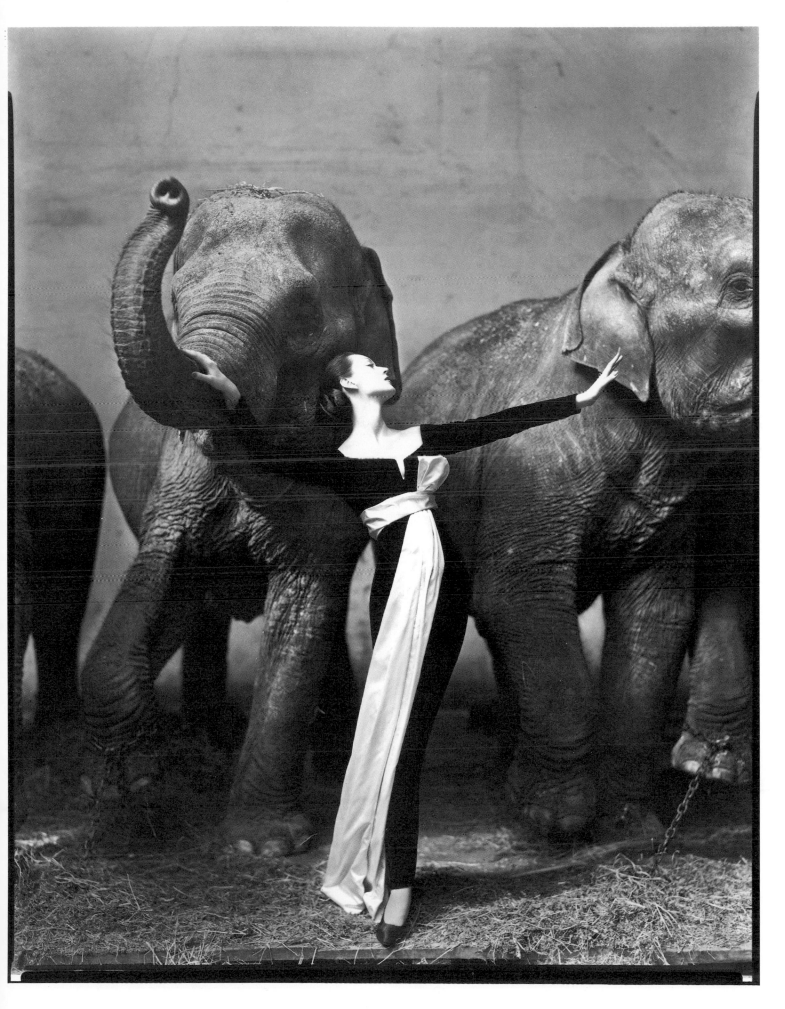

As an example of a former photojournalist he cited Martin Munkacsi. Munkacsi had been persuaded to join American *Harper's Bazaar* in 1934, forsaking his career as a reportage photographer in Europe. He was the first consistently to apply snapshot techniques to fashion photography: the shock caused when, on his first session, he instructed the model to *run* along the beach is now legendary. The *Bazaar*'s great competitor, *Vogue*, soon felt left behind in the race to respond to what was felt to be a new kind of woman, active and liberated; to meet this challenge they had to look no further than a young woman photographer already on their staff, Toni Frissell, who was already providing society snapshots in an unposed, natural style. She was soon applying this approach to fashion reportage with conspicuous success.

It should not be supposed that the informal snapshot took over entirely. In fact the history of fashion photography, right up to the present day, might be seen as a continual tipping of the scales between the formal and the informal. When Richard Avedon first worked for *Harper's Bazaar* in 1944 Munkacsi no longer worked for the magazine and his influence there had faded, though it was to some extent perpetuated by Louise Dahl-Wolfe. Still Avedon felt that the type of fashion photograph that prevailed was too static, the women too unreal. Remembering the lessons of his youthful admiration for Munkacsi he re-invented action. It is astonishing how often a device such as conveying movement – or the impression of movement – could be reinvented. *Art Direction* magazine, for example, reported in 1964 that *Harper's Bazaar* had broken with 'the stand there and look pretty school' in a feature with the title 'Bazaar + Avedon = models in action.' It was as though this had not been a preoccupation of Avedon's for the previous 20 years.

In the 1950s there appears to have been a feeling that *Vogue* magazine was again falling behind the times. The haughty

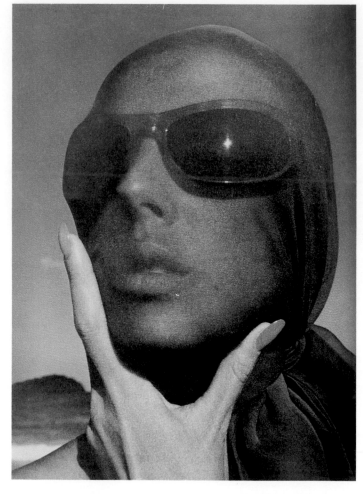

Below left Shock tactics were Chris Von Wangenheim's hallmark, as typified in this beauty shot made for Dior in 1976. (Courtesy Christian Dior, New York.)

Below John Lennon and Yoko Ono, 1980, taken by Annie Leibovitz during the last photo-session before Lennon's death. (Courtesy Sidney Janis Gallery, New York.)

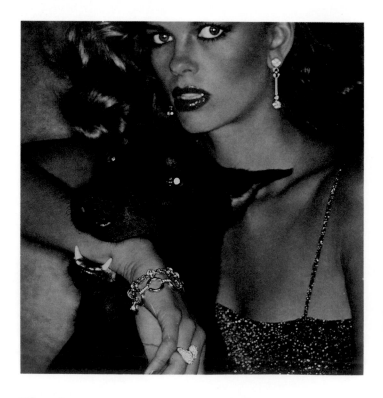

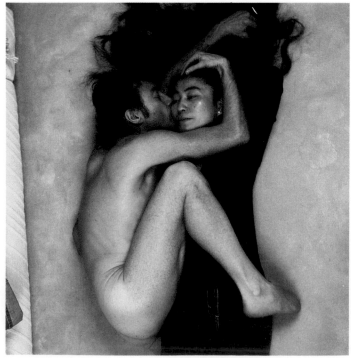

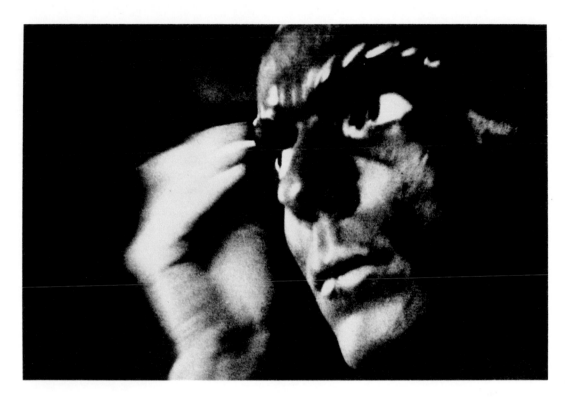

elegance they still purveyed was out of key with the youth movement and rock and roll. The art director Alexander Liberman (who had replaced Agha in 1941) took the bold step of signing up William Klein in 1955. Klein, who had never shot fashion previously, proved a great success, in spite of his irreverent attitude to the whole business. He managed to retain a lot of the freshness of his street pictures in his fashion work, mostly working outdoors, though of course with the major difference that here the action was directed entirely by Klein. Liberman took a similar risk with Bruce Davidson a few years later. Oddly, he asked Cartier-Bresson if he thought Davidson would make a good fashion photographer, and received the advice 'if he can photograph Brooklyn Gangs he can photograph fashion.' Davidson only shot fashion for *Vogue* for three years, and his pictures were successful precisely because of his lack of aptitude for the world of *Vogue*. Obliged to produce something from his early fashion sessions he was forced to turn the sittings into something as close to reportage as he could make it. He used the same equipment and techniques, a Leica and high-speed Ektachrome, that he would for reportage work. The result was some of the grainiest, fuzziest pictures ever to grace the pages of *Vogue*, and also some of the most vibrant and thoroughly natural.

Over the last 30 years fashion photography has continued to exist in most affluent parts of the world, despite the feminist movement and the lessening power of couturiers to dictate styles. The most interesting fashion photography has usually been produced by individuals who have shared something of William Klein's irreverence to the business. Only a few of these have photographed fashion exclusively. Most notable among this minority are Helmut Newton and Guy Bourdin. By the early 1960s they were both sufficiently well established to be able to push magazines (particularly the French

edition of *Vogue*) into accepting work that closely corresponded to their own visual and sexual obsessions. They had found in fashion photography, once they could bend the rules, the perfect vehicle to express themselves. Neither was a

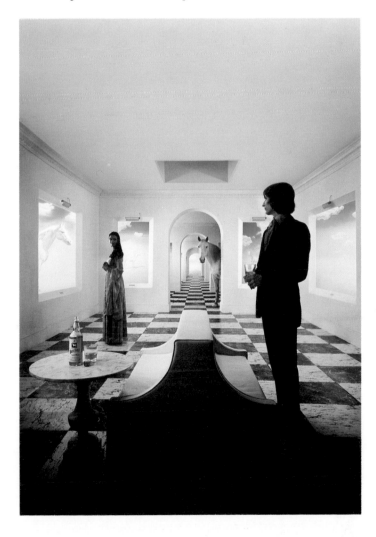

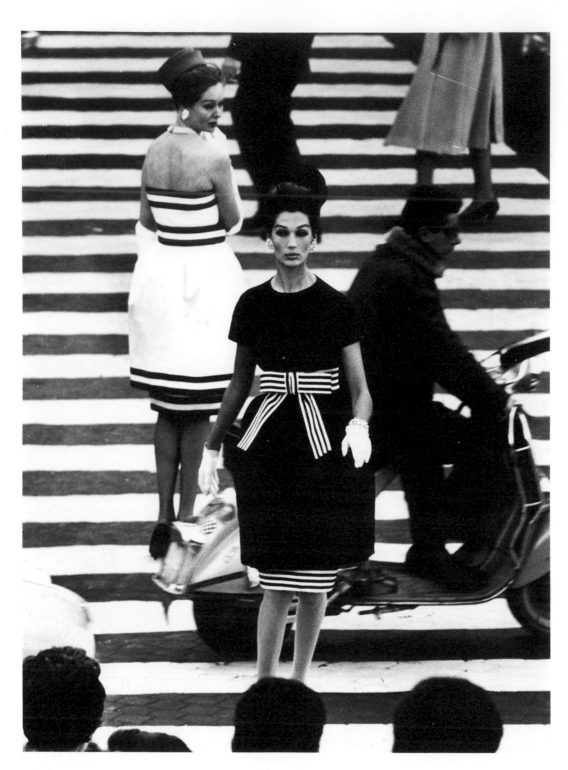

Left *Rome,* 1960, by William Klein for *Vogue* introduces elements of streetlife photography into the remote world of *haute couture* (© William Klein.)

frustrated landscape photographer or portraitist, they work-ed in an environment of chic eroticism that was essential in creating the sort of images they most wanted to make. New-ton has stated frankly 'how else could I draw on the services of the best make-up artists, hairdressers and models that the world has to offer?' Such was Guy Bourdin's prestige at French *Vogue* by the 1970s that he was able to dictate that his photographs would run in sequences, each over a double page spread, suggesting a filmic narrative. He was also re-sponsible for a revolutionary advertising concept for Charles Jourdan shoes in which the actual product occupied only a tiny proportion of the picture frame: what attracted the read-er was a graphically subtle Bourdin photograph, which again

suggested an undefined but intriguing narrative. As the high fashion magazines have become increasingly conservative in the 1980s (the United States dictates largely in this field and is catering for the new middle-class yuppies) it is ironically in advertising photography rather than in the editorial pages of magazines where some of the most innovative fashion photo-graphy is being done.

Few of the best postwar photographers to get involved with fashion have stayed in the business for any length of time. Bruce Davidson, who only stayed three years, said the pictures 'were my pictures, but I felt removed from the world they represented, and at the same time attracted to it.' Duane Michals first worked for American *Harper's Bazaar* in 1963, at

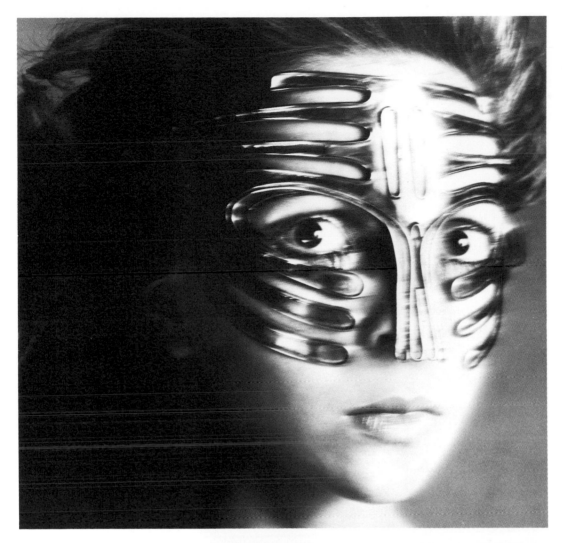

Left *Penelope Tree, Mask by Ungaro,* Paris studio, January 1968, by Richard Avedon. Tree was one of a small group of models whose faces came to symbolize the break with convention in the 1960s. (Photograph by Richard Avedon. Copyright © by Richard Avedon Inc. All rights reserved.)

Below Terence Donovan, who took this picture for Alexon in 1985, was closely associated with Bailey and Brian Duffy. The work of 'The Terrible Three' was dominant in the frenetic 1960s when London was the style capital of the world. (© Terence Donovan; courtesy Saatchi & Saatchi Compton Ltd.)

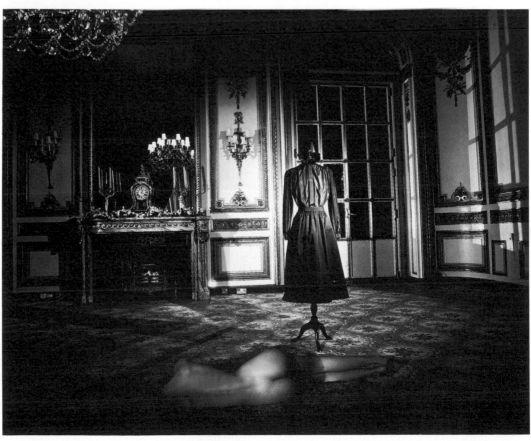

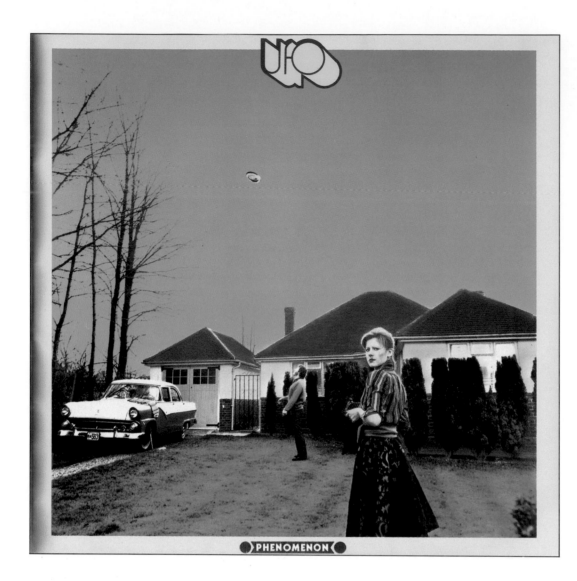

the invitation of two young art directors, Ruth Ansel and Bea Feitler, who had recently taken over from Marvin Israel, and who maintained his sensitive and elegant approach to layout until the magazine opted for mediocrity in 1972. Michals is even less equivocal than Davidson, believing that his fashion photographs have nothing whatsoever to do with the 'serious' body of work by which he is much better known to the photographic fraternity. The disavowal of his commercial work is not, presumably, a defensive ploy, since his fashion photographs, certainly in the 1960s, are quite accomplished in their own terms. Some of the techniques he used – such as partially blurred imagery – parallel or perhaps even prefigure experiments along similar lines in his personal work. None but the earnest delver into back numbers of fashion magazines will probably even know of this aspect of Michals' career, but in the light of his interest in narrative the way in which he succeeded in grafting these concerns onto some of his fashion pictures is at least intriguing, and does not deserve to be completely omitted from his photo-history.

Fashion photography is, just as much as any other branch of the medium, perfectly responsive to the application of art-history techniques, though these methods have rarely been tested. To take a few examples. Richard Avedon's career at *Harper's Bazaar* took off in 1944: the leaders of the earlier generation of fashion photographers left the scene at almost exactly the same time – Hoyningen-Huené, for example, retired from fashion in 1945, Baron De Meyer died in 1946, and Munkacsi's best work was behind him. It is surely no accident that Avedon became arguably the greatest fashion photographer of the century by being the first to combine the classical elegance and compositional rigor of Huené, with the feeling for movement and realism associated with Munkacsi.

Britain in the 1950s produced few fashion photographers of real merit. The best known is John French. Not especially innovatory as a photographer he is nevertheless revered for his charm and patience as a guide and mentor, by models and designers as well as photographers. Many of the young British photographers who helped revolutionize fashion in the 1960s trained with John French, most notably Terence Donovan and David Bailey. As Bailey has testified 'during the eleven months I was with John French I learned more about attitudes and how to deal with clients than about photography,' and it was this grounding in what makes fashion tick that provided the solid platform from which Bailey and his colleagues could rebel. You didn't get to work for *Vogue* in 1961 simply because you wore jeans and had a shaggy haircut, and it was French who supplied the fashion know-how.

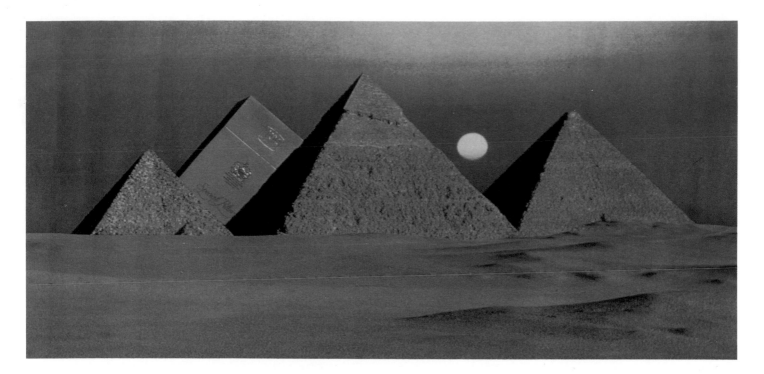

One of the leading European fashion photographers today is Peter Lindbergh. His photographs are graphically powerful, dramatic and sexy, often conceived as mini-narratives in series he pursues for perhaps several months at a time. These are characteristics his work has in common with both Helmut Newton and the late Chris Von Wangenheim. These three are possibly the only German-born photographers to achieve prominence in fashion, and it cannot be coincidence that their work exhibits some marked similarities. Lindbergh's narrative concerns intriguingly hark back to Bob Richardson, an American who achieved prominence in the 1960s by telling poignant stories of detached, rather sad women in eight-page dramas in which fashion reporting was – or so it appeared – a secondary concern for the photographer. Peter Lindbergh must similarly exercise a lot of subtle persuasion with magazine editors to be allowed the freedom he needs to make his kind of pictures today: perhaps most remarkable is that he is able to work almost solely in black and white, at a time when fashion magazines are almost entirely orientated towards color production.

The leading American photographer now is Bruce Weber: he will not undertake any commission which involves compromising his own photographic interests. Consequently he has hardly ever worked for the American edition of *Vogue*, but has ironically been offered the license to shoot what he wants by sympathetic advertisers such as Calvin Klein and Ralph

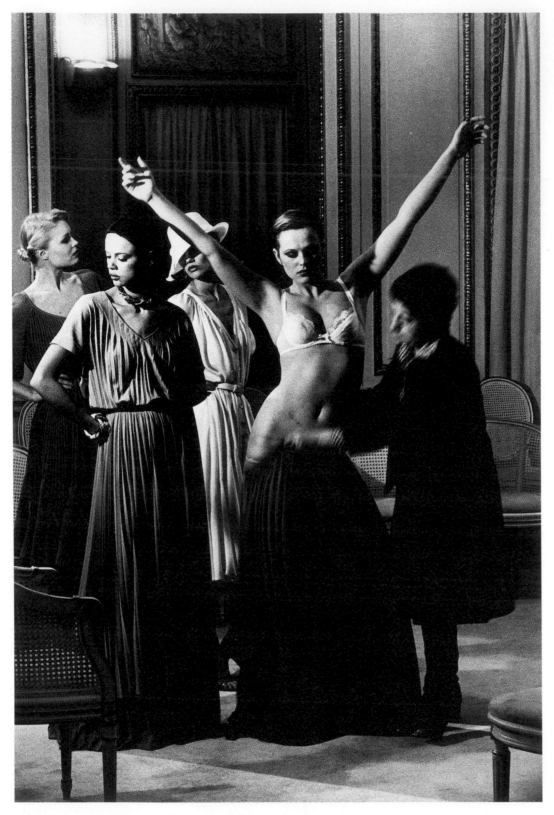

Right Linking fashion to social and sexual mores is Helmut Newton's signature. Taken for French *Vogue* in 1975, this picture reverses expectations and displays woman as the aggressor. (© Helmut Newton.)

Left Playing with and questioning traditional concepts of femininity, Helmut Newton structures his pictures into narratives, with beginnings and endings left to the viewer. Taken for French *Vogue* in the salon of Jean Patou. (© Helmut Newton.)

Lauren. Photographs made solely on his own initiative he publishes in books or exhibitions, and in a sense his commercial endeavors help subsidize these extracurricular activities. As the creative opportunities offered by fashion magazines become increasingly limited there is a growing tendency for fashion photographers to look for other outlets for their work. Deborah Turbeville, for example, who is rarely seen in English magazines, is nevertheless well known in Britain through her books such as *Wallflower* and *Unseen Versailles*.

Some commentators have suggested that fashion photography came to an end in the 1960s: in the sense that fashion itself has been largely 'retro' since then they may have a point. Hiro's space-age visions of Courreges' clothes were perhaps the last forward-looking moment. But new names and innovatory approaches are constantly appearing and the fashion photography refuses to go away: in many ways it appears to have more to do with our everyday lives and yet its real function is, in Irving Penn's words, to sell dreams.

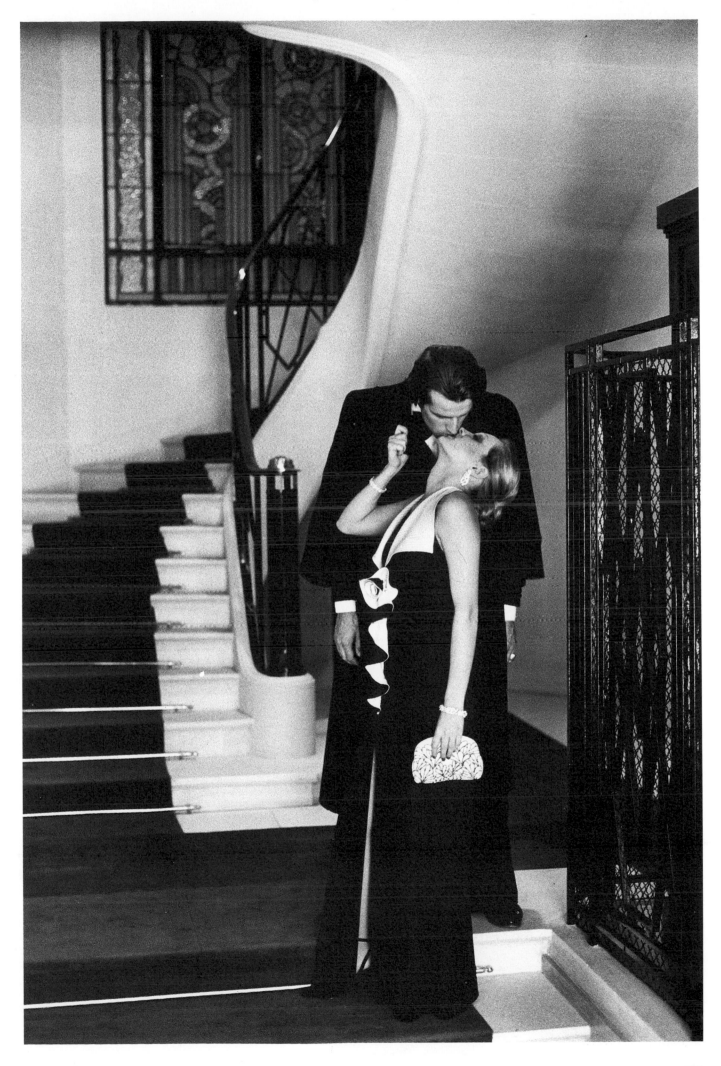

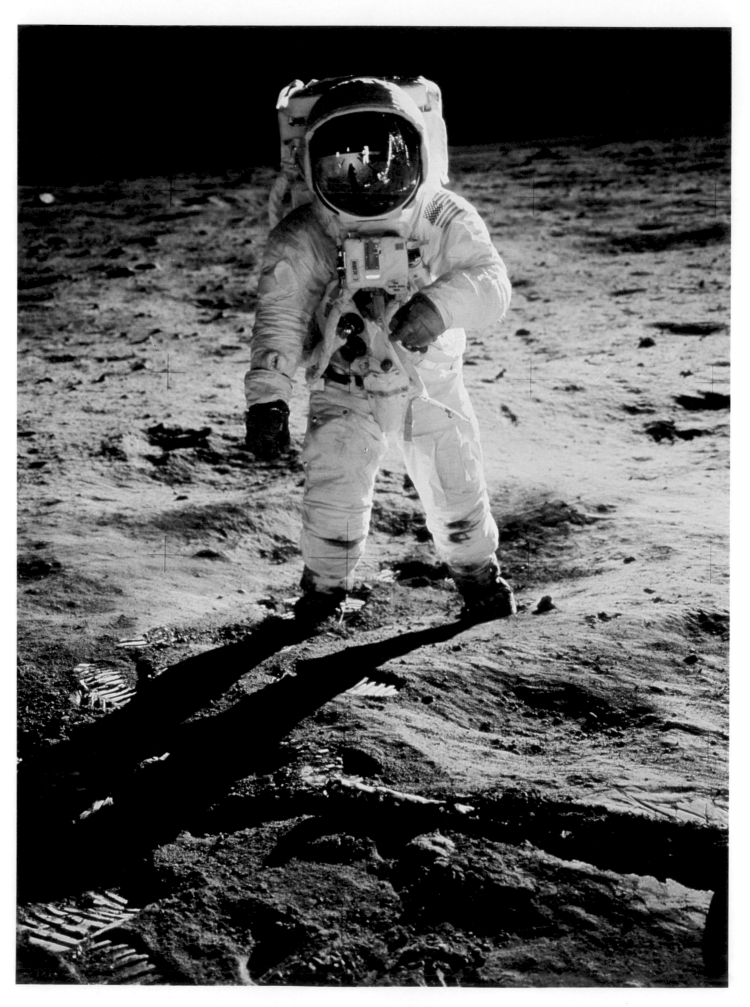

CHAPTER TEN

In Search of the Invisible

Photography and Science

From the beginning, photography has been linked with science. Significantly, Daguerre's invention was first announced at a joint meeting of the Académie des Sciences and the Académie des Beaux-Arts in 1839. But scientists recognized the potential importance of photography long before they were able to exploit it. Initially, photography's main use was the simple reproduction of the visible world. It could record more precisely and more immediately than a draftsman's hand the way the world looks to the human eye. Even this basic function has been of immense value to science. For disciplines such as entymology and geology, the mere compilation of photographic data provides objectively agreed 'type specimens' against which variants can be judged. Photography thus becomes an arbiter of scientific truth.

Scientific photography has become crucial to the communication of scientific ideas and discoveries. From the 1840s, scientific journals then proliferating throughout the western world were carrying photographs that enabled scientists in distant lands to compare research and judge findings with a speed and detail hitherto impossible. Through photography, the major modern scientific developments have been made accessible to millions of people almost instantaneously. Images of the first nuclear explosion in New Mexico in 1945 and the first hydrogen explosion in the Pacific in 1952 demonstrated to the startled populations of all countries that a new power had entered the world, what the inventor of the bomb, J Robert Oppenheimer called, quoting the *Bhagavad-Gita*, 'Death, the Shatterer of Worlds.'

Photography plays a critical role in introducing the medical student to the world beyond his or her immediate experience. In 1852, in the Surrey County Asylum, the first systematic photographic record of patients was started. Later, the US Surgeon General's office produced a six-volume compendium of photographs of Civil War wounds. The science of anatomy soon made great strides through photography. Where pioneers like Leonardo had to painstakingly draw what they saw in the process of dissections and autopsies, modern scientists are able to reproduce in limitless quantities the most exact replications of any anatomical subject.

But photography's greatest contribution to science has not been simply reproducing what is already visible to the human eye, but in providing information inaccessible to it. It has revealed views of the world hitherto unseen, often startlingly unexpected. From the earliest daguerrotypes to the latest digitally-encoded computer-reconstructed images, photography – in its broadest sense – has broken the boundaries of vision imposed by the limitations of the human retina. With microscopes and telescopes, it has expanded our perceptions of scale. With high-speed and time-lapse photography, it has expanded our perception of time. With ultraviolet and

Left Buzz Aldrin photographed by Neil Armstrong on the moon's surface, 21 July 1969 – a twentieth-century icon. (NASA.)

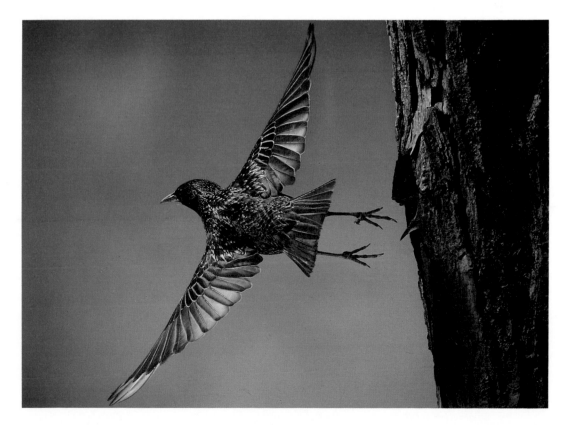

Right A starling frozen in motion by high-speed flash becomes sculptural. By Stephen Dalton. (© Stephen Dalton/NHPA.)

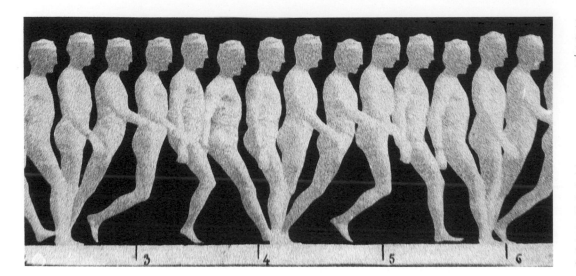

Left A pioneering chronograph describing movement by Etienne Jules Marey c 1883. (Musée Marey, Beaune.)

Below Sequential photography disproved nineteenth-century theories of animal locomotion. From a series by Eadweard Muybridge, 1884/5. (Eadweard Muybridge Collection, Kingston upon Thames Museum and Art Gallery.)

infrared sensors it has expanded our perception beyond the limits of the visible spectrum. Photographs have been taken in deepest space, in the depths of the ocean and inside the human body, depicting realms previously envisioned only by wild flights of imagination. In the process, photography has produced images of both scientific value and astonishing aesthetic beauty.

In 1880, in a speech to the Société Française de la Photographie, the astronomer P J C Janssen praised the art of photography from a scientist's viewpoint. 'The sensitive photographic film is the true retina of the scientist,' he said, 'It faithfully preserves the images which depict themselves upon it, and reproduces and multiplies them indefinitely on request; in the radiative spectrum it covers a range more than double that which the eye can perceive and soon perhaps will cover it all; finally, it takes advantage of that admirable property which allows the accumulation of events, and whereas our retina erases all impressions more than a tenth of a second old, the photographic retina preserves them and accumulates them over a practically limitless time.'

It was in the field of photomicrography that photography made its first scientific venture. Pioneers Talbot and Reade photographed wood shavings, insect wings and fly's eyes with the aid of microscopes. But a constant technical difficulty in those days was insufficient light. Microscopes and cameras would have to be conjoined either in bright sunlight or by the illumination of oxyacetylene torches. Only in the 1850s was J B Dancer at last able to produce photomicrographs on glass of sufficient definition to be of scientific use. It was not until 1903 that a monochromatic emulsion equally sensitive to all colors was produced. This was essential to recapture what was seen through the microscope without

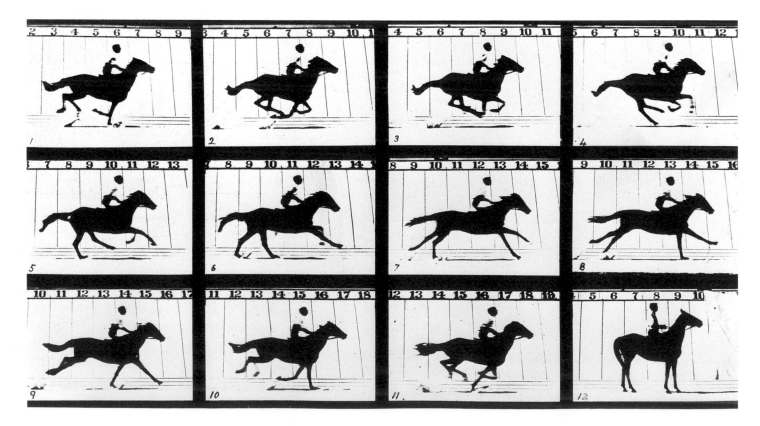

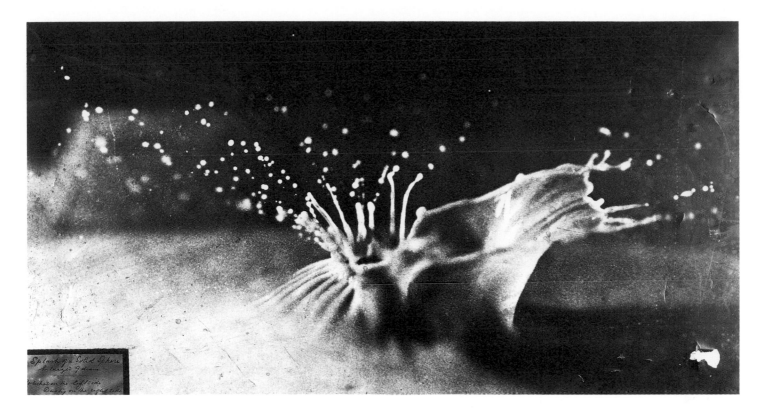

distortion. Where microscope technology led the way, photomicrography soon followed. The electron microscope was developed in the early 1930s and the first electron micrographs were taken in 1934.

In the 1930s nuclear physics was transformed by the discovery of new particles. Though the neutron's existence had been postulated theoretically, it was only confirmed by photographic evidence in 1932. Other subatomic particles –

the positron, the deuteron, and the enigmatic varieties of quarks – were all discovered photographically at a later date. This is because the only evidence for the existence of subatomic particles is the trace left by them on supersensitive nuclear emulsion. Through photography, nuclear experiments, involving thousands of infinitesimal moments and infinitesimal events could be rapidly recorded and later scrutinized at leisure in the laboratory.

Above From the first ever sequence of high-speed photographs of splashes. By A M Worthington, c 1900. (Science Museum, London.)

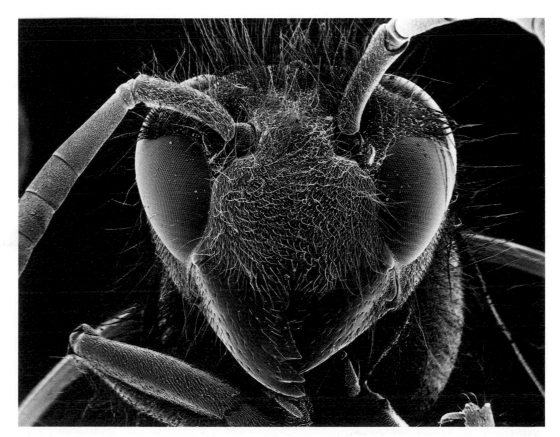

Right Magnified out of recognition by an electron microscope, a wasp's head takes on a fearsome appearance. By Gordon Leedale and Helena Cmiech. Magnification ×46. (Biophoto Associates.)

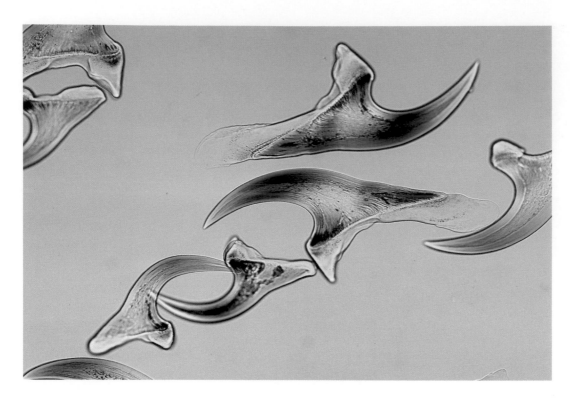

Left The hooks of a hookworm magnified into elegant abstraction. Magnification ×50. By Jan Hinsch. (Jan Hinsch, Microlaboratory E Leitz Inc, Rockleigh NJ USA.)

Scientists had postulated the idea of the virus in order to account for what they had observed in their studies of illnesses. But it was only in 1942 that the existence of the virus was confirmed by photographs taken through an electron microscope. So refined was photomicroscopy by the late 1960s that detailed photographic studies could be made of the process by which genes – which are made of DNA molecules – transmit and transcribe their essential hereditary information. Amazingly, the configurations revealed by the photographic image matched those postulated by diagrams which had been drawn on a purely theoretical basis.

With the aid of ever more powerful and complex microscopes, photographs of ever smaller units of matter have been obtained. The existence of the atom had been asserted theoretically for over 2400 years, but it was only in 1960 that E W Müller was able at last to produce a clearly defined image of the atom. These first atomic photographs, taken through the newly invented field-ion microscope, actually showed the contours of individual tungsten atoms – looking like small spots of light. Since then many images of atoms have been produced with the aid of scanners, electron-wave holographs, and increasingly powerful electron microscopes.

Right A colorless subject (a cervical smear) photographed by interference contrast which involves the use of polarizing filters and Wallaston prisms, which bend the light, give color and create a 3-D effect. Magnification ×300. (Marian Hudson/Charing Cross and Westminster Medical School.)

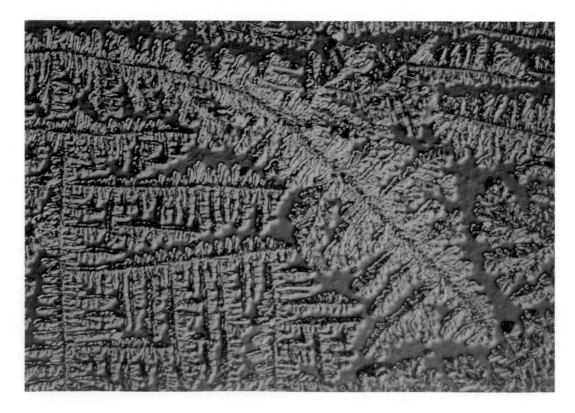

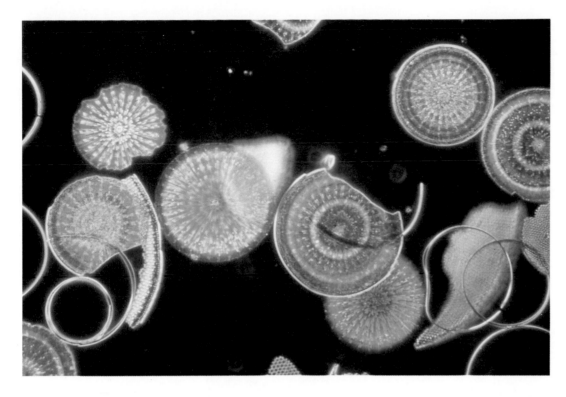

Left Centric diatoms made visible through dark ground light microscopy by Gordon Leedale. Magnification ×50. (Biophoto Associates.)

Through the agency of photomicrography, what had been merely an object of theoretical speculation, the building block of the universe, has been perceived and analysed.

Not only minute spaces, but equally minute passages of time have been photographed to reveal aspects of reality invisible to the naked eye. In the 1850s Thomas Skaife in London introduced the world to his 'pistol camera' which took 'pistol graphs.' In announcing his startling invention in the pages of *The Times*, Skaife stated that 'epochs of time, inappreciable to our natural unaided organs or vision, can be made evident to our sense by a photographic camera as

decidedly as the presence of animalculae in blood or water.' To prove his point, he published a picture of a cannon ball apparently frozen in mid-flight.

But it is Eadweard J Muybridge who is most closely associated with the wonders of high-speed photography. His famous studies of horses at the gallop, undertaken in the 1870s, were commissioned by horseowners in an attempt to answer the age-old question of whether a galloping horse at any moment lifts all four of its hoofs off the ground. Muybridge's experiment, conducted in California in 1878, consisted of a battery of twelve cameras connected to trip wires

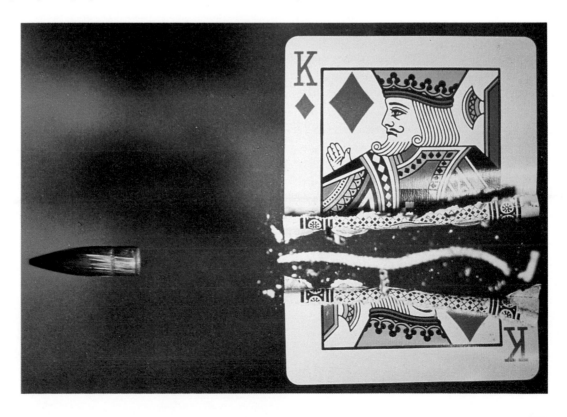

Right Impossible to witness without photography, a flying bullet is halted by Dr Harold Edgerton and a high-speed flash. (Science Photo Library.)

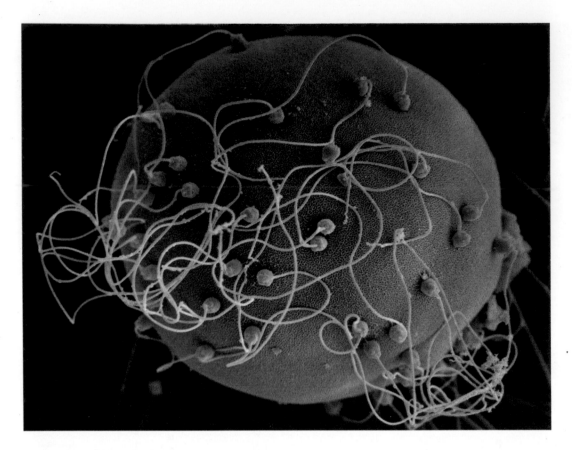

Left Sophisticated scanning electronmjcroscopy gives detail at massive magnification. Here a clam sperm is shown fertilizing an egg. Magnification ×6000. (David M Phillips, The Population Council, New York.)

which were triggered by horses galloping past against a calibrated background. These studies revealed the complexity of the horse in motion for the first time. After centuries in which painters had portrayed horses at full stretch with forelegs and hindlegs spread in opposite directions, Muybridge showed, by photographically breaking the motion down into a succession of instantaneous images, that they had got it completely wrong. Horses do indeed lift all four hoofs off the ground, but not in the way the old artists thought. Muybridge's work with sequences of images laid the foundations of cinematography (see Chapter 3).

Another to see the value of high-speed photography in making visible the invisible was the physicist and philosopher E J Mach. In Prague in the 1880s Mach devised an ingenious photographic set-up to record the shock and supersonic waves produced by the movement of a bullet through the air. Inadvertently, his work proved of considerable use to the rapidly developing study of ballistics; the sardonic Mach remarked that 'to shoot in the shortest possible time as many holes as possible in one another's bodies [is] the most important affair of modern life.'

It was the Frenchman E J Marey who exploited most cleverly the possibilities of high-speed photography in the era following Muybridge. His 1894 study of a cat being thrown off a ledge and righting itself before landing on all four paws showed how photography can analyse and explain familiar movements too fast to be understood by the naked eye. His later photographs of smoke streams in a wind tunnel were a major advance in modern aerodynamics.

A M Worthington published his fascinating studies of one of the commonest occurrences, the splash, in 1908. They revealed a world of complex movement and countermovement. He published the photographs, he said, in order to share with the public 'some of the delight that I have myself felt, in contemplating the exquisite forms that the camera lens revealed, and in watching the progress of a multitude of events, compressed indeed within the limits of a few hundredths of a second, but nonetheless orderly and inevitable, and of which the sequence is in part easy to anticipate and understand, while in part it taxes the highest mathematical powers to elucidate.'

Worthington's work anticipated that of Harold Edgerton, whose work includes studies of bats in flight. In Edgerton's system the movement of the bats themselves set off the electronically-controlled flashes which exposed the moment-by-moment manipulation of their wings. High-speed photography has developed to such an extent that even the movement of light waves can now be captured with the use of laser-triggered shutters. The exposure time is less than a picosecond – a million millionth of a second.

Time-lapse photography is the mirror-image of high-speed photography. Here a prolonged or repeated exposure is used to capture phenomena which happen so slowly that they are invisible to the eye. In this way, the sun's analemma – the figure-eight described by the changing position of the sun at its zenith over the period of a year – was recorded with astonishing clarity in a twelve-month experiment conducted between 1978 and 1979 by Dennis di Cicco.

Fox Talbot, the great pioneer of photography, correctly predicted that one day, 'the eye of the camera would see plainly where the human eye would find nothing but darkness.' This prophecy has born fruit with the development of emulsions sensitive to parts of the spectrum not visible to human eyes, that is, wavelengths at frequencies lower than 'red' or higher than 'violet.' J W Draper, a professor of chemistry at New York University, led the way with early experiments in which he set out to analyse what he called 'the constituents of the sun beam.' Draper exposed his daguerreotype to sunlight concentrated through a telescope and diffracted through a prism. This revealed previously invisible parts of the solar spectrum.

But the greatest innovation in apprehending the non-visible spectrum was the discovery of X-rays by the scientist Wilhelm Röntgen, who in 1895 produced the first X-ray photograph showing the ringed, skeletal hand of his wife. News of the discovery – the rays that allowed humans to 'see through' objects – spread fast, and X-ray photographs of virtually everything under the sun soon appeared in print.

Above all, however, it was as an aid in examining the living human body that X-rays made the greatest impact. The first use of a 'tracer' (an element resistant to X-rays and therefore visible in a radiogram) was in 1896. The element was injected into a cadaver's hand to produce the first arteriogram (an image displaying the arteries). The first composite X-ray picture of the whole human body had been made before the end of the century.

Other uses for X-rays were developed in following decades. X-rays diffracted through crystals left patterns on photographically sensitive film which could be analysed, raising crystallography to new levels. A similar process involving organic molecules enabled scientists to examine the innermost details of nature. In the early 1950s photographic patterns left when X-rays were diffracted through DNA molecules revealed DNA's now-famous helical structure.

Right An electron microscope transforms a grain weevil into a vision of a grotesque underworld. By Gordon Leedale and Helena Cmiech. Magnification ×70. (Biophoto Associates.)

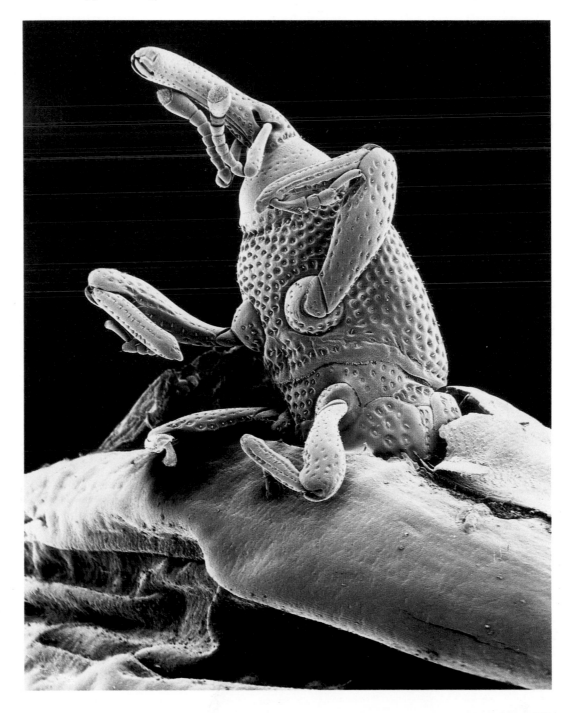

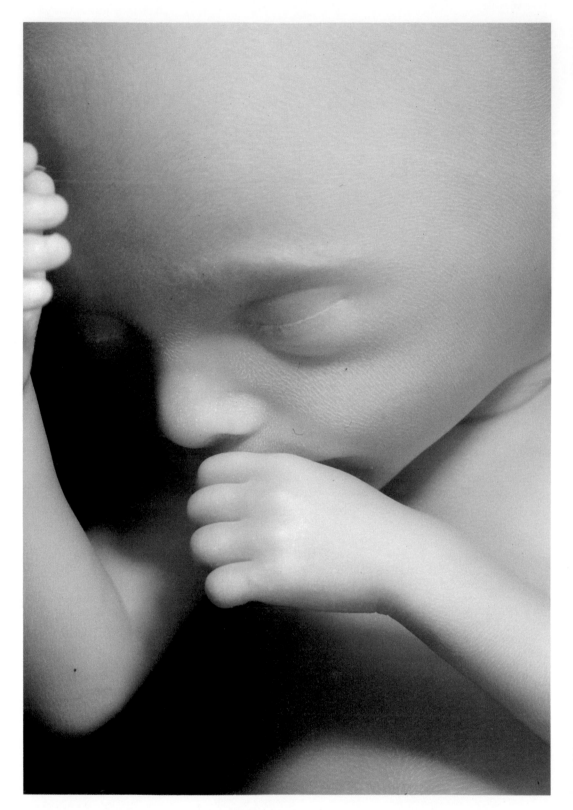

Left A human foetus photographed at 20 weeks, sucking its thumb. (Marian Hudson/ Charing Cross and Westminster Medical School.)

Far right top Thermogram showing hand temperature. The hand had been cooled and is reheating; finger tips are warmest and knuckles coolest. (Francis Ring/Royal National Hospital for Rheumatic Diseases.)

Right First complete X-Ray of the human body, made in Germany, 1896. (Deutsches Museum München.)

Other parts of the invisible spectrum have also been photographed. Ultraviolet studies have proved useful in analysing the composition of the atmosphere, for charting interstellar gases, and in dermatology. Even more important, infrared photography – first foreseen in the 1860s but not fully developed until the 1930s – has assisted in scientific endeavors as various as meteorology, geology and cardiology. Aerial infrared photographs of the earth can reveal varying degrees of vegetation and rock, as well as long-range weather developments. Thermography, a type of infrared sensor which de-

picts small variations in surface temperature, was originally spurred by military demand for weapons detection, but has been put to more constructive use in the early diagnosis of breast cancer and strokes.

Recent developments include the speckle interferometer camera, which can produce images of remote stars enabling scientists to measure their mass and luminosity. Aerial data collected by multispectral scanners can be converted by computers into images which show valuable mineral deposits for which geologists would otherwise have to search on the

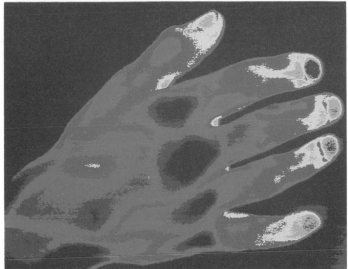

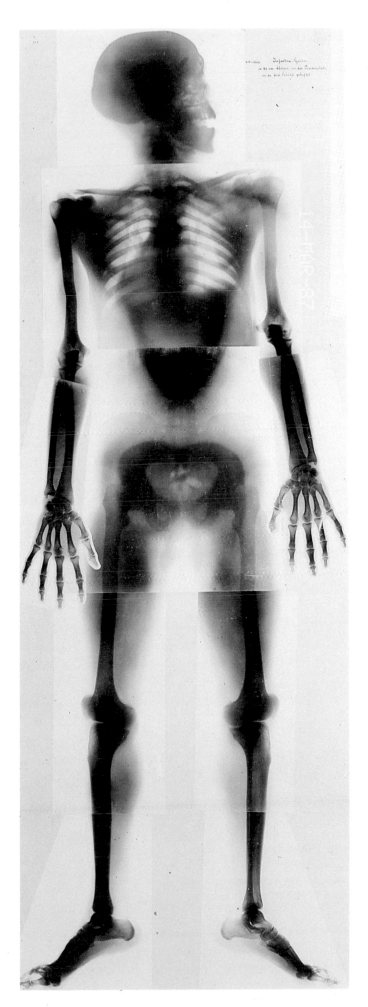

ground for years. Photography has taught us that there is a great deal more out there than the relatively small band of wavelengths which we perceive as 'light.' In the late 1960s, a photographer used infrared sensitive film and a set of filters to reveal an invisible – to humans – 'bow' in the rainbow, an additional hue adjacent to the deep red, present from the dawn of time, but only recently visible to the human eye with the aid of the camera.

Photomicrography, high-speed and time-lapse photography, as well as X-rays, infrared and ultraviolet techniques have all contributed to an unprecedented exploration of the human body. In the 1880s, E J Marey used a single camera with a rapidly rotating shutter to analyse human movement as Muybridge had analysed equine motion. His 'chrono-photographs' of a running man enabled scientists to analyse the continuous flow of human legs and arms. X-rays, of course, are used for a plethora of diagnostic purposes. The technique has been supplemented by the development of angiography, demonstrated in 1927 by the Portuguese scientist Egas Moniz. He injected a non-toxic contrasting agent directly into an exposed artery of a living human and then took a radiogram (X-ray photograph) of it to reveal, for the first time, the complex web of cerebral blood vessels in action. More spectacularly, in 1929, Werner Forssman defied the prohibition of his surgical director to demonstrate on himself the viability of the catheterization of the heart of a living human being. He tricked his nurse into helping him and produced six radiograms of his chest displaying the heart and the catheter reaching directly into it. After further refinements this technique has become a major diagnostic tool, enabling doctors to visualize the operation of parts of the body not revealed by X-rays.

But perhaps it is the field of endoscopy – the visualization of the inside of the living body – that has produced the most startling results. Various instruments for looking into the stomach, bladder and lungs and so on been developed but it was some time before photographic technique could preserve clear images of the inside of the body. The first color photographs of the inside of the stomach were produced in 1956. In

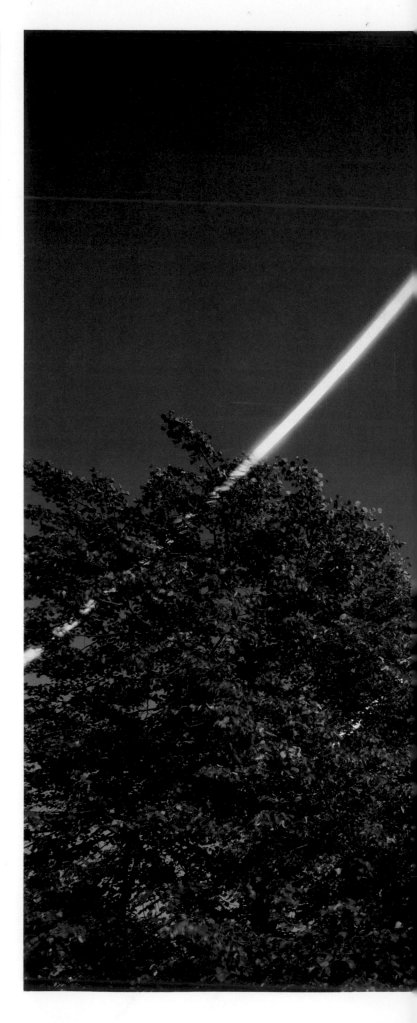

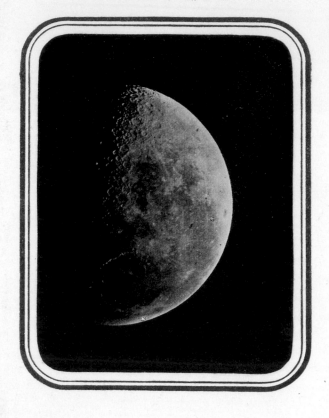

OBSERVATORY, Cranford, Middlesex.

NORTH LATITUDE......... 51° 28′ 57.8″
WEST LONGITUDE......... 1 37.5 Min. Sec.

ENLARGED PHOTOGRAPHIC COPY

OF A PHOTOGRAPH OF

THE MOON

SEPTEMBER 7, 1857, 14—15 HOUR

The Original Collodion Positive was obtained in five seconds,
by means of a Newtonian Equatoreal of thirteen inches
aperture and ten feet focal length.

Sir John W. Herschel Bart.
with Warren De la Rue's
Compliments

Sept 22/57

Above The moon, photographed by Warren de la Rue in 1857; five years earlier he had been the first person in England to make a lunar photograph. (Science Museum, London.)

Right Some 48 separate exposures of the sun made weekly by Dennis di Cicco on a single sheet of film shows the eccentric nature of earth's orbit. (© Dennis di Cicco.)

1965, using an ultra-wide angle lens and miniature flash on the tip of an endoscope, a photographer in Stockholm produced the first vivid, striking photographic images of a living foetus in the uterus.

The camera has also revealed to land-based humans the rich, mysterious world undersea. The first underwater camera was tested off the French Riviera in 1893. But the

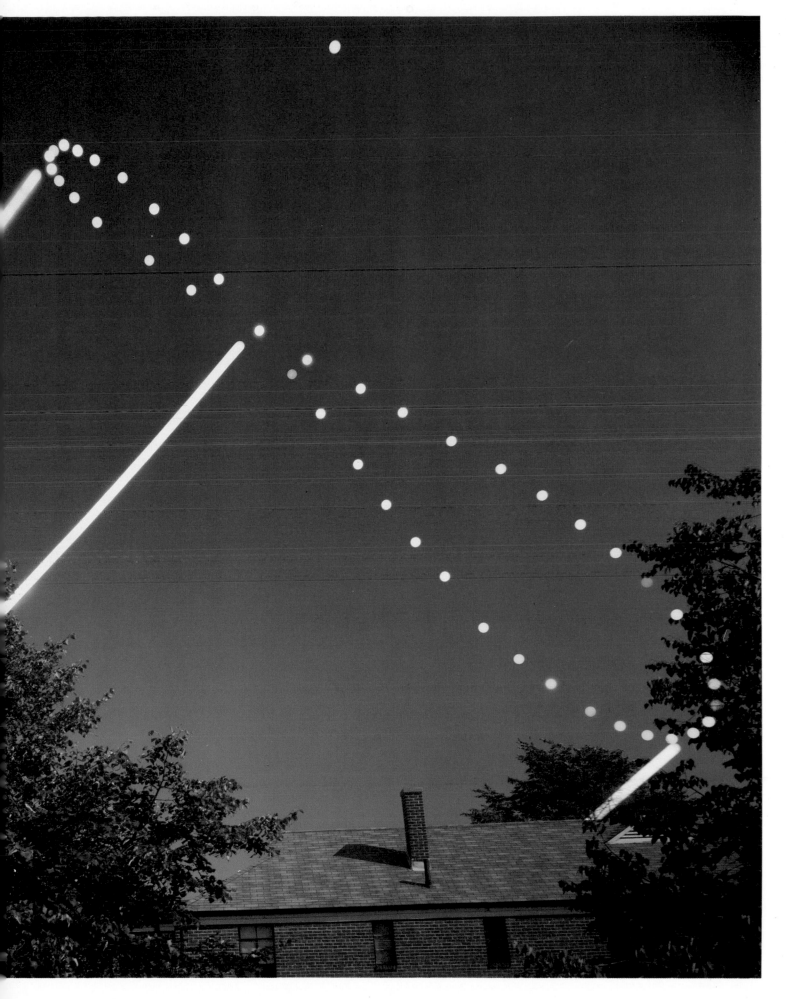

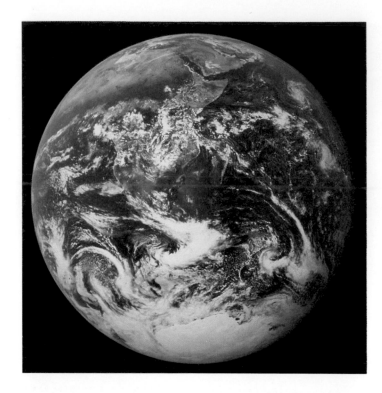

outstanding achievement here has been that of Harold Edgerton of MIT, who invented watertight casings capable of withstanding incredible deep sea pressures and temperatures, special electronic flashes to illuminate the darkness, optical correctors to compensate for water distortions, and the sonar 'pinger' for positioning an unmanned camera accurately at depths of thousands of meters.

In 1954 Edgerton took the first photograph of the legendary tripod fish standing on the Mediterranean Sea bottom at a depth of 1600 meters. This animal had never been seen *in situ* before. Since then numerous other species have been recorded in this fashion. Edgerton was also involved in photographically mapping the ocean bottom and revealing the rocky crevices which later confirmed the long-discounted theory of continental drift.

Today cameras patrol the depths of the ocean and have uncovered oases of life in an otherwise deathly cold environment. Images of many species which can only be seen undistorted in their natural habitat have been obtained by new technology in which electronic impulses from beneath the sea are assembled into color images by computers.

More than any other realm, the heavens have been unlocked for us by photographic technique. J W Draper took the first daguerreotype of the moon in 1840 and the sun in 1845. A single star was first photographed in 1850 and a planet, Jupiter, in 1851. Solar eclipses were an early preoccupation of photographers. As a transient and rare event that could not be directly observed by the naked eye an eclipse was the ideal subject for the new technology. In 1860, photographs at last confirmed that the 'luminous prominences' observed by the eye during eclipse were in fact excrescences of the sun and not an optical illusion as had long been surmised.

Above Planet earth photographed from Apollo 17 during its lunar landing mission in 1972. (NASA.)

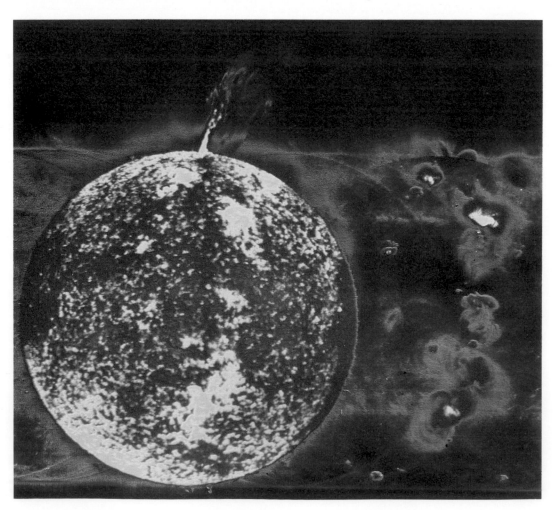

Right A computer-enhanced and colored view of the sun, taken through a solar telescope on board Skylab, the American observatory in space, 1973. (NASA.)

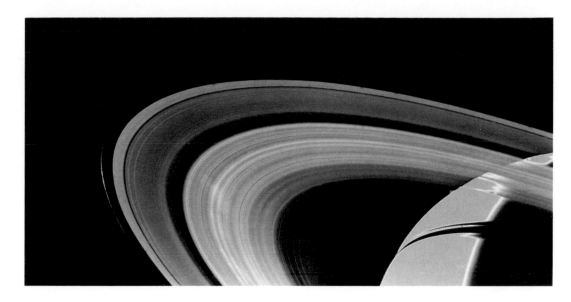

Left Saturn's rings, photographed by Voyager 1 in 1980, 930,000 miles from the planet's surface. (NASA.)

But it was not until the advent of a dry and relatively simple photographic process later in the century that astronomers began to exploit photography in earnest. A systematic photographic map of the sky was initiated at an Astrographic Congress in Paris in 1887 and completed – with the co-operation of 18 observatories in various countries around the world – in 1891.

In 1892 photography showed its superiority to human vision when a comet, hitherto undetected among the millions of heavenly bodies, was discovered accidentally in the course of examining a blur in a long-exposure photograph of the sky. In 1930, after a nine-month painstaking search based on mathematical probabilities, the most distant planet in the solar system, Pluto, was at last located by a systematic photo-mapping of designated sections of the night sky. Here was the first but not the last example of a major astronomical discovery made possible solely by photographic technique.

With the naked eye, the stars and planets appear to have very little coloring. But with the development of a color emulsion effective in long exposures at low light levels, it became possible to record the colors of various stars, galaxies and so on. Here photography has emulated a visual response which does not actually exist and cannot be checked by the human eye.

In the late 1950s space exploration created a new era in scientific photography, yielding image after image of breath-

Right A once-impossible chart of earth's ozone layers, made from Nimbus-7 in 1978. Blue and white show high ozone values, black and red are low. This project disproved the theory that ozone levels were lowest at the equator. (NASA.)

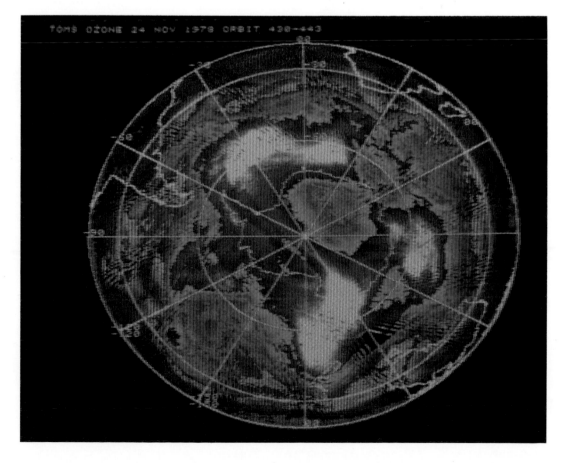

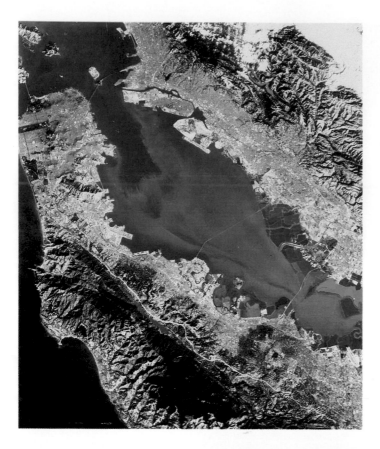

taking beauty as the hitherto unseeable heavens yielded up their secrets. The Soviet satellite Luna brought back the first photographs of the dark 'invisible' side of the moon in 1959. In 1965 Mariner 4 sent back photographs of Mars showing the existence of inexplicable craters on its surface. In 1971 Mariner 9 sent back photographs of Mars' Mons Olympus, a volcanic peak towering to three times the height of Mt Everest with a base spreading 600 kilometers wide. The Mariner probes also confirmed the existence of dry water channels on Mars, thus confirming an observation long thought to be wildly speculative. Like the craters and volcanic peaks, they still defy scientific explanation.

The Viking space probes sent back images of Venus taken with ultraviolet- and infrared-sensitive cameras, which revealed details of its atmospheric composition and surface temperature. Voyager sent back a series of dazzling images of Jupiter, its moons, Saturn, and its rings. Here the visual detail is aesthetically striking – particularly the swirling patterns which make up the Great Red Spot of Jupiter (several times the size of the earth) – but far from resolving age-old disputes, the pictures have simply added to the number of enigmas puzzling the scientists.

The dilemmas faced by scientists attempting to construct accurate images of extraterrestrial bodies is well illustrated by

Above San Francisco and the Bay area seen from Landsat 4, a mapping satellite, 1982. Due to a computer error the famous Golden Gate bridge appears kinked. (NASA.)

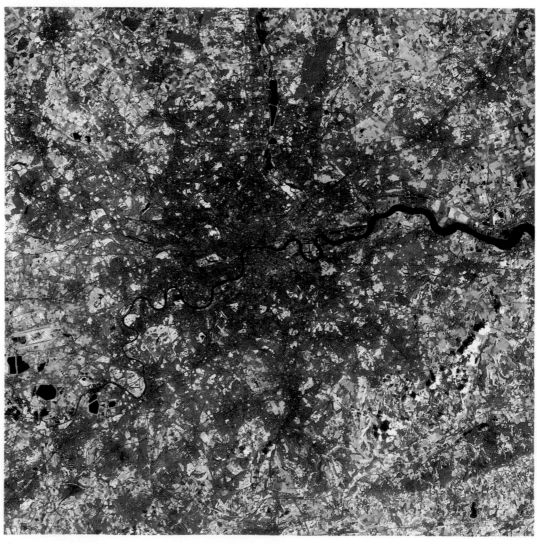

Right Landsat 5 thematic mapper image of London, 1985. The river Thames is clearly visible, as is Heathrow Airport, on the left edge of the frame. (NASA.)

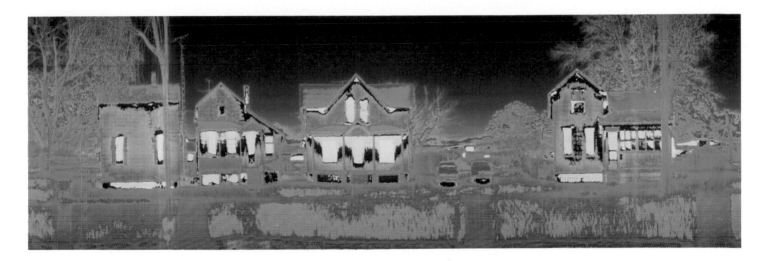

the story of the first color photographs taken on the surface of Mars by Viking 1 in 1976. Using a 'facsimile' scanning camera which transmitted a line-by-line impulse to earth, where the impulses were reconstructed and color-coded by computer, NASA scientists obtained the first picture of Mars surface as it would be seen by a human being standing on it. The version which they first released showed a rocky, high contrast landscape under a blue sky – very much like something one might see on earth. However, after further investigation, they realized that they had incorrectly 'tuned in' the impulses from Mars, and allowed their earth-bound preconceptions to color not only their judgments, but their 'photograph' of the planet. After correction, the landscape of Mars appears a dusty brown, with a salmon-pink sky created by particles suspended in the Martian atmosphere.

Whether or not the images produced by new processes such as digitalization, false-color computer reconstruction, linear scanners, and so on are 'photographs' or not is a moot point. New techniques of 'imaging' may be replacing the traditional chemically-based photographic process, but the results produced are similar, and the dissemination of the electronically produced imagery still relies on photographic techniques. The lesson to be learned, as true of Draper's first shots of the solar eclipse as of the Viking images of Mars, is that all visual evidence requires interpretation and reconstruction. Photography, while it has confirmed many scientific discoveries and provided clues for many more, has also confirmed the age-old fact that the presence and methods of the observer are as much a part of the final result as the observed phenomenon itself.

Above A thermograph shows domestic heat loss and thus pinpoints insulation needs. (VANSCAN® Continuous Mobile Thermogram by Daedalus Enterprises, Inc. USA.)

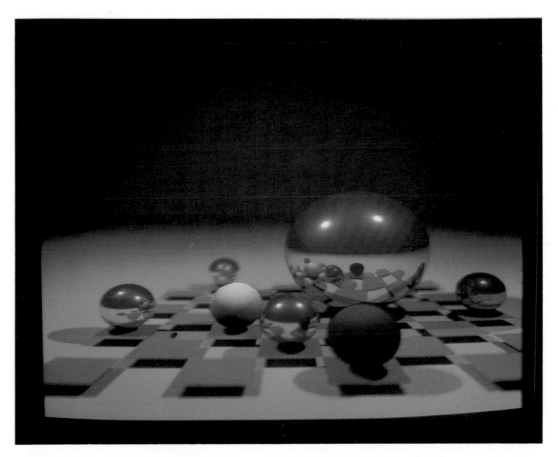

Right Computer graphics can create cameraless works that may be manipulated at will. It is predicted that photography's future lies in electronic imaging systems. (INMOS.)

CHAPTER ELEVEN

The Liberated Image

Towards a Contemporary Photography

As the 1960s gave way to a new decade, the flushes of enthusiasm for their medium which kept street photographers up and running took on a different hue. Social, political and cultural changes were taking place that altered both the kinds of photographs being made and the reaction of the viewing public. An expansion took place whose proportions were beyond the imagination of even the most heady dreamers of the 1960s.

Tom Wolfe described the 1970s as the 'me generation' and its climate fitted photography, at least the freshly emerging 'personal' photography perfectly. Within this cradle, photography as art came up from the Underground and was put before the public as a major, mature medium of personal expression. And with the exposure that followed came all the signs and trappings of success – galleries opened, museums collected, critics debated, hierarchies developed and factions were formed. To photographers this seemingly meteoric leap for their medium – near obscurity to public acclaim – and their own promotion to rank with 'serious' artists seemed nothing more than a natural (if overdue) course of events. In retrospect a series of events can be seen to have conspired to attract attentions beyond traditional notions of photography as a mass medium inseparably wedded to the printed page. The events begin with education and end with politics.

In Britain photography gained a kind of legitimacy by being part of its 'swinging' image. No sooner had the King's Road, Chelsea, Carnaby Street, the Who, the Beatles and Rolling Stones, Mary Quant, Vidal Sassoon and political and social satire as a way of life been thrust into international consciousness than photographers were absorbed into this contemporary fabric. Suddenly and briefly Britain, or London at least, was style capital of the world. Photographers who mirrored the image were given top ranking in magazines like *Town*, *Queen*, *Vogue* and the *Sunday Times*. They might be working class (like Don McCullin or David Bailey), middle class (like Robert Freeman or Sam Haskins) or even members of the aristocracy (the marriage of photographer Anthony Armstrong-Jones to Princess Margaret in 1960 lent the medium a new kind of credibility) but all were thrust into a media limelight. Photographers were a new elite and this inspired and encouraged a generation below, who began flocking to art colleges and polytechnics in search of a way into the new pantheon.

Equally, photographic education in the United States experienced an uplift. Higher learning was the ideal legitimate escape from conscription and the war in Vietnam. In 1968 alone six million students enrolled in higher education. Between 1966 and 1970 the numbers studying photography or

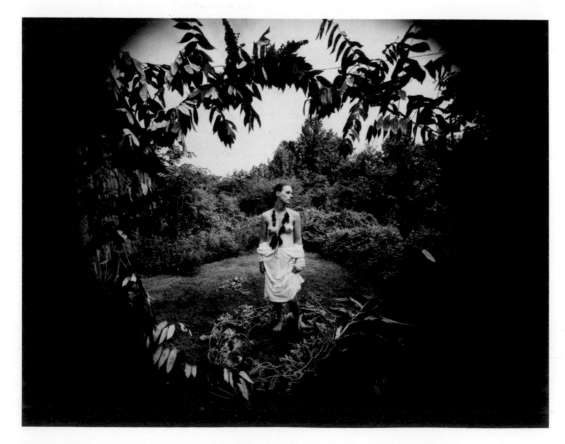

Left *Edith, Danville, Virginia*, 1971, by Emmet Gowin, who gave what was private (a relationship) a broader and public meaning. (© Emmet Gowin.)

Right *Untitled*, 1974, by Ralph Gibson, one of the first to take advantage of the new enthusiasm for photography in the 1970s. A would-be photojournalist, he became a successful art-gallery and museum exhibitor. (© Ralph Gibson.)

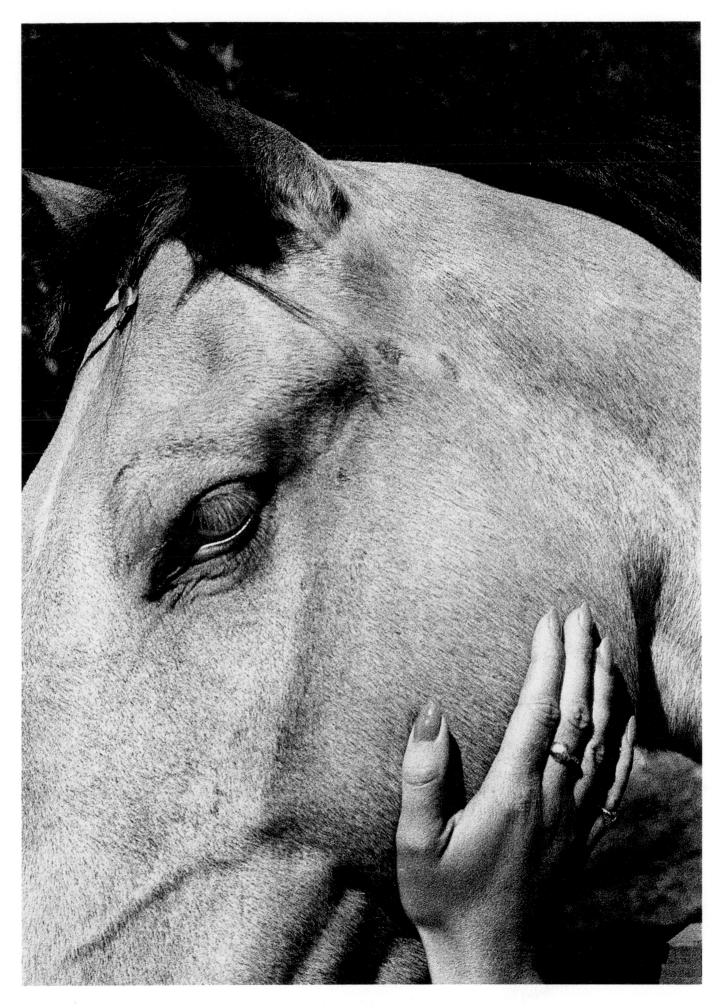

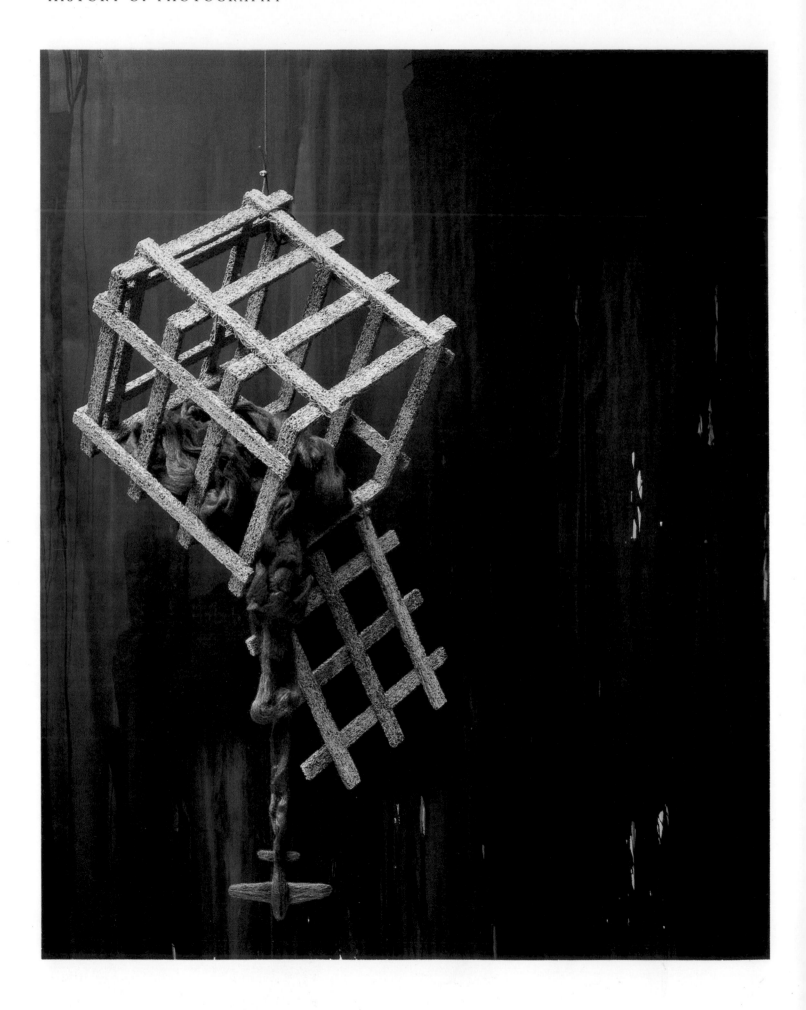

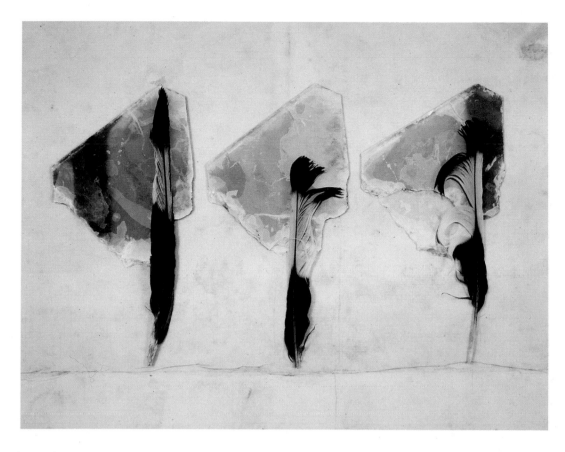

Right *Three Feathers, Three Crystals*, 1981, by Olivia Parker. Somewhere between photography and sculpture, this image highlights an awareness of formal issues by contemporary photographers. (© Olivia Parker.)

results of institutional support; there a National Endowment for the Arts (NEA) had given public funding to artists *and* arts projects since 1965. By the early 1970s, Lane was able to see the results – public funding created work, public education, a sense of national culture and made perfect sense as a sponge to absorb the outpourings of a recently schooled multitude. In tandem with the numbers of new photographers and pressures they brought, private galleries were opening – Lee Witkin began a highly successful showplace in 1969 and was followed two years later by Light Gallery – both sited at fashionable Manhattan addresses. Meanwhile existing, often prestigious, painting, graphics and sculpture venues turned their attention to photography – Castelli, Sonnabend and Marlborough were most prominent.

As well as practitioners, museums too were recipients of NEA largesse. Like the Arts Council of Great Britain (and similar bodies in Europe, Canada, Australia, New Zealand and later Latin America) the NEA was anxious to make its

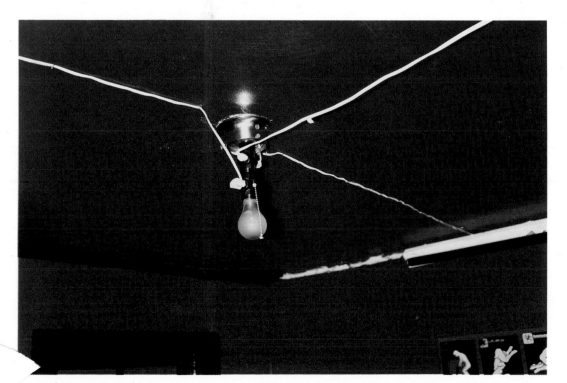

Left *Red Room, Greenwood, Mississippi*, 1969–71, by William Eggleston. Lyrical, recondite and accomplished Eggleston is a serious color photographer. (Middendorf Gallery; Victoria and Albert Museum.)

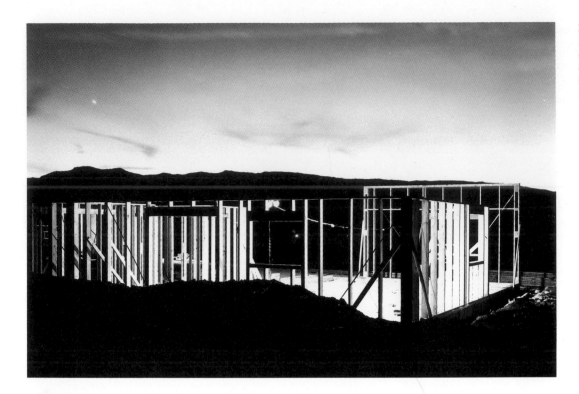

Left From *Nevada,* 1978, by Lewis Baltz, a leader in the move towards defining a new form of documenting man's excursions into the landscape. (© Lewis Baltz.)

expenditure of public funds as evident as possible. Giving individuals grants to work was a necessary but somehow hidden exclusive activity – helping museums show works gave the whole movement a broader credence. And photography had a popular edge, was inexpensive and was beginning to take on an aura of fashionability that encompassed education *and* art's avant-garde. The medium boomed, collectors loomed, critics were appointed to newspapers and magazines and suddenly photography was the talk of the town. It was a fragile enterprise, underpinned more by faith and enthusiasm than any firm base as A D Coleman, probably the best writer on photography for the *New York Times*, *Village Voice* and *Popular Photography*, pointed out when he introduced a collection of his critical essays: 'So much seemed to be happening in photography at that point and my knowledge of and background in the medium were so scant.' Coleman was

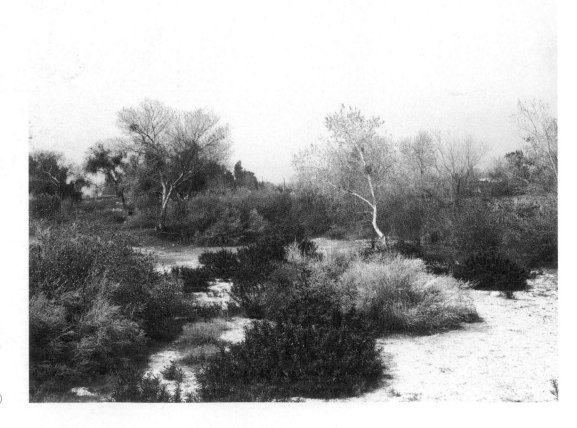

Right *Santa Ana Wash, Norton Air Force Base,* 1978, by Robert Adams – more redemptive in attitude than many 'New Topographic' photographers, Adams shows the land enduring. (© Robert Adams.)

excited by what he saw, enthused about it in the press, but had to realign his thinking to incorporate the very weight of images, ideas and possibilities coming down on him. From time to time he would muse on the negative potential of all this attention being paid to a young medium and fear for the future, but the rush went on.

In 1972 Princeton University set up a chair in the History of Photography and offered it to Peter Bunnell, former curator at the Museum of Modern Art, New York. During 1973, noting the sudden rash of works on or by photographers, the authoritative *New York Review of Books* commissioned a leading intellectual, Susan Sontag, to write a series on the medium. In 1974, perhaps in reply to the movement away from photography's traditional home on the pages of magazines, Cornell Capa, an established photojournalist, set up the International Center for Photography, New York, to keep alive the humanist principles of 'concerned photogra-

phy.' The same year *Newsweek* magazine devoted its cover and its extensive editorial space to the medium's new status and in 1975 the University of Arizona set up a major scholarly research archive and exhibitions area, The Center for Creative Photography in Tucson. By 1976 interest had reached such a pitch that *Artforum*, most weighty of the art journals, devoted an entire issue to photography.

As Coleman predicted in 1973, a rapid ascendancy was not to be without problems – amid the new cultural splendor of photography in the gallery came such a rush to be involved that eventually the ship carrying photography to a new port became swamped and nearly sank (bailing out began in the late 1970s and goes on to this day). Coleman's prescient view was succinctly stated when he observed that students asked him 'pointed questions about Making It with their Art. What kind of work, they wanted to know, is being shown and published and collected? What is the coming thing?' The

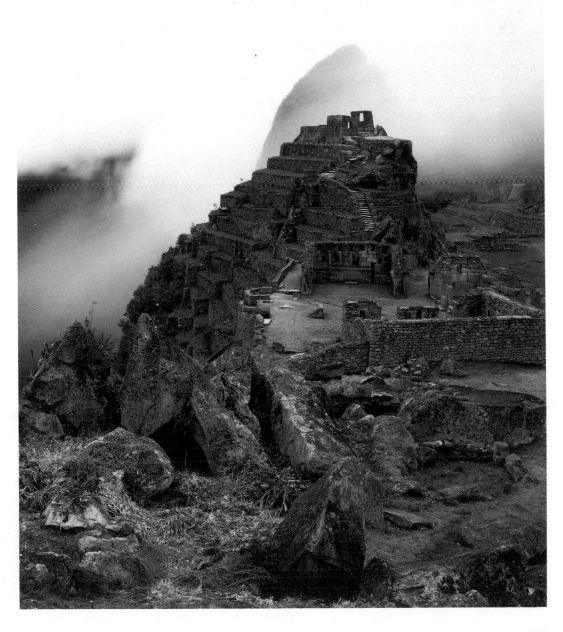

Right *Machu Picchu, Peru,* 1984, by Linda Connor, who leans more toward evocation than her contemporaries, but maintains a strict formality. (© Linda Connor.)

211

Right *Vary Cliché/Fetishism*, 1978, by Robert Heinecken, introducer of a broad range of print-making methods to staid silver-printers. (© Robert Heinecken.)

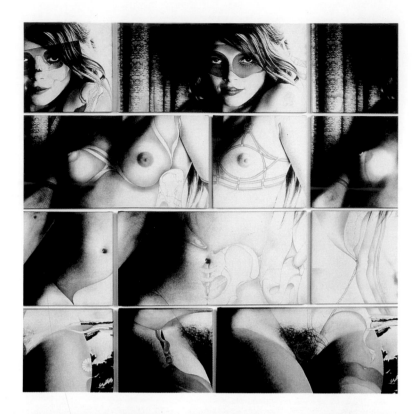

Below *Untitled*, 1980, by Joyce Neimanas, a multiple exposure composite, created from individual Polaroid SX-70 images. (© Joyce Neimanas.)

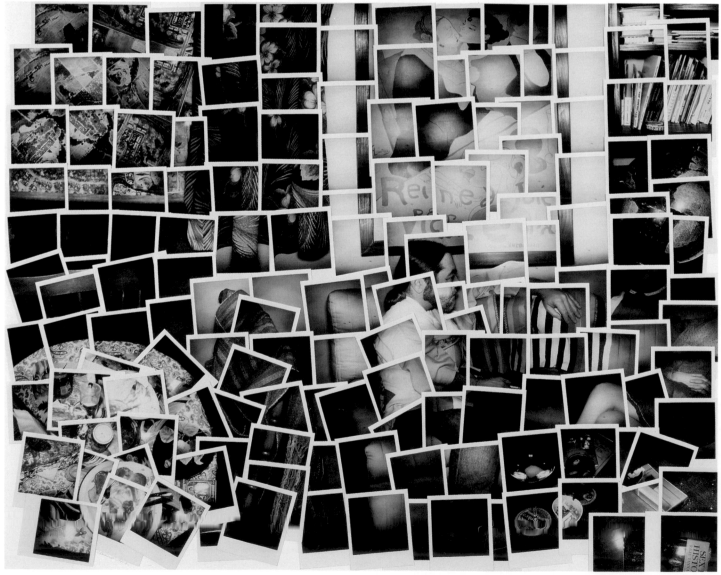

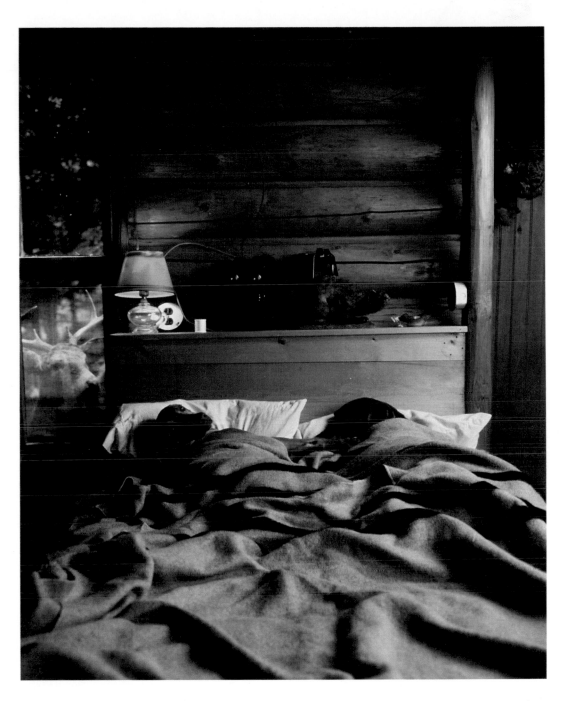

Right *Ray and Mrs Lubner in Bed*, 1981, a Polaroid by William Wegman, a conceptual artist using photography to propose witty conundrums. (Courtesy Holly Solomon Gallery.)

market place, show business and hype were joining thoughts of creativity in the minds of young photographers. As college and university classes filled with eager would-be super stars it slowly became apparent that photography was incapable of sustaining its overly hasty elevation to peerage in the art world. Mature work by image makers like Robert Adams, Lewis Baltz, William Eggleston, Ralph Gibson, John Gossage, Emmet Gowin, Robert Heinecken, Duane Michals, Joel Meyerowitz, Nick Nixon and Stephen Shore could keep successful company with conceptualism, minimalism, 'earth art' and the constructed, linguistic-based pieces that ruled the avant-garde roost. But as Vicki Goldberg, a contemporary critic, pointed out in 1984: 'Students, legions of students, all wanted to do what the teacher did, or else what commanded a high price in the galleries. So we got conceptual and what might be called semi-conceptual photographs by the carload, turned out by people who really didn't have any concepts . . .

After conceptualism we got role playing and the media, which were actually important issues until five thousand photographers decided they were the road to originality . . . We got self expression which a just god would have spared us, and in which many a photographer has indulged . . . We got mixed media, which is the cheap and snappy way to look like an artist . . . We got cute funk and pseudo comic strip literary efforts . . . and some of us got tired.' Education had worked like pyramid selling – stalwarts of the 1960s (Nathan Lyons, Jerry Uelsmann and Van Deren Coke among them) had persuaded a future influential group of photography's importance and were now gazing amazed as the process of teachers teaching skills which had little use outside the classroom moving into a self-perpetuating and dizzying spiral.

Curiously enough, in Europe only Britain made significant claims to much organized photographic education, and little of what was on offer could compare with the frenetic zeal

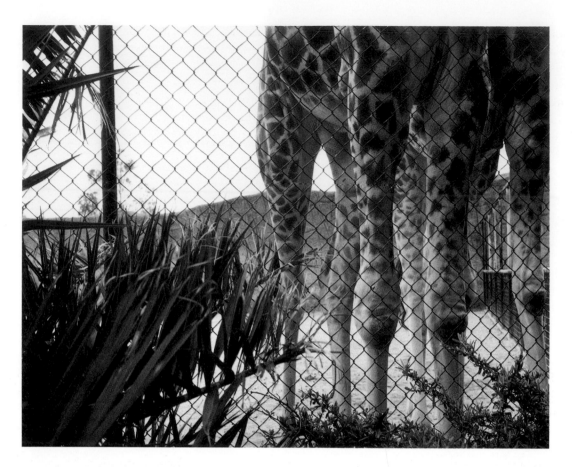

Left *The Zoo, Melbourne, Australia,* 1977, by Heather Forbes. (© Heather Forbes.)

Below *Manali,* 1977, by Max Pam; Australian by birth, internationalist by nature, Pam reviews his world from perspectives only offered by the camera. (© Max Pam.)

with which ideas of creativity were pushed in the United States. Exceptions, though, proved the rule as Bill Messer – photographer, traveller, gallery director and writer – made clear in an extensive article on photography he contributed to *U.S. Camera Annual* in 1977, the high spots in fact were easily comparable: 'In 1966 a man sat behind a desk at the Derby college of Art and Design, smack in the middle of the British Midlands, sending out letters, orders for books, requests for printing and offers for exchange exhibitions all over the world. He called what he was doing the Derby School of Creative Photography; he didn't quite know what he meant by that but he was certainly going to find out. Through the better part of the next decade, largely eschewing the various local photo scenes (including London's), finding encouragement from America, this individual was largely responsible for conceiving and nurturing (in his own words) "the largest photography department in Europe", the first English diploma course in Creative Photography, and the shining light of British photographic education.' The educator concerned was Bill Gaskin, who took his lead from the United States and began to import American teachers – John Mulvaney, a recent graduate, was followed in 1973 by Thomas J Cooper who bowed out in 1977 to be replaced by Chris Sieberling. All were from the University of New Mexico. Gaskins presided over a course with two centers – Derby and Trent, a polytechnic in Nottingham, and for a while the intensity of teaching, producing and proselytizing seemed to overtake British photography. Paul Hill, a successful press photographer and photojournalist who had become disillusioned with 'media mediocrity' and taken up a more contemplative

work, joined Trent's staff and became chief local protagonist in the fight to raise British photography 'from the Dark Ages.' He was soon joined in his fight by Raymond Moore (see Chapter 9).

While one group pushed and pulled for British photography to align itself with international art movements, another wanted visual roots more properly examined. David Hurn, photojournalist, Magnum member, and highly successful, abandoned what had been an exemplary career in reportage

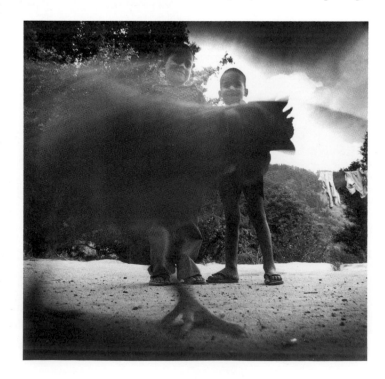

(with occasional excursions into fashion) to start a course in Documentary Photography in Newport, Wales. Hurn, Welsh born, felt that British history, geography, climate and light could not sustain a borrowed vocabulary. Instead he advocated the factual, sometimes low-key but always pragmatic way of doing things that had marked British photography as particular but no less personal since before World War II. Like Gaskin, Hurn introduced multiple teaching elements into his course – from Keith Arnatt (a conceptual artist who used photography) through Ron McCormick (a talented photographer and sometime gallery director) to Tom Hopkinson (ex-editor of *Picture Post*).

His attitudes were not misplaced, they came at a point when Britain was discovering its photographic past and gaining a renewed sense of national photographic culture. Historians such as Margaret Harker and Arthur Gill had been hard at work on the history of the nineteenth century, filling in gaps and putting flesh on photography's first bones, now a new group were coming forward, asking questions about the more recent past and trying to assemble a sense of tradition that was wholly indigenous. Prime movers were Val Williams and Andrew Sproxton. In 1972 they opened Impressions, a gallery in York, which was only the second purely photographic space in Britain, and began to revive interest in work from such neglected photographers as Cecil Beaton and Peter Rose Pulham. Impressions was joined by the Half-Moon in London (soon to rename itself Camerawork); The Photographic Gallery at Southampton University, set up and run by Leo Stable; Side in Newcastle, created by Murray Martin, a filmmaker; Stills in Edinburgh, directed by Richard

Hough; and Ffotogallery in Cardiff, whose first curator was Bill Messer. Meanwhile grander institutions were taking an interest. In 1972 Roy Strong, then Director of London's National Portrait Gallery, appointed Colin Ford as the gallery's first Keeper of Photography and Film (Ford was later made director of Britain's National Museum of Photography which opened in 1983). And in 1975 the Victoria and Albert Museum was given the responsibility of caring for a National Collection of the art of photography. This museum already had substantial holdings (indeed, Mark Haworth-Booth, who was given charge of photographs, has remarked with evident pride that the Victoria and Albert must be the only 'museum in the world in which a photograph by Mrs Cameron can be labelled "Given by the Photographer"'), but it quickly began implementing a major acquisitions policy designed to give some coherence to the collection as a whole.

A rising national consciousness about British photography was marked in 1975 when the Arts Council staged 'The Real Thing: An anthology of British Photographs 1840-1950' and opened it at the major London venue, the Hayward Gallery. As well as being the first substantial overview of British photography most people had seen, the exhibition marked a departure from current photo-exhibition practice. The works were selected by Ian Jeffrey, an art historian with a developed interest in photography, and he attempted to use the works shown as signposts down a broadly cultural highway rather than individual, pleasantly visual objects. As Jeffrey, joined by David Mellor (also an art historian), worked at the process of establishing a cultural context for the medium, a Marxist group was sifting through writings by

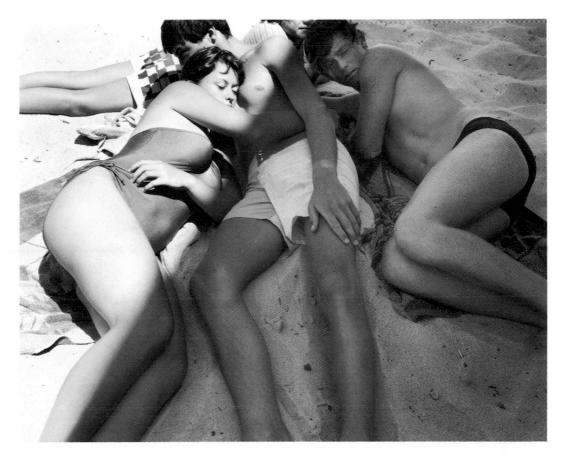

Right *Manly Beach, Sydney,* 1985, by Fiona Hall, a leading Australian practitioner of personally directed image making. (© Fiona Hall.)

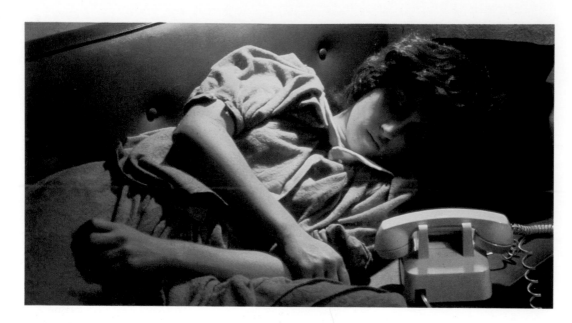

Left *Untitled,* 1981, by Cindy Sherman, who used herself as the subject to question the line separating fact from fiction. (Courtesy Metro Pictures.)

Walter Benjamin, Roland Barthes and other such radical philosophers and aligning photography with semiology, sociology and linguistics. Marxist ideology came into currency on the back of student unrest in 1968 and slid into education as the one-time dissenters joined the academy. Led by Victor Burgin, a substantial artist, their concern was for the politics of representation, and photographs were construed as 'sites of meaning' to be 'decoded' and 'deconstructed.' In Europe and the United States, Marxist critics came to dominate one sector of photography, establishing through their writing and lecturing a new visual form, 'Image and Text,' which subsumed expression into a broader political desire. By 1979 yet another Arts Council Hayward

Gallery exhibition announced the state of the British photographic nation. Called 'Three Perspectives,' it promised even-handedness by asking a leading figure from each of the groups vying for domination to select photographs representing their viewpoint. Each chose a banner: Paul Hill used 'Photographic Truth, Metaphor and Individual Expression,' Angela Kelly 'Feminism and Photography' and John Tagg 'A Socialist Perspective on Photographic Practise.' Significantly Hill and Kelly were photographers and Tagg an art historian turned theorist.

Left-wing politics gave the appearance of flavoring much late 1970s and early 1980s work on both sides of the Atlantic, if only because Marxist critics were keen campaigners

Right *Construct NYC-17,* 1984, by Barbara Kasten. A post-modernist work, it looks back to machine-age works of the 1930s. (© Barbara Kasten.)

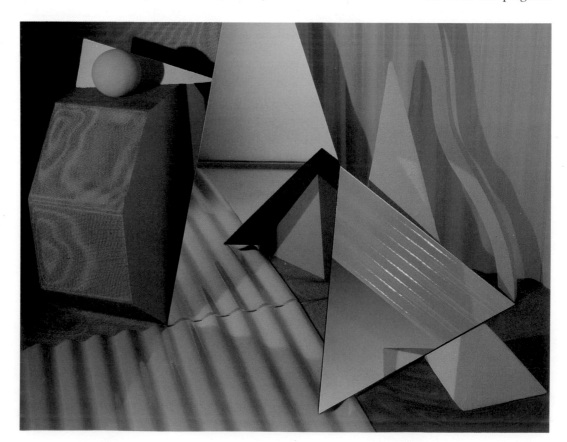

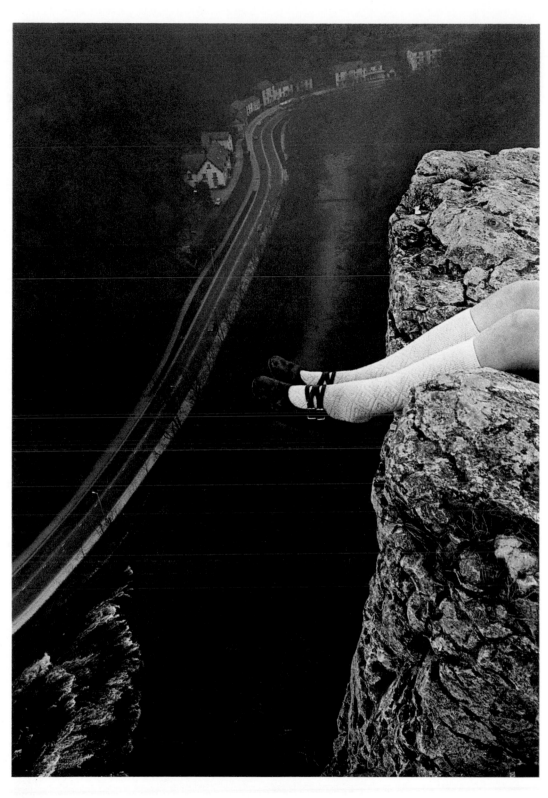

Right *Legs Over High Tor, Matlock Bath,* 1975, by Paul Hill, whose viewpoint changed a passive view (a child at rest) into an image charged with tension. (© Paul Hill, The Photographer's Place.)

whose dismissal of notions of 'connoisseurship' (valuing some photographs above others for aesthetic reasons) was met with praise by radical art journals who disliked and mistrusted photography's sudden elevation. Sadly, for its protagonists, their selective appropriation of works to fit theories (rather than constructing theories to fit works), zealous didacticism and use of a socio-linguistic and philosophic jargon which excluded understanding from all but their peers made for a limited appeal. But alongside politics and theoretical obscurantism, other issues were coming forward, and new photographic stances.

As galleries and museums began exhibiting photographs on a large scale, and dealers selling them, the fact of the medium's reproducibility caused problems. Some photographers, with an eye to the marketplace, chose to limit their prints to 'editions' in the manner of etchers or printmakers in the hope of enhancing their value. Others found such practices reductive, and beginning in 1970 a boom in books began – mainly self-published or within the parameters of small presses, though by the end of the 1970s large publishers were on the trail. The single, signed, limited edition fine print seemed constraining on a medium with serial, sequential potential. One of the first to seriously explore this region was Ralph Gibson, whose book *The Somnambulist* (1970) heralded the advent of photographic book works as a serious rival to gallery walls as a legitimate home for photographs. To publish this work, a sequence of 42 images, Gibson set up Lustrum Press. Lustrum Press later published many of the decade's most important books – Larry Clark, Robert Frank, Michael Martone, Neal Slavin and Danny Seymore were all featured in their list. Lee Friedlander (see Chapter 9) began publishing too, restricting Haywire Press to his own works – beginning with *Self Portrait* in 1970 – and *Aperture*, now managed by one of Minor White's students, Michael Hoffman, added book publishing to its role as a quarterly magazine. As a book publisher it favored classic monographs by major figures such as Edward Weston, Paul Strand and Diane Arbus but soon began to add books by younger photographers to their list. Book and magazine publishing caught hold in Europe too – houses were established in Britain (Travelling Light), France (Contrajour), Germany (Edition Marzona and Mahnert-Lueg), Sweden (ETC) and Italy (Punto e Virgola). On the magazine front *Light Vision* in Australia, *European Photography* in Germany, *Photo-forum* in New Zealand, *Photo Vision* in Spain, *Printletter* in Switzerland, *After Image* in the United States and *Camera Austria* were all set up during the 1970s. In Britain the Arts Council was also briefly

active as a book publisher; it began a series which hovered between book and magazine *British Image*, published monographs on John Blakemore, David Hurn and Chris Killip, then an anthology *About 70 Photographs* by Chris Steele-Perkins. Direct publishing soon turned to subsidy and monographs under the Gordon Fraser imprint were made available. Fraser's, who also published photo books of their own, produced retrospective monographs on George Rodger, Thurston Hopkins and Bert Hardy – all stalwarts from immediate postwar photography.

Admission of photography to an inner ring, the gallery network, had another and separate effect on the kinds of photographers being produced. Photographs moved out of their enclosure and rediscovered the avant-garde. Suddenly, or so it seemed, photographers, painters, sculptors, video and performance artists had something in common. Photography's traditions and its self-assigned role within the province of evidence were set aside as image makers using cameras invaded the art world. In Britain Hamish Fulton, Keith Arnatt, Boyd Webb, John Stezaker, Roger Palmer, Ian Breakwell and several others became engaged in photographic works, generally with a conceptual basis. Similarly, in America Tom Barrow, Robert Heinecken, Robert Cumming, John Baldessari, Sol Lewitt, William Wegman, Lucas Samaras, Jan Groover, Eve Sonneman and later Cindy Sher-

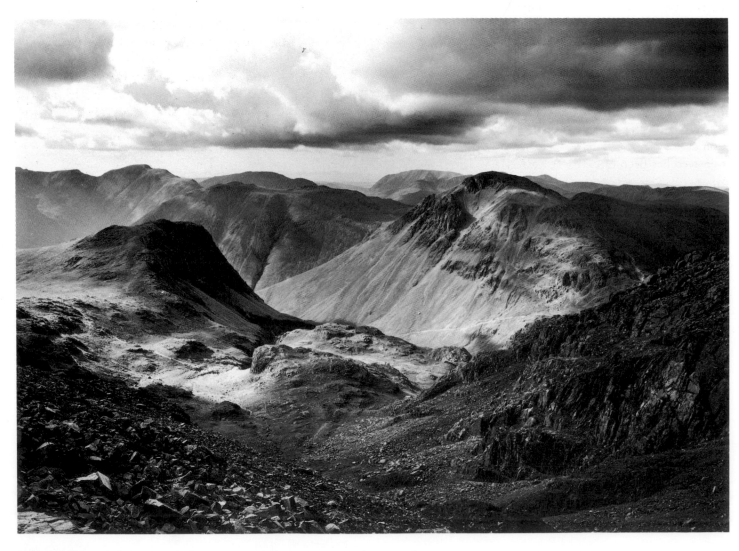

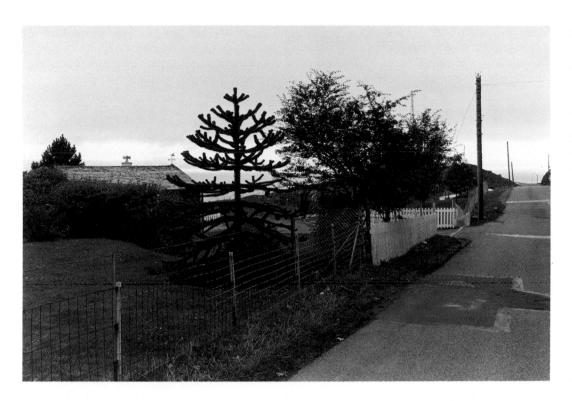

man took photography into areas previously thought of as belonging to the other visual arts. Eventually evidence itself came under scrutiny as a conceptual as well as a material fact. Fact, fiction, construction and concept were all digested and absorbed into the photographic arena.

Color had also previously been ignored by serious photographers – it carried an odor of triviality, gloss, commerce. As Robert Frank had made plain almost 20 years earlier 'black and white are the colors of photography.' In the somber 1970s all this was to change when the Museum of Modern Art, New York, gave its blessing by mounting a solo exhibition of 75 color prints by William Eggleston in 1976. What followed has been called 'The Rush to Color,' though little work of consequence emerged. Unlike Eggleston, most photographers seemed unable to handle color as a descriptive tool and they lapsed into decoration – though recent works by several photographers, notably Martin Parr and Paul Graham in Britain and Alex Webb and Joel Meyerowitz in the United States, are indicative of color's growing maturity.

Throughout the 1970s and into the 1980s, aside from a strong school of landscape photography prompted by works from Thomas J Cooper, John Blakemore, John Davies and Fay Godwin, Britain held resolutely to its documentary bent with Chris Killip and Graham Smith leading moves away from a rigid narrative style into a more fluid and authentic record of contemporary life. And after its flirtation with art-imitative styles, American photography too began a return to documentation. Conscious of works made in record by conceptual and land artists and in reaction to the excesses of the 'me generation,' a small group of photographers began making pictures of a kind that recalled their medium's original brief – to describe. With a coolness, detachment and sense of irony which contrasted violently with the work of their contemporaries they set about rejecting 'style' or 'form' or

'presence' as subject matter. Their works, which continue to be highly influential, were brought together for an exhibition in 1975 at the International Museum of Photography George Eastman House called 'New Topographics: Photographs of a Man-Altered Landscape.' Contributors to the show were Robert Adams, Lewis Baltz, Bernd and Hilla Becher, Joe Deal, Frank Gohlke, Nicholas Nixon, John Schott, Stephen Shore and Henry Wessel Jnr. 'New Topographers' used nineteenth-century survey photography as a model, particularly the work of Timothy O'Sullivan (see Chapter 2), with all its sense of objectivity, mapping and uninflected description to set present reality against past myth, and explain their sense of alienation from the very core of human experience – the land.

The frenetic activity described here (at best a very partial account) during a decade when more photographs were made and seen than at any time in the preceeding 130 years, created a precedent for the medium that photographers found hard to follow. In pulling itself up by the bootstraps, as it were, photography overextended itself – its bubble had to burst. When the burst came, roughly in 1980, the scene altered: growth turned to cut-back, passionate interest to mild recognition. As suddenly as they started, galleries, museums, publishers and public funders either stopped their photographic activities or 'reviewed' them. Just as quickly as the star arose it fell. But decline, surely linked to a depressed world economy and avowed lack of interest in the arts by world leaders who now seem ready to measure civilization in unemployment statistics, has not been without its uses to photography. Out of the limelight, away from stardom, photographers of all kinds have been forced to reassess their commitment. The success of the 1970s was a bonus which only served to fuel their conviction that photography is after all life, and well worth living.

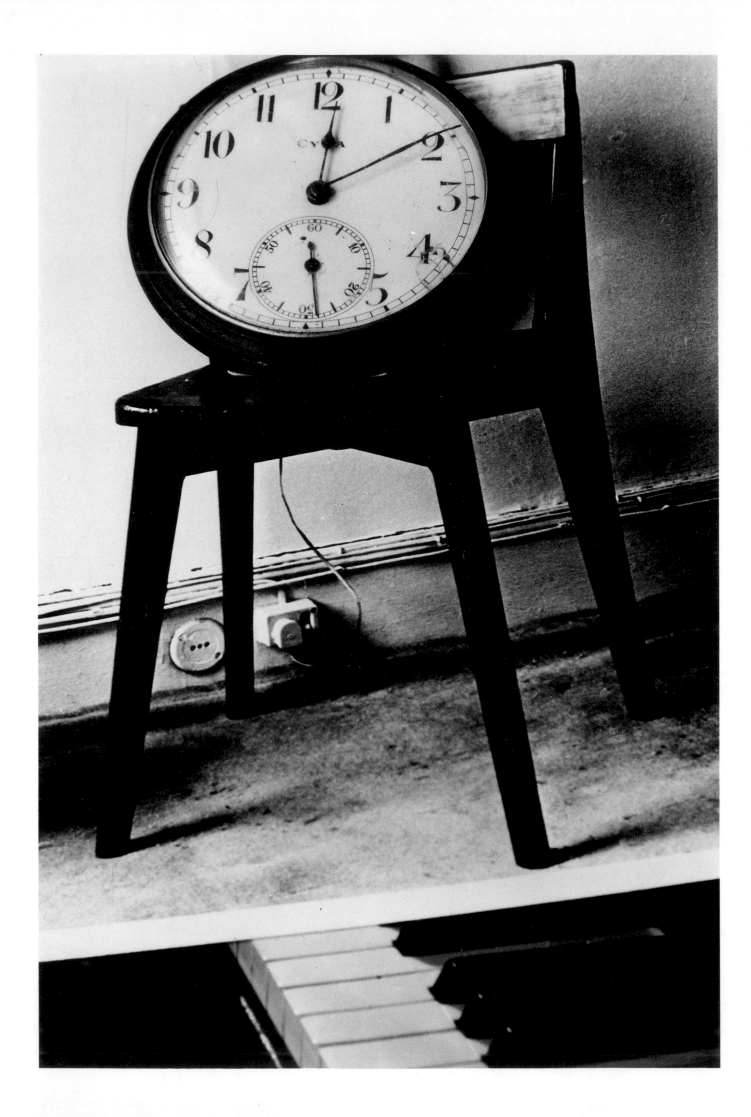

Select Bibliography

General Histories

Bensusan, Arthur D, *Silver Images: A History of Photography in Africa*, Cape Town, H Timmins, 1966

Coke, Van Deren, *Avant-Garde Photography in Germany 1919-1939*, New York, Pantheon Books, 1982

Gernsheim, Helmut and Alison, *The History of Photography from the Camera Obscura to the Beginning of the Modern Era*, London, Thames & Hudson, 1969 and New York, McGraw-Hill, 1969

Green Jonathan, *American Photography: A Critical History, 1945 to the Present*, New York, Harry N Abrams, 1984

Greenhill, Ralph, *Early Photography in Canada*, Toronto, Oxford University Press, 1965

Hall-Duncan Nancy, *The History of Fashion Photography*, New York, Alpine Book Company, 1979

Harker Margaret, *The Linked Ring: The Secession Movement in Photography in Britain, 1892-1910*, London, Heinemann, 1979

Haworth-Booth, Mark (ed), *The Golden Age of British Photography, 1839-1900*, London, Victoria & Albert Museum, 1984 and New York, Aperture, 1984

Homer, William Inncs, *Alfred Stieglitz and the American Avant-Garde*, Boston, New York Graphic Society, 1977 and London, Secker & Warburg, 1977

Jeffrey, Ian, *Photography: A Concise History*, London, Thames & Hudson, 1981 and New York, Oxford University Press, 1981

Kahmen Volker, *Photography as Art*, London, Studio Vista, 1974 (pub New York, Viking Press as *Art History of Photography*, 1974)

Knight, Hardwicke, *Photography in New Zealand, A Social and Technical History*, Dunedin, John McIndoe, 1971

Newhall, Beaumont, *The History of Photography from 1839 to the Present*, New York, Museum of Modern Art, 1982 and London, Secker & Warburg, 1982

Rosenblum, Naomi, *A World History of Photography*, New York, Abbeville Press, 1984

Tausk, Peter, *Photography in the 20th Century*, London, Focal Press, 1980

Williams, Val, *Women Photographers: The Other Observers, 1900 to the Present*, London, Virago, 1986

Visual Anthologies

Beaton Cecil & Buckland, Gail, *The Magic Image: The Genius of Photography from 1839 to the Present Day*, London, Weidenfeld & Nicholson, 1975

Bernard Bruce, *The Sunday Times Book of Photodiscovery*, London, Thames & Hudson, 1980

Campbell, Bryn, *Exploring Photography*, London, BBC, 1978

Doty, Robert, *Photography in America*, New York, The Ridge Press, 1974, and London, Thames & Hudson, 1974

Eauclair, Sally, *The New Color Photography*, New York, Abbeville Press, 1981

Fabian Rainer, & Adam, Hans-Christian, *Masters of Early Travel Photography*, London, Thames & Hudson, 1983

Hopkinson, Tom, *Treasures of the Royal Photographic Society 1839-1919*, London, Focal Press, 1980

Jeffrey, Ian (with David Mellor), *The Real Thing, an Anthology of British Photographs 1840-1950*, London, Arts Council, 1975

Naef, Weston, *The Collection of Alfred Steiglitz: Fifty Pioneers of Modern Photography*, New York, Metropolitan Museum of Art/Viking Press, 1978

Nori, Claude, *French Photography from its Origins to the Present*, Paris Centrejour, 1978, New York, Random House, 1979, and London Thames & Hudson, 1979

Scharf, Aaron, *Pioneers of Photography: An Album of Pictures and Words*, London BBC, 1975

Shudakov, Grigory, *Pioneers of Soviet Photography*, Paris, Philippe Sers editeur, 1983 and London, Thames & Hudson, 1983

Szarkowski, John, *Looking at Photographs*, New York, Museum of Modern Art, 1973

Szarkowski, John, *Mirrors and Windows: American Photography since 1960*, New York, Museum of Modern Art, 1978

Szarkowski, John, *The Photographer's Eye*, New York, Museum of Modern Art, 1966

Turner, Peter, *American Images, Photography 1945-1980*, London and New York, Viking Penguin, 1985

Critical Writing

Adams, Robert, *Beauty in Photography: Essays in Defence of Traditional Values*, New York, Aperture, 1981

Barthes, Roland, *Camera Lucida, Reflections on Photography*, New York, Hill & Wang, 1981 and London, Jonathan Cape, 1982

Coleman, A D, *Light Readings: A Photography Critic's Writing, 1968-1978*, New York, Oxford University Press, 1979

Goldberg, Vicki (ed), *Photography in Print: Writings from 1916 to the Present*, New York, Simon & Schuster, 1981

Newhall, Beaumont (ed) *Photography: Essays and Images*, New York, Museum of Modern Art, 1980, and London Secker & Warburg, 1981

Sontag, Susan, *On Photography*, New York, Farrar, Straus & Girous, 1973, and London, Allen Lane, 1978

Stott, William, *Documentary Expression and Thirties America*, New York, Oxford University Press, 1973

Thomas, Alan, *Time in a Frame: Photography and the 19th Century Mind*, New York, Schocken Books, 1977

Tractenberg, Alan (ed), *Classic Essays on Photography*, New Haven, Leete's Island Books, 1980

Index